STICK FLOAT
WIZARDRY

JIM BAXTER

1889 books

Cover artwork © 1889 books. Photo by Mick Rouse
– many thanks for this permission, Mick
Cover font ©2001 Nerfect Type Laboratories
and Britton Walters – thanks guys

www.1889books.co.uk

ISBN: 978-1-915045-08-9

Dedicated to Dick Ward (1934 – 2018)
– a fine angler, stick float pioneer and true gentleman.

Contents

Introduction

Unlike my first book covering the waggler, a float attached to the line at its bottom end only, this part-historical, part-instructional book concentrates on the stick float and similar floats fastened at each end, or "top 'n bottom" (a.k.a. 'double rubber,' as silicone rubber tubing holds the tip and base of the float in place). It offers a very direct way of fishing with the float controlled from the tip.

On any river this can give us a distinct advantage over the first float, particularly when the water is icy cold and fish are lethargic: we can change the trotting speed at will by checking or releasing line in different degrees and at the precise moment or point we desire.[1] At the business end of the line the baited hook can tantalise the fish to take, by the bait lifting when the float is stopped then falling slowly again once line is released.

And there is something special about trotting a stick float, to watch that speck of float tip gliding downstream before it disappears as a fish takes; hearing that familiar 'clunk' on a successful strike as the float erupts onto the water surface, then feeling the determined resistance of a good fish. It takes longer to master the stick than the waggler it's fair to say, with more precision involved, but most would say the prize is worth the effort as the rewards can be spectacular.

The feel of a well-used stick is evocative of memorable days on the river. I can still pick up the 7 x no. 6 original Pete Warren float that I used years ago on the Burton Joyce Road stretch and re-live those times. This popular stretch of the Trent frequently had a favourable wind (over the right shoulder) and catching roach and sometimes chub living on a gravelly bed was made easier using this light float.

Float choice makes for considerable debate, and much of it is about feel. We look at a wide spectrum of popular stick floats and why one might be better than another. But we can

---

1 A waggler, too, can be successfully held back, of course, to slow the bait down but it will dip underwater if the line is held tight at the reel. Once line is released the float re-appears and might then go under again with a fish taking. While this might be a useful tactic at long range, it hardly compares with the precision of the stick for a slowed down presentation.

only lay out the stall; it is for you to decide which ones suit your purpose.

We will see how the float has evolved over the half-century since its inception, and chart the styles of the pioneers and masters of the technique. Other top and bottom floats like the Bolognese, Stubby Carrot and Lightweight Topper will also be covered here. The vogue float of today is the Bolo,' but the stick still has a mighty fan base on rivers UK-wide.

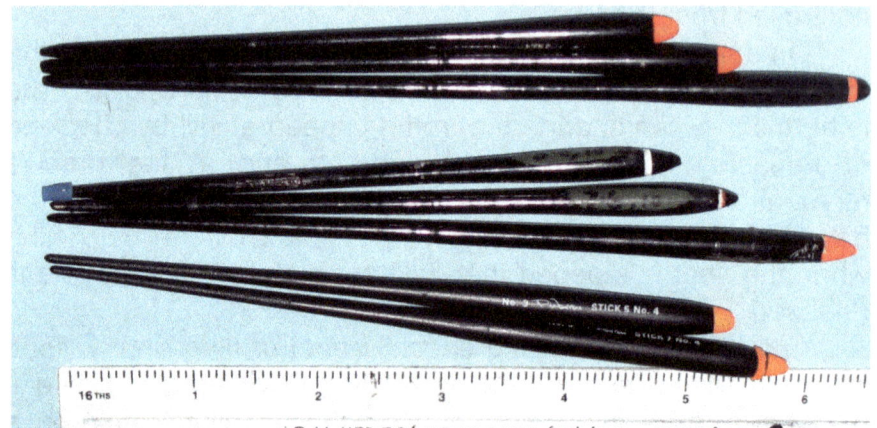

Pete Warren originals manufactured by Gerry Woodcock (top to bottom): dome tops, pointed tops and the stockier Mark II Middy version with plastic stem

The writing team draw on their experience to analyse different stick designs and why one might be selected over another, and it is quite subjective. Is a heavy base preferable or not – and would that choice be wood, wire or plastic? What size of float is best for a given swim, and where are the shots ideally placed? Even among the angling greats, opinions differ widely.

The species most associate with stick floats is roach, alongside chub and dace where they exist. I am a roach lover myself, happy catching them from rivers or lakes, and still fish with an urgency based on years of competitive fishing where every second counts. The contributors, too, are almost all from the same mould, but I trust this does not pigeon-hole the book. The stick float can be enjoyed by river anglers of all kinds and the themes and advice apply equally to those who fish purely for pleasure.

Billy Makin, a former student of the maestro Benny Ashurst, confirmed why he thinks the stick works so well in a recent reflective article in *Match Fishing* magazine. In referring to a greenheart-based float built from a tapered cotton spindle – a heavy wood that sinks but only just – he said: "the unintentional beauty of the stick float is that it always points directly at the bait because of the neutral buoyancy of the stem." There is indeed much truth in this as we'll come onto, but whether the float *always* points at the bait, i.e. with bait preceding the float as it travels downstream, is debatable. Even the material and weight of the lower part of a stick float is a matter of conjecture.

An internet search shows greenheart has a specific gravity of 0.99 which means it barely floats in water (rated as 1.0 SG), though I have seen it as low as 0.80, and Dick Ward, a toolmaker by trade, and another Lancastrian Trent ace in his time, refers to both a floating and sinking type. He writes about his approach with a greenheart float and how the *bulk* of a stick mightily improved bait presentation over the lighter feather and porcupine quills of former times.

Despite making many stick floats and enjoying a few career highlights with them on rivers, I'm not sure I ever fully appreciated the importance of the float's *balance*. Let's say I was a shade cavalier with my stick float approach for a long time compared to the waggler. The late John Illingworth, a top Yorkshire angler and England International, once told me that the base portion of a stick float should always cock to some degree, enough to break through the surface film when thrown onto water, unshotted. I tried to build this into my own float creations from then on, but while some floats balance nicely and their further cocking motion is in unison with the string of shots, others lie too flat, while those with a heavy base wood, cock too suddenly for some. The pros and cons of each type are considered by the different contributors.

But if I have any slight regrets about my Trent days, it is a) that I never tried Warren-style with a dome-topped float over-shotted; and b) I never really took to the centrepin reel in adverse conditions, a weapon that led at least two of the book's champions to many victories.

My research has taught me more about bamboo, alias Tonkin cane – Benny Ashurst's original base wood that he matched with the balsa. Benny said it was 'heavy,' yet researching the specific gravity of different woods in comparison tables, I found a discrepancy. I'd also wondered why some garden canes in a batch would sink (as used in the original Pete Warren sticks) when others floated? Although I found examples of cane rated as lighter than water, Ray Gould, a US rod-builder, claimed it as heavy as 1.13!

Calum Gladstone, a cane fly rod builder for Hardy's, solved the riddle for me. He explained that the bamboo used to make split cane rods was from the close-knit 'power fibres' on the outside of the plant whereas the lighter pith on the inner side is a floating material. They dry the bamboo out in an oven, and certain float-makers have also done this. He sent me some samples and they sank as fast as lignum. Ironically, it was not until reaching middle age when fishing a stick float on a lake (and believe me, a stick can be very successful on still water as will be revealed) that I really started to make better-balanced floats and fully appreciate the difference.

It has always fascinated me how every fishing day is different, just like every snooker game, round of golf or set of tennis. On a river especially, the water is constantly changing – it may be fining down, getting cleaner after a flood, or rising fast with mucky floodwater. Externally, a cold wind may spring up to kill sport, or it may help improve flat calm conditions. Temperature may also change for better or worse. No two anglers ever fish quite the same even with an almost matching set of tackle, and Lady Luck also plays a part with fish never evenly spread throughout a river. Surely these differences add to the intrigue because we never know what each new day at the waterside will bring. Unlike ball games however, we are competing against nature, which adds another dimension.

As the great John Dean says, the first man (with the correct tackle and bait) who finds out how the fish want to feed should in theory be the winner. If he doesn't get the right presentation the fish want quickly enough, someone else surely will, and he may come second (in a top swim) or come nowhere, but this is only the half of it.

What species is the optimum to target on that particular day on that water... will they feed close in or far off... on or off the bottom... what bait, method and tackle to use... grade of line, size of hook... and that key link from rod to hook, what float? These are all big questions for the angler. One's experience and confidence help us make the right decision, but every new day at the water is still a challenge. At worst, when we cannot get a bite for love nor money I liken it to playing snooker without a white ball – crazy. Then a fish takes and we believe there is a God after all!

There are many different ways of going about putting a good catch of fish together; fortunately two anglers side by side can use contrasting tactics and baits to catch an almost identical weight. Back in the golden years of the big matches, the difference between a winning catch and coming nowhere could be slight and every dram of weight counted; a win often came down to exploiting short bursts of feeding fish, and a subtle change at the right time often gained someone top honours. It was always satisfying to come out on the right side of those close battles we often experienced.

Are you an attacking angler who feeds heavily, or a more measured, light feeder? – either approach offer an element of profit and loss. Do you err on the light or heavy side with your float? Do you back-shot the stick in a downstream wind? Most top Trentmen would, but Dave Thomas never did, and few could better his match record.

Do you like a fine tip to your float and a pronounced shoulder for holding back Allerton-style, or a blunt, dome-top, shotted almost level to the surface to do the same? Tiny hook or bigger? Some swear by a Mitchell Match reel, others a closed face ABU or similar, or even a centrepin which has something of a 'Marmite' factor about it? With stick floats and all tackle items it all comes down to confidence in the end. The spectrum can be studied here but the choice is obviously yours.

At the end of the book we briefly come on to the pole. Why is it that pole floats have a sensitive fine bristle in the top and a stick float usually doesn't? Would a very fine tip or 'inserted' stick more like a pole float shape, help us catch more fish, like those used to defeat upstream rollers on a river? I'd wager it would, so in a postscript we contemplate whether the stick design could be improved even further.

Finally, we must pay homage to Benny and that first group of Lancastrians back in early sixties for laying the foundation for all that the stick float became. We say that fishing is more than just catching fish, but could it be this 'revealing of the hidden' then seeing that live creature slide into our net that is the true thrill of the sport. This may be what keeps us wanting more and maintains my passion for it, whilst the stick remains a marvellous float to enjoy the experience.

Even today after 50 years of keen angling, I can truly say that every day spent on the bankside is still as fulfilling as it was when I was a young 'apprentice' of 16. I was so excited back then at the prospect of a bus and train journey to fish the River Witham, that sleep never came easy with a head full of dreams about what the big day would bring. No money can buy it; a lifelong pursuit of angling makes us rich as kings. Hope you enjoy reading the book as much as I did writing it.

Chapter 1
Benny Ashurst – the Mastermind

Of the stand-out match anglers of the 20th century, in terms of their contribution to future generations by passing on skills via books and magazine articles, I'd name five men before all others: Frank Oates, Billy Lane, Ivan Marks, Kevin Ashurst and the godfather of competitive angling: Benny Ashurst, Kevin's remarkable father. All have good instructional books to their names but as wide-ranging and progressive as their teachings were, it is Benny's book of ideas that has made the greatest impact in the long run.

Benny, born in 1916, was possibly not the first angler to use caster as bait, but his name is synonymous with it, which is why he deserves the credit for championing its use. It is unlikely, too, that he was the first to develop a cane-based, balsa-topped float, but he promoted it as a stick float and put his name to it. This was a man on a mission, who starts his book of 1968 with the words: "I had the same mild interest in fishing as any other young lad but I didn't take it seriously until I was 19. This sudden enthusiasm came when I married and moved to Leigh in a house close to Fir Tree flash" [an adjacent lake, though for many young married men it works the other way round!]

In these pre-war years Benny was unable to source maggots near his home so was compelled to fish mainly with bread. But enthusiasm was his byword and Benny applied himself to 'fishing every spare minute' he had from his job as a miner. And his dedication paid dividends when, twelve months after he began fishing in earnest, he beat 200 men to win his first match on the local canal with 1lb 14oz. But at that time matches were two hours long and, being Benny, the same afternoon he fished another match on another section of the canal and won again.

"This was in October", said Benny, "and the main club contests locally had already been fished that year. The colder weather soon puts canal fish off the feed and, traditionally, fixtures were concluded before the bad weather came. But during the winter months I fished the canal at every chance. There was a warm water outfall from Plank Lane Colliery which ran into the Leigh Canal and I fished close to that warm patch all winter. My two wins had made me so keen I was determined to practise all I could and be ready for the next season.

"At that time few anglers fished in the winter. I used to creep quietly to the water not wanting others to see me. They would have thought me stupid to fish at that time of year. But I was steadily accumulating knowledge that would stand me in good stead the following summer."

The starlet progressed rapidly from there and after winning all eight of the Fir Tree AC club matches he stepped up a level and joined the Leigh Angling Society. He won the first match he fished with this club, then won four more including the big annual match. By now he had solved his maggot shortage by breeding his own. He was also travelling further afield to rivers like the Weaver and Severn... and frequently making the prize list.

The war then intervened and burst Benny's balloon just as he was starting to fly. A near-death car accident in 1951 almost stopped him fishing for good. He suffered head injuries, a broken leg below the knee and a fractured wrist. He'd earlier been forced to retire from the pit after an accident underground, but he turned this to advantage by becoming a commercial maggot breeder. Benny's nightmare start to the Fifties would turn out lucky after all.

Ashurst on the River Nene

In 1953 he started experimenting to see what results he could obtain by trying to produce sinking casters as a loose feed for roach. Casters are full of protein, and he found that when a tray of casters was left out at his maggot farm alongside a tray of maggots, rats would only eat the casters. He also supplied some to a miller who fed half his chickens on them. The caster-fed birds grew plumper and reached maturity sooner than those given only normal poultry food.

Benny first put the caster to test on the River Weaver in 1956. And what a fabulous season it was: he won eight big open matches, five association matches and a score of sweepstakes. He broke the Weaver match record with 17lb in four hours, repeating the feat on the Leeds-Liverpool Canal with 8lb 5oz, and smashing the two-hour record on the Adlington Canal with 5lb 11oz. In the same year he designed and created the first stick float.

In his 1968 book, *Match Fishing with Benny Ashurst*, written by Peter Collins – he explains the concept behind the design.

"Each float I have in my tackle box is a specialist float made for a certain function. I know exactly what to expect of it, how it will behave due to the properties of the material from which it is made, its casting power, how it holds up and its exact shot-carrying capacity. I don't have a single float in my box that I have bought from a tackle shop. I am certain that I can make much better floats than I can buy. And part of the pleasure in fishing, for me at least, is to consider the problems posed by a certain river and then to design floats capable of combating the problems of that river.

"Most of my success in canal fishing has come by casting to and fishing near the far bank. And the bites have come while the bait is still falling through the water after the cast. Thus I want a float that will gradually tilt and settle to the pull of the shot on the line. It must be in register with the shot and tell me when a fish is taking.

"I found the answer to be the stick float, which has proved so popular all over the country. I designed this float some 12 years ago, when I hit on the idea that a buoyant top and a heavy base incorporated into a float would provide this pendulum action. The buoyancy of the balsa in the tip holds it up to the surface while the heavy cane sinks through the water in an arc. I found that high density Tonkin cane was the best material for the base.'[2]

"By varying the length and diameter of the balsa in the tip in relation to the cane I was able to make a number of floats with a variety of shot-carrying capacities. This range extends from a minimum of a single BB and one dust shot (or 0.4g+) up to one AAA and a dust shot (0.8g+).

"When shotting for canal fishing I place the BB tight up under the float and the single dust shot is placed on the line a foot from the hook. The BB shot is up near the float simply to add to the weight and to increase casting power. The same float could also be used on a flowing river like the Trent, but in that case the shotting would be different. Instead of placing the BB under the float I split that weight into either three no. 6 or two no. 4 shot and space these equidistant along the length of line below the float.

"Trent fishing doesn't usually entail casting more than three rod lengths out and therefore there is no need for that extra shot near the float. Instead, the weight is placed further down below the float to all the bait to be presented in a natural fall, thus offsetting the effect of the flow of the river on the bait.

"It is a simple matter to learn the behaviour pattern of this float after it has been cast. It is possible to time the float's movements as it cocks and any variation from the usual must bring a prompt response. Whenever the float either dips sharply or fails to settle in the normal way a fish is usually responsible. The strike is made at once and a fish is hooked.

"I shape these stick floats so that the balsa tip which protrudes above the surface has been sharpened down almost as fine as a pencil point. Thus the amount of float above the surface is very small indeed and bites register instantly.

"The length of these floats varies between six and nine inches, the depth of water being the factor dictating the final choice. If the canal is a mere eighteen inches deep then I use the shorter float, whereas I use the longer one on the Trent where the depth is greater. The thickness of the floats can be varied so that both the long and short floats have the same

---

2 Although Benny describes Tonkin cane in his book, his original stick incorporated a porcupine quill base with a balsa top, as described in a 1957 Midland Angler magazine article entitled 'King of the Canals'. This was confirmed to me by Kevin Ashurst, but later Benny no doubt realised that cane was heavier and would therefore cast better

shot-carrying capacity.

"These stick floats must be fished what I call 'double-rubbered.' That means being fastened to the line both at the top and bottom. When bites are being registered 'on the drop,' to fasten at the base only upsets the pendulum action of the float and its advantages are lost. And, of course, there is a further advantage in this double-rubber fishing, for it means the float can be changed at will, either for a different size or for one with a different coloured tip if the light should change.

"If I am fishing with a shot tripping the bottom of the river I prefer to use a stick float with a blunt tip. The shape of float has greater buoyancy in the tip and this helps it to hold up to the surface instead of dragging under with the flow."

If any other sticks were made by Benny's friends around this time it hardly mattered, for he had seized the unwritten patent. The stick float became Benny's legacy and has benefitted river anglers since, particularly when combined with caster on the hook.

Today there are any number of stick floats available, made from various materials both natural and man-made. But whether they incorporate wire or lignum, balsa or plastic, the principles and techniques involved in fishing with them remain precisely the same as when Benny Ashurst created his original.

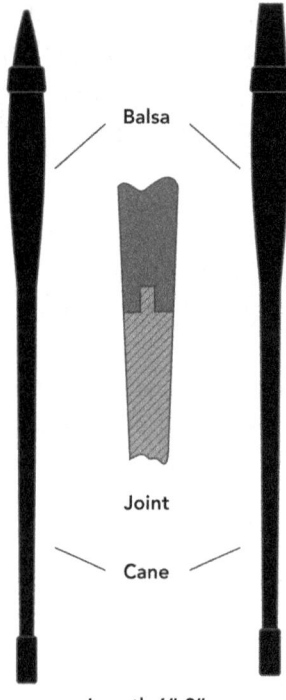

Benny's Stick
Designed in 1956

Balsa

Joint

Cane

Length 6"-9"
Swim depth dictating choice

Benny Ashurst's two original river stick floats in cane and balsa. Elliptical balsa shape, one with a pointed tip, the second with flat tip, the former for still or slow-moving water, the latter for faster water – blunt tip coping better with turbulence and flow. Sizes ranged from 1 x BB or 4 x no. 6 and a dust shot (8) up to 1 x AAA or 8 x no. 6 and a dust. The joint (centre) showing cane spigot would or should have been at least a half-inch or more long (see Pearson).

Chapter 2
Kevin Ashurst – the Prodigy

If ever an angler was destined for greatness it is Kevin Ashurst. Born into the Benny Ashurst 'angling academy' in Leigh as it effectively was, and learning fast from his dad's every move, he was already beating men to win canal matches while still at school. We could fairly say he was at angling degree standard by the age of twelve, but being born in the right place at the right time takes nothing away from the future 1982 World Champion's host of achievements. From the start he showed a great will to win; second place was never contemplated.

It was on the semi-polluted North West canals where

Kevin developed the scratching style that would eventually help him gain a World Championship title, along with several near-misses. His individual gold medal came on Ireland's Newry Canal on pole and bloodworm, but that's jumping ahead of the story. Kevin's talent really blossomed when it came to fishing stick float and caster on the Trent.

Kevin led the way for Stoke in the 1969 National

To be introduced to stick floats aged sixteen, when his famous father, ever the fierce competitor, was performing at his peak and using this new float to dominate local canal matches, was most fortuitous. It was as though Kevin and the stick were made for each other. He'd go on to smash the six-hour Trent record with 41lb 11oz from Shelford shallows in 1965 and, in a far harder test, he conjured over 8lb to take fourth in the 1969 Trent National. Many of his early big wins in his career fell to the stick and caster combination.

Now a veteran of 80, Kevin still competes in matches, mostly around Enniskillen, Northern Ireland, where he lives part of the year. I asked him about the record catch from Shelford shallows back in 1965. Was the key to success making the fish compete for the caster, for example?

"The swim was only four-foot deep and I caught roach

steadily throughout the day. The stick was a 5 x no. 4, with a no. 8 tell-tale and no. 4 shot, strung out with the last one immediately below the float. The river was perfect and carrying a little fresh water which improved the shallows, and I used a 16 hook (the popular Mustad 90205 caster pattern). What some anglers perhaps didn't cotton onto then was when the roach came to the surface, leaving the warm river for cool air, they didn't kick and bounce like they would normally and so could be lifted straight to hand which saved time.

Kevin at full stretch lands a good roach at Hazelford on Trent.

"Yes of course, making the fish compete for the bait was, and is always, vital. I fed up to twenty casters per throw, but only two and a half to three pints of casters over the six hours. Most fish came as the rig was fully settling, at two to three rods out, trotting halfway down the peg, but by extending the 'drop' – the tell-tale shot to hook distance – from twelve to eighteen inches, meant I could at times also catch fish trotting further down the peg.

"Harold Booth, brother of Manchester ace Ken, was next peg upstream and he pushed me close with 39lb 0oz. This left him ounces behind Ivan Marks' runner-up net of 39lb 14½oz from the peg above Harold. So it was a memorable battle. I thought later that Harold was wise for sitting on his basket to fish while the rest of us stood up, as his low profile no doubt helped in such shallow water."

In Kevin's book of 1977, ghost-written by Colin Dyson, he describes the stick as a 'simple float' then asks: "so how come only a small percentage of anglers fish well with a stick, and only a handful are what could be considered outstanding with it?" He then says: "I know the answers but I'm blowed if I can put them into words. I can watch two men fishing apparently well with a stick and know, somehow, that one or both is doing it wrong. I can look at my own swim and that little voice in my mind tells me what to do. I can give you umpteen approaches to try with the stick, but I can't say method A is the way to tackle such and such a swim or that B is the way to crack a different problem, for what is right one day can be wrong the next in the same swim.

"I can recall a practice session on the Trent in five feet of fairly pacey water. My travelling partner chose to fish with a fair amount of lead down the line, which could not be considered wrong as a starter, but something told me to tackle it light. I knew he was shotted wrong when I started to catch and he didn't. I told him but he didn't believe me until he switched to my shotting and started to catch straight away in a swim he thought was empty [compare diagrams below]. In a match he would have been slaughtered, and gone home blaming the swim. The daft thing is his method might well have been right another day.

Kevin's simple rigs for a shallow swim

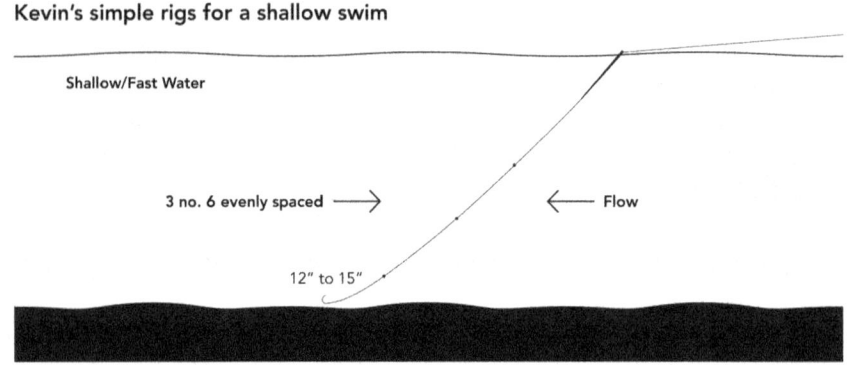

Kevin Ashurst and two rigs for fast, shallow water around two feet deep, simply shotted shirt button-style. The smaller float takes 3 x no. 6 evenly spaced with the tell-tale a foot or more from the hook.

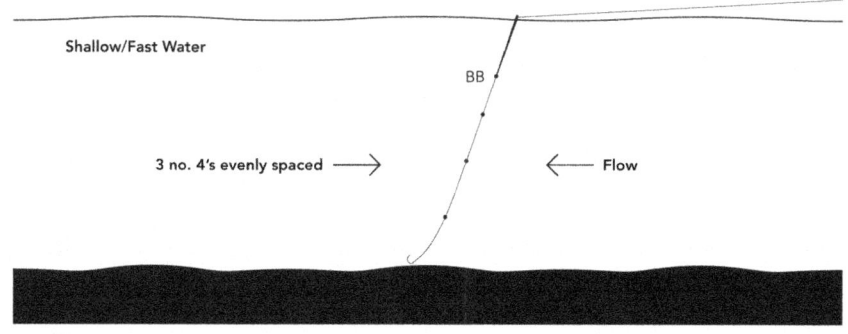

Shallow/Fast Water

BB

3 no. 4's evenly spaced ———>   <——— Flow

The larger a BB shot and 3 x no. 4 evenly spaced for longer casting. The light float is fished up to eighteen inches overdepth; the proviso with the heavier float is it can only be fished a foot overdepth.

(source: World Class Match Fishing, Cassell 1977)

"I did, after all, grow up with people who pioneered the stick *[mild understatement! – ed]*. Combined with the question of control, shotting and presentation, is the need for precision feeding. You need to know exactly where the feed is going and how the fish are behaving in response to it. When you get it all right the rewards are tremendous.

"In the good old days on the *Trent [he no doubt refers here to the 1960-65 period]*, drop fishing in good swims produced roach records for good stick men which may never be beaten. We just dropped into a deadly rhythm, and it all seemed so easy. It probably was easy then. Now there are not so many roach and they do not come off the bottom so often. We are struggling on most occasions, and low double figures win a lot of matches. Sometimes these weights are put together by painful effort; other times in one fast burst before you either catch them all or scare them off. But in either event the need to fish really well when it matters is vital. On rivers like the Trent you can't afford to start wrong or go wrong later, since there are too many who won't put a foot wrong at all. [Kevin would acknowledge that by the mid-seventies there were new forces on the Trent who were outstanding with the stick: Warren, Thomas and Dean in particular.]

"There are many approaches which are all right on their day, but one or two that prove effective more often than most. One is 'just overdepth' with the conventional string of no. 4s set a foot apart, with 2 x no. 6s nearest the hook in a swim depth of three to six feet, with the tackle set over-depth by six to twelve inches and allowed to run through at the speed of the current. An alternative to this is to fish 'well overdepth' with a lighter float taking 3 x no. 6s plus a no. 8 about a foot away from the hook. In a swim around three feet deep the float would be set at five feet and this tackle would be put through slowly and fully checked occasionally to allow the bait to stay ahead of the rig and the bait to swing up in the water. It is difficult to fish this much overdepth over an uneven or snaggy bottom but when the nature of the swim is right the method can be a killer."

Light or Heavy Stick?

What size of float to start with is a judgement call every river angler has to make, and if we get it wrong we need to recognise it smartly and make changes. It is when we need to draw on experience. The fish might want a slowed-down bait one day, or run through as fast as the flow allows the next; they may stay close to the bottom, or could start there but quickly rise up the column of loose feed as the swim develops. I once watched Bill Hughes, of Leigh, fishing next to Alan Mayer, of Stockport, at Dunham. Alan was fishing heavier than Bill and I thought he was looking the more likely of the two to do well. But Bill, on a 5 x no. 4 stick, won the match with 15lb of roach and left Alan trailing. They were both on caster, but the fish came up in the water for Bill while Alan used a bit too much weight to capitalise from it. But because Bill and other Leigh anglers had stepped up from fishing canals, our danger was sometimes trying to fish too light. We had to avoid falling into that trap and through experience we learned that in slightly different conditions Alan's rig would have been right.

In shallow, fast water like that encountered on the River Severn, Kevin might only use 3 x no. 6 down his line, or 3 x no. 4s on a heavier stick to cast out further if necessary. And for longer casting into deeper water an even heavier stick employing an AAA shot immediately under the float, a BB at half depth and 1 x no. 4 tell-tale only. But his heaviest, described in the book, takes a AAA under the float, 3 x BB shot spaced out down the line with 2 x no. 4s below them. This would be fished in seven feet of pacey water of the kind often found on the Severn. He also makes the point about the importance to add a back-shot when fishing the stick in a downstream wind, usually placing 1 x no. 6 shot a foot behind the float and sinking the line from float to rod tip.

Of all Kevin's wins on premier waters at home and abroad, from catching Trent roach or River Severn chub to Fenland bream, to big pole catches on Irish festivals or his hard-earned World title win with less than 2lb from the Newry Canal, it is a day on the tidal Trent that he most fondly remembers.

Most memorable match

"We were at a Rotherham four-hour match at Dunham Bridge, and I was having a lean spell. I told Ken Booth of my frustration, saying: 'I'm not coming here again, am sick of struggling.'

"Ken fired back that I was simply drawing badly: 'You want the straight above the bridge and it'll all come right, you'll see.'

"As it happened I drew five pegs below the bridge – flier! A bit too embarrassed to go to my peg early, I went late to avoid the inevitable comments, and the match could not have gone any better. I hardly missed a bite or lost a fish and won with 23lb of roach from 4-5oz. A magic day!

"The next Dunham match, the river fished terribly, but, drawn at Laughterton, I won with just 4lb after a switch from caster to maggot; and the one after that I made it a hat-trick of wins. The lesson is we should never give up."

After finishing as joint worst team performer (five-man team) in his debut World Championship in Holland in 1970, Kevin became the mainstay of the team and would finish as best (five times) or second-best team points scorer in eight of his next eleven appearances up to winning the individual title on the Newry Canal, NI in 1982. That impressive consistency included widely different waterways in eleven different European countries.

In this period Kevin helped England to six silver and

bronze medals but they never managed the gold. But from 1984 onwards under Dick Clegg's management, their fortunes improved dramatically, notably when winning their first gold medal on Italy's River Arno in '85 and denying the home team by a point! They added two more team gold medals before the Eighties were over with Kevin always in the thick of the action. In short, they replaced France as the World's top team, with Kevin ably supported by the likes of Ian Heaps, Dave Roper, Bob Nudd, Denis White, Tom Pickering, and the emerging forces that were Steve Gardener and Alan Scotthorne to follow.

Wire vs Wood?

Kevin said back in 1982 (in *Coarse Angler* magazine) that he did not use a wire-stem stick float. He stayed faithful to the conventional cane base in a turbulent swim but would turn to a thicker/heavier float for extra stability. His stellar record with the float justifies his confidence in it.

Yet Billy Lane, match legend and 1963 World Champ, writing a decade earlier (in his 1971 *Float Fishing Encyclopaedia'*) said he was no great fan of the cane-based stick, preferring a wire stem version. This is surprising as Billy set great store by an Avon float built from cane running through a balsa body.

He called the stick a 'most limited' float, and one for trotting where it is not too difficult. He warned that wind conditions must be simply perfect for its use: never in a facing wind or one blowing downstream. A few famous Trent anglers might dispute that. Billy did concede though that he had an 'increasing regard' for the wire-stemmed stick, citing better control between rod tip and float as the reason.

Chapter 3
Dick Ward – the Method man

Dick Ward on the Witham

Born in 1934, Dick Ward, of Stockport, grew up in the shadow of all that was happening in terms of stick float development in the Manchester area, with Benny Ashurst leading the way. Dick sadly passed away in 2018, but I had the privilege of knowing his friendly personality for years, and got the chance to meet up with him and delve into his main fishing diary before he became too unwell. The contents revealed plenty about the float and the skills of the men behind it, obviously including Dick himself. For the benefit of those too young to know, Dick and his North West contemporaries mastered the stick float and caster method throughout the sixties before the rest of the angling world began catching up.

Considering Dick spent three years working in Africa as a young man (Rhodesia, 1957 to 1960) where he caught catfish and tigerfish before returning to England, it's tempting to think he was a late starter on the home front. But he had enjoyed some early fishing adventures as a schoolboy. He kept a diary from the age of sixteen and in one of his first ever matches – the 1955 National Championship on the River Huntspill and King's Sedgemoor Drain – he made a stunning debut. He caught 12lb 6¼oz comprising seven bream and a roach of 1lb 6½oz to win his section for a first medal and provide his team's second best weight. Not bad for age nineteen!

That first diary entry of March '53 told of a catch of '26 small rudd and a 2oz perch' from a local pond, mostly on maggot. The second entry described a trip to the River Idle where he caught '14 roach up to 12oz, all on maggot... total about 4lbs.' In these detailed writings he includes the hours fished and the weather conditions. He was showing an eye for detail that would figure highly both in his career as a toolmaker and his match-fishing life. Dick set up a company called Method Tools after which his team was named. He also wrote articles and match reports for several newspapers including *Angling Times* and the former *Angling Telegraph*, a Sheffield Newspapers' monthly publication.

Around 1961 Dick teamed up with Ken Booth, a Bury tackle dealer, and fellow Stockport anglers Alan Mayer, Bobby Watson and Frank Read. Ken would buy a gallon of caster maggots from Benny Ashurst's farm and turn casters for the regular team of four. "Depending how the maggots turned we'd sometimes end up with little over a pint of casters each. But we could catch by feeding sparingly at that time and half a pint would often be enough to catch double figures of roach," said Dick.

This team of five struck gold in the 1963 1,500-peg Trent Championship, with Ken winning the individual with 16lb 7oz, Dick coming third with 12lb 14½oz and Alan seventh with 11lb 8oz and, with a little help from the other two, they also secured the team trophy with 47lb 11½oz.

This was a serious breakthrough as they were up against the country's finest river match anglers including the Northwich Loco team led by Benny and Kevin Ashurst which made second place with 40lb 2¼oz.

Dick described his pal Ken as the best Trent angler on the

circuit using the stick and caster method at the time, but he was obviously no slouch himself, and this was only the start of some wonderful days on the river.

Three of the 'Method' team: Alan Mayer, Dick, and Ken Booth.

What made these anglers and their method quite remarkable was that they lived over eighty miles, roughly a two-hour drive, from the Trent, so they could never be classed as locals. Nor was there a river in the Manchester area anything like the Trent on which to practise: it was all down to long weekend journeys to the Trent itself.

In this same year, came the first of the Nottingham vs Manchester challenges, and again Dick came good. It seemed only right that the stick float pioneer Benny Ashurst won the individual with 17lb 8oz to spearhead a Manchester win, but Dick, despite wasting some time taking pictures to cover the event for *Angling Times*, made second with 12lb. As the news of this event spread far and wide, anglers generally saw the marked difference between the Manchester approach with their modern casting reels, stick floats and caster bait, to Nottingham's centrepin reel and maggot combination. The stick was gaining momentum fast.

For the locals to get turned over on their own river by these Northern invaders with a new method that they were still not fully familiar with, would have both shocked Nottingham's finest and dented their pride. One can imagine much head-shaking and chuntering from their peers.

In the winter of '63 however, Nottingham gained revenge in a six-a-side challenge at Fiskerton. Their star angler of the day, Jim Sharp, silenced the pin-reel's critics with top spot, closely followed by an emerging talent, the in-form Johnny Toulson. Benny and Kevin Ashurst teamed up with Dick's team of four – soon to call themselves 'The Method,' but stick and caster lost out to centrepin and maggot, fed with groundbait. Not even the stick and caster could win every time!

But gaining confidence by the week, Dick led his four-man team to victory in the George Jones Memorial on the Bridgewater Canal with 3lb 9oz of their 8lb 15½oz total, and not long after he pushed Benny Ashurst into second in a Castleford AA open at Southfield Reservoir with 12lb 7oz of roach on caster to Benny's 9lb 1oz.

With the Notts vs Manchester contests all square at 1-1, a decider was inevitable and early in 1964 they staged another battle of 12-a-side. And again it was the Ward-Booth combination that set Manchester up for victory. Dick won with 20lb 12oz, Ken Parr made second for Nottingham with 19lb 0¼oz, just ahead of Ken Booth's 18lb 9oz for third. Lancashire's eight double figure weights proved too much for Nottingham's five, boosting their total to 153lb 9¾oz for a near 23lb winning margin.

Dick's later successes included winning *The People*'s (newspaper) Northern Championship in a match on the River Wharfe at Tadcaster with 7lb 0¾oz of chub on wasp grub; and top spot in a 'three-man team' open, involving 34 teams on the Trent at Holme Marsh with 15lb 7oz, when along with Ken Booth and Alan Mayer – scaling 11lb 9oz and 9lb 6oz respectively, they cleaned up by winning all three sections under the team banner Stockport Waltonians.

The match Dick rated as his best came in a downstream wind on the tidal Trent at Besthorpe with a net of quality roach for 20lb 14½oz, despite apologising afterwards for not doing justice to a flier and calling himself 'rusty' for losing 5lb of fish off the hook! Teammate Alan Mayer came second on 17lb 12½oz, and Alan Tremethick third on 13lb 9oz. Other big names in the top 10 were Howard Humphrey on 11lb 1oz and John Illingworth 9lb 2oz.

Although Dick fished for Warrington Anglers Association and was not picked by Benny Ashurst for his winning Stoke National team in 1969, when Stockport took the Division 2 National title in '74 with the spectacular points total of 1,161 from a possible 1,380, Dick was a leading team member and took the third best score.

His best Trent match weight was 23lb 11oz in the 1972 Burton Joyce Saturday series, which pushed Pete Warren into second with 18lb 8oz. He also took his skills to the River Witham and won the Grimsby 450-pegger in 1973 with 12lb 0½oz, the Boston Open in 1974 with 7lb 2oz of roach, and the 1975 Lincoln Open with 12lb 15oz of bream.

Frank Read and Bobby Watson might not have made as many headlines as Dick or Ken Booth, but they still played a key part, and match colleague Harry Jackson said Bobby was the tidiest angler he ever saw fish a stick float. So it begs the question: in a match between Dick's team and their nearest rivals, Abbey Hey from Gorton, who would have won? I put the question to Ian Heaps who, after a lengthy pause for him, said: "It would have been very close."

In the next chapter Dick reveals how he fished the stick and caster back in the day, and how he shotted his greenheart-based stick so that it pulled line off the reel to trot smoothly. How a float's *bulk* affects trotting is a feature that we possibly sometimes take for granted. Every float, in a river situation or not, has to boss the conditions presented on the day so don't make the mistake of using one that's too light. See what you make of it.

Chapter 4
Essence of the style – Dick Ward

The following two short articles were written for Angling Times way back in July 1967, when Dick Ward and his friends from the greater Manchester area were on red hot form, fair cleaning up the Trent match prizes and showing the locals a new method that could beat their long-established centrepin reel and maggot approach for roach. This was a milestone year for myself when, aged 17, I won my first little match with 21lb of Fenland skimmers (Popham's Eau drain). I drew a good swim that day but was still very much a beginner and it took me a while to win another club match. Had I read articles like these early on, however, I'd have shotted my float better, for a start, and advanced quicker. Dick and his North West colleagues pioneered the stick float and caster and the records show they dominated for over a decade. Although cleaner and clearer water means the Trent fish will now rarely feed as close in as described, and lead shot in no. 5 or 6 size is now banned, the basic advice is still as relevant as it was in the Trent's heyday.

1) TROTTING TACTICS FOR ROACH

Most of what is written on trotting for roach deals with the subject on the basis that the angler is using a centrepin reel[3] to catch fish feeding near the bottom some distance downstream, and the fish will only take a bait held back against the flow.

While appreciating that such tactics work well on most rivers and result in impressive match and pleasure weights, a totally different approach is required when fishing the River Trent.

In discussing tactics for the Trent one feature of the river which must be borne in mind is the relatively high temperature of the river in winter, caused by hot water being pumped into it by the many power stations along its banks.

Whereas in other rivers the cold weather slows down the

---

3 Elsewhere Dick calls the centrepin the traditionalist's reel, adding that in his opinion a fixed-spool reel with line loaded right to the spool rim is superior as it allows much more smooth trotting

fishes' active search for food, this does not apply on the Trent when the river is at normal winter level.

Should there be heavy rain or snow, then for a few days the river temperature will drop, putting the fish off for those few days.

Lightweight rod

The basic equipment will not vary from that used on any other similar river. A light rod with a stiffish action with a length of 11 to 12 feet, balanced with a fixed-spool reel, loaded with 2½lb line, with the spool filled to the top of the rim is needed. This spool filling is vitally important in all forms of fishing, but in river fishing is even more important – being the difference between smooth and jerky trotting.

The next item of equipment to be considered is the float. In ninety nine per cent of the matches on the Trent, the winner will be using a stick float. Although originally designed in Lancashire for fishing canals, this float has been adapted to river fishing and with its increased popularity has been produced commercially. It can be bought at most good tackle shops.

Originally the stick float was made with a balsa top and a piece of tapered slow-sinking greenheart for a stem. However, with a shortage of greenheart, the commercial float manufacturers have replaced greenheart with cane, without spoiling the float's performance.

By varying the proportions of balsa to cane, stick floats can be made to carry various amounts of shot, and when shotting up for the Trent the principle to work on is one no. 5 split shot per foot of water.

The top shot is placed immediately under the float for one main reason: the stick float with its slim shape is held in place by rubbers at the top and bottom, meaning constant striking could slide the float down the line, altering the depth. This shallowing up effect could cause the bait to pass over the feeding fish, which the shot under the float prevents from happening.

The shot under the float therefore acts as a depth marker. It enables the angler to try fishing deeper and when bites are not forthcoming, by leaving the shot in its original place, the angler can bring his float back to the exact previous depth.

It is a good idea to use three rubbers on any float without rings, one at the top and two at the bottom. One of the two as the base acts as a spare if one of the others snaps. This saves having to break down the tackle to put on another rubber.

But why is the stick successful?

Many people use a stick float without bothering to wonder why it is so successful. By reason of its inbuilt weight it can be cast a long distance without much shot on the line, but as most Trent swims are fished just beyond the rod-end this is not the reason.

The float's buoyancy is greatest at the top, whereas in many other floats the top is less buoyant. Therefore there is more to it than sensitivity. Why then is a stick float carrying 5 x no. 5 shot more suitable than a porcupine quill a third of the bulk, but also carrying 5 x no. 5 shot?

Bulk is the answer. By reason of its bulk in relation to its shot-carrying capacity a stick float will draw line from the spool of a fixed-reel, overcoming the friction of the line over the spool and through the rod rings without slowing its movement downstream or lifting it higher in the water, which would make bites more difficult to see.

On the Trent in a swim around 4½-ft deep, with this depth range in mind, a stick float taking 5 x no. 5 shot is the most popular choice, with the shot spaced approximately every 12 inches and the bottom shot 12 inches above the hook.

Then there is the question of suitable hooks. There are literally thousands of shapes, sizes and colours to choose from and many are suitable for casters.

If the hook you are at present using is bronze with a wide gape and a long shank and a spade end, then there is no need to change. Generally speaking a size 18 tied to 1½lb line will do to start with, only changing to finer tackle if the fish are difficult to tempt.

The basic idea of the tackle arrangement and rate of feed, which I will discuss later, is to get the roach feeding off the bottom and on the drop, i.e. as the bait falls. This method can produce, and has produced, spells of fishing providing 10lb to 12lb an hour, but it is very rare to keep the fish feeding at this rate for more than one to one and a half hours. But it is in this brief but hectic spell that the bulk of a winning weight is made.

2) BAIT PRESENTATION

Having discussed the tackle last week, now to outline the actual presentation of the bait. As previously mentioned, an average swim on the River Trent is four and a half feet deep, weed free and has a steady flow.

At the start of a contest quickly plumb the depth four feet beyond the rod end and adjust the float to carry the bait six inches off the bottom.

Having set the float correctly, throw twenty casters immediately in front of you and four feet beyond the rod end. As soon as possible after the casters have gone in, cast the float two feet beyond and three feet downstream of the spot where the casters hit the surface. When the cast is made, make sure that when the float hits the water the rod tip, float and hook are in a straight line.

As the tackle lands on the water keep your finger on the spool of the reel so that no more line is given. This will cause the bait to slowly sink towards the river bed and to swing into the bank at the same time. Before the bait has reached the bottom the float will have swung into line with the casters previously thrown in.

Rise and fall of the caster

When the fish are feeding really well, bites can be expected 'on the drop' while the bait is swinging round and, as the tackle is in a straight line, it is only necessary to tighten on the fish to drive the hook home.

If a bite does not result then, as soon as the float reaches the point immediately downstream of where the casters were thrown in, line should be allowed to run off the spool. The bait will now be falling towards the fish in a similar way to the feed casters.

If a fish takes the bait before it reaches the bottom the float will not fully settle. This is a lift bite and should be struck immediately. Once the bait has reached its lowest point and all the shots have registered on the float, however, most of the bites will be signalled by the float disappearing.

If the float travels four feet without a bite, stop giving line. This will cause the bait to rise and often produces a bite. After the float has been held long enough to cause the bait to rise two feet off the bottom, more line should be given, allowing the bait to be fished on the drop once more, producing lift bites as before. This lift and drop method can be used to explore the whole of the swim.

To avoid frightening the fish, any fish hooked should not be drawn through the length of the swim or allowed to splash, on the surface, but should be quickly drawn towards the bank and then brought upstream along the edge of the bank where it cannot affect the swim.

The sequence of twenty casters per cast should be continued until the fish are drawn into the swim and then feeding is reduced to six-twelve casters each swim down, to keep the fish interested but without overfeeding them.

Dotting the float

Bites can be very shy, particularly with casters, and, to make sure the bites show up for easy detection, the float must be shotted so that 1/16" or less is showing above the surface.

This means that since the bait is off the bottom and if the float goes under it is usually a bite. It will sink quickly after the fish takes the bait and gives the angler more time to strike before the fish feels the drag of the float. With so little float showing, bites on the drop are just as easily seen since an increased amount of float above the surface is quickly apparent.

Naturally this style will need to be practised so that the sequence becomes automatic, but regular practice will bring its reward in increased catches.

Chapter 5
Local rivals Abbey Hey: two Ians
– Heaps & Alcock

As the stick float style gained momentum, other anglers were quick to join the party, notably from one Manchester Working Men's Club: Abbey Hey AC. From their regular Sunday bus trips to the Trent emerged four top men in particular.

As a youngster, Ian Heaps was tutored on Stockport's Peak Forest Canal by his father, Jim and, like Kevin Ashurst before him, he matured into a good angler at an early age. He would go on to win the World Championship individual title in 1975 and represent England several more times, including being in the team that won England's first gold medal in Italy – no mean feat. But long before that he made his mark in Trent matches as a member of Abbey Hey AC's top team of four. His river skills were boosted when, as a keen 18-year-old, he walked the bank as an eager spectator at one of the Nottingham vs Manchester challenges. Two anglers who impressed him that day helped him devise a new shotting pattern which proved invaluable for his Trent matches and every other river where he presented a stick float. Ian Heaps remembers the occasion…

The match was billed as a Centrepin reel vs Casting reel challenge, Nottingham and Manchester respectively, but it was really about their maggot approach to our caster style. And I was fortunate to see the skill on show with both. A fascinating encounter, the local Nottingham team caught the most fish on maggot, but Manchester won the day by catching better quality roach on caster.

I watched Benny Ashurst, skipper of the Manchester side, whose approach was efficient and precise: smooth without rushing anything. His stick float was shotted shirt button style with no. 8 shot 6" apart. If memory serves me right I believe he won the match. His float went through the swim nice and straight and he certainly looked the part. When he hooked a fish he'd turn his rod parallel to the bank to coax it into the edge before pulling it upstream to avoid disturbing other fish in the shoal. But I left Benny, eventually, thinking "I can do that."

I then watched Albert Badder for the home (Nottingham) side whose method was a total contrast to Benny. He was using a crowquill Avon with a big bulk shot – a fixed, round drilled 'bullet,' around 20" from the hook and 1 x no. 8 dropper. He was holding his float back to half the river's speed, unlike Benny who ran it through at pace, and instead of loose casters was feeding a walnut-sized ball of groundbait with maggots behind his float every trot down. I remember that he finished about fourth – taking more fish than Benny but smaller and including dace and gudgeon.

My overriding thought about the day was how both styles had been brilliant in their own way – the finesse of Benny and the cruder but efficient Badder impressed me equally. "If only I could manage to combine the two I'd be unbeatable," my brain was telling me.

Back to the drawing board, I made up a rig of 10 shots including 9 x no. 8 shots spread out above a no. 10 tell-tale placed 4" from the hook. I placed a no. 8 five inches above the no. 10, 2 x no. 8s bunched together six inches above that, 3 x no. 8s together seven inches above those, then reverse tapered back to 2 x no. 8s, and finally, 1 x no. 8, placing these last two shots 5" apart. The principle of this pattern, with the heaviest shot in the middle, could be compared to a double tapered fly line in miniature, but if more weight was ever required I'd add more single no. 8s above the top one.

With the challenge still fresh in mind, and my new rig good to go, a fortnight later I was booked on a canal match with my pal, Nev Roscoe, but the match was cancelled as the canal had iced over. We managed to book two late tickets for an open on Newark Dyke instead. And surprise, surprise, I won the match with 13lb 15oz, pushing Benny Ashurst, no less, into second with 13lb 7oz!

It could be said that day was a breakthrough for me, a leap forward. The lovely thing about the shotting pattern, too, was when cast overhead in windy conditions the rig never tangled, and it served me so well I've never felt the need to change it.

I remember the windy Trent days at Winthorpe when

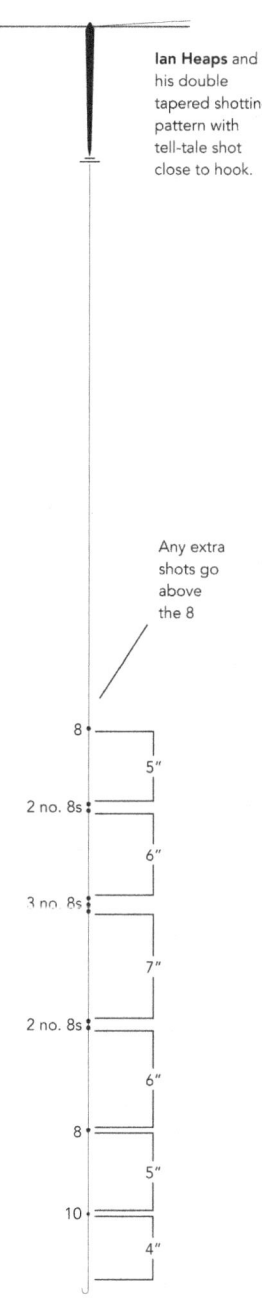

Ian Heaps and his double tapered shotting pattern with tell-tale shot close to hook.

Any extra shots go above the 8

8

5"

2 no. 8s

6"

3 no. 8s

7"

2 no. 8s

6"

8

5"

10

4"

distinctive-smelling sugar beet effluent from the nearby Newark sugar factory soured the bottom of the river and brought the fish up in the water. I turned this to advantage with a 5 x no. 4 stick, shotted as described. This short float, up to 6" maximum length, was sometimes given a fatter balsa top to increase its shot capacity, plus a domed tip or a flat tip. I'd always start by presenting the caster hookbait 1" off the bottom. For my home-made floats I knew about the heavy greenheart cotton spindles liked by some of my friends, but I preferred a sinking green cane with a flat side that could be obtained from florist's shops.

The secret to fishing the dome top float was to over-shot by a no. 8 amount and this forced you to fish the float properly, holding back slightly to keep the float up top, and the friction of the line going through the rod rings would just provide enough tension to keep it up top in a dotted position.

I'd buy a gallon of maggots every Monday and turn them to casters for the following weekend. By keeping them in damp old sawdust, adding half a cupful of water every day, we'd end up with big fat juicy casters.

We mostly loose-fed casters on the non-tidal, but on the tidal at Dunham Bridge we had a trick up our sleeves with groundbait. We studied the tide tables and I had a mix of brown crumb and sugar syrup at the ready whenever we knew of a split tide coinciding with the match hours. As the flow stopped on the ebbing tide the river might hold still for a half-hour or more. The fish seemed to enjoy this period and would always show themselves on the surface, but usually a fair way beyond the normal catching distance. By feeding several hard balls of this sticky groundbait, and switching to a bigger float for a longer cast, set deeper, it was possible to catch a quick 5-6lb before the tide turned and the river flowed upstream. And as you know 5lb in half an hour in those days was often the difference between winning and coming nowhere. Such happy memories!

Ian's lateral thinking and originality would surface again in big matches years later, like when he broke the World record match weight with 723 roach for 166lb 11½oz from the River Erne at Enniskillen. The day before the event, he cobbled a big pole float together by running a cork body onto a slim

Robert Tesse 'carrot' balsa and bristle which boosted it to 2.5-gram size, while at the same time improving lift bites from any roach that held up his 3 x no. 8s which were bunched as a tell-tale. There were so many roach in the swim that they had little room to swim off after taking the bait, so he got more bites that held the float up or lifted it slightly. He had likely learned this fish behaviour years earlier in his Trent apprenticeship when drop fishing with that small stick float.

Ian Alcock's finest hour

Ian Alcock upstaged his friend and Abbey Hey match colleague, Tony Knight, by winning the 1966 Trent Championship in that outstanding year for English football. Ian, now 78, should feel mightily proud whenever he dusts off his silver replica of the large trophy he was presented for his 22lb 11oz catch of roach that September, for he had topped over 1,000 anglers including the cream of Trentmen, aged just 22.

Ian drew a swim on Shelford Shallows which, with 12" of extra water on the river, always made this area a potential winner. Of course, drawing a fancied peg is only the start of trying to win such a prestigious event, but even though Ian was still learning his trade, helped by his experiences on the Abbey Hey winter bus Trent matches, he rose admirably to the challenge. The win put Ian among an elite group of North West anglers to claim the Trent title. Only a National Championship win could offer more prestige.

Ian never realised that his four-hour total fell only 10oz short of Coventry's Harry Wills' record weight for the event set back in 1953, a record incidentally that stood for over 30 years! But let's allow Ian to take up the story:

"The area of Shelford Shallows I drew was on the bend downstream of the stones, opposite the High Hawthorns section. In those days we were fishing mainly for roach and gudgeon; very few chub were seen. I only found 2½ foot of depth where I started fishing at three rod-lengths out, and that was with an estimated near foot of extra water over normal. Closer in I'd only around 2' of depth, but the water held a good colour which you wanted when standing up to fish shallow water as we did back then with the bait on the basket top. Standing above fish in clear, shallow water is never good. So I began at three rods out with a light greenheart stick taking 5 x no. 8 shot spread out shirt button-style, and caster on an 18 hook.

Abbey Hey AC – back to back team winners of the Aberlour Shield : Pat Bielderman, Tony Bielderman, Rob Palmer, Ian Alcock and Harry Jackson

"I was feeding twelve or more casters every trot down, with the rig set a fair bit over-depth, and during the first hour caught small roach steadily from around ten yards down the peg. The plan was to work the fish closer in and up the peg, and the constant caster feed starting taking effect in the second hour. The roach were on the small side but they kept coming. In the last two hours I'd got the fish at closer quarters and in the last hour I was getting a bite and catching almost as soon as the float had settled. In the later stages it became a fish every chuck. I fed two to two and a half pints of casters in all, and was naturally happy to break the 20lb barrier. I should add that our casters were always top notch from Norman Gresty's maggot farm, and you could bury an 18 (Mustad) caster hook in them easily. I've always stayed faithful to burying the hook in the shell."

When two of Abbey Hey's original team of four left and went their different ways, and Bob Palmer and Harry Jackson were recruited as 'supersubs,' Ian would continue his winning ways with a double team triumph in the Aberlour Shield on the Weaver in 1969 and 1970, as well as becoming one of Benny Ashurst's banker selections for his Stoke National winning team of 1969.

As for the Trent Championship, in the 1967 event, Newark's Martin Dobson matched Ian's feat by winning with 23lb 3oz of roach, once again threatening Harry Wills' record, but then disaster: the disease Columnaris struck and the roach stocks seriously declined leaving Ian to lament: "The river was never quite the same again."

Confirming Ian's prophecy, Mancunian John Ebbrell, who made his own greenheart sticks, lifted the 1969 Trent Champs trophy with its lowest ever winning weight of 9lb 4½oz. He drew below Hazelford weir and fished caster under a 5 x no. 6 stick. The previous year Leigh's Dick Bowker jnr. won it with 11lb 8½oz. The river did not always show its best face.

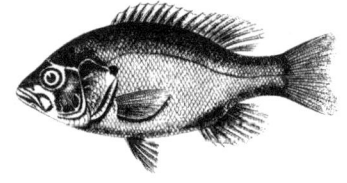

Chapter 6
...and two Tony's – Knight and Bielderman

Tony Knight and bumper catch

Stockport's Tony Knight (born 1939) started fishing while still in short trousers, when his granddad George took him to the 'Bridgie' (alias Bridgewater Canal) at Agdon Bridge. He never caught a fish which was not the ideal start but, far worse, he was rushed into hospital the following day with chicken pox and scarlet fever!

Once Tony had fully recovered, George encouraged him to try his hand again, this time at 'the beautiful' Lymm Dam, as Tony remembers it, where he fished an inviting spot in the shadow of the church. He was becoming despondent after two hours without a bite, when the float suddenly went under and he recalls shouting to his tutor: "my float, I can't see it!"

"Lift up the rod," said granddad, at which point Tony proudly played and landed his first fish – a 3oz roach.

For the next few years fishing at weekends became a keen interest. Granddad was a member of the Abbey Hey Working Men's Club AC, and, although still a schoolboy, Tony was invited on one of the club's matches. He had to try and find a place to fish apart from the competitors but he loved the experience and asked to go again.

One season soon led to another and along the way Tony found a like-minded youngster on the trips in the shape of Ian Alcock, who a few years later was to graduate to the senior four-man Abbey Hey match team. Ian got a major boost by winning the Trent Championship individual title in 1966 and the two of them spurred each other on. "We have been friends for 65 years," says Tony, now a veteran.

After learning a few skills from the old hands at the club, Tony found himself winning the odd club match locally, before embarking on more trips to the River Trent in winter with Abbey Hey. "I couldn't understand why the fish were not cold on frosty days, and it wasn't until my fourth visit to the river that one of the lads told me how the power stations took cold water from the river only to replace it with warm water," he said. This is why the river steamed of course, and the fish generally fed well even in freezing air conditions.

Aged 20, Tony met another angler, local to him in Stockport, a bit older and more advanced in terms of experience: His name was Dick Ward. "I think this was my lucky break," said Tony. "I had started to gain confidence and win a few club matches, but had never fished an 'Open.' Dick came round to see me and asked about my progress, and why I didn't fish open matches. Soon after his visit he showed me the stick floats he'd made which was a big boost to my learning curve.

"Considering Dick's words about bigger matches, and copying some of his stick floats myself, we managed to get the club to run an open match on the Trent. Another youngster, Jimmy Colecliffe, came second and I made third, which probably surprised us both, but I think this was the result that led me to concentrate on match fishing seriously. Thereafter I started fishing opens all over Lancashire, to the Trent and beyond, and never looked back. I set out on a river match path that lasted years, including my best seasons on the Trent and sometimes the Severn from 1968 to 1980."

As Tony's confidence grew with each match success, he and Ian gradually won the respect of the Abbey Hey stalwarts and they were destined to make up half of one of the best four-man Trent teams to ever fish the river. Joining Tony and Ian were Stockport colleagues, Tony Bielderman and Ian Heaps, the future 1975 World Champion. "Tony B was the brains of the team, being the general organiser and booking us onto matches etcetera. He also developed a heavy stick style for fishing on the tidal Trent at Dunham when the wind was awkward, blowing in and downstream," said Tony.

Abbey Hey colleague Harry Jackson described Tony (Knight) as the "best angler in the club" once he got established, whilst Ian Heaps revealed that the four-man team decided to share their winnings whenever they fished together. "Trouble was Tony won more than anyone else," said Ian, "so we had to change the rules so the money winner kept half his winnings and shared the rest."

Two stellar National Championships confirm Tony's river credentials. In the 1973 Relief Channel National he won a bronze medal for third out of the 1,500 entry, with 20lb of bream, and almost repeated it in the 1974 Warwickshire Avon National, but had to settle for fifth among 115 teams of 12 with 18lb 10oz of chub. His catch and great support from Dick Ward and others spearheaded Stockport to a classy victory with an emphatic 1,161 points. Years later Tony won his third National medal as a member of the winning team on the Boston drains.

While Tony used bigger sticks or all-balsa floats at times on the Trent when conditions dictated, he generally preferred to fish lighter than most, favouring a 5 x no. 8 size stick wherever he could get away with it. And he used this float size to score what he considers his *best* match win. One might have thought his winning 23lb of roach net in a big Worksop Open, that pushed a 21lb chub catch from the next peg into second, would take it, but not Tony. His choice was a low weight day when he had to work hard for every fish: "I'd have to pick the Rotherham Fur and Feather at Dunham on the tidal with 300 fishing, when I drew a few pegs below Dunham Bridge with the river over two feet in flood. I managed to jam my seat box in between the rocks in the margin and sit down to fish. I inched the light stick down the side, a method that some refer to as rock-hopping, easing it through over-shotted, and won it with just a few roach for 2lb 8oz."

Bielderman – the General

When Tony Knight described his colleague Tony Bielderman as the brains behind their four-man team it was not without justification. Tony not only took the lead in booking the four-man team into matches, he had a habit of coming good with a big weight when the competition was most intense. After gaining experience fishing Nationals for County Palatine AA from 1963 to 1967, he was called up for duty in Benny Ashurst's 1969 victorious Stoke team and took their fourth best weight on the day.

In that same year he won the Rotherham Open at Dunham with 20lb 3oz, and in '68 he won the 500-peg Northern CIU Championship with 16lb. Tony Knight also credited him with pioneering the bigger stick floats they sometimes used on the tidal Trent.

Fishing for Warrington, he won a bronze medal for third in the 1972 Division 1 National on the Bristol Avon for 21lb 12oz of mainly chub, then in the '75 Division 1 on the Nene, he went one better with a runner-up 48lb 8¾oz of bream. He smashed his 80-peg section and might have fairly expected to take the title, but Rotherham's Michael Hoad-Reddick had other ideas and found even more bream to deny him with 63lb 7oz.

Tony was also a long-serving stalwart of Stockport and District Angling Association, holding both the post of match secretary and, ably supported by wife Pat, junior section coach for 25 years. Together they built many strong junior teams that figured highly in the NFA Junior National. In recent years their daughter Bev and husband Jim Smith have taken over the helm.

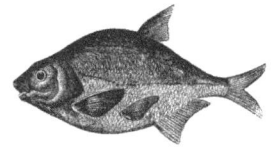

Chapter 7
Sixties stick culture – Ken Giles, Harry Jackson & Ian Heaps

Ken Giles 1976 National third place catch

A time of great change

"The younger element can't be expected to appreciate how vastly different things were with regard to tackle in those early years of the sixties. When I started experimenting with stick floats there were no instruction books and anglers did not have the car transport that exists today. Neither, other than in the All-England match, did they ever meet anglers from other counties, so knowledge therefore spread a lot slower.

"We (loosely) named our floats 'sticks' but had little to go on in terms of good design in the West Midlands, so progress was made only by trial and error; some early models were successful, others rubbish, and getting the right balance took a while. This was also pre-silicone rubber days and we'd fix our floats in place with bicycle valve rubber. Even getting hold of the right glue wasn't easy initially. This was years before Benny (Ashurst), king of the loose feed, and Billy (Lane), king of groundbait, began spreading their wisdom about floats. These two kicked the sport along. But we learned and improved. Nothing was out of reach if you put the time and effort in and, really, there were no superstars. Both individually and team fishing with Shakespeare Professionals it was a wonderful time and we lived the dream!" – *Ken Giles, BAA and Shakespeare star and England International.*

Home-made greenheart sticks

"The early sixties were exciting times on the Trent when I first travelled on the Abbey Hey winter bus, often to Gunthorpe or sometimes to the tidal at Dunham Bridge. I was only seventeen or eighteen then and a rookie on the bus. We looked up to the old hands like Joe Dickinson, Dicky Bowker (a friend of Benny Ashurst's from Leigh) and Tony Knight, who was a bit older than myself and the best of the younger anglers. Friends Ian Alcock and Bob Palmer also travelled with us. The bus was full every Sunday. We all made our own stick floats as they were not available in tackle shops. I made the float bases from garden canes, drying them twice in a hot oven before shaping them. This tightened the fibres and removed any air pockets. Ideally the cane had to penetrate the surface film as soon as it hit the water so the float cocked slightly and was fishing immediately.

"We bought the balsa for the floats and the square section catapult rubber to make our own catapults from a modelling shop. Anglers had to be adept at making or modifying most tackle accessories back then as the quality was often lacking in items from the tackle shop.

"We used only short sticks to begin with, particularly in places like Shelford shallows where swims were less than two feet deep, or the Cherry Orchard – floats taking only 2 x no. 8 shot up to 4 x no. 8, as we fished very close in. A long stick at the time would be seven inches up to a maximum of eight if we wanted to cast well out, but bigger floats like the 'paintbrush'[4] were made up later for the more powerful tidal water at Dunham.

---

4 Detailed in chapter 10

"Around '64, possibly '65, Kevin Ashurst gave me a handful of cotton spindles. My eyes lit up as this was like a gift from the gods. These greenheart spindles suddenly grew popular because: a) they sank, and b) they were perfectly tapered from 3/8" down to a 1/8" point, so didn't need any shaping other than carving a spigot to attach to the balsa top. Helped by the fact I owned a lathe, I turned them into five floats, gifting some to Ian Alcock, who in return made some for me.

"Hooks were always size 18 buried in the caster and we found some Mustad serrated shanked hooks which served us well. This hook would easily bury inside the quality casters we got from Ted Barloga at Norman Gresty's maggot farm. We also did things like shortening the stem of Mitchell reels by half an inch to make for a more comfy stretch to the spool with the forefinger. I changed one over for Dick Ward and a few others who had short fingers. Dick had helped me out with lifts to fishing venues before I had my own transport.

"The Trent was nothing like clean and sewage would find its way in when flooded, but the fish were plentiful, mainly roach and gudgeon. If the wind was downgate and awkward, which it could be there, casting was restricted anyway, but feeding lightly with casters, we held our own. At that age we could not afford much bait, but we rarely needed a lot. A pint of casters was ample, and a half-pint could produce 10lb-plus of roach, which might win the match. In a flood we'd be fishing for a lower weight of gudgeon.

"With the river's warm winter temperature on icy days we'd stand in the edge and not suffer cold feet, and we wore cheap ex-army tanks suits which were snug in all conditions. The army stores was next to the model shop close to Piccadilly station which was so convenient!" – *Harry Jackson, Abbey Hey*

Cane and balsa

"I preferred to make sticks from a sinking (dark green) cane available from Florist's shops. They were not fully round but flat on one side, but this didn't matter. We were so keen to learn the method, I spent hours making floats. I'd go for an average size of 5 x no. 4 – one shot per foot of depth – with a domed or flat top. The flat tip would combat more turbulent swims without being pulled under, and was good for holding back without it lifting up from the surface. I liked to over-shot by 1 x no. 8, which forced me to fish the float right, holding back hard enough to keep it up top.

"One strange thing about making floats that's hard to explain is why, from a batch of ten new sticks, only four, or six at best, would perform well on the line, yet the rejects looked almost identical!

"I'd always plumb up and start with the bait an inch off the deck. It was no good fishing full depth on the Trent as sugar beet effluent lined the bottom and the fish didn't like it. In the seventies this improved and the river got cleaner, which is one reason why the fish moved further out and bigger floats like wagglers became popular that would cast the distance to reach them." – *Ian Heaps, Abbey Hey*

It's a Fact

For a wood, plastic or other material to sink and be suitable for a stable stick float base it needs a specific gravity that is higher than water, which is 1.0. Below are some examples of woods suitable for the job:
〰 Lignum Vitae 1.37 – the fourth heaviest wood
〰 Bamboo (or Tonkin Cane) 1.15 – the cane used to make split cane rods.*
〰 Greenheart 1.04 - the stiffest wood in the world

Density of four of the World's top 10 heaviest woods:
1st/ Black Ironwood 84.5lb/cubic foot, 3rd/ African Blackwood 79.6lb, 4th/ Lignum vitae 78.5, 9th/ Kingwood 74.9

*Note: To discover that Bamboo's SG is higher than sinking greenheart may come as a surprise. The Manchester anglers told me how well the latter works as a stick float base. Some grades of cane do float, however – so amateur stick makers may need to shop around for the heavier variety.
With regard to wire stems, aluminium is approx. twice the weight of the World's heaviest wood – Black Ironwood – pound for pound, which explains why a length of 1/16" diameter aluminium wire will cock most sticks as easy as a fatter shaft of lignum even though lignum is rated highly for its casting power].

Chapter 8
Nottingham v Manchester Trent challenges
1961 – 1969

Manchester's Domination

The build up to the first of the Nottingham vs Manchester series of challenges started after the National Championship (formerly called the All-England) in September 1961. Unfortunately no pictures could be found of the match, but here, gratefully reproduced from the files of John Essex, is a copy of what the report in *Angling Times* had to say:

"In the 1961 All-England, two teams from the Manchester area – Groves and Whitnalls, and Warrington – finished in third and fourth places. Nottingham anglers, well beaten on their own water, shrugged off the Mancunians' success as the luck of the draw, but the Lancashire lads were so confident of their ability to fish the Trent, that they decided to give the Trentsiders a chance to get their own back.

The result was a 50-a-side friendly challenge match between the two cities that proved to be as much a contest of styles as well as ability. The Nottingham men stood up and used centrepins, the Lancastrians sat down in comfort and used fixed spools. The venue, naturally, was the Trent at Gunthorpe – scene of this year's championship – and although both teams included a National champion (newly-crowned winner Ron Lye (Notts) and Bill Hughes (Manc), the Nottingham side appeared to have the edge. Among their team were such well-known Trent experts as Ken Parr, Johnny Moult, Stan Roberts, George Smith and Peter Mansfield.

But paper form is not a good guide on the Trent and Nottingham were soundly beaten. Manchester's top 20 men not only won with 163lb 6¾oz to Nottingham's 124lb 7oz, but also rubbed salt in the wound by filling the first five individual places with Benny Ashurst (17-15-0); R Ward (12-4-8); D Owen (11-12-8), R Watson (11-2-8); and K Booth (10-10-0)."

Stick float supremo Benny Ashurst mentioned the match and his weight briefly in his book of 1968, only adding that he won it "*by a very wide margin.*" Dick Ward made second, despite spending some time taking pictures for *Angling Times* (lost in the mists of time), and his weight was also given.

Bobby Watson and Ken Booth also performed well, as did members of Dick's four-man team 'the Method,' all of which confirmed that Manchester had the winning method using the modern reels with stick float and caster. The Nottingham team did not place a man in the top five.

Nottingham's Revenge

Two years elapsed before a 'new' challenge was arranged at Fiskerton in December, 1963. This was prompted by the new Trent champion, Ken Booth, a tackle dealer from Bury, North Manchester, who boasted both on Radio Nottingham and in an *Angling Times* interview with Bill Barlow, that Nottingham had fallen behind: "The Nottingham centrepin is beautiful to watch but is hopelessly out of date," adding: "the fixed spool reel is twice as fast as the centrepin."

In their defence Nottingham's skipper Bernard Thompson replied: "We are not averse to fishing the fixed spool in slow or still water." The after-match report said the river was moving at a: "spanking pace, and in front of the first six pegs there were plenty of little eddies and swirls as the water hit the stones that guard the bank of the river."

It's fair to say Thompson was stung by Booth's remarks, a man who was noted for his brashness, never shy at sticking his neck out, and of whom, even his pal, Dick Ward, observed was brilliant but had a big mouth! Bernard picked up the gauntlet. A six-a-side match was arranged and the line-ups announced. In the red corner were: Benny and Kevin Ashurst, and Dick Ward's foursome – Ken Booth, Frank Read, Bobby Watson and Dick himself. The blue team was represented by Jim Sharp, Harry Shaw, Johnny Toulson, Johnny Dexter, Keith Hardy and Bernard.

Unlike the Gunthorpe reaches, Fiskerton was a little bit off the Manchester team's radar, and according to Johnny Toulson, "the stretch had hardly ever seen a caster," a factor which would play into the hands of the Nottingham men. Fishing with centrepin reels and maggot combined with small balls of groundbait, Jim Sharp won the match for Nottingham with 22lb 11½oz just ahead of teammate Toulson on 22lb 6oz. Only a couple of fish short, the latter could say he was a shade unlucky as he hooked a 1¼ lb trout at one stage that jumped out in the fight and scattered his roach for ten minutes.

While the Manchester team found some better quality roach on caster, they didn't catch anything like the numbers their opponents caught on maggot. A mid-match switch to maggot by Kevin Ashurst saw him make up ground on the leaders to finish third overall, but the Nottingham team were too experienced and too far in front for him to catch. Kevin, who drew the downstream end peg, admitted: "I stayed on the caster too long. I changed to maggot in the last hour and it was murder" (meaning he was catching very fast).

Another style difference noted in the match report was that to a man, the Nottingham team "overloaded their floats with shot, and then held back slightly to hold the top of the float above the water."

The casting reel did not appear faster than the pin at all, if anything it was slower on the small roach as observed by bankside spectators. According to *Angling Times* reporter, Dave Thorpe, Jim Sharp, who incidentally was drawn upstream of Benny Ashurst and beat him easily, was observed batting his reel to bring his float back from the bottom of his swim in three seconds, while Ken Booth took a fraction over four seconds to retrieve his on the fixed spool.[5] Toulson described Jim Sharp as "the best in the world on a pin" at the time.

After the result was announced Ken Booth went over to Bernard Thompson and shook his hand and said: "Very good Bernard." But afterwards he said: "I don't think anyone could have got fish out faster than I did – when I was catching them. It took me time to get them going on caster but when I did there didn't seem any point in changing."

The two-page picture spread in *Angling Times* called it: "The Trent match that set the whole country talking," and Ken Booth was made to eat his words when the headline stated: "Who said the centrepin was out of date?"

Result: Nottingham: J Sharp 22-11-8, J Toulson 22-1-0, A Badder 17-8-0, H Shaw 14-10-12, B Thompson 14-4-12, G Woodcock 10-12-0.

Manchester: K Ashurst 20-6-12, K Booth 19-3-4, B Ashurst 14-14-0, R Watson 12-13-0, F Read 12-2-8, D Ward

---

5 So certainly quicker than the 'half as fast' claim

11-13-0.

Nottingham 102lb 5oz / Manchester 91lb 5oz

The Clincher

It was obvious that a decider match was required and this was arranged for a few weeks later at Shelford. This time it would be for 12-man teams of National Championship size, and this time Nottingham would take Manchester on at their own game and fish caster. The six Lancashire lads drawn in to supplement the Fiskerton team were: Bill Hughes, Alan Mayer, Dave Owen, Dick Bowker, Eric Harrison and Keith Chapman, while Nottingham would retain Sharp, Shaw, Toulson and Thompson, but bring in some fresh talent in the shape of: Ken Parr (the 7-hour match record holder), Gerry Woodock, Archie Tizley, George Robinson, Mick Ryans, Johnny Moult, Ken Orchard and Stan Roberts.

This time the fixed spool reel and caster prevailed and Manchester won fair and square, putting a spring back in Mr Booth's step. The Ashurst's performed well, but it was three of Dick Ward's team who were more instrumental in the win – Dick topped the field with 20lb 12oz which he later said was his "best match," Ken Booth was next with 18lb 9oz (third overall) and Alan Mayer was fourth best (seventh overall) with 13lb 0¼oz. Splitting them was Leigh's Bill Hughes with 15lb 9½oz (and fourth overall).

Ken Parr, the Trent's seven-hour weight record holder with 50lb 3oz from Shelford, filled runner-up spot and proved he was still a force to be reckoned with, but Manchester returned seven double figure weights to Nottingham's five and this gave them their comfy edge.

Result: Nottingham – K Parr 19-0-4, G Shaw 16-10-4, G Woodcock 15-10-4, A Tizley 12-14-12, J Toulson 11-13-8, J Sharp 8-13-8, G Robinson 8-8-12, M Ryans 8-8-4, J Moult 8-3-0, B Thompson 7-5-8, K Orchard 7-2-12, S Roberts 6-0-0.

Manchester – D Ward 20-12-0, K Booth 18-9-0, B Hughes 15-9-8, A Mayer 13-0-4, D Owen 12-4-8, R Watson 11-2-0, F Read 10-3-4, B Ashurst 9-8-0, D Bowker 8-2-12, E Harrison 6-14-12 and K Chapman 5-4-4.

Nottingham 130lb 12¼oz / Manchester 153lb 9¾oz.

The striking statistic for me were the modest returns for

Nottingham of Jim Sharp and Johnny Moult – two of the Trent's best ever, and of the skipper Bernard Thompson.

The Washout Finale

It was not until the winter of 1969 that the two sides met again for another battle, 25-a-side this time at Clifton Grove. By now the Trent's form had sadly slumped, hit badly by the 1967 roach disease Columnaris, and ominously, in the September '69 Trent National, only 32½lb was enough to secure the (12-man) team title. In the biggest challenge so far, some new faces joined up with the originals. Unfortunately, the river was flooded like it had been in the National and the match became something of a lottery. Eddie Upton won it for the home side, but Manchester won again thanks to their strength in depth and better back-up weights.

Result (top 10 per side): Nottingham – E Upton 10-8-0, J Lockyer 5-3-0, D Hallam 4-0-0, M Lowe 3-11-0, E Stokes 3-8-4, A Steggles 3-1-0, J Moult 3-0-0, B Shelton 2-8-8, B Richmond 2-2-12 and H Gretton 2-0-8.

Manchester – I Heaps 5-6-12, K Ashurst and R Fenton both 5-5-12, J Cottam 5-2-12, D Brierley 4-10-0, D Sharpe 4-3-12, A Mayer 4-3-0, J Heaps 3-7-4, T Barloga 3-6-12 and F Read 2-10-0.

Nottingham 64lb 5¾oz / Manchester 67lb 3oz

Series Analysis

I was always given the impression that Manchester won these challenge matches almost without having to try, and that the fixed spool reel was infinitely better than the centrepin, as was the caster's superiority over the maggot. But the results hardly bear this out. Match 2 proved that Nottingham's centrepin reels were excellent tools in the right hands and could land fish at speed, and the caster was found wanting in what became a small roach race: maggot and groundbait having the edge. Match 3 showed the skills of a very confident caster team and the best team won, but eight double figure weights to five is hardly a thrashing. Match 4 was a grueller, fished in a flood that could have gone either way. On this day the likes of Pete Warren, Johnny Toulson, Roy Toulson, Harry Shaw, Terry Dorman, Gerry Woodcock and Frank Barlow – top class to a man, all caught less than 2lb, and Benny Ashurst, Ken Booth and Tony Bielderman weighed in ounces. This proves that the state of the river was a leveller and a greater degree of luck entered the equation. I'm sure Manchester would not have taken much credit for this win, but the stats say they won the series 3-1.

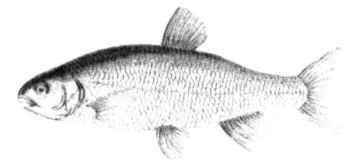

Chapter 9
Benny's triumph with the first
pro' team – the '69 National

Benny's dream had always been to win the National Championship individual title. However, no one could expect to win the National without a degree of luck, and he acknowledged in his book of 1968, that in a match of 1,000 or more entrants the first essential was to draw a favourable peg. In 1945, at his first attempt, he felt he had got over that hurdle, but although weighing in 10lb of small fish, he lost six good chub and came up 6lb short of the winner, believing his inferior line and hooks let him down. Bear in mind that this was before nylon line was introduced.

But after many Trent victories using the stick and caster method throughout the late 50s his confidence was sky high. In 1961 he was second in the CIU National with 19lb 11oz, and he won the first Nottingham versus Manchester challenge by a wide margin with 17lb 8oz that same year. In 1964 he won on the River Calder with a thumping 40lb 5oz on stick float. By 1967 Benny, 50, was arguably still near his peak and hungry for one more shout at the title.

He had a keen eye on the next Trent National in '69 as a last chance of victory on his favourite river, when along came an unexpected setback: the UK's roach stocks were suddenly hit with Columnaris disease and went into widespread decline. But with a champion's positive outlook he approached the Stoke DAA president, Alex Profitt with a proposition. If allowed to field his own team of 'crack' anglers, he told Alex, they'd bring home the team trophy.

Now Mr. Profitt was a successful businessman who drove a big Mercedes, quite a limousine at the time. Though I have no evidence to prove it, I suspect that he made a deal with Benny along the lines of: 'I like your idea. Let's go for it and win, providing you pick me in the team.' The decision to allow Benny to bring in outsiders at the expense of Stoke's top locals was obviously controversial and, interestingly, Profitt was the only Stoke representative.

It's fair to say that this team drew on the best talent available in the whole of Lancashire – Benny's selection was almost a county team, including his already well-established son, Kevin, and the cream of the top angling clubs in the greater Manchester area. Never before had the National seen such a team of 'ringers,' all of whom were hell bent on winning it.

Practice had shown there were roach feeding, but on the big day the river was carrying two feet of floodwater so it was not going to be easy. But, from a huge field comprising 114 teams of 12 anglers, Benny delivered on his promise. Benny, Kevin, and Bill 'Ginger' Pennington, all Leigh men from the stick's birthplace, led from the front and finished in the top ten individual list, with their combined 23lb 2oz contributing more than two-thirds of the team's total and more on its own than second placed Long Eaton's total weight of 21lb 7¾oz!

For three men in the same team to be in the top ten in a National of 1,368 hopefuls including many champions in their own right was incredible, about as spectacular in its way as the feat of a dozen Spaniards overwhelming thousands to take the Inca empire! Bill Pennington was allegedly not really considered a Trent angler by his fellow team members, but the skipper obviously knew better. Proving how tough a test the river was, Ken Booth won his section with a level 2lb. It all underlined the supremacy of the method and the confidence of the men behind it.

As Kevin's reward for delivering the team's top weight, he was selected to make his debut appearance for the England team, as was the custom for the best performances in the National's top few teams at that time. Later Benny modestly remarked that "caster was the key." So, while Benny's ambition to win the individual National title remained unfulfilled, as far as team fishing went it was the stand out moment of his whole career.

It was Lincoln's Roy Else won claimed the title and gold medal with just 9lb 7¾oz from a fancied draw in D section at Holme Marsh, but the majority of anglers struggled to top the 1lb mark. It was reported that Roy fished a 'cane and balsa float.' Whether this was a form of stick or an Avon-type we can only speculate.

A young Pete Palmer, representing the Long Eaton side, struggled for just 9oz, but he would go on to become a star of

Notts Fed a decade later. Joe Brennan, fishing for Wolverhampton's Whitmore Reans club, was another future big name who had to settle for 1lb 5oz. And Stoke's Ian Heaps, who'd win the World title in 1975, slumped to a 7oz return. Alex Profitt was ironically Stoke's worst performer, yet obviously thrilled with what the others had done for his town, he celebrated by treating them all to several bottles of expensive champers!

The Stoke team card read as follows: Benny Ashurst 7-8-0, Dave Bove 0-4-8, Kevin Ashurst 8-1-0, Brian Lees 1-0-0, Ken Booth 2-0-0, Ian Alcock 1-3-4, Bill Pennington 7-9-0, Tony Bielderman 2-13-0, Ian Heaps 0-7-0, Alex Proffitt 0-0-4, Dave Owen 1-1-8, Vinnie Walsh 0-2-0. Total 32-8-8.

This win proved the turning point for many other teams deciding to change the old selection systems and begin 'importing' anglers from far and wide into their National Championship sides. Not every team agreed with this, but the loyalty element of many in only selecting anglers who lived within a short radius of their home town would soon fade into oblivion.

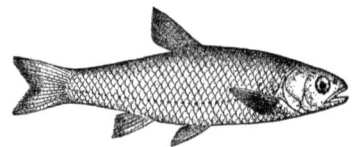

Chapter 10
The Dunham Dynamo – Harry Jackson

Frank Barlow nicknamed our next contributor the 'Dunham Dynamo' for twin successes on the tidal Trent venue as you'll discover presently. But although Harry Jackson cut his float fishing teeth on the Trent with the mighty Abbey Hey AC and their winter bus trips out of Manchester, he's won big open matches on the River Witham, Weaver, Holme Pierrepoint rowing course, and several other waters. He won the Weaver Championship with 28lb of bream that stood as the river record for years, and he also once hauled in a massive 86lb of bream on pole to break the venue match record at Holme Pierrepont. Harry also has the distinction of being included in the first four-man team to name themselves Barnsley Blacks. When Denis White was a man short for his team at a Dunham match he asked the Stockport angler to join them, and they duly won the day with his help.

I'd like to describe a special memory for me from the Trent's big match era: Rotherham's Connor Cup back on 13th October, 1974. I drew a peg upstream of Dunham Bridge just before the clapper gate where there was a feature of hawthorn trees behind the flood bank stones. I could not believe my luck, there was nobody downstream on the next peg and an upstream wind was blowing – an easterly and rather cool, but perfect for fishing a large stick float.

With the tide running off all day I set up a greenheart stick float taking 8 x no. 8 shot on my 13ft rod; my reel was loaded with 1.7 lb Bayer line combined with an 18 hook to 1lb trace. I started fishing at 2-3 rod-lengths out, where it was 8ft deep with a steady flow, running the float through at depth and feeding six to eight casters every other run down. I was so confident I was fishing for a double figure weight, but was having a major rethink when, after almost three hours, I'd still not had a bite!

I changed my shotting to a bulk 2.5 feet from the hook, put another 18 inches on my depth and slowed my presentation down. But after another hour and numerous rig changes, alarmingly, I still had no bites. With just over an hour to go, I decided to change again in order to at least contribute to our team (of four) weight. I put the rest of my casters – 1½ pints – into a brown crumb mix with added molasses. This sticky mix would go straight down which it needed to as by now the flow had picked up pace. I proceeded to put three tennis ball-sized balls of groundbait filled with casters down the edge. I then ripped off my stick float rig and put on a bigger 'paintbrush handle' stick float.

To digress slightly regarding this float, it was made from a paintbrush handle. This came from a day when I was tidying my children's room and spotted some discarded paint brushes. Thinking some would make a good base for a big stick float for heavy water like the tidal Trent, I stripped a couple down to clean wood and noticed they had a very close grain. I made two floats by first drying the wood in an oven before stripping it down and carving a spigot at the thick end to attach the balsa top. The wood seemed like a dense type of cane.

The following weekend I went to try them out with Ian Alcock at Dunham. The river was carrying some extra water which was perfect for testing the floats. They worked so well that when I got home I raided my children's stock of discarded paint brushes with a view to making more sticks, hence the name, though in truth it was my Stockport pal, the late John Farrer who insisted on calling them paintbrush handles. The sizes varied from 5½ to 7½ inches long, the lower portion would be 1/8" to 3/16" diameter going up to a max. 3/8" wide, about ¾" below the pointed float tip. We also supplemented these floats with some 6 x BB to 8 x BB all-balsa jobs made by Oldham float-maker, Dave Brierley, for the Bristol Avon. This river is famous for an upstream wind which stops a small stick float trotting through, whereas a bigger float with a heavy bulk weight at 2/3-depth will catch the river's gradual flow and travel naturally on the current.

I plumbed up on this margin line at six feet deep, but before I shotted up this new rig I cast out a leger on my quivertip rod over the groundbait. I was pleased to get a rattle on the tip while I was still making the change. I missed the bite but now knew there were fish on the feed as I came back with a frazzled caster. This bigger float would normally take 8 x BB shot, but I over-shotted it with 11 x BB in a block, 2.5 feet from the hook, plus 4 x no. 8 shot below as droppers. Finally, twelve inches behind the float I added 1 x AAA back-shot.

Checking my watch, there was just short of an hour to go. I lowered the rig in at the end of my rod with three feet of line to my float, holding back against the large back shot to stop the float still, and inching the rig downstream until the rod reached ten past the hour. I then started at the rod end with a firm ball of groundbait the size of a pigeon's egg every other chuck. The second put in, the float went under and my first roach of the day was quickly netted. Then, to my surprise and delight, more roach followed, almost one a chuck during this last period of the match. Two fellow anglers came up at this time and asked how long I had been catching? "Last hour," was my reply, as the float went under once again. These willing roach just kept on coming.

As the match neared its end, the comment: "Five minutes to go" came from behind me. I set my rig ten inches deeper and paid out another yard of line to put the rig lower down the peg, looking for a bonus fish. So on the last chuck of the match I would have been twelve to fourteen inches over-depth. As I did this there was a comment from one of anglers behind me which I ignored. Within three minutes I hooked another fish that was holding strong in the current. This turned out to be a 14oz skimmer that I netted just as the 'all out' was announced.

The two anglers told me that very little had been caught and I would likely make the frame. One of these anglers was the brave man who spoke to Harry Race on the way back to match headquarters. As for catching all the fish so late, I was not the only one to be surprised. Walking back to the draw after the match, I got to the bridge and heard Harry (a fair giant of a Rotherham steelworker) enquire of an angler who sat behind me what weights there were upstream. He replied: "I have just watched a youth catch nearly 9lb in the last fifty minutes," to which the big man boomed back in his deep voice: "Nobody has caught that on this river today!" This prompted my witness to say: "I sat and saw it for myself." I had no wish to get involved at all, for Harry seemed annoyed and was shaped like Arnie the Terminator, so I quickly made a hasty retreat to HQ to learn of the outcome.

As it turned out that last-minute bonus skimmer was the

key to victory. Our team also managed to win, which rounded off the day perfectly.

Result: H Jackson. 8-14-0, 2nd J Shakesby 8-8-8, 3rd H Race 7-0-8; Team: 1st Abbey Hey 18-6-0 (Ian Alcock, Rob Palmer, Tony Knight and Harry Jackson)

Connor Double

Twelve months later in the same event I drew a good peg above Dunham Bridge just below the Dubs, number 112. The river was a good level as the tide had turned about an hour and a half before the match and started running off for the rest of day, nice and steady. This was a good area and I fancied I could win the match in spite of the tight pegging.

I started with one float rod 13-ft. long with 1.7lb reel line to 1lb hooklength and a size 18 hook, baited with caster. I mixed a small amount of groundbait feed in case I needed to bring the fish up the peg. I had 1½ pints of casters to loose feed. I plumbed up to find 8ft of water having set up a 6 x no. 10 greenheart stick float full depth with a 1 x no. 8 back shot.

Just before the all-in I noticed the angler above me had a set of scales and he asked if I would assist in the weighing-in as he was a committee member. "No problem," I replied, though I was always a shade suspicious how committee members seemed to draw good pegs to order back in the day. The match commenced and within 15 minutes I caught my first roach and began getting a feel for the peg.

After the first hour I had a dozen roach, but then the man above considered that his peg continued 2-3 metres below my standing position. That's all I needed as he was using a large crow quill and every time he struck the splash frightened me. I asked him obey the NFA ruling and not fish into my peg, encouraging the reply: "Don't worry, I will make it right when I weigh you in." This got me so annoyed that I warned him I would take his terminal tackle off him and throw it up the bank the next time his float entered my peg.

A short while later as I was unhooking a roach his float passed me again. Trouble brewing. This time I dragged his float out and broke it and the rig off and threw it up the bank. He never said a word. After this incident I was able to get on in peace and finished with a net of pristine roach weighing 18lb 7½oz. I must say the committee man did apologise fully knowing he was in the wrong. Fortunately I won the match!

This was a proud moment retaining the Connor Cup with back-to-back wins, but it was probably one of the easiest matches I have won – good conditions and a text book day. For icing on the cake my Stockport Fed team also won the day by a mile with 32lb 0oz, this time joined by Ian Alcock, Tony Bielderman and Rob Palmer.

Result: 1st H Jackson 18-7-8, 2nd P Hill 9-14-0, 3rd M Thacker 8-14-0

Harry Left Feeling Over The Moon

Harry had not known John Farrer for long, but John had told him of a good spot on the River Weaver where he had caught a few nice bream. Harry drew the same area the following summer in the 440-peg Weaver Championship at Northwich – peg 62, nearly opposite the boatyard below Marshall's Wood. For the first 90 minutes he caught nothing, at which point a spectator arrived, an older gentleman he knew called Dave Gill.

"Hello Mr Gill," says Harry.

"Hello young Jackson," says Mr Gill "Caught anything?'

"Not much yet," says Harry, though his hopes were raised as he usually caught fish whenever he saw Dave.

Little had been caught in the section other than a single bream to two anglers nearby, so with nothing to lose, Harry promptly mixed up a bowl of soft groundbait and added plenty of casters. While setting up his swingtip rod, the bream story John had told suddenly came to mind, and so he went for it, balling the whole 6lb mix in. He cast over the groundbait and soon caught a bream, then another, and over the last two and a half hours of this four-hour event took a winning 28lb to break the river's match record. Dave followed Harry to the match presentation and, thrilled for him, said: "You will not forget this day as long as you live."

"Oh yes?" queried Harry.

"No, never, because you've won on the day man landed on the moon!" smiled Dave.

Harry had been so intent on fishing the Weaver he'd forgotten all about what Neil Armstrong achieved for mankind in the early hours of that morning 20th July 1969.

(Harry's record lasted around 10 years before Liverpool's Chris Diamond broke it with 40lb).

Chapter 11
Gerry Lees – the lad from the cotton mills

Hailing from Failsworth, near Oldham, Lancs. in that swathe of Northern countryside which housed the 'dark satanic mills' of the old textile industry, Gerry Lees was originally a member of Failsworth Cycle Club AC, a top club in the Ashton and Oldham Angling Association. The club would enter as many as five teams of five in the Trent Championship. After teaming up with his local tackle dealer and Halifax team skipper, Jim Gilder in 1966, the duo built up an impressive Trent match record from then onwards through the seventies.

The stick float was all the rage when Gerry bucked the trend in favour of a stocky little float of his own: the Carrot. The float's design was based on a float used by a friend. He called it the Arch. While Jim and Gerry pooled their ideas and plundered the Trent match circuit, some of their rivals thought the float peculiar and didn't give it much credit, but Gerry had total faith in this little float with the shouldered tip. Nottingham's Rob Taylor was one well-known Trent angler who saw its potential in Gerry's hands, and, one match win later became a convert, ordering many more of the floats from Jim's shop in later seasons.

Jim was fourteen years Gerry's senior and once they'd joined forces his experience rubbed off on Gerry who quickly became a regular winner. At the Trent match Mecca, Burton Joyce, Gerry was tagged 'the lad from the cotton mills' by match organiser Roy Toulson. Here is Gerry's story of the 'carrot' and the other big reason why he was eternally grateful for knowing and befriending Jim Gilder...

As far as I know the Carrot float design was born in the early sixties. Teddy Catlin, a good friend of mine and a member of the Cycle Club, first mentioned it to me. When I got to know Ted, I discovered that the way he fished was different to everyone else I knew: a method called 'the Arch.' At the time he could not find any floats heavy enough for how he wanted to fish, so he asked another club member who was pretty good at making things to come up with an answer. Ted Jones was a bit of a legend in the Oldham area. I still have a couple of model fish that Ted made, either carved or moulded – a 2lb 10oz roach and a 25lb salmon caught on Brighouse Lake by Jimmy Gilder, a record at the time of capture (1977).

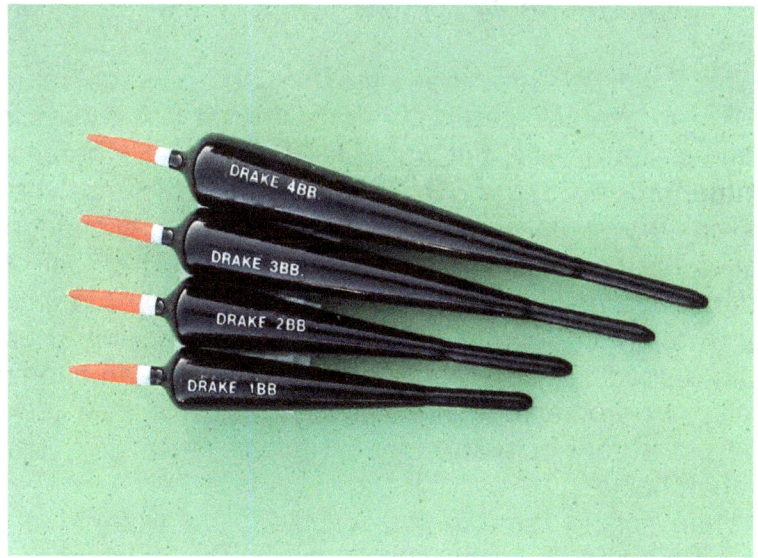

A modern take on the Gerry Lees carrot from Oldham company Drake, with extra fine tips

But regarding the original float, Ted and his father got their heads together and came up with the Carrot. The early sizes as I recall went from 2 x BB up to 3 x AAA. Ted was after a waggler-style float to suit the Arch style as mentioned. He would cast this bottom only-attached float upstream and follow it downstream in an arc, without releasing much line from the reel – in and out all the time. His way of casting upstream did not seem legitimate in a match setting, but that's another story.

When I started fishing the Trent and Calder in the sixties there was very little choice of floats in the tackle shops other than quills. I remember one of the first shops I went in and the dealer showed me a card with a dozen floats on of various types. They were called Belglow and not one was suitable for the Trent or really streamlined. Of course, by the end of the decade this all changed with a fair explosion of different brands of sticks and peacock wagglers.

I could not quite get to grips with the stick floats that had just come on the market, so I adapted the Carrot float to fish double rubber. I found it to be quite stable and hold back without riding up when long trotting. When Jim started having Carrot floats made commercially for the shop he ordered sizes from 1 x BB up to 5 x BB. My favourite sizes were 2 x BB for the Trent (seems a bit light now) and 1 x BB for the Calder. For trotting down twelve to fourteen yards I always felt in full control.

The 2 x BB Carrot that I mostly used on the Trent was ideal for an average depth of 5-foot. I never had a prescribed shotting pattern really, but would start with no. 8's nearest the hook then no. 4's and a BB. After as few as two trots through the swim the shotting pattern might start to get changed to adapt to the conditions – flow and wind etc. The floats were not difficult to make: a slim cane pointed at the top inside a three to four-inch length of balsa body shaped like a carrot, leaving a short spigot of cane at the bottom. As an alternative to balsa we sometimes used elder pith. This was tricky to shape but a very buoyant material taking more shot, size for size, than balsa.

When fishing the Trent and Calder the weather always played a big part. In a downgate wind, as the Notts lads called it, good float presentation was difficult. To keep the float away from the stones and travelling in a straight line I always used the longest rod available. My first match rod was a 13-ft Milbro Enterprise followed by a 14-ft Hardy Matchmaker. I had a very strong right arm for my nine and a half stone! They were my rods for a few years, before Jim bought a 16-ft Bruce and Walker CLT carbon that weighed in at 1lb 10oz, then soon fell out with it, finding the lead insert in the butt end too heavy, so I ended up with a lovely 16-ft carbon for free! At the time it was the longest rod in the country and it was perfect for my style of fishing. Paired up with a 4 x BB Carrot, holding back in a downstreamer afforded good presentation, and this set me up for the rest of my angling career. By the way I still have the treasured rod.

The one limitation with the Carrot was its casting ability. A stick float made with a heavy base material like lignum, or a metal stem, or a balsa with more weight down the line, would cast further. But my second favourite method got over this limitation big style: the mighty peacock waggler. This float could be cast anywhere. Benny and Kevin Ashurst used to deliver maggots to Jim's shop, and on one occasion told of how the day before they had got their backsides kicked by a bloke called Johnny Rolfe (legend). Benny admitted to Jim: "he was fishing with a piece of peacock 18-inch long, waggling all over the place." So the bottom-only waggler became my second favourite float, and a boss float (i.e. beats the conditions well) anything from 2 to 4 x SSG.

My best result with the Carrot has to be the Trent Championship, a huge match at its peak and second only in prestige to the National with 1,250 entrants in five zones from Burton Joyce down to Holme Marsh. I weighed in 13lb 10½oz of roach in 1973 only for Bradford's Kevin Armitage to pip me to the post with 13lb 13½oz. The 'Bradford Babes' as they were called were a strong Trent team, but, oh, the agony. I'm still trying to get over that 3oz! However, thanks to good back-up weights from Jim Gilder, Pete Warren, Peter Hill and Teddy Catlin, we (Failsworth UFO) won the team event with 42-2-4.

Roy Toulson called me the Lad from the Cotton Mills which I suppose was a kind of compliment. One of my best results came when fishing with Notts Fed in their 'Copper Kettle' Championships fished over eight matches on different

Trent stretches. I won the individual twice in three years, beating the illustrious John Dean in one. I also had a good run in the Midland AC series of eight matches at Hoveringham and Caythorpe – winning four and taking two seconds, with nets from 8lb to 16lb.

For a best performance, I'd have to claim my 529 gudgeon from Caythorpe in five hours for 14lb 15oz, on my 14-ft Hardy Matchmaker (not the lightest rod), but I was 'ounced' again when Johnny Rolfe two pegs away tipped 15lb 1oz of roach on the scales!

Caster Men

Top choice of bait for me and Jim had to be casters. On our trips to the Trent and other mainly river venues we would take from six to eight pints of casters each. Casters would produce a better stamp of roach. We might only feed two to three pints on average but six or more on a flier. I remember with great amusement, Rob Taylor, an out-and-out maggot man, coming up and kicking my caster pot and asking: "What you going to do with them, youth?"

"Give you a good hiding," I replied.

He smiled and said: "Not today."

A youthful Gerry Lees with a nice catch of roach from Kelso, River Tweed

I finished the match with 21lb of pristine roach; he had 9lb of bits. Rob was speechless.

The line we used back then was always Bayer Perlon – 2.6lb on the reel for the Carrot (3.2lb for waggler), and 1.1lb or 1.7lb hooklengths. I had a short spell fishing for gudgeon when the Trent was solid with them. One master of the gudgeon was a good Long Eaton angler, Bill Cartwright. He fished an 18 Mustad gold hook to 1.7lb trace. Bait for gudgeon was four to six pints of white maggots and 10lb white bread groundbait. There were no fancy groundbaits back then. The float was a 5 x BB Carrot with 4 x BB, bunched a foot from the hook and 2 x no. 6 droppers six inches away. The reel was an ABU 508 but the rod was used like a whip line to hand. We'd hardly even time to chat during a gudgeon battle. I had an old chap behind me, talking in the match described, and I never turned round so never knew what he looked like.

Teamwise, Jim and I enjoyed our best National in the Division 3 on the Huntspill in 1976. This was before carbon poles had entered the match scene. In practice we caught tiny eels and skimmers. As Halifax captain, Jim advised us to fish the 'new' 8-metre pole and equip ourselves with a Polynet micromesh keepnet for the eels. The plan worked, we came fourth overall and just missed out on the medals. But the following year we toppled the mighty Barnsley Blacks at Burton Joyce in a Yorkshire area final. Mel Smith, another tackle dealer with two shops in Halifax and Huddersfield, was a leading member of that team, along with old mates like Brian Worsnop, Mick Bottomley, Jack Warne and Freddy Fox.

Angling provides so many happy memories. I have never warmed to top anglers unless first and foremost they are decent human beings. Fortunately, most anglers from that period were very good lads, but here is a shortlist of the many people I admire: Johnny Rolfe, Ted Stokes, John Moult, Roy Toulson, Pete Palmer, John Dean, Frank Barlow and Terry Dorman. All were great anglers but most importantly great blokes.

Finally, a word of thanks to my mentor for many years, the late Jim Gilder. He was a brilliant innovator and leader, as keen as mustard, who lived for his fishing. He drove me everywhere to matches for years. My introduction to Jim was to change my life forever. He opened a tackle shop in 1966 in Failsworth with his wife Beryl and daughter Pamela. A few of the lads started going in to buy their bait and word came back that there was a 'little cracker' behind the counter (Pamela). So I and my mate went to investigate. Meanwhile, Jim had a trophy made to present to the club. On presentation night Jim could not attend so Pamela came instead to present the trophy. The club doors flew open, in walked the 'green goddess' as I called her. Pam and I started dating and, once engaged, Jim obviously became my father-in-law. Pam is my long standing/suffering (!) wife of fifty years this year.

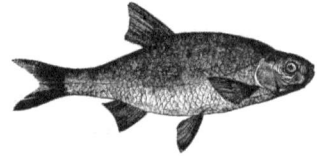

Chapter 12
Stockport Fed reign supreme in Div. 2 National

In 1974 Kevin Ashurst predicted that Stockport Federation would win that year's Division 2 National on the Warwickshire Avon – the second biggest ever contested by 115 teams of 12, and would do so with caster. He knew each member of the team and their capabilities, having a fresh memory of four of them from their great win with Stoke – Ian Alcock, Tony Bielderman, Ken Booth and Ian Heaps, but was also aware of the skill and consistency of the other eight.

Under the new divisional system the great match was now decided on section points and when Stockport absolutely blitzed it with a total of 1,161, it confirmed Kevin's good judgement and more besides. The 1969 Stoke team had long disbanded, Kevin had moved on to become an England International and, with Leicester star Ivan Marks, they became the biggest names in seventies matchfishing, one with a weekly column in *Anglers' Mail* and the other in *Angling Times*.

Interestingly, Stockport drew peg 28 on the day, close to the number 26 from which Stoke had won the Trent National; could it be a lucky omen? It certainly appeared so when at least half the team began plundering chub, roach and bream on various sections of the Avon matchlength with the methods they'd refined and polished back on the Trent.

With the big match now split into divisions and being decided on total points instead of weight and with one hundred and fifteen teams of twelve competing, this Stockport team caught well enough to record the best National Champs performance to date, scoring 84.1 per cent of the total section points on offer.

No fewer than seven of the team finished in the top fifteen in their sections, each having beaten at least a hundred other competitors to do so. Tony Knight and Ian Heaps both won their sections for 115 points and Dick Ward came seventh in his for 109 points. Backing up this terrific start came: Ian Alcock and Trevor Lovatt both 106, Geoff Kirk 104, John Farrer 101 and Bob Redfern 100. Young John Farrer had taken Harry Jackson's place in the team after he had to rule himself out, and delivered.

It has to be said that the Avon was not just a stick float contest for these anglers more used to the top and bottom style: they adapted to a combination of stick and waggler, though to a man they fished with casters. Tony Knight, for example, drew upstream of the bridge at Eckington and fished waggler and caster for 18lb 7¼oz – an all-chub net, bar one bream, that earned him fifth overall. Ian Heaps meanwhile, won the end section 'M' at Twyning with 12lb 2oz on a slider.

The captain and senior angler in the team was Jim Heaps, Ian's dad, who performed creditably himself to bag 95 points. The lads were most proud to win it for the veteran who was a very popular figure in Stockport having coached many young anglers to put them on the right track throughout his life.

Stockport finished 69 points clear of Lyttleton on 1,092 and Reading-based King Heron on 1,065 who took silver and bronze respectively. It was a magnificent performance, but for at least ten years most of these guys been developing their skills and gaining confidence on the Trent. They now had experience to go with youthful enthusiasm and it all came to fruition.

Man of the Avon, and England International, Ken Giles, in praising Stockport's performance said: "There are always good and bad draws in any National of twelve big sections, so some found it harder than others, but this team obviously fed the river right. They knew how to keep the fish coming with 'little and often' feeding. Go too heavy on the feed on the Avon then, and the fish would switch off after three hours. I dare say a pint of casters, never two, was the way on most sections to get the most out of the swim, so they sussed it out perfectly."

Section Points Scores: 'A' Dick Ward 109, 'B' John Farrer 106, 'C' B Redfern 100, 'D' Geoff Kirk 104, 'E' Jim Heaps 95, 'F' Trev Lovatt 106, 'G' Ken Booth 83, 'H' Alan Mayer 38, 'J' Ian Alcock 106, 'K' Tony Knight 115, 'L' Tony Bielderman 89, and 'M' Ian Heaps 115. Total 1,161 PTS.

Let us now briefly examine some of this team's big match credentials:

Jim Heaps, Method men and Abbey's best

Jim as the skipper and elder statesman in the team, together with the experience and enthusiasm of Dick Ward would have brought vast experience to the younger team members and the points show there was no weak link. In fact it was two of their most consistent anglers who did least well: Ken Booth and Alan Mayer.

As good as the team was, any bookie would have given long odds on Ken Booth finishing in the last two team places, and for Alan Mayer to be their back marker on 38 points suggests he and Ken drew badly. Ken was, after all, rated by Dick Ward as the best man on the Trent for several seasons who excelled on the stick and caster, the bait which dominated this championship. Alan Mayer, too, was a third member of the successful four-man team called 'The Method' in the line-up.

With or without a good draw on the day, having chippy Booth in the team must have spread a super confidence throughout the ranks. This was the man who a year or two before had bagged the Trentman title and three other big match wins in a fortnight – how he must have urged them on. Anyone with the ability to win the Trent Championship and three other big matches inside a month at that time, and was long used to team success, had to be a huge inspiration to others; and, to a man, they were experienced enough to handle their tag as favourites to win.

Geoff Kirk and Trevor Lovatt

Two more of the team whose catches made a big contribution to the win were Geoff Kirk, alias the 'Bollington butcher,' and Trevor Lovatt of Northwich. They were as sharp as their favourite porcupine quill floats.

In the sixties, the swingtip decade when bream largely ruled throughout Fenland, some anglers forsook the chance of an average four or five bream to win or frame in a big Witham match, and targeted the more reliable small roach wherever they drew. One such group was Northwich Loco's team of four, distant travellers from Cheshire. They based their style on annatto gozzers, annatto being the dye that colours butter. Home-bred by Trevor on chicken heads, the yellow maggots were fished close in over groundbait and squatts.

They won numerous team events on the Witham, Welland and Nene, tempting one reporter to say after one success: "As usual Northwich Loco won the team event." Trevor and Geoff were their most successful anglers, along with Graham (Trev's brother) and John Proctor. The group had learned their craft on the shallow Macclesfield Canal and the River Weaver when they were tough, the Weaver slowly recovering from pollution. Trevor won the Weaver Championship with a modest 3lb 9oz, and won with as little as 1lb 9oz on the Macc' Canal.

When they tried this small roach 'scratching' method on the Witham and Welland they found both rivers also suited the style perfectly. But they had a trick up their sleeves that others did not try: raking the swim before starting to fish. Trevor adapted a garden rake to fit on a fourteen-foot landing net handle and the other team members followed suit. This was especially helpful on the weedy margins of the Welland, but also on the Witham in hot summers.

They fed regular nuggets of groundbait containing plenty of squatts, and each team member would carry four pints of the feeders and be prepared to get through around 7lb to 12lb of mix. It was good enough to win Geoff the Tetley Gala on the Welland and get Trevor second spot to Austin Clissett in the 1963 Welland Championship. It also earned Trevor a rather special 11lb of roach in a Chesterfield open on the Witham. His best two fish that day scaled 2lb 5¼oz and 1lb 12½oz no less, and the larger specimen earned him the £5 'fish of the week' prize in the Sunday People newspaper. Geoff chipped in by winning the Peterborough Hospital Cup with 23lb of bream on the float on the Nene's North Bank.

The story later emerged that the big roach brace Trevor caught in the Chesterfield match were no fluke: the team often took a bigger roach or two to add to the small ones, and they found them on or close to the bottom.

This form team of the period regularly caught from 5lb – 8lb of roach per man in the Fenland opens when 20lb+ was always a handy team weight. And what float did they select as best for the job? A three to four-inch, slim porcupine quill taking just 2 x no. 8s down the line, occasionally scaling up to one taking 3 x no. 6! These two anglers proved they had the confidence and adaptability to fish caster on the Warwickshire Avon.

Chapter 13
Pete Warren – the Beeston bricklayer

In one month, just prior to Christmas 1974 to Jan 18th '75, Pete Warren set the Trent scene alight with seven wins, three seconds and a fourth, plus a fourteenth from three hundred in a Worksop Open at Winthorpe. It appeared, for this stick float ace from Beeston, as though all his Christmases had come at once, but this kind of consistent success was becoming almost predictable. Such was Pete's dominance, that Long Higgin match organiser Steve Toone showed his frustration one day by announcing: "His float looks no different to mine and a few others as it travels downstream; the big difference is Pete's keeps coming back with a fish on the end, ours don't."

A wind of change was blowing down the Trent valley. The river was gradually becoming cleaner and cooler, and less of a semi-polluted brown soup as fish stocks recovered from the 1967 Columnaris disease. That close quarters area around the rod tip where the Manchester anglers had reigned supreme for a decade with small stick floats and casters was now less reliable; the fish were becoming cautious, moving further out into the flow requiring heavier floats to reach them. The waggler at distance would increasingly become a winning method.

'Leathered' the opposition: Pete in his pomp with winning catch

The Ashursts and friends had already trialled the waggler in practice for the 1969 National and only floodwater conditions on the big match day ruled the method out while their faith in the stick gave them team glory.

All good runs have to end sometime though, and if the Northern invaders were getting a shade complacent, then other anglers were more than ready to fill their shoes. One local above all others would redress the balance and generally pave the way back for future Nottingham teams. He was Pete Warren, a bricklayer by trade and a self-taught angler.

Even in the early sixties the North West men did not have it all their own way. There were always outstanding individuals who could spring a surprise. But in the heart of Nottingham old habits die hard and the transition from pin to casting reel and maggot to caster, took time. And although Nottingham's top anglers had advanced since the day Ken Parr and Archie Tizley travelled to the River Weaver on a spying mission where they saw Dick Ward and friends wielding the stick, they remained in some disarray. Johnny Toulson and Johnny Moult were consistent star performers, but neither were true to the original stick float design. The former's float of choice was a loaded balsa and the latter excelled at bottom-only style.

Although Pete Warren had won some matches on a porcupine float fished close in, he would undergo a style transformation before the sixties ended. It was a draw next to the great Leicester skipper and star all-rounder, Ivan Marks, at Dunham Bridge that did more than show him the way forward, it rocket-propelled his angling career.

"I'll never forget it," said Pete. "Ivan was drawn upstream of me with his pet dog for company. We used crow quills and porkies and centrepin reels back then, but I'd never fished a stick float. I was beating Ivan on the inside line until he set up a stick float and cast out to three or four rod-lengths. I just couldn't compete. The experience changed me completely. I went and had a look at his rig and everything afterwards, and the next day bought some stick floats and a fixed spool reel and started fishing it. It opened my eyes, that day next to Ivan."

Pete was unhappy with the early stick floats that were sold locally, believing they were either too heavy in the base or too light. "The heavy ones would cock to vertical before the bait had sunk so you couldn't always see bites on the drop, and they were so heavy to cast they'd overtake the shot in the air and cause tangles; the lighter ones wouldn't cast well at all. I wanted a happy medium: a float that would cast well and settle in a line with the descending shots, because you used to get a lot of bites on the drop. I wanted a float that would give me the best chance of catching those fish."

Soon after the lesson, Pete had drawn a design for a stick float and presented it to Nottingham's top floatmaker Gerry Woodcock, a National angler and no mean Trentman himself. In short order he was making the floats to Pete's liking. And the commercial 'Warren stick' was to become the template for almost all other sticks that followed up to the end of the century. Pete himself promoted the float in the best way possible: he won match after match with them!

At the start of the seventies other Nottingham anglers were fast improving too, and Pete pays credit to the skills of Pete Palmer, Roy Toulson (no relation to Johnny), John Rolfe, Ted Stokes and Frank Barlow as prime examples, but Pete was leading the way, sowing the seeds for future Notts Fed glory, particularly at his favourite stretch, Long Higgin.

I was impressed by an early seventies *Angling Times* picture of Pete clad in black leather jacket and holding his winning roach net stretched out for the camera. This was cool; never before had I seen a winning angler in a coat he might wear to go to the pub. The headline read: *'The Beeston bricklayer.'* The report described how he caught 20lb of roach on just a half-pint of casters, and again this appealed to my imagination. Drip-feeding was the order of the day.

Pete with wagglers and a selection of his Mk 2 Middy stick floats

There were days and certain seasons on the Trent when roach were simply not feeding in numbers. At such times anglers would have to resort to 'gudgeon bashing' and I have known Pete put 10lb or more of these fingerlings on the scales to make the frame.

Showing his dedication to the game, Pete, like Dick Ward before him, shortened his Mitchell Match reel stem to easier reach the spool with his forefinger. "I've got rather short fingers so I cut between ½" and ¾" from the pillar that connects the reel seat to the body. Then I glued it back and strengthened the joint with two countersunk screws, ensuring first that the bale arm still cleared the reel seat," Pete wrote for *Angling Times* in 1975. He would later change to a closed face model, though he did not always rely on the line leaving the spool for smooth trotting anyway.

"Paying line off with your hand was the smoothest way, although with closed face reels I often used to trot the float by following it with the rod then pay off a full rod's-worth of line in an upstream sweep and following it down again, repeating the process until I'd trotted the full length of the peg," he said.

Pete, now 78, recalls how he won 50 matches in 1974 when fishing three matches a week mostly on the Trent, and believes he'd have won the Kamasan Matchman of the Year title easily had it existed at the time. Without equal on a good stick float peg until the river changed in the mid-seventies and bronze maggot became the bait of choice, he estimates his open match wins run into the hundreds but has not kept count over a long career.

Surprisingly, his most memorable match is a win in a winter league semi-final on the Warwickshire Avon at Pershore, where he broke the venue record with 70lb-plus of bream: "It was something different for me. I fished the tip with bomb and double red maggot and the bream were just there. We won the team event too as a bonus. It is always enjoyable on a flier when it happens."

Despite the enduring success of the Nottingham Federation team, including many anglers Pete had inspired in their youth, he stayed faithful to Nottingham's rival team, Notts AA. "Good times with a cracking bunch of lads" is how Pete remembers those team fishing days.

A keen teenage observer of Pete Warren, who became a leading matchman himself a few years later, was Wayne Swinscoe. This is what he said about Pete in a 1993 magazine article when he was then established as a top river angler:

"I have been lucky because I have been able to watch who I consider to be the best stick float angler there has ever been. In all my years fishing I don't think I have seen anybody who came close to him, with the exception perhaps of Don

Slaymaker. People talk about John Dean, and though there's no dispute that Deany came from another planet light years away, I still have treasured memories of watching Pete Warren; talk about poetry in motion! Pete seems able to make the stick work in any kind of conditions, often when others have given up the ghost. I recall him winning six good matches on the trot at different Trent venues including Shelford, Burton Joyce and Long Higgin, quite incredible."

DO'S AND DON'TS from the Pete Warren stick float manual

⌣ The fish always dictate the way the float should be presented. In summer on the Trent (or other rivers) with the fish willing to feed and chase the bait, we can expect to run it through at the flow speed. In winter however, I'd be more likely to hold the float back seven days out of ten.

⌣ Size of stick? For rod end work I'd use a 4 x no. 4 float, then for distance and deeper water a 6 or 7 x no. 4. As a rough guide I'd work on equivalent to a no. 4 shot for every foot of depth.

⌣ Shotting patterns vary according to the angler but shirt button-style is my starting point. For close in work in three to four-foot of depth I'd use no. 8s only with the tell-tale starting 9" from the hook. For casting further out into double that depth I'd still use a no. 8 tell-tale but string out no. 4s above it.

⌣ Balance is the key to a good stick. You want it to cock in line with the shots falling. Lignum does not do this as well as sinking cane or certain grades of plastic/nylon in my opinion. A cane stem catches fish both on the drop and on the bottom, and a forward lean on the float when held back, pointing towards the hookbait is desirable which is why I don't want the base too heavy.

- Back-shotting is essential in a downstream wind allied with sinking the line from float to rod tip. I will use two number 8s above the float to keep the line down, though I have used as many as four.
- Hook sizes for caster? – I would advise a fine wire 18 as standard but occasionally a 20 can work better on shy fish, buried in the caster.
- In winter try over-shotting the float by 1 x no. 4 shot and hold back to just ease it down the peg. We used to call this putting the bait in the fish's mouth. But remember that every day is different; I did not always over-shot if the fish would have the bait running faster to them.
- Ref feeding, it is half the battle to get the feeding right and little and often will take you far with casters. My old Trent method was half a dozen casters and a little pinch of groundbait every run down. It worked everywhere I went. Many times I could lay the float on the water, run it a yard and it would go under!
- Feathering: before the float lands on the water stop the line to feather the float down quietly and this also straightens the shotted line below the float.
- Controlling the line: cast the float to where you intend it, then use the rod to lift any loose line and flick it upstream to sit directly behind the float to start the trot (ie. with consideration to point 5 and wind factor).

Chapter 14
Frank Barlow & the mighty Notts Fed team

Eyes down on the stick at Long Higgin

If Terry Dorman was the court jester of the great Nottingham Federation, alias Trentmen, squads of the 1970s and beyond, then a few others were also good at responding with the one-line witty quip. These were anglers with a sense of fun to match their undoubted skills. Apart from being a wag, maggot breeder Terry was also known for the quality of his baits which were famously tagged 'Dorman's donkeys.'

The team fished National Championships under their official banner Nottingham and District, and their motto was 'Win or lose, have a booze.' Two others who could crack a joke while keeping a deadpan expression were John Rolfe and Frank, aka 'Boris,' Barlow. While John became the original Trent waggler man, Frank's results on the stick float inspired his colleagues. As for the boozy image, I dare say they didn't drink more beer than other teams; they had a winning mentality but were not bad losers and could take a bad result on the chin. This, I think, was really what the motto meant to reflect.

But one man in particular deserves most credit for starting the local stick float and caster comeback, the outstanding motivator for the good anglers to follow: Pete Warren. From the early seventies his winning consistency was second to none, and soon others were getting in on the act; confidence was rising with each passing season and the victories were coming for new names on the Trent circuit.

A nucleus was in place already: Johnny Moult who had long been a winner anyway, Rolfe, the stand out performer on waggler in 1971, John Toulson, a known big-weight angler, and Ted Stokes who set the five-hour Trent weight record in 1965. Adding to this quartet was the aforementioned Barlow who was now regularly clipping the wings of the Northern invaders on the stick float.

While Warren remained loyal to Nottingham's rival team, Nottingham Anglers AA, his protégé, young Wayne Swinscoe would soon become a leading member of Fed's squad. As the Fed' team grew in strength it became a badge of honour for any local to be able to say he fished for them.

Another big name was Pete Palmer who ran the Burton Joyce Saturday matches with his talented friend Roy Toulson (no relation to John). Pete would go on to take the 1977 Gladding Masters title and for a few seasons was almost invincible. But for a while as the seventies dawned it was Warren and Barlow who were often toppling the mighty Mancunians.

Was it man landing on the moon in 1969 that finally made Nottingham's best realise that anything was possible, I wonder, because their run of Trent dominance started around this year. Don Slaymaker, nicknamed 'Sledgehammer' was another born winner

Jan 'the man in red' Porter: not just flamboyant but a quality angler

whose Fenland float results on bream, were also impressive. When the quiet but deadly John Dean and one-time travelling partner, Paul Cope, joined the gang it could be said they upskilled an already good squad into a great one. Charismatic Jan Porter, 'the man in red,' was improving fast and on course to join the group. Jan had the benefit of working with the great John Moult.[6]

Frank captained Notts AA to Division 2 National victory with 806 points in 1978 on the Trent which he described as his proudest moment, but was with Fed' for their finest hour when taking 1980's Division 1 team title on their home river with a record-breaking 883-point score, while in the intervening season he won a remarkable 20 open matches! He was described as 'one of angling's greatest characters – built like a rugby prop forward, his size belies his skill with which he controls the finest of tackle.'

Pete Palmer steered the team to victory on a good river in the upper Trent National in 1983, including Steve Draper's near title miss with 40lb-plus, ounces behind champion Dave Howl on 42-9-8. As the eighties wore on, first Jan Porter (1987 Trent team win) then the much-respected Ted Stokes took over the skipper's role, with Ted spearheading their fourth Trent win in 1992. Now something of a father figure, Ted, aided by Jan, would inject a little more professionalism into the young squad, which was now sponsored by Daiwa in spite of the experienced trio of Barlow, Slaymaker and Swinscoe having transferred to Shakespeare's Superteam. But the re-shaped team didn't disappoint.

---

6 I travelled with Jan Porter over two winters in the eighties to the midweek Normark League at Evesham. We both enjoyed some good results and the journeys alone were fun, sometimes with Tony Greaves or Mick Fisher joining us. Jan was flamboyant but far more than an angler who wore all-red outfits. The Notts Fed skipper had played guitar in a band and often fished and won matches while wearing Walkman earphones playing Big Country tracks! Johnny Moult, the brilliant but unorthodox Trent legend, often entered our conversation. Jan was apprenticed to Johnny in the engineering shop at Rolls Royce and so found the perfect (fishing) mentor. Johnny was renowned for his quirkiness - he carried a fishing box for years with a hole in the side plugged by a towel, but he was never short on finesse with size 20 hooks and impressed on Jan to always 'get the business end right' – the float to hook section of line.

With Jan Porter and close friend Steve Draper in the squad, along with the likes of Roy Henson, Les Melbourne, Col Perry, Colin Walton and Steve Handley they were always dangerous. Fresh talent came later in the shape of Terry Moroz, Tony Barker, Denis Bonner and Joe Green and the list went on. Fed prided themselves on local county talent, unlike some pro' squads who observed no boundaries, but all-rounders like Neil Parkinson (ex-Goole) and Mal Talbot (an RAF star) proved an exception to the rule. All these anglers could conjure up winning bags of roach on a stick float.

Frank Barlow had also turned his hand to writing a humorous weekly article in *Angler's Mail*. He had a nickname for all his regular bankside characters – 'Rip-off,' 'Cyanide Frank,' 'yellow wellies' et al, and importantly he remained committed and successful on the match circuit which validated the column.

For plain common sense in his approach to the stick. I have re-worked a few lines from a chapter he wrote in the book *'The Match Fisherman'* edited by David Hall, starting with the float's shape:

Float design

Judging by the many anglers I see using a stick float when conditions are all wrong, or even using sticks that are not up to the job, let's start by looking at what a stick float is and what it's supposed to do.

First, the ratio of cane to balsa. Unless this combination is correct, and it should closely approximate 2:1, a stick is useless as it will not sit correctly in situ. Another problem is the use of light cane for the stem. The widest part of the float

The ever popular Ted Stokes

should be around 5mm or ¼" below the tip of the balsa[7] and the base should be of heavy tapered cane.

The stick was originally designed to fish the far bank of Lancashire canals with a minimum of shot down the line and so they were designed to be cast reasonable distances. If the shape is wrong or the same thickness runs throughout its length, then obviously it will not cast properly. Make no mistake there are no instant stick float anglers, it is a method that takes time to master, but it's considerably easier if using a float that is made to do the job.

Realistic distance

It often surprises me when famous anglers advise that the stick float should never be cast more than two or three rod-lengths distance. Some of my best catches have been taken five or even six rod-lengths from the bank, although the conditions have to be right, of course; you can't do that into the teeth of a gale!

Shotting myths

Another popular misconception about stick floats is that you should always string them out along the line, which is not true. If fishing a waggler you would not do that, so why does it have to apply to the stick? Further, when fishing a waggler the bulk of the shot goes either side of the float, so why can't we put an extra shot under a stick?[8]

This I think is where many people go wrong, thinking that because it's a stick float the shots must be evenly spread. For a simple example, let's assume I am fishing at Burton Joyce in a swim that requires fishing four rod-lengths out. The type of rods we use with soft tops help us to flick the float out that far and, given a depth of no more than eight feet, I'd be confident in tackling it with a light 4 x no. 4 float. My shotting would be 2

---

7 This makes a float ideal for casting, and one that will sit at half-cock as soon as it hits the water. Consequently less shot is required on the line and bites on the drop are easily seen. Most shop-bought floats are the wrong shape and have too much balsa. [Luckily for today's anglers, this is no longer true!

8 Ivan Marks, similarly, would often place a BB shot immediately under his stick for extra casting weight; he neither shied away from using extra weight to beat tricky conditions.

x no. 6s directly under the float, 6 more no. 6s spread out evenly from a point around halfway between the float and hook down towards the hook, and finally a dust shot (no.8) 12" from the hook. In the event of the wind getting up I'd switch to a five x no. 4 stick with the extra shot going directly under the float, leaving the business end of the tackle as it is.

Frank and a bumper chub net

Float range

My stick floats range in size from 3 x no. 4 up to 8 x no. 4 and these fulfil everything I want to do. When people start talking about stick carrying AAA shot then I think it is asking a stick to do what it was never designed to. When fishing this method you should be able to present the bait at all levels in the water and I don't see how this can be achieved with so much lead on the line. I am not a great fan of the wire-stemmed stick by the way, believing that a traditional cane stick can do all I need it to.

Shotting a stick, as in all float methods, is important. But it is also a personal thing, for while most anglers will shot up basically the same, each will have little things which are peculiar to his style. For the most part, given reasonable conditions, my shotting is as described above, except that I also like to put one x no. 4 shot below half depth (as something to hold back to, should the need arise). Below that I have no. 6 shot tailing off to 1 x no. 8 and finally 1 x no. 10. With this pattern I feel I get three bites at the cherry – the chance of catching on the drop, on the bottom or holding back. If the peg has a bit of a boil, however, I would go to a heavier float and instead of a single no. 6 shot I'd use 2 x no. 6s below the no. 4 to get that extra bit of stability, but would leave the 8 and 10 alone. Under these conditions I would not expect to have to cast very far.

Being adaptable

There can be nothing rigid about shotting patterns because no two swims are the same and, more important, the fish don't

always want to intercept a bait the way you want to give it to them. So having started out with your tried and tested pattern you have to be prepared to change, and this is perhaps in this area that the difference between the club angler and the open match anglers is most obvious. The clubman will often reason that because he caught 20lb of roach on one method the previous week the fact that he cannot catch this week is because the fish are not feeding or he has drawn a barren peg.

Don Slaymaker: popular amongst his peers, Don always did it with a smile

This may be the case but it's far more likely that the fish just want the bait presented differently.

In the first hour of any match the open angler is looking for the most productive method, and this involves juggling shot about, altering the depth, first trying single maggot and then trying to tempt better fish with a double maggot combination – all these things are tried. When some anglers sit behind me and see me move a shot and start catching, they might conclude I have a secret formula, which of course I don't. It is just a combination of application and experience working to present the bait the way the fish want it on that day.

Over-shotting

Since the stick float's conception there have always been anglers who have had a natural affinity with the method, who could make the float 'talk' as we say. Inexperienced anglers might watch them, however, and because what they are doing looks so easy they think they can do it too. Nowhere is this better demonstrated that with the over-shotted stick float. If it's not done properly it is a totally unproductive method. It requires total control or the float sinks, so obviously this severely limits how far out and down the swim this can be fished effectively. It is ostensibly a method that has to be fished close in, held back and inched down the swim, giving perfect presentation on days when the fish will not intercept a bait travelling

Always dangerous on fish: Wayne Swinscoe

85

at the same speed as the current. Pete Warren was a master of this technique.

Back-shotting

Back-shotting above the float is a way of combating an awkward downstream wind when the fish want the bait held back slightly. The casting position is critical and the answer is to cast downstream and half a rod-length past your intended target area, then to wind the float back into position with part of the rod tip underwater. This sinks the reel line out of harm's way and you can then start the trot with a straight line from rod tip to float.

Stick float royalty: the Notts Fed 1980 National winning team celebrate their record 883-point winning score. Johnny Moult holds the trophy sitting on the shoulders of skipper Pete Palmer

A Typical Match Scenario:

So let's imagine I'm at Burton Joyce, the conditions are OK, and I'm faced with a steady flow and a swim 8' (2.4m) deep. I decide on a 5 x no. 4 Pete Warren float and start by feeding a line two rod-lengths out with a quarter handful of maggots; hookbait is single maggot on a size 20. As I suspect 20lb could win the match, a couple of 1lb chub in the first half hour would be very handy. To make a winning total I have to attract some fish into the swim and feeding is the key. If chub did show early, I'd continue feeding a quarter handful every run down. To catch any fish on the second or third run down would tell me where they are and then I'd continue to feed that line confidently. There are many days when it seems chub will eat all the bait you can throw at them, but if I started catching roach then I'd reduce the feed to just eight to ten maggots per cast. Roach are less greedy and I've lost count of the times I've had a double figure bag by feeding only two to two and a half pints.

So how do I decide what line of river to base my main attack? My answer is I pick the line where I can run my float down best under full control, and on a shallow outside bend with a favourable wind it will probably be several yards further out than a deeper peg on an inside bend. Other than the red-letter days when the fish might come on my original line all day long, it is more common to catch around 3-4lb of fish before the swim starts dying. When this happens I have to start work and respond: changing the depth, moving shots, fishing further out etc.

Experience on the Trent has taught me that a couple of casts further out will often get me a bonus fish or two. The important thing is to keep the main swim alive while plundering other swims. Two hours in and I'd be looking to put 6lb of mainly roach in the net, but after that it is getting harder.

Shallowing up by an inch brings me a roach, a change to the shotting pattern brings another. I try reducing the feed and go biteless for ten minutes, then increase the feed and catch a bonus chub! But it is a false dawn with no more to follow, and it is roach I'm really after as I know I can't get 14lb of chub from this peg. In the second half, the swim hardly ticks over and my final weight is a modest 7lb 15oz.

On a good day I might have kept enough roach coming to scrape double figures for a low frame position as the last hour can often see bites return and a marked improvement. This is a time when the angler below you might have lost heart and packed up early, thus giving you a double peg, or the light level may have dropped to encourage the fish to feed again. An angler with few fish in his net with half an hour or less of the match remaining, can always gamble by feeding heavily with nothing to lose, and, hey presto, this can occasionally produce a big fish or two, and a match take an unexpected turn.

Chapter 15
John Toulson and a heavy approach for roach

It is not entirely accurate to describe our next Trent ace as a stick float angler, as none of the floats he used quite conformed to the standard design. But despite his admission that he has never bought a stick float in his life, his home-made balsas had a piano wire stem set deep inside the base, making them self-cocking and stable, so we can safely say they functioned almost identically. In order to maintain the logical sequence of the Nottingham anglers' role in the stick float story it seemed right to include John's contribution in this section and not group his float with the balsas.

Some anglers like to fish as light as the conditions on the day will allow; others almost relish the chance to fish heavy, no matter how often words like *delicate* and *finesse* are linked to float presentation. Like Billy Lane before him, our next angler falls into this category. He was never scared of putting heavy lead down his line in any Trent swim he found himself in. This man is Johnny Toulson, Trent ace and leading member of the BAA team, triple National Champions in the seventies.

Matchfishing legend, Ivan Marks often referred to many anglers making the mistake of fishing too light for the conditions, but singled out John Toulson as an exception because he knew how to make lead work, implying that he always fished a big enough float to boss the wind and water conditions. He added that shotted correctly the heavier floats are just as sensitive.

Johnny's style was about all-out attack: feeding a ball of groundbait and casters every trot down combined with a heavy rig to get his bait to the bottom quickly. It is no secret that big shots like AAAs or SSGs down the line never troubled him, and he relished the challenge of deep water swims. When I met him on the Trent at Winthorpe back in the seventies his float for the day carried 3 x AAA shots spaced out eighteen inches apart, but I did not recall seeing a dropper shot. John recently assured me that he did use droppers, however.

The key difference with Johnny's floats to the all-balsa models used by anglers in deep or turbulent swims, was extra stability provided by the wire that both added weight and helped the float to cock in line with the descending shots. He'd sand down the top quarter to half-inch of float to a point or dome shape, and taper the rest of the float down to a fine point at the base.

The finished floats were on the short side – from three to six inches only – and squat, taking from 2 x AAA+ right up to a monster 6 x SSG (swan shot), with the heaviest being five-eighths of an inch in diameter at the widest point. When thrown into a bucket of water all the floats would cock to halfway up their length. Johnny's whole approach to fishing the Trent was about catching fish on the bottom with enough lead to get the bait down quickly. By using AAA shot down the line, he did not expect to get bites on the drop as he'd total faith in catching better fish on the deck. He described the logic: "hooking a fish that is coming up head first to intercept a bait at mid-depth is less secure than one with its head down feeding on the bottom."

A standard rig for fishing a steady ten-foot swim on his old stamping ground, the Burton Joyce Road stretch, would be, working up from the hook: a 'dropper' of up to 4 x no. 6 shot (or a BB equivalent) bulked together between six and twelve inches from the hook, then 1 x AAA shot two feet from the hook and a second AAA eight inches above that. In adverse conditions a heavier float would be used with SSG shot replacing the AAAs. This amount of lead is not dissimilar to the positive way anglers fish the Bolognese method today, and was far heavier than most would fish for roach in the Trent's heyday.

"I'd try to fish it like a pond, casting as far as comfortable, pulling some line off the reel and throwing a loop of line upstream and behind the float. The float would be set to put the tell-tale just on the deck, and I'd hold the float back and ease it through slowly, catching roach to 10oz when it went to plan," he adds.

Another key part of Johnny's technique when the Trent was at its peak for roach was regular groundbaiting. A butcher by trade, he used sausage rusk – aka 'pab' – a very fine bread rusk, and he probably bought more than any other butcher in Nottinghamshire. For Johnny would take up to twenty pounds of the dry cereal to every match he fished. The upper limit was for days when he'd be getting a bite every cast and was on for a netful.

In the summer period, however, from the start of the river match calendar on June 16th onwards, the Trent could be a difficult river to master. John remembers how many matches were won then with 3-4lb of small fish. His explanation was linked to water temperature: "Warmed as the river was from the power station outfalls, the water was probably too warm in summer for the roach to respond properly. But as soon as the first frosts arrived in autumn and the river steamed as the warm water met the cold air, their hunger kicked in and big weights were possible."

Grandstand finish

John won many autumn and winter matches in the sixties with 20lb or more of roach, with a personal best all-roach 47lb 4oz coming from Hoveringham in a six-hour Nottingham Post Office AC match in 1966. On a previous sortie to this venue he'd found four feet of depth on top of the shelf at the rod tip, then a bit further out it dropped off to ten feet. He made his play in the deeper water and caught roach steadily, but in the last hour of the match he found some better fish on the closer line, on top of the shelf. Armed with this knowledge for this second match, he started close in, on top of the ledge, caught 10lb in the first hour and never had to search further out.

John said in summary: "Fishing deep swims at that time was right up my street, but I obviously had to try the close in shallow swim first. After such a good start I knew a big catch was on. The weight briefly gave me the six-hour record previously held by Kevin Ashurst with 41-11, but a potential bigger weight was on as the fish were coming very fast in the last hour. Given another fifteen minutes I'd have smashed Ken Parr's seven-hour weight record of 50lb 3½oz. In the minutes up to the final whistle I was swinging net-sized roach of 10oz – 14oz to hand, using a 14 hook buried inside a large caster."

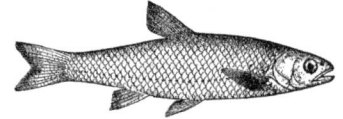

Chapter 16
John Dean – the Selston wizard

/2. 1975

'n from the Force

4th

ABOVE: Sailing down the river . . . this brolly, belonging to an unlucky angler in K section, was just one of the casualties in a string of keepnets, bait boxes and umbrellas claimed by the Force Nina gale!

LEFT: It was predicted that M section would produce the chub . . . and Mick Cresswell, of Derby's NCB No 5, included these useful specimens in his 7 lb net.

RIGHT: Ripley's John Dean took this 10 lb 1¾ oz roach catch while his neighbours at Holme were struggling against the wind for consex. You can see the swim which produced John's fish on page 11.

LEFT: Goole's John Allerton had to cast out five rod lengths to find any depth of water to his shallow 2 section pop. But he fought the wind — and won — to take a third-placed 11 lb 5 oz of small roach and gudgeon.

The inimitable Billy Makin, canal ace and character from Leigh, Lancs. is the former owner of the popular Makin's carp fishery, and a one-time top match angler. He is now spending his retirement in Thailand. In a series of Facebook reminiscences he recalled the days when he was bravely trying to beat John Dean on points to win the Matchman of the Year title:

"Back in the late 70's was a time when John Dean and I were once again locked head to head in a race for the Matchman of the Year competition. Ah... John Dean. This was a bogey man – a man that kept grown matchmen trembling in a state of permanent fear and anxiety – a man who ate new born babies for breakfast – a man who was seemingly unbeatable on his local River Trent.

"The time was mid-winter, and John now held all the aces in what was becoming an annual duel for the coveted title. It was the coldest winter known to mankind. All stillwaters had a near 12-inch ice lid on them, and the only matches being held were on the Trent. This was John's home – this was the river from which he had been spawned following a liaison between two of the river's roach. At an early age he had left the river and moved to Selston. Week after week, no-one could even get a bite, conditions were so bad. John Dean could: he had relatives living in the river. In reality, John was a quiet unassuming guy who never realized just how good he was. I would have given my right arm for half his talent."

Billy's fantasy encapsulates the aura John had built for himself at that time, although the year previously Billy had pipped John to win that very title. Billy's accolade was but one of many used to describe the 'Selston Wizard's' fishing ability over the years. In his short match career, a little over 10 busy years on the Midlands circuit before going into the tackle trade with Colin Perry, he ruled the Trent with phenomenal success. He ran rings round the opposition on float, conjuring up frame results from average pegs and reliably winning from good ones. Notching up a 4th, 2nd, 1st and 1st in four consecutive Matchman of the Year competitions, fishing against the UK's top anglers was exceptional. I still can't believe he was only picked to fish in one World Championship in 1981 in which he performed well!

In recent years I have enjoyed fishing with John as two match veterans and I trust I've a few points to add to his story which may surprise you still. For one, he once threw an ABU 506 reel into the Trent in frustration over its failings. "The line was sticking and bedding in all day and I couldn't pay the line off smoothly enough for my liking. So when the match ended, into the Trent went the reel," he admitted.

Most of those who know John will never have seen him, the ultimate 'Mr Cool,' show any sign of a temper. Outwardly he was always fully in charge of his emotions. He loved the ABU 507, but was obviously far less impressed with its smaller cousin!

Brilliant as he was, even John didn't always get it right, nobody can. In a 1981 magazine article he revealed how he was beaten by Dave Thomas at the next peg, saying: "Dave was getting twice the number of bites that I was and at the end had double my weight. At the after-match inquest Dave explained he had strung his shot out like me but put his tell-tale six inches from the hook where I stubbornly kept mine eighteen inches away. The fish were mouthing the bait and Dave was spot-on with his presentation. It illustrates the point that although you can catch fish on the majority of outings with a basic shotting pattern, there will always be days when the fish want the bait put to them in a totally different way. The moral is that whenever you're not catching, keep ringing the changes."

Fishing can never be an exact science, though it is a shade ironic that John describes a rig in the book with a very close tell-tale shot to hook, while Dave reveals a preference for a good gap before placing that nearest shot. But bear in mind these are outstanding anglers with the confidence and versatility to change seamlessly to a different presentation when the conditions demand.

To illustrate what John could do with a stick float, let's look back to start of the 1980 Trent summer season. Fast out of the blocks, an opening day practice session at Burton Joyce rewarded John with 30lb of fish. This was confidence booster for the opening match two days later.

"I remember that match very well, 18th of June 1980, first match of the season, Notts Fed were running some Wednesday Opens as practice for the National Championship later in the year. I drew peg 252 on the Road Stretch at Stoke Bardolph. The river was carrying 18" of extra water and there was a downstream skimming wind.

"I started on a stick float two rods out shotted with 4 x no.4 shot, 3 x no.6 shot and 1 x no.8 near the hook. Double bronze maggot on a 90340 size 18 hook. I caught from the off – 12lb or so in the first 45 minutes; then disaster as my main line (1⅔lb Racine Tortue) broke near the reel. I had a spare rod set up with a waggler – tried that – no good at all. I then set a stick float up on this rod (2¼lb Racine Tortue) and could not catch.

"Then I stopped fishing and re-tackled my stick float rod with the finer line and a slim wire stem float shotted with 7 x no.6 shot and 1 x no.8 tell-tale near the hook. This was the key to float control in the nasty wind. I weighed in 41lb 6oz in the five-hour match, all roach except for a couple of small chub

(27lb 6 oz was second from the Ferry Field stretch). [Note: In 1965 the great Kevin Ashurst set the six-hour river record on stick float with 41-11oz].

"It is my best roach weight but I did win one of the Saturday opens in 1984 – again on the stick with 44lb 2oz of small chub from the Ferry Field – a Saturday match record at the time. After that 41lb, I won the following Wednesday's open match from peg 127 with 31lb 13oz, and then the following match I was second with 22lb 1oz from peg 171. Not a bad run that."

John retired from the match scene shortly after the latter match. I once asked him how he felt about scaling the colossal 41lb to win by a street but he didn't show even a glimmer of satisfaction. The perfectionist in him could only admit he felt annoyed about the time wasted after breaking his line that cost him an even bigger potential catch.

The other highlight that same year was the Division One Trent National in autumn, when the dozen members of the Notts Fed team showed their prowess by breaking the points record with 883 points, averaging a top 10 place from the 80 anglers in each section. It was fitting that John, the team's new star performer, led the charge with a section win, while John Moult, in the twilight of his career but still brilliant, achieved a second place in his.

I was sent a cutting of a December 1980 match where Billy Makin watched John Dean struggling to get a bite with the Trent in flood. Billy had come away from a cancelled canal match with ice spoiling the show. When he'd reached John he'd nothing in his net, leading to some jibes from Billy like 'the jockey's fell off' etc. But to his great surprise when he saw the match report in *Angling Times* days later, John had won the match with 7lb 11oz, mainly thanks to a late 6lb 8oz carp on stick float. The headline read *'King is back on the throne.'* This was a shade misplaced, as you can't return to something you've never left, and the stats tell us that John did indeed hold all the aces at that time.

In little over six months since that first win on June 18th up to Dec 31st he was outstanding with 13 wins and six seconds. He did have the occasional slip, of course; for example, on Oct 12th he fished a rather special Holme Church Charity open when 51lb took the top prize from the Weir Field, but John could only manage a modest ninth, with 32lb 6½oz! His diary entry read: "Drew peg 127 down from Holme village, caught 20lb of chub to 3lb and 12lb of roach up to 1lb 6oz on a 6 x no. 4 wire stem fished off his rod end, fed seven pints of maggots. 350 fished."

He took home £11.38p. "Pegging was tight, with 10 yards being a long peg there in those days," added John. In fairness the best Weir Field pegs were golden draws back then as National results proved. But overall John's skill, versatility and consistency were unparalleled at a time when match entries ran into hundreds, and to win four opens in a whole season was classed as doing well. John would not lose his Trent crown for a while yet.

Now, when it comes to centrepin reels, and there are many river aces who have long disowned or forgotten them, John's eyes light up. He is a bit of a collector and the two favourites in his collection are Harlow models. I confess to being a closed-face reel fan myself, though I do own a couple of pins in mint condition, an unused Adcock-Stanton included. I showed it to John and he was honest enough to say he didn't like it. And when he then showed me his favourite Harlow pin I could instantly tell why. It was not what some might be inclined to think: that it spins endlessly. To the contrary, John wants his reel to turn at a moderate speed only, just fast enough for the line to leave the spool cleanly in the slowest speed of current.

His Harlow has the patina of long use, but is half the weight of the aforementioned and has no handles on the drum to get in his way when trotting. But best of all, there is a hardly discernible gap between the drum and its housing. 'Perfect' is his word for this fine piece of engineering, and few could dispute it. The fact that Dave Thomas is as big a fan of the pin as John should really tell us all something. I have to think I was myopic in my rating of this reel throughout my river match career, because for these top anglers it was always called into service when extra water was on the river!

But John is modest and philosophical about all the fish he's caught on the Harlow: "It was just another method really that worked well when conditions demanded it."

John, now 74 and a very keen pleasure angler, explains that the pin reel came into play in boily swims or when extra water was colouring up the river and the fish could be caught close in. It was just another method he stresses, but on every occasion when he'd set up two stick float rods (and a third rod for waggler), the Harlow pin would be on one of them. His late close friend and teammate, Malcolm Levy taught him how to overshot the stick and inch it through the swim, and it didn't take John long to master it.

John's pin reel collection, no. 1 Harlow top left

Something you'll notice from my interview with John (below) is how light he shotted to fish the Trent when he could entice the fish to come up off the bottom; for they didn't always feed in the bottom two feet of depth. A four-inch float is one that I never owned in my Trent years, but in every hour he spent on the bankside, John never stopped experimenting and found most of the answers necessary to stay one step ahead of the opposition.

John retired in '83 while at his peak after taking on Mansfield Angling Centre in partnership with Colin Perry. To make a success of the shop he had to sacrifice Saturdays to work, which meant he could no longer practise the river with the same intense dedication, and it cost him his sharpness. Second best would never suit this perfectionist who had reached almost every angling pinnacle.

To his Trent rivals his loss was undoubtedly their gain, but we can only imagine the extent of what he would have achieved had he continued performing in matches into his forties when many matchmen reach their peak, even more so given the career longevity of stars like Bob Nudd or Denis White.

Finally, thanks to John keeping a detailed log of his matches in a diary from the seventies onwards, we can all be sure there is no memory failure which can at times distort or embellish the truth. Here's our interview that took me back to the Trent's golden years when King John II ruled the roost:

1) The Float

Q: Your sticks included plastic stem, wire stem, pointy tips and more domed ones, which type did you prefer in say two contrasting Burton Joyce swims 6' deep or so?

Sticks from John's own collection (plastic paintbrush handle bases)

– I would usually set up two stick float rods, sometimes three. One with a heavy rig – mostly a 5 to 8 x no. 4 shot float with the lead concentrated in the bottom one third of the rig. This was a dome top float, either a stick or a wire stem in more boily swims, often fished with a centrepin reel. The other rig would be much lighter with a pointed top, perhaps 5 to 8 x number 6 shot, spaced out over the whole rig.

It often worked swapping between rigs when bites tailed off. The fish would come up from the bottom, which is when the lighter rig worked.

Q: What size stick in relation to depth did you generally choose for the Road stretch for example?

– The size of float depended not just on the depth, but also the flow – any extra water on – and the distance out from the bank the fish were at.

I caught lots of fish very close in with a float only 4" long, trickled down the edge with a centrepin reel. The float was vastly overshotted and held hard back.

On a normal river, in the middle of the Road stretch, a 5 x no. 4 heavy rig and a 6 x no. 6 light rig would be a good starting set-up. But they were always subject to change as the day progressed.

Q: What was your favourite stick of all-time?

– Probably a 5 x no. 4 size.

Q: Did you always add 2 x no. 8s as back-shot?

– No, I always used 1 x no.8 back-shot a few inches above the float. A second number 8 was added in adverse conditions.

Q: Shotting – describe a 'go-to' starting rig for say a good peg on gravels of BJ Road – ideal conditions: normal river level, wind over right shoulder?

– I would start with this set-up but move the shot about if it was not working. A number 10 at three inches from the hook, then 1 x no. 8 six inches above that, then 1 x no. 6 six inches above that, 1 x no. 4 six inches above that, then 2 x no. 4, then 3 x no. 4.

All of the shotting in the lower third of the rig but it is always subject to shuffling about. I can't stress enough how moving the shot about works.

Some days a shot very close to the hook (two to three inches) worked. If I was missing bites then the shot nearest the hook would be moved away, the rig changed. Other days the fish would want a long tail, especially big roach.

A short tail can produce lots of indications but missed bites, a long tail far fewer indications, but a fish on when the float went under or a sucked maggot. Every day is different: the angler who finds the answer first, wins.

The light rig would have 1 x no. 8 about nine inches from the hook with equally spaced out number 6 shots above it.

Hook lengths were always 24" with the stick float. (36" with the waggler on the Trent and 60" with the waggler on a slow river or lakes). I discovered many years ago when waggler fishing at Butterley Reservoir that a very long hooklength produced better results. The roach then could be difficult to catch and very shy biters. I believed a long fine hooklength allowed the bait to behave more naturally.

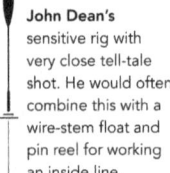

John Dean's sensitive rig with very close tell-tale shot. He would often combine this with a wire-stem float and pin reel for working an inside line.

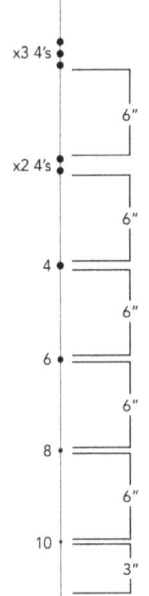

It's very different today with a six-inch hooklength often producing a bite a cast!

Q: Taking the water temperature was a big part of your routine back in the day. What temperature did you hope to find for a double figure or more catch?

– Above 42° F was best. Below that could be a real struggle for roach although the chub would feed.

Q: Was it always evident that the fish came up in the water better the warmer it got; and did you see it get colder in your experience from the sixties winters when it always steamed on a cold day?

– Yes, the roach would come up in the warmer water then, but after the power stations started to close down the water was definitely cooler.

Q: Rods have improved so much in the last 30 years, if you could zip back to Burton Joyce in a time machine with today's equipment, would you use say a 15' or 17' rod, to replace the old Bruce & Walker 'John Dean' 13-footers you put your name to, for better line control? And what else might you upgrade knowing all about recent advances?

– Yes, modern rods are fantastic, I have four Drennan Acolyte rods –

100

wonderful compared to what we used back in the day.

Q: In a recent magazine article Alan Scotthorne disclosed how he shotted up a 70cm length of .20mm diameter line to make a 'leader,' in effect with all his working shot on. In this feature he was using a 2-gram mini Bolo' with 28 x no.8s on the leader which terminated in a 'Quick Snap Swivel' for easy change of his 12-inch hooklengths. Apart from being a time-saver, he says the thicker .20 line is also less tangle-prone in winds?

– This is not for me. I preferred to make up my rigs on the bank. I always found that the finer and lighter lines I used produced more bites. My general choice was 0.004" (0.10mm) hooklengths of 24" long and 0.005" (0.12mm) reel lines. As for tangles, well no, I cannot remember many tangles.

Still, I cannot deny that fishing has changed so much over the last 40 years and the new methods work for the modern angler.

Q: Feeding – I know it's a 'how long's a piece of string' question, but, on an average BJ peg, say on the Rack, looking for 10lb or more in autumn, calm and normal level, how many maggots would you expect to feed, and same for casters? And, how many per cast at the start – approx.?

– I would take at least four pints of chrysoidine maggots with me and a few yellows (this is before the red maggots took over). I liked a variation in the colours: a darker orange maggot from the week before was often good, as was a chrysoidine-dyed yellow maggot as a change hookbait.

I never counted how many I fed, just played it by ear as the fish responded (or not) to the amount I was feeding. It depended on how many fish I was catching as to the amount of bait I put in. The important part is to feed regularly, every cast or more often than that.

On a cold winter river at Holme Marsh, back in the early 70's, I remember watching Bill Bartles from Sheffield, legering and feeding one maggot at a time. That always stuck with me, regular feeding – not the quantity – was more important.

Q: On a low and clear river, on the Road once again, how far out would you start on stick, or would you automatically think waggler?

– I would set up both, probably two stick rods and two

waggler rods – experimenting to find out which worked best.

Q: When the river was say 12" up and coloured and drawn on gravel, how close in would you start?

– At the rod end with a centrepin reel, float vastly overshotted and inched down the peg. This was a method Malc Levy taught me in the 1960's, and it won me a fair few quid.

Q: Did you always hook the maggot lightly at the fat end, or not necessarily, and how did you hook the caster? Many of the original caster anglers never changed from burying an 18?

– Yes that's me – maggot at the thick end and bury the hook in a caster.

Q: If we can fast-forward a generation and look at the match scene now, the long pole has made a bigger impact on rivers combined with the typical continental groundbait barrage, and/or with hemp on the hook. Tony Scott told me how Nigel Bull had a good run in 2019 at Burton-on-Trent with the heavy groundbait and long pole/short line tactic, out-performing running line methods. Is this natural progress that is at times making the stick redundant, or is it as much about water abstraction, and a slower flow on rivers when not flooded?

– Sorry, I do not know. I've never fished like that so I cannot compare it to the way we fished in the 80's. The Art of Angling has always been one of change through the ages. Fish populations and their behaviour are constantly changing, new and different methods of catching the fish are always evolving.

Q: You mentioned the Mustad 90340 in sizes 18-22, also a 'secret weapon' change hook, the gilt Au Lion D'Or 1206 hook in a 22. What was your banker starting size in the 70s/80s on stick and maggot?

– I would start on a size 18 (90340) and as the match went on and bites became harder to get, change down to a 20 and then a 22. The 1206 was a lighter wire and was what I might turn to when bites were few and far between.

Q: What's your favourite river other than the Trent and why?

– I liked the Witham in the 1970's when roach catches were good. I was never very good with bream.

Q: Name your all-time most enjoyable match or session?

– Not sure I can do that: so many good memories.

Chapter 17
Colin Perry makes a good impression

A famous angler once said that "some anglers catch fish; others catch reporters." Mansfield's Colin Perry is one of the former, but spending years in the shadow of his former business colleague and fishing partner, the illustrious John Dean, he made fewer headlines. Ironically, it was in fact John who claimed that some anglers could make news while others, no matter how deserving, couldn't. True or not, the ever-cheerful Colin was certainly underrated. He won forty club matches before entering his first open, and has since won over two hundred. Apart from four wins at Burton Joyce in the Trent's heyday, he set the weight record for the River Idle in the Idle Champs at Bawtry, with 74lb-plus of bream and skimmers, and also set the River Torne record with 18lb of roach.

My Rice Impression – the 1990 Evesham Festival Team match
The Team event of the August Bank Holiday Evesham Festival is always held on a Sunday between the John Smith's Final and the Wychavon Final. The Smith's final was not great for me. I drew one above Denis White, near the culvert below the bridge, and just pipped him by 3oz with almost 6lb.

As part of the festival it was usual to have an evening buffet at the Boat Club, which most competitors attended. As the evening progressed I spoke to many friends about the day, but ended up in a corner chatting to a lad I did not know named Andy Burt. He told me how he had watched me and Denis for a while, and had a few questions for me if I didn't mind.

I said I didn't and he told me he had been following the match scene for a while, during which time he had been watching and sitting behind Pete Rice on every match that he'd fished in the last three weeks. My ears pricked up as Pete was on a brilliant run just before the festival with some big roach weights from the Avon up to 20lb-plus.

Andy had observed that Pete was not fishing too far out, using a stick float about 5 x no. 4 size, subject to the depth and flow. He was shotting the float with no. 8 shot in a shirt button string from just below the float every two-three inches at first, then to four-inch gaps, then to five and six, with the last shot being around eighteen inches from the hook. This was revealing. At this time, we were still into BB's, no. 4's and 6's, with a no. 8 being the standard tell-tale shot nearest the hook. At least this was the case on the Trent where I did most of my fishing. The Avon has a much slower pace than the Trent, however, so I could see how this could be working. The story got better when he explained to me how he was fishing!

Pete was feeding hemp and maggots in equal amounts, but his feeding pattern was very different to the norm – thrown in front before trotting down the swim. He explained how he was laying the float in at the desired distance with the hook downstream as normal, and then as the float was settling, would feed hemp and then maggots on top of the float. Pete would hold tight to the float in good control, with the float shotted so that it left a mere dot on the surface when the tell-tale shot settled.

It was really important that he knew when the bait had fully reached the bottom and was tripping through steadily. Once the float had fully settled, if no bite occurred within a couple of feet of trotting, he'd drag the float back upstream to pull the hookbait back up into mid water, and then feed again on top of the float, which by now may have been six to seven yards down the swim. Then he'd repeat the process to the end of the swim. This meant that he might be feeding three or four times until the float was out of range to feed, then he'd run the float to the end of the peg but keep dragging back every time the float had settled correctly.

Pete expected bites as the float settled or just after but, occasionally, as the float settled, he experienced sharp, quick bites that suggested bleak. But the bites were from big roach, some being over a pound!

Andy had given me great food for thought and although it had gone 10 p.m. by the time we got back to our accommodation, I scrambled into the back of the car to find my stick float rod, floats and shot. Luckily, I had a 5 x no. 4 stick already set up, and just had to adjust the shotting which didn't take too long. The event organiser, Dick Derrington, had changed the rules slightly for the Team event, so now, for half of the match, you had to fish the pole. This was a fairly new thing to river fishing then, as the pole in the UK was in still its infancy and many of us were still learning the method.

I looked through my floats. What pattern for the pole? Many of the pole floats I owned in those days were rubbish by today's standards. In the end I decided to use a stick float of the same size as that on my rod, shotted exactly the same as explained by Andy. This would mean I had two identical rigs – one on the rod and one on the pole.

By 8.30 a.m. I was on the Crown meadow looking for my teammates. I was fishing with a scratch team that Dick Derrington had put together, but we would be up against it, with Barnsley, Dorking, Starlets and local teams to beat. The draw was made and I was handed a peg on Whitehouse bend, below the town waters, which was not ideal because the town waters above the bridge were always the favoured area.

Anyhow, I set up and plumbed the depth on the stick rod at just over six feet and discovered on searching around that the bottom was flat as a pancake. The Avon, if you don't know it, can be all sorts of depths and the bottom can be 5ft on one peg and a couple of pegs down it can drop to 10-12 ft deep. So I was happy. I adjusted my shotting slightly by adding 2 x no. 8's so that just a blip was showing, as Andy had described. The rule on the day meant fishing the pole only for the first half of the match and any method afterwards. I set up two pole rigs, both at seven metres, line to hand – an olivette rig of 1g with a couple of droppers, and my stick float rig as described, adjusting the shotting pattern slightly to duplicate that on my rod. Feed was hemp and maggot of which I had six pints, standard for those days. I had a few casters too which I was hoping not to need.

I started the match on the pole stick and fed as Andy had explained. First run down the float buried and... gudgeon. But yes, I'd had a bite. I carried on and, for the first half-hour, caught small fish quite regularly, but it was not hectic, so I decided to try the olivette rig. It worked and I began to catch faster, still dragging the float back every couple of yards and, although my fish remained small, because it was a team event I was happy to keep them coming. Every now and then I'd change to the stick rig but the bites continued to come more quickly on the olivette rig.

We were nearing the halfway stage when the shout, 'Any Method' came down the bank. Instantly out came the stick rod. I estimated that I had around 4lb at this stage and things were going OK; no thoughts of winning the match, but happy to be catching steady for the team.

I cast the stick about three rods out and as it was settling I fed my maggots, around twenty, then a similar smattering of hemp on top, by which time the float was almost settled. This was slightly further out than my pole line where the wind was a little trickier, but just as the float settled under it went and a chunky 6oz roach came to the net. Another cast, and on the second draw-back and-feed I hooked another nice roach, then another.

For the next half-hour it was small fish, one or two better roach, then back to small fish but the better fish were gradually showing more and then it happened. I had just fed my hemp around the float which was two-thirds settled and it shot under quickly. I missed it. I recast and trotted down to take a gudgeon. In again, and as it was about to settle it shot under and a 12oz roach came to the net. These bites were right under my feet, and the rod was working much better than the pole.

Because the fish were so close, I began to feed slightly further down the peg for an easier and slightly better presentation, and to avoid playing the fish in the centre of the swim. Another big roach, perhaps 14oz, next graced the net and then suddenly it was a fast bite almost every drop. I didn't hook them all, but when I did it was from 6oz up to a pound fish every time. I was now building a weight.

By now there were a number of spectators behind me but I was oblivious to them – completely in the zone. The tempo was slowing though, and the fish seemed to back off further down the swim. The wind had also got up slightly, making presentation more difficult, but a few fish kept coming until the final whistle. With the big roach in the net I thought I must have double figures, always a good score at Evesham. I had not even thought about an individual placing, just hoped that I had done OK for the team.

I started to pack my gear away, the crowds had now all disappeared to watch the scales. The weigh-in always took place from the downstream end by Huxley's Cafe and then worked up to the pegs at the top of the town. I could see the scales coming now about three pegs away, so I strolled down to see what was happening. "10 lb 4oz," I heard Dick Derrington shout, and a few moments later "12lb 6oz." The river had obviously fished very well today.

My turn, and as I lifted the net I heard a voice from the crowd: "This lad will beat them." I had my doubts, but on the scales they went...and "13lb 12oz... Section Win!" came from Dick. Great stuff.

Information from another angler can lead us astray because we all fish slightly differently, but I could now see how Pete Rice had been doing so well. He had perfected a method for the roach and Andy had given it to me in a nutshell and I had simply tried to replicate what he had told me.

After packing away my gear, I drove off to Crown Meadow for the results and presentation. After an initial talk from the Mayor of Evesham who thanked everyone – anglers, sponsors and spectators alike for attending the Festival, Dick got down to the results. He began with the individuals first, to keep the tension of the team placings on until the end. "In third place... " Applause. "In second place... " Applause. And then the magic words: "In first place... Colin Perry" and I was up on the staging for my trophy and winnings. What a great feeling. The Evesham Festival in the eighties and nineties was the pinnacle of the West Midlands match scene and this was the third time I had collected the winner's cheque. These are memories you never forget as a match angler. I would win the John Smith's final again in 1993, but this match was up there as one of the most enjoyable, with everything pretty much going to plan. I saw Andy later, bought him a pint and thanked him once again for the help he gave me. As for the Team event? Sorry, can't remember.

Chapter 18
Roy Henson – a *styl* of his own

One of the unsung heroes of the great Notts Fed (alias Trentmen) teams of the eighties, was Roy Henson. Starting out as a 15-year-old with Gotham British Legion AC, he won almost all the club's trophies inside three years, and this tempted him to enter the Trent opens. After he won a match with 26lb of roach from Radcliffe Viaduct, Wayne Swinscoe invited him to join Trentmen and he jumped at the chance. Attending the first squad meeting, he was a little awestruck to see an all-star cast with the likes of Frank Barlow, Ted Stokes and John Dean in the room. Roy would soon establish himself in this esteemed company, though figuring in many team victories with his own unique stick float approach. He gained a National section winner's medal for Fed on stick float, with 11lb 13oz from a peg above Stoke Ferry weir, and won another on the Leeds-Liverpool canal.

In recent years Roy, now 74, has left his rods behind in the garage and turned to golf. He's obviously got a talent for that too, playing off a regular 5 handicap.

My wife would drop me off at Burton Joyce in the early days for Roy Toulson's Saturday matches, and I'd take the opportunity of watching other anglers while waiting for the lift home. Dave Thomas would continue after the match sometimes, and he stood out as impressive for how he fished the stick well out at three to four rods and with a high work rate. I also learned how to cast better by watching Ted Stokes make a loop cast to land the rig in a straight line and downstream of the float, poised for the trot.

I began experimenting with styls[9] instead of shots and would make up rigs at home and put them on winders like pole

---

9 French cylindrical Styl weights are slim and streamlined leads which are easiest attached to line with special pliers. They are curiously numbered in the opposite direction to shot sizes with a no. 7 being the smallest (.01g) up to a no. 20 as biggest (.258g].] With split shot, of course, bar the bigger sizes SSG, AAA and BB, they decrease in size the number gets bigger – from a number 1 (.28g) down to a tiny no. 13 as the smallest (.012g.) The weights converge at no.10, both weighing . 034g approx.

anglers do, for different sizes of stick – 3 x no. 4 up to 7 x no. 4 mainly. This started with a two or three styl bulk of size 12s around the halfway point, then tapering them down towards the hook – sizes 11, 10, 9, and 8, a few inches apart, and ending with (the smallest) no. 7 on a 15" hooklength.

The exact position of this last styl was always the most adjustable. To my knowledge none of my peers used styls, but they gave me confidence. I thought they were more hydro-dynamic, which I'm sure is the term. On windy days when I had to sink the line above the float, I also used styls as back-shot.

The original Pete Warren sticks were my favourites until the day John Dean made me a set of his own with wire stems and more pointed tops; from then on I'd alternate between the two according to the nature of swim. The lads called me the 'rock-hopper' because I always dropped a few maggots close in and would often catch down the edge at some stage in the match.

I fished bronze maggot and hemp (where allowed, as in those days it was banned on some stretches) or caster, depending on the venue, and liked to vary the colour of the hookbait: some days the roach preferred a dark bronze shade, other days a light one, whereas at Long Higgin a red maggot served me well and would also tempt the odd skimmer or bream.

The styl method helped me in winning the Soar Championships one year with 42 roach for 17lb-5oz from Abbey Meadow. It was not the highest rated area, but my peg held quality roach on the day. They didn't want much feed though, and I fed only two casters and eight grains of hemp per cast. The following year in the Home Ales Brewery charity open I drew a bit of an unknown area and a local in the draw queue put me off by saying it wasn't worth going to. Well he didn't know that much; I took 19lb-4oz of roach to win, not doing a lot different to the previous win, and beat Barry Chaplin by a whisker. He was well choked having caught a tremendous 19lb-2oz of gudgeon that he must have thought was enough!

Were the styls superior to shot is the burning question, but the difference is subtle so it is hard to tell. Pete Palmer, a teammate and I drew about four pegs apart on the Road stretch one day and both caught steadily. I edged it something like 12lb to 9lb which proved nothing, but occasions like that always boost your confidence, and it probably made me fish better for a few weeks after. Ultimately a high confidence level is what every angler needs to make good decisions at the right time, enabling us to make the most of any draw.

Many great memories, but If I have one regret it was the AT Winter League final at Evesham on the Avon. We had practised and got a good feeling for the match, but heavy rain on the Thursday and a rising river looked like changing things. Expecting a flood and a feeder match by the weekend, skipper Jan Porter dropped me and put in Colin Walton – a super all-rounder so no complaints. But on the day Colin drew a lovely slack and won the match... on stick float! Knowing how the peg would have been right up my street was hard to swallow, but that's how sport can get you.

Colin Walton landing a quality roach

Chapter 19
Stick Float Memories (and 'Gobbing')
– Pete Hobson

It is rather a hazy memory of when I first met Pete Hobson (no relation to Barnsley's Keith) but it was somewhere at Burton Joyce in the seventies, and then only briefly. He didn't have a Yorkshire brogue or give me any clue that he came from Leeds. Smart and articulate, I mistakenly thought he was local to Nottingham. Both of us were new on the match circuit and what struck me was his eager smile and great enthusiasm. As if drawn by a magnet, he eventually moved to live close to the Trent in Nottingham at which time he joined the up and coming Birmingham team, Starlets. Such was his dedication to angling business, on his wedding day he put a stick float in his suit top pocket instead of the traditional buttonhole! Now living in Cambridge, I only recently caught up again with Pete for this story. Here he takes us back to those early days, then finally describes an unusual method which he put to good use in a Severn team event…

In true Yorkshire tradition, growing up in the 1950s and 60s, we weren't allowed to utter the word 'Lancashire' until we'd reached voting age. As far as we were concerned, Lancastrians were primitive: no schools or hospitals, and illiteracy reigned.

Consequently when, as aspiring young anglers, we heard rumours of something called a 'stick float' emanating from the North West, we assumed that the locals were breaking twigs from trees to use as makeshift floats.

Come 1968 (age 18) I was finally allowed to explore the world. My fishing partner, Graham Lister bought himself an old Vauxhall Victor, and together we embarked on a whole new dimension of angling adventures, notably South to the legendary Trent. Through the pages of the *Angling Times*, I learned about the rivalry between the anglers from Lancashire with their weird-sounding casters and the classical Nottingham protagonists with their centrepin reels and maggot hookbaits.

The only book about match fishing I had read at the time was by Yorkshireman, Frank Oates, and it contained more porcupine quills than the animal itself! However, around this time I came across a brand new book called *Match Fishing* by Benny Ashurst. It was a revelation.

Apparently the so-called 'stick' was a spigoted combination of balsa and cane. At that time there was no chance of buying one in a shop and so we diligently set about making crude imitations to try out on our native Yorkshire rivers. Despite the fact that (by today's standards) they looked horrific, they worked really well. They cast better, rode the flow better, and were certainly better for holding back in the current. With apologies for the cliché, I was neatly hooked in the top lip!

And so my stick float education began. I managed to get hold of an angling catalogue published by the famous Nottingham tackle retailer, 'Tom Watson's' and its pages revealed a multitude of tackle items that were completely unavailable at that time in Yorkshire, including some beautiful-looking 'Trentcaster' stick floats. Graham and I just had to know more so in summer of 1970 a pilgrimage to the shop was made.

Watson's tackle shop was managed and run by the legendary 'Gentleman' Jim Sharp, the finest Trent angler of his generation, and a man whose calm, confident good nature I have yet to see equalled. As a competitive angler he was in a league of his own, but the most noteworthy aspect of his skill was that, dressed in tweed jacket, shirt and tie, he could demolish a field of competitors with 40lb-plus of roach, and be so neat, clean and tidy at the end as to comfortably attend church without raising an eyebrow. In contrast, many of the other anglers of the day would finish a match so caked in groundbait, slime and mud that you could easily believe they'd had to wrestle their catches into submission.

On a hot, busy Nottingham Saturday, this was the man we nervously approached with a request to view the famous Trentcaster sticks. Our aspirations were high but, in truth, our funds were quite limited and whilst we both knew that we intended taking a bundle of assorted cane and balsa creations home with us, we were determined to maximise our opportunity to ensure that no 'secret' models were missed in our haste to buy. The Trentcasters were too special to be on display to all and sundry and my abiding memory is of Jim

Sharp laying out a succession of wooden drawers from the back of the counter. These were full of elegant and glossy slim-line, dome-topped floats and we two callow youths from Leeds pored over and poked through them in silent wonder.

The shop was a heaving, hollering embodiment of a busy afternoon tackle shop, with dozens of local anglers, kids and browsers buying bait and bits and pieces for their weekly outing on the Trent, but Jim must have sensed how much that day meant to us. He gave us his undivided attention, asked our opinion, made suggestions and recommendations and left us alone to talk and finally, when we eventually handed over our cash for our accumulated collection threw in a couple of extras 'for luck.' A great retailer, a great angler and a wonderful man.

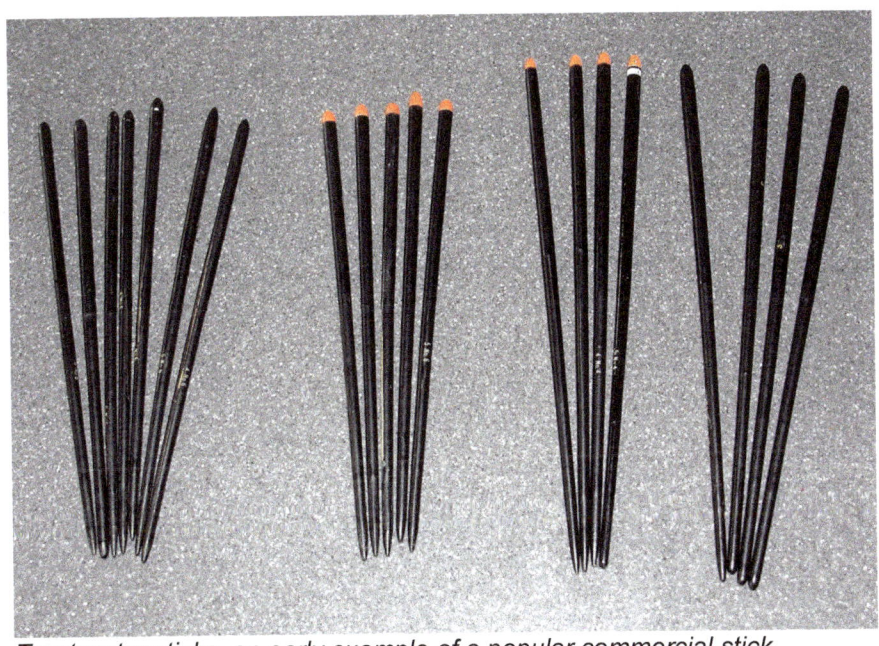

Trentcaster sticks, an early example of a popular commercial stick

Now, well inspired, Graham and I also travelled to matches in Nottingham as spectators, specifically to watch the best exponents of the time – the likes of Pete Warren, Frank Barlow, Ian Heaps and then, latterly, John Allerton.

On one occasion at Holme Marsh, we were discreetly stalking a succession of competing anglers, noting any move or method of significance, when we were stopped in our tracks by an imposing young man. We didn't recognise him but he was fishing so impressively with a stick float that we were transfixed. Feeding with tiny balls of groundbait every cast, he exerted such float control that, despite the fresh breeze, the end tackle might just as well have been fixed by wire. This impressive command of the conditions seemed to emanate from a unique and bizarre arrangement of rod and reel. Using the established and popular Mitchell Match fixed spool reel, it had been somehow doctored to point crazily up at the rod.[10]

The line was captured in what can only be described as a 'funnel' of no less than 10 rings whipped on the butt section of the rod alone. A unique and unusual combination to be sure, but it was incredibly effective, and the angler was certainly outperforming everyone else around him. In complete ignorance of the angler's identity, we watched in awe for the rest of the match, before engaging him in conversation whilst waiting to weigh his fish.

That angler was John Allerton, little older than we were and relatively unknown at the time; he would progress to become one of the country's top rods and a continuing mentor and role model through much of my subsequent career.

Around that time I remember taking over thirty pounds of dace, roach and chub from my favourite peg at Boston Spa on the River Wharfe with a neat little stick float I'd made the day before at home in Leeds. The float wasn't properly sealed which meant that through the day I had to keep removing shot as it absorbed more and more water, but this taught me that in moderate depths and flow you don't always need as much lead as was recommended by some of the older fishing books.

So, after many years of trial and error, I finally settled upon an approach which has served me well. For me, the reel of choice is a closed face. I've used centrepins and open-faced fixed spools, particularly the Mitchell Match, but find that a large closed face such as the Abu 508 (I'm left-handed) gives me the ease of use and the line control that I'm looking for. My rod back in the day was a 13-foot Shakespeare President with six rings on the butt (à la Allerton) and an extra ring added an

---

10 Pete refers to how the angler had managed to bend the reel's stem to lift the spool of line closer to the rod, making for an easier reach to control line with his forefinger and at the same time reducing the risk of line being blown behind the spool and tangling in a facing wind. The extra rod rings were also about maintaining close line control.

inch below the tip ring which reduced wrap-round tangles. With regard to line, I rarely go above a 1.7lb or 2lb BS reel line as this matches the type of rod I am using and the roach, dace and chub I am after.

From this point on, everything is open to almost forensic scrutiny. Microscopic attention to detail can make a significant difference to outcomes over time. The float should be attached to the line by two different diameter pieces of silicone. One at the top to snugly fit just over the dome of the tip, and a bottom piece around three quarters of an inch long to support the cane or lignum base. Many anglers will use any old float rubbers to attach the float, but I think this is worthy of attention.

Next, I only ever use No. 8 lead shot below the float. Most floats are marked up as how many No. 4 they take, but I never use No.4s. I find that using only No. 8s in ones, twos or bunches, allows me maximum flexibility with my shotting patterns. I can fiddle around endlessly through the day in order to get just the presentation that's needed.

One of these combinations was to prove exceptionally useful to me on my first ever appearance for the 'Starlets' after moving to live in Birmingham. The winter league match was at Stourport-on-Severn and, proudly dressed in my new blue Adidas jacket with Starlets badge sewn carefully on the front, I walked straight into a tree branch! Blood was flowing copiously from my forehead and I had neither hand towel nor handkerchief to hand. Now, please understand, we are talking a serious lesion here, no little scratch or scuff, but this was my day, my opportunity to show that I was a worthy contributor to one of the best fishing teams in the world.

I'd been enlisted by Mark Downes at a fishing seminar a few months earlier. The Starlets represented everything I loved and aspired to in the competitive angling world and I'd be damned if some inconvenient bump on the head would stand in my way now. My allotted peg was a dream: flowing steadily left to right and about six feet deep, two rod lengths out. So I set up a 5 x No.4 stick float with 11 x No.8 shotted shirt button-style. Armed with the 'on trend' gallon of maggots at the time, I added some turmeric to the bait and set about feeding up the peg and fiddling with depth and shot to maximise the peg's potential.

It started steadily enough. Dace, dace, a nice roach and frequent chublets (very small chub). There was a bit of an upstream breeze, making presentation particularly pleasurable and I was enjoying myself. River conditions were perfect but my instincts were that I was not catching fast enough or big enough to make much impact on the section or the match. So I embarked upon a series of changes to try and improve the situation.

Two thirds of the way through the match I hit on 'the method,' one I've only used occasionally and have hardly ever seen other anglers trying. It is called 'gobbing' and only works occasionally, but when it does it's deadly. I took all 11 of my No. 8 shot and arranged them one millimetre apart at exactly half depth. This means that in a six-foot swim you'll have three feet of shotless line above the hook. It's not great for casting, but if you are only fishing an easy swing from the bank, which I was, it's more than manageable.

A generous handful of Terry Dorman's finest maggots was fed into the swim and two juicy ones impaled on the hook. A gentle underhand cast and two yards down the swim the float buried! There was the satisfying resistance of a decent roach, fooled by the free falling bait, and a fish of around 6oz was netted. Next cast, same again. And again. Suddenly I was in business!

I weighed in 17lb something and was feeling very pleased with myself, when one of the Starlets' runners who was following the scales grimaced and said: "Pete, have you seen the state of you, mate?"

Face, hands, arms and proud new jacket were covered in an evil mix of blood, bright orange turmeric and maize meal. It's the dirtiest, messiest match I've ever fished – but I impressed the Starlets boys enough to become a fixture for the next ten years.

However, to put my messy but good day into perspective, the late, great Clive Smith was fishing for Cofton Hackett and drawn two or three pegs above me. He weighed in with 37lb-plus. I wandered up for a chat.

"How'd you catch 'em Clive?"

"On a little stick just off the rod end."

"Use much bait?"

"Just over half a pint of casters, mate."

And his clothes were immaculate!

Chapter 20
John Illingworth, Geoff Scollick & the 'Babes'
– by Tim Worsnop

John Illingworth poised ready for a bite, looked on by friend Pete Baron and other Bradford colleagues.

"Anybody with even the tiniest knowledge of fishing could not have helped but be impressed by him. When you watched him you just thought, this guy can REALLY fish." – *Scollick on Illingworth.*

John Illingworth as recalled by Geoff Scollick

June 2020 marked the 10th anniversary of John Illingworth's death. He was just 65 and up until the short illness from which he died, was still very much at the top of the fishing game. Over five stunning decades he was revered at home and abroad, feared at the water's edge and listened to in awe when he held court at the bar.

His journey from novice to genius was remarkably short. It began around 1960 when change swept the country and the template for modern day fishing was laid. Away from the sluggish rivers of the Fens where the swingtip came to the fore and bream ruled, this was *the* era of float fishing and true angling legends.

From first meeting a 15-year-old Illingworth, former Bradford City teammate, early mentor and holder of no fewer than five Trentman badges including a first, second and sixth individual, Geoff Scollick watched John's angling career mature and blossom with huge interest.

"There was no mistaking his ability even from that first time I saw him," said Geoff. "It was June 1959, and the annual junior match on the Leeds-Liverpool Canal at Apperley Bridge, Leeds was underway. I was walking along and suddenly came across this ginger-haired lad flicking a top and bottom porcupine quill float under the far bank. I knew the instant I saw him, and how he was casting so accurately despite using a centrepin and a rod that looked too long for him, that he was going to be very good."

Geoff, nine years John's senior and recently turned 84, regularly saw John at Bradford City matches on the Ure at Boroughbridge – where he would arrive in a motorcycle and sidecar with his non-fishing dad, Bill (who would later catch the fishing bug, too). The two became friends, and when Geoff bought his first car in the 60's the pair would travel to matches together.

"It was all about the float in those days. I'd learned from some very good anglers including Kenny Kendall, and I taught John as much as I knew. But it's fair to say it didn't take him too many years to reverse the roles. In the end I took the view that to come second to him was good enough for me."

John won matches everywhere, from drains and reservoirs to deep and shallow rivers and canals. In later years, after he left Bradford, he and his travelling partner, Pete Baron, joined the talented Doncaster team, perfecting slider fishing on the fast-improving River Don and later on the same venue the pole and flat float. He was second in an NFA Division 1 National on the Ancholme – the best ·of many outstanding national championship performances.

Punch in to your search engine 'Park Drive Match Fishing To Win' and who's that picture of concentration on the cover with co-authors, Billy Lane and angling journalist Colin Graham, during an international friendly match in France in 1972? Found it? Of course, it was John who emerged that day with the top weight!

John was a great innovator, forever tying hooks and making floats and was always ready to embrace change. Geoff remembers fishing a match on the tidal Trent at Dunham Bridge in the early to mid-sixties. Stick floats were already being used to win matches, mainly by the Lancastrians, but on this day Geoff spotted something different:

"I watched Rodney Pegden and Leonard Harmes, two good Hull anglers, do well with a type of float I'd never seen before. It was like a forerunner to the modern Topper which of course is a lightweight body around a crow quill or pheasant quill. These had a balsa or pith body with a wooden stem and were in the shape of a Topper but were not fished with bulk. They might have taken 3 x BB shots which were then spread out as number 4s.

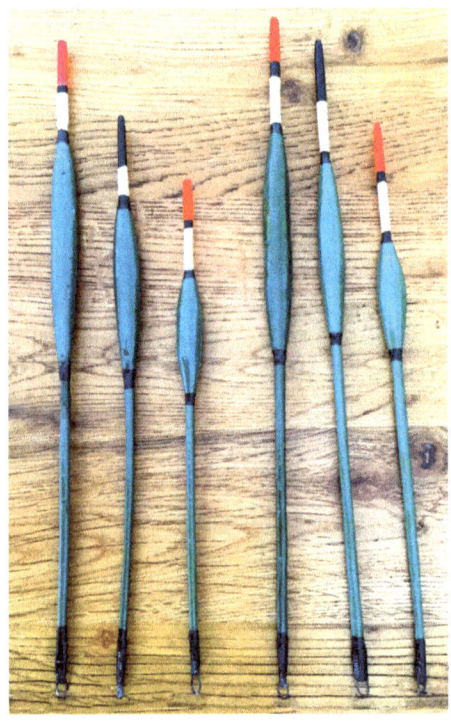

"The weight and I suppose aerodynamics allowed you to fish well out and the floats were particularly good at holding their position when you checked the line. They also rode very well in the water. They came at a time when everyone was striving to fish light, but these allowed you to hold the line well out for that vital extra second to attract a bite. I was told the floats came from Jack Clayton (the famous Fenland bream angler and swingtip inventor) at his shop in Boston.[11] I jumped in the car and drove down

11 Research shows this float was a Jack Clayton Wyndjammer [sic] with a greenheart stem – picture courtesy of Robin Jackson

there and bought three sets – two for me and one for John.

"Not too long afterwards, Dick Ward, one of the top Lancashire anglers, pulled me to one side to ask who the young bloke was that had been at the next peg to him? Dick had been very impressed at how John, now in his early twenties had managed to fish so far out and with such success despite using a centrepin reel. The answer was innovation (the new floats I'd given him) and a supreme level of ability that was now manifesting itself regularly in the very best of company.

"The emphasis at the time seemed to be on lightness but you have to remember that parts of Dunham can be 10-foot and deeper. This heavier float definitely gave you another string to the bow and in depth more control."

The turnout of angling luminaries at John's funeral where Geoff presented the eulogy, was testament to the high esteem in which he was held. He was rated among the best ever, certainly in the eyes of the late and great Ivan Marks. And his success was all the more impressive because it was achieved alongside a job that required him to travel the world. Remarkably though, he still managed to get home to fish matches on Saturday and Sunday. Then, on Monday, often twice a month, he'd be back on a plane heading to the US.

His mastery of moving water, be it with a porcupine quill in the early days on Yorkshire's fickle rivers, full-bodied balsas and Toppers on the Severn and Bristol Avon, or a stick on the Trent, was equalled by his expertise with the waggler, his slickness with the slider and his prowess with the pole. He was exceptional at everything he did.

"We eventually got him to come over to the Fermoy Festival on the River Blackwater in Ireland which is all about stick float fishing for roach and dace," adds Geoff. "He won the festival, and I remember in the bar one night watching as a group of anglers gathered round him. They were asking questions and listening intently to what he had to say and looking at him as if he was a God. It really made me smile."

On another occasion Geoff recalls turning up for a Yorkshire Winter League on the Calder at Brighouse, a match that John couldn't make. His absence didn't go unnoticed and gave Leeds' Charlie Grimshaw the chance to have a joke.

"He sauntered over and said: 'They say you've only got half a team today lads, we might have a chance of beating you!' The league was teams of 12 and was decided on weight in those days and the inference was that John's weight would have been equal to six other anglers."

With the world at his feet, John's reputation grew quickly: "Quite simply he was that dangerous you didn't really want to draw next to him, anywhere. Given half a chance he would win, and nearly always he'd pick up money. On Bradford City matches at Boroughbridge the match HQ was the Crown Hotel, and in our little group it was always understood the one who won the most bought the first round. It is funny looking back but in those days we considered ourselves better than John, after all he was still a kid, yet he was always the one at the bar first!

"He was the first person I can remember to need two weighs in a match at Boroughbridge – remember we were using pan scales back then – and his net of 13lb of roach and dace at Roecliffe was unheard of. Often 6lb would be enough to win. You can imagine the stir afterwards.

"It used to make me laugh but the consensus after matches he'd won or done well in always seemed to be that the wind had been in John's favour or some other excuse, when the truth was that he was just better."

Leeds were still the dominant force in angling at the turn of the decade. They had won the national on several occasions and counted star names like Kenny Kendall, Freddy Friend, Henry Pollard, Norman Seal and Horace Seed in their ranks. They were the equivalent of today's Barnsley team.

But, as the sixties began, new teams with new stars were chipping away at their dominance. And one of them was just down the road. A cabal of forward-thinking matchmen had become friends, chiefly through the Bradford City club and matches at Boroughbridge. They included Geoff and John.

In 1964 they fired a warning shot across the bows of the big guns from Lancashire, Nottingham and Leeds when Geoff won the Trent Championship. It was fair reward after previously finishing runner-up to Leeds' Pete Hardcastle, also taking a sixth place overall. John won the Gunthorpe section while Leslie and Richard Stanley, and Jonny Widdop chipped in with good weights for Bradford to win the team event on the day. In what was considered the most prestigious match on the calendar this was a huge achievement.

Bradford 'Babes' at their peak with trophies for a second Trent Championship win: Richard Stanley, John Illingworth, Les Stanley, Geoff Scollick and Jonny Widdop.

"It raised a few eyebrows I think it's fair to say. The established teams weren't sure what to make of it," said Geoff.

It was a huge entry with over fifteen hundred anglers split across five zones from Stoke Bardolph on the way to Nottingham, to Fiskerton near Newark. Geoff remembers travelling down in Les Stanley's car with Richard, while the two Johns shared a car. Despite the amazing outcome it was a day that began in pure slapstick, as Geoff recounts:

"Part of a team prize won the previous year was a set of wellies each, and Les, Richard and myself were all strangely size 8s. Les was in a bit of a rush to get us to our pegs to give himself some time and I ended up with two left feet. Les got two right feet and the only one smiling was Richard.

"It was a bad wind that day as I recall. You were not allowed catapults and if you couldn't loose feed you put it in with groundbait. You were also only allowed one rod. The business end of the gear was a light, top and bottom, white porcupine quill float (they were more buoyant) fished upside down, flat end on the surface – which was what I liked to do.

"It took 5 x no. 4's equally spaced and a couple of dust to within six inches of the hook. I always set up with the float overshotted and then removed no. 4's until it showed. I used a Milbro Trophy rod, a centrepin loaded with 2lb Racine Tortue main line, and a 20 hook to 1lb bottom.

Bucking the bait trend

"The thing people have to remember was that in those days the Trent was heavily polluted and carried a lot of colour. On the sections having an average depth and flow, there was nothing to be gained by casting a long way. You concentrated on the rod end or not too far beyond. The Lancastrians had just started to introduce casters at this stage, but I tended to fish with maggots died yellow with auromine when I guess most would have used white maggots.

"Interestingly, I chatted afterwards with Kevin Ashurst who'd come runner-up and he was surprised that I'd caught on maggots (I don't think we knew much about casters at the time except for putting the odd 'chrysalis' on the hook as we called them). He said he was certain he'd have caught little, if anything, had he not been fishing casters. He said he just didn't have any confidence in the maggot.

"I started fishing dead depth and had a run of gudgeon. The river had a lot of them at this time. And then, after a while feeding little but often, I took six inches off and the roach were there in the 4oz to 6oz bracket – real weight builders. I caught all match but I'm a really laid back angler and I wasn't sure what weight I had. I always seemed to have more than I imagined, even now it's the same.

"There was a guy who had been watching me and I remember him congratulating me in a back-handed way, saying I'd done well but that Jim Sharp (one of best Trent anglers at the time) would have had 10lb from the peg. When the scales arrived I had 14lb 4oz.

"Back at the draw we'd had some great results. I managed to grab one of the stewards and asked him what had won

Gunthorpe and he said the young lad on the end peg (which I knew was John) with 9lb 6oz. The steward said the photographer had wanted to get a picture of him with his net but John had declined, saying he wanted to return the fish to the water so there were no fatalities.

"Colin Dyson said he'd worked out that we'd definitely won the team title and wanted a photo of us, adding that Kevin Ashurst had won the match with 13lb 6oz. I looked at him and said: 'I don't think he has.'

"The sheer size of the event meant that the formalities had to take place later. The organisers had said that because we had done so well they'd bring the prize-giving show to Bradford instead of Nottingham and that's what happened. And it was a good night I can tell you."

More than that, the victory proved the catalyst for a Bradford City team that would become one of the most consistent at national level for many years.

The team would include: Pete and Stuart Baron, Alan Tremethick, Richard Stanley, Dave Wall, Kevin Armitage, John Widdop and Malcolm Leeming mixed with a few older heads like Tony Ramsden and Arthur Nicholson. At their heart was former Naval Petty Officer Les Stanley, Richard Stanley's father, a butcher by trade, a great angler in his own right and the captain who ran a tight ship. And, of course, John and Geoff.

The sixties was a melting pot of ideas and a wonderful period in which to be a match angler. As Bob Dylan sang 'The Times They Are A-Changin,' indeed they were in angling. Innovation gripped the sport like never before. Fishing was becoming more and more popular and a burgeoning match scene demanded the best tackle. The split cane of the fifties was now replaced by longer and lighter glass fibre rods, and excellent fixed spool reels were now available making fishing at distance far easier.

Float evolution too started to advance as the porcupine quill – which had been embraced by anglers for decades – became more obsolete with the invention of early stick floats made from balsa and cane.

"The Lancashire lads brought casters to the front line and then were the first to introduce what came to be called stick floats," says Geoff. "Not long after I won the Trent Championships I can remember getting a real hammering from Ken Booth, another top Lancastrian on the Trent. He'd used casters and had 17lb of roach to my 12lb on yellow maggots. It was the first time I'd been beaten out of sight by a caster angler. But he'd also been using a home-made stick float. He sportingly gave me a couple and they were a start.

"I left them on the bank one evening at Burley-in-Wharfedale where I often would go after work. When I realised I'd left them I ran back and only went and stood on them! I guess like everyone else we all began making our own stick floats then. Shops stocked cane and balsa and providing you could spigot the cane, fit it neatly into a (drilled) balsa top then shape it, you were away. A dab of glue and a few licks of paint and you had a float."

Mr Scollick himself

Geoff had worked with fishing tackle for many years. Following a spell with Bradford sports retailers H J Knutton, he opened his own shop in Shipley. Recognising the growing demand for stick floats he discovered a float maker in his home town, Shipley, who would make them for him and his shop exclusively.

"He was called Charlie Makaitis, and his floats were superb. I got them for a lot of the Bradford team. I'm not sure if Charlie was Polish or Latvian but he'd settled here after the war. The floats were a little heavier than we'd been used to, made from balsa and the hardwood skewers that they used for bailing wool. Bradford was a textile centre and unfortunately in those days the industry was in decline and there were literally millions of these skewers to be had.[12]

"Charlie figured a way to split them and then splice them at an angle with the balsa. They all came in the same base colour which was a sort of battleship grey/green. They had two colours of tops – orange and black. I think they cost a shilling each, but it was money well spent because they were very hard wearing. My favourite colour top was orange, but the black tops were brilliant for the Trent because in those days there were no trees to cast a shadow and black was easier to

---

12 These skewers were most likely the greenheart cotton spindles

see on such a wide expanse of water.

"They were a little heavier than a lot of people were using but we felt they gave us greater control. They came in four sizes from around 3 x BBs to 4 x no.4s but it wasn't a precise science. They stood us in good stead for several years before the wire and aluminium stem floats of the nineties changed everything. I don't think anything has come along since to improve on them. My float of choice now is always a wire stem and I've had loads of success with them, especially on the Calder."

Up until a couple of years ago Geoff was still winning matches in good company. In his 80th year he won the Fermoy Festival for the second year running and his third time overall. Geoff, who lives with his wife Wendy in Shipley, began his angling career in the late 1940s.

Despite enjoying overall good health he now suffers from impaired vision, which makes fishing difficult. It is a huge blow to such an accomplished angler and one of the true gentlemen of match fishing. "I can't ever see me winning again," he says.

Turn the clock back 71 years and it probably seemed unlikely a 13-year-old Geoff would win either, when he turned up unannounced for his first ever match. It was 1950 and the depths of winter, and Geoff gate-crashed a competition on the Aire at Saltaire in the company of some of Leeds' finest anglers. It was a day when fate, as often happens, played a huge part. He won with just over 6lb 9oz of roach.

"I'd actually set off to go to Doe Park, a reservoir in the hills above Bradford. But having got as far as Bradford I was waiting for another bus when a kindly man stopped his car, asked where I was headed and explained that Doe Park was frozen over. He suggested I went back to Saltaire and fished there... (Geoff later learned his guardian angel was none other than his future captain and pal, Les Stanley).

"I turned up not realising that there was a match on. But an angler called Leslie Telford said there was a spare peg going and very kindly gave me two shillings for the pools. I pulled out the very end peg 60 which was by some new tennis courts. The problem was I only had a very small keep-net with one ring at the bottom, and a top which required a knot to stop the fish getting out. When I caught a fish I popped it in the net and then redid the knot. But it was so cold I eventually couldn't undo the knot and had to put a fish back. It was then that Joss Smith, who lots of people will remember as Bradford City match secretary, came to me and asked what I was doing.

"I explained what had happened and he very kindly lent me a net. With his help and coaching I managed to win the match and it took another five years of fishing for me to beat that weight. I won £2 which was a lot of money in those days and in the euphoria I forgot to give Leslie back the pools money he'd lent me."

It was the start of a lifelong love affair with match fishing which would see him develop a winning mentality, particularly on Yorkshire's fickle waters including the Ure at Boroughbridge, the Wharfe at Ulleskelf, the Ouse above and below York, and later the Calder at Brighouse, Dewsbury and Wakefield. Then as is now, information was the key to success and to do well you needed to glean what you could from other anglers, with or without their permission.

"I decided one day to go and watch Kenny Kendall, who was the best angler around at the time, and an absolute wizard with the float. It would have been the middle 1950s and I knew he was taking part in a match at Ulleskelf on the Wharfe. I had to catch a bus from Shipley to Bradford and a train from Bradford to Ulleskelf (wherever that was!) From there I hadn't a clue where to go," said Geoff.

"I managed to find the pub where the draw was and someone told me where Kenny was pegged. It was a heck of a walk. I found him somewhere near what they called Fielding's Point – a good area – and, wary of casting a shadow on the water, I sneaked up and lay motionless in the grass watching him work his magic."

True to form Kenny, won the match with more than 15lb of dace caught on a lightly shotted porcupine quill. So was the trip worth it?

"You bet," recounts Geoff. "I noticed that he was netting every fish he hooked, even the small ones which was unusual. I wondered if he was using very light gear or maybe a small hook. When the match finished he looked behind and said: 'You can come out now lad.' (He'd known I was there from the moment I'd arrived), and he showed me the net of fish. 'Were you using a really small hook?' I asked (a 20 was as small as you could buy then). He looked up immediately and asked how I worked that out. I said because he had been netting so many small fish. Then his look turned to a smile and he said: 'That's between you and me now!'

Kenny and 'Young Geoff' as he would call him, somewhat tongue-in-cheek in later years (there was only about ten years between them) became lifelong friends and the pair often fished together, travelling to midweek Trent matches in the nineties. The day at Ulleskelf taught him a valuable lesson and he has always since erred towards fishing light and with small hooks.

The late fifties and sixties were a heyday for match angling and Yorkshire was no exception. Big matches were generally on a Sunday and were shared between the likes of Leeds, Bradford City and York on the Ure, Ouse, Swale, Derwent and Wharfe, and when the River Calder around Brighouse came on song, the Bradford No.1 club slotted in too.

These were club events not opens (serious match anglers held several club books) – but they were huge, nothing like the meagre turnouts we see these days. The Ouse would accommodate upwards of four hundred for Leeds matches (pushing a thousand for the annual Ouse Championships), Bradford City would have as many as four hundred on its events.

"Jonny Widdop won the Bradford Telegraph and Argus Cup at Boroughbridge with just 6lb and there were four hundred people fishing," recalls Geoff. "Smaller venues like the Wharfe, Swale or Calder would see in excess of two hundred."

Some of Geoff's big wins on the Yorkshire circuit included two North of England Championships, two Victory Cups at Ulleskelf, and the Middle Calder Championships two years running to name a few. He has enjoyed an exceptional match career and has few regrets save for the time he lost two bream in 'cabbages' in the 1962 National Championships on the Welland, finishing seventh with 10lb in a match that was won with 14lb.

A self-confessed float fishing addict, Geoff has seen more top and bottom styles come and go than almost anyone. Porcupine and goose quills, fluted floats, carrots, chubbers, and sticks, with every stem imaginable from cane to lignum, quill, wire and aluminium. But regardless of float design, any float is only there to do a job, he stresses. The real skill and expertise is in that sense of timing and control, the confidence to know the precise moment to check the float, hold it and let it go again. It's something that he and John Illingworth did time and time again with real panache.

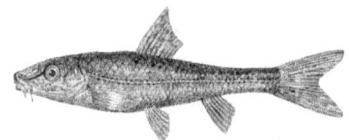

Chapter 21
My way with the Stick – Dave Thomas

Dave Thomas became a bit of a hero of mine after watching him perform on two consecutive Saturdays in the Trent Opens on the famous 'golden mile' at Burton Joyce matches which attracted sell-out entries from the cream of the Midlands match circuit and far beyond. In the first he had not drawn anything like a good peg. He was in the Nelson Field, near what's called the 'stone bridge,' on an inside bend in a pacey swim, but managed 10lb of fish on stick float, which put him third overall. I knew there were far more than two better pegs than his on the day. The following week he did draw well on the Road section and won the match with over 20lb of roach, but it was the way he caught the fish, notably his work rate with

feeding that impressed me. He fairly demolished the opposition drawn either side of him; it was as though he drew all the fish from their swims into his. This was a fair few years before he fished for England in 1981 on the Avon at Luddington and won the World individual title. He was never given the chance to defend it, which seemed a bit unjust. A very confident angler, Dave would always be in my all-time four-man 'dream team' of stick float anglers.

'It ain't what you do, it's the way that you do it, that's what gets results.' This line from the old song is certainly a fair analogy for most aspects of our sport, but none more so than with stick float fishing. A perfect example was the River Trent back in the 70s – a time when there were very few chub around and the predominant species was roach backed up by shoals of gudgeon in the margins.

The river below Nottingham was so prolific it came under huge angling pressure in those days. On both days of a weekend if you turned up to pleasure fish you'd be lucky to find any popular stretch not 'matched up.' Consequently the fish were hard to catch – everything from feeding the swim to tackle presentation had to be spot-on or you would finish up as an 'also-ran.' I used to say that to get it 90 per cent right might produce a 7 or 8lb catch, but to hit the 12 to 15lb you needed to win, the approach had to be 95% right or more. This meant that attention to detail was paramount. Whenever you floatfish on running water you only need to get one thing wrong for your returns to suffer heavily, especially on hard-fished venues.

Feeding
The first thing to get right is your feeding. Whether it is roach, dace, or chub that are the target species, you are looking to create and maintain a situation where the fish are having to compete for the free offerings, say maggot or caster. This means feeding just the right amount in the right areas and at the right frequency – usually meaning at least once every cast. Making those vital choices comes only with lots of experience and learning from your mistakes. As a general rule I would err on the side of caution, for overfeeding can quickly ruin a peg. The amount of feed can always be stepped up later if

necessary, especially where chub are concerned – habitually greedy, but feeling your way into a heavier feeding pattern is my advice. In most river situations I'd expect to feed every line I might conceivably catch from. At least until a pattern emerged.

On the Trent the pace of the river would dictate the choice of these lines. In swims where the flow increases the further out you go, I'd not feed beyond a point where the flow suddenly gains significant pace, but would in fact feed up to at least a metre short of it. This offers a shoal of fish a safe haven to back off into while not losing contact with the 'freebies' in the feeding zone.

Based on observations from bridges over Yorkshire rivers, I often found that fish in a shoal will pick a safe place in the flow to settle, whereby if feed is introduced a metre or so to one side they will drift across the flow to intercept it, each time the swim is fed.

On one occasion I stood on a bridge over the River Nidd watching a pal fish a stick float from the swim above. I could see the swim was full of good quality dace eagerly snapping up all his loose feed but ignoring his hook bait. Had I not been there this could have gone on indefinitely, leaving my pal convinced that the fish weren't there. After a few tackle adjustments we got it right and from then on it was a fish a cast.

The above and similar experiences always remind me that anytime we are not catching fish it does NOT mean they aren't there and eating all we throw at them. In the Nidd example there was clearly nothing wrong with my mate's feeding or his rig – float, shotting etc, it was just a case of finding the right depth to fish at. His swim that day was barely four-foot deep, so imagine the scope for error in deeper water.

Shotting
The story emphasises the importance of taking the trouble to make continual minor adjustments to the depth your float is set at; also paying attention to shotting which is just as crucial to bait presentation. I like to keep my shotting simple, mostly shirt button-style. It used to be no. 6 shot evenly spaced, but since the lead ban on larger sizes I now use no. 8s. The 'tell-tale'

shot, or one nearest the hook, is usually a no. 10 in my book, and its placing regarding distance to the hook needs to be experimented with. I found on the Trent at Burton Joyce in its heyday it had to be at least two feet away; any closer and you would not catch consistently. It being so crucial to get this right, I'd try moving it inch by inch if ever the bites stopped. The same applies to any other venue really. If there is a strongish undertow in a deep swim I like to concentrate more shot towards the bottom half of the rig, still spaced out evenly but with closer gaps. The depth, as illustrated, is again essential to get right, often inch perfect to get the best results, and this also needs to be constantly adjusted if and when the bites dry up.

When roach fishing, and it can equally apply to dace and chub, it is rare to catch all day long without making minor adjustments to shotting and depth as described. Hook size and hook length diameter are also very important, for as well as being 'shot-shy,' fish can also be 'hook' and/or 'line-shy.' I used to assemble four float rods for a match – say three carrying stick floats and the other a waggler – to cover all eventualities. It is like playing a game in which the fish keep changing the rules, and to win you need to quickly determine what the new set of rules is, and it's guaranteed they will change during a five-hour session. Failure to comply can mean the fish eating everything you give them except the all-important hookbait!

Dotting

Talking about shotting, brings me on to dotting. I like to really dot my float down to a mere pimple on the surface and believe only a stick float is perfectly balanced this way. This means that apart from gaining better float control you will see the most delicate indications when a fish moves that tell-tale shot, bites that would likely not be detectable with even ¼" of float showing. On the Trent I'd look at the float in situ and ask myself if it would take another number 10 shot. Even when it looked doubtful it would carry one, I'd often try it and find that it would. With the bare minimum of float on the surface you may ask how it is possible to see it for any distance downstream when trotting, but it's surprising how our eyes adjust enough to know when that 'dot' changes size or disappears. The resistance felt by a taking fish is reduced in this way and this obviously means, confident bites and more fish in the net.

On his way to winning the section in the 1980 Trent National

One thing I notice with some anglers is that they stick to the same line all day (and I mean feeding area not reel line). I think you'd be very lucky to catch on the same line indefinitely. Fish move both in and out of the flow as well as up and down in the water, especially after you have caught a few from a shoal and aroused their natural caution. Coming back to earlier points about feeding, you can accommodate this by feeding more than one line constantly. This means that when the fish move off one line there will always be some feed to attract them on another line. With practice you can even cover a far line and a middle line with the use of a catapult, as well as feeding the near line by hand.

Another vital point is to always feed downstream on a river. Just how far depends on the depth and pace of the swim, but always try to make sure that by the time your float fully settles your hookbait coincides with the point where the loose feed has reached the bottom. By feeding upstream in anything like a slow to moderate flow the fish are likely to move up towards it, and by the time the float has settled, you have gone past them. The only time I'd feed directly in front of my standing position, or to the upper limit of my peg is if it seems obvious the feed is not getting down in my swim. But be wary in this regard of falling into the trap of thinking you should feed upstream in deep water.[13]

Float speed

The only way to find out how the fish want the bait presenting on the day is by experimenting until you hit on it. It can vary from running the float through at the speed of flow, to holding it back hard and all the variations in between. You must get it right to build anything like a decent catch. For many years when I started fishing in Yorkshire as a teenager, it was all about holding back and slowing the bait down as it progressed through the swim. This applied to our main five rivers – Wharfe, Swale, Ouse, Derwent and Nidd. Dace were abundant then, but could take some catching, especially on the Wharfe at big match venues like Tadcaster and Ulleskelf.

There was a lot of skill in this style of presentation to get the float to go through the swim smoothly on line and at the

---

13 I once did a feature for Improve Your Coarse Fishing magazine about slider fishing on the Yorkshire Ouse, on peg 6 at Thorpe Underwood. The swim was 19 feet deep and I fed only very slightly downstream. As this method incorporates a bulk shot, the float settles very quickly. I caught nearly all my 15lb of roach that day within a yard of where my loose feed was hitting the surface. There was a steady flow on the river and I was sure my feed could not possibly get down so quickly in that depth, yet the fish were sitting right under it, proving that had I fed two or three yards upstream to allow for the depth I might only have caught a few stragglers. I have seen this on many occasions, it's as if the fish move above the feed to be directly under where it is going in, but in 19-ft? We can only speculate as to what is going on.

required pace that the fish wanted. For me this is where the centrepin reigned supreme, and I still think it is unbeatable within its range.

By now you will have realised that there are no fixed set of rules when it comes to stick float fishing, just basic guidelines as mentioned. A prime example came during my early forays on the big match scene shortly after I'd decided to abandon club matches (aged 28) and have a crack at the opens, entering a match at Caythorpe-on-Trent. I drew a pacey swim, as most are at this venue, only to suffer a frustrating day of finicky bites; and despite a 9lb total I knew the peg was worth more. I thought I had put my float through the swim beautifully with my trusty centrepin – slowing it down and easing it through the swim it had looked perfect. But relating my experience to my pal Stuart Thompson who, together with Stan Haigh and myself had also started fishing the Opens, it was clear that he had come to the same conclusion. Then Stuart hit the nail on the head in saying: "you know I'm not sure they wanted it held back?" I knew immediately that he was right. Talk about a light bulb moment! It explained everything about those finicky bites I'd missed.

Milestone

That day proved a massive turning point for me. It wasn't the end of holding back the float by any means, but from then on my weights in the opens significantly improved by running the float through unhindered at the speed of the flow. Certainly in good conditions on this area of the middle Trent, below Nottingham, it was absolutely vital. On some days, however, under ideal conditions, I'd get to a point when I thought I should be catching with the float going through this way, yet the bites weren't coming well. This was when I'd reach for the waggler rod that was set up behind me at the ready. It was as if there was a slight, undetectable difference in the speed the waggler went through compared to the stick. As suggested, the fish can be most discerning in the way the bait comes to them. Sometimes it worked the other way round of course, when a switch from waggler to stick was necessary.

I think stick float fishing is an individual thing and firmly believe that no two anglers do it quite the same. That is why it is essential to develop your own style, to work at it and keep asking the key questions: how do they want it? Am I too deep or too shallow? Is my shotting right and how should it change? Would a smaller hook and lighter hooklength help? Is my float staying on line etc?

With experience and following your own gut feeling you will develop an instinct for knowing when to change something, and when not. Whenever you have a thought, a nagging voice inside your head that you need to try something, then respond and do it quickly. You can always change back if it doesn't work, but this is how you learn and develop as an angler. Don't be lazy, make the effort, it's a great feeling when your hunch comes off and if it doesn't you have still learned something.

In a match, I could usually tell whether the angler above me was likely to catch by briefly observing his float as it travelled through his swim towards me and by how he fed. Back in the pub after a match I won at Burton Joyce I overheard the angler who had drawn above me saying to his mates: "But I did it just the same as him..." I smiled to myself and thought: "Oh no you didn't."

Feeding is key
Coming back to feeding, the thing I notice most is that some anglers neglect to do it, or maybe feed every third or fourth cast only. In other words the frequency is irregular and is therefore not likely to hold a captive audience of fish. It has to be at regular intervals to keep any shoal interested. It happened a lot on the Trent. In some matches you could go three hours for next to nothing, then suddenly the float would bury and you would experience that wonderful feeling of a good roach on the hook. You could then expect to continue catching, probably right to the match finish, with double figures on the cards in the last two hours leading to a possible win or frame placing. Had you not fed consistently and regularly in that blank three hours, then you would not have caught in the last two, the equation was that simple.

For sheer enjoyment, running a stick float through would be the choice of most anglers, like myself, brought up on running water. I used to revel in matches on hard venues where you would need a 10lb weight to win and every fish had to be earned. This was invariably the case on hard Trent matches, but a good example comes to mind from the Avon at Evesham. I drew a peg just below Huxley's café one autumn and caught good quality roach but they were extremely finicky. Bait presentation had to be spot-on before they would look at it and they were quick to reject the bait, making it a match of half chances. I was proud of my 10lb that day which was good enough for second, behind a net of chub that usually won on this stretch. It had been an immensely interesting and enjoyable day's fishing, right up my street: 'proper fishing' as we call it.

Another time we travelled to an open match on the River Nene at Oundle. This was a fair drive from Leeds and none of us had ever fished that high up the Nene before. I drew my peg only to be told it was not a very good area. But the river in front of me looked idyllic – picturesque with a nice steady flow: perfect for a stick float and roach. I plumbed up to find nine feet of water about a rod and a half out. I could tell it was a situation for a softly-softly approach, delicate presentation and light feeding. It was an easy peg to fish in terms of holding back, slowing down or stopping the float. The fish were cagey but I managed to keep them going over an immensely enjoyable five hours before tipping 10lb on the scales. That put me second in the 120-peg match, just 'pipped' by a 54lb bream catch! The moral of the story is that every other angler I could see that day fished a waggler which was obviously the popular method with the locals. I saw it as crying out for the stick and a more controlled presentation, and it illustrates how an outsider can sometimes teach the locals a new trick.

Stick vs waggler

Another waggler-rich area used to be Lincolnshire which is understandable since most of their venues – the Witham and other fenland rivers and connecting drains, are very slow moving most of the time. But even with the slightest of flows that look to suit out-and-out waggler, the stick can often beat it hands down. For example, I once fished a 50-peg Lincoln knock-up on the Witham at Southery. It was back end-ish, maybe November, and the river was barely flowing. I did not see anyone using a stick float that day and the waggler looked on the face of it the best option. Although I set one up and tried it, the day turned out to be one of those eye-openers. From my first cast with a stick float I was able to control my float and put it through in what could only have been a fraction slower, but the difference was incredible. My float kept going under, those of the opposition's didn't and I won comfortably with 12lb of roach.

Days like those described are the ones I enjoy the most, when everything has to be so precise even for a low, double-figure winning weight. I also recall one summer on the Witham's main matchlength at Kirkstead, in the days when 300 anglers would line up for the match. We would often gamble on the bream not showing which, on some days, they didn't in numbers, and fish the float for roach and eels. My travelling companion at the time, Tim Harrison, had a good run, framing several times with eels on the stick, again on a barely moving river. He found that the eels for some reason took the bait properly when presented under a stick, whereas on the waggler the bites were notoriously difficult to hit. Once again the difference in the way the bait presented must have been minute, yet the difference in return was huge. Only the fish know why.

Of course there are times when the above works in reverse, when an apparent stick float swim produces to the waggler and, to stress the point once again, we can only learn this by experiment and searching for the answers. So often a seemingly minor change makes all the difference and we get that Victor Meldrew moment when we say to ourselves or out loud to friends: "I don't believe it!"

Float choice
We all have our favourite floats and over the years I have had mine. For some reason, often impossible to explain, we can discover a one-off float that just works better than any other. I first found this with the traditional cane and balsa sticks. I had a home-made one taking 7 x no. 6 shot that won me a fair few matches. I could never quite analyse why but it just fished superbly. Maybe it was the perfect balance between the two materials, who knows? Whenever I hit upon such a float I'd always try to make another just in case I lost it, yet curiously

the replica never performed quite the same as the original – same shape, same shotting capacity, but *not* the same in terms of control and presentation.

The original commercial cane and balsa sticks were not suited to the venues we fished so we had to make our own. It was essential to use sinking cane and I would buy a bundle of garden canes, throw them in a bath of water and only select the ones that sank. My choice of balsa was always on the soft side to give good shot carrying capacity. It was a laborious job, working mainly with sandpaper and razor blades, but there was much satisfaction in winning a match with your own float.

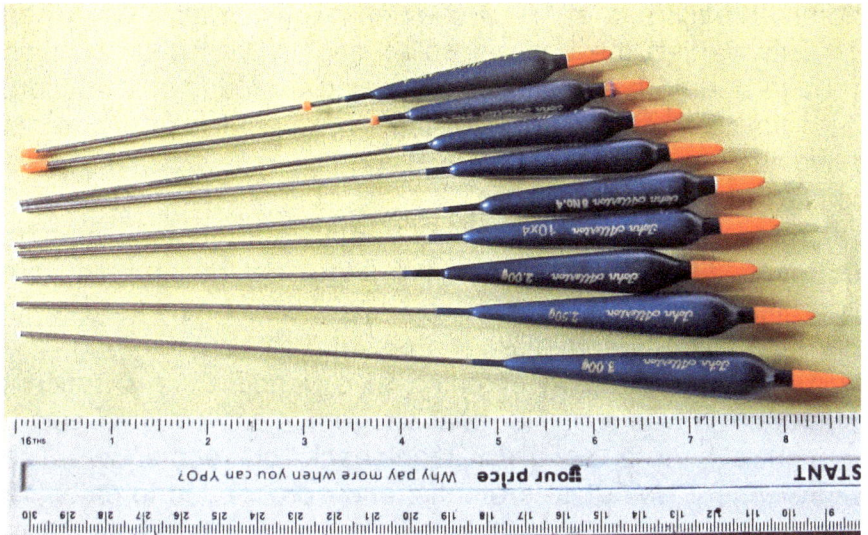

John Allerton's Mark II range made by Jimmy Leach, ex-Barnsley Black. Given a bit longer stem than the originals, they scale right up to 3g which we can fairly class as a Bolo float

The first good shop-bought sticks I liked were the John Dean range. The stems were a nylon material which was totally consistent and they were well balanced. Pre-dating these were the Pete Warrens which were also very popular. These had a more domed top and they undoubtedly worked very well. I generally preferred a more pointed top, but we all do it differently and Pete's floats obviously complemented his style as he was one of the Trent greats.

I later put my name to a range of sticks, incorporating

green nylon stems of a slightly heavier grade than John's, along with a wire stem model that I used quite a lot. This one had a nice shape with more of a shoulder than previous floats. Then came the John Allerton range. I liked these and won several opens using them. Choosing the right float for the conditions was always the key. The wire-stemmers seemed best for shallower, pacier swims; the more traditional sticks generally came out in steady, deeper water.

One excellent example of the importance of float choice came during a long ago pleasure session in the Ferry Field at Burton Joyce. Conditions were good and I chose a swim with an inviting 8-9ft depth at 2½ rods out. I set up an alloy-stemmed stick and at first it seemed okay. It was a day when the fish wanted the bait controlled slightly, not quite running through but more a case of just leaning on the float a fraction. But I got to the stage where I thought my catch rate was not doing justice to the swim: I was getting a few fish but was convinced it was worth more.

After playing around with my depth and shotting nothing improved. I couldn't quite put my finger on the problem, but something told me it might be the float. I changed to a standard nylon-based stick, and as soon as I put it through the swim without changing anything else, I noticed a significant difference. It was a bulkier float altogether and seemed easier to control, more solid to lean back on somehow. The improvement was quite dramatic, and I proceeded to catch 12 fish in as many casts! I went on to bag a very good weight of roach that day. It is experiences like this that have convinced me over and over again how critical bait presentation is and the importance of experimenting until you find the winning formula. This occasion was incredible, but other differences can be just as subtle and making the right move is often the difference between a good catch or failure.

I do not want to leave the impression that I lost faith in the alloy-stemmed sticks by the above experience. Indeed nowadays for fishing the Yorkshire rivers I rate the Drennan alloy sticks highly. They go up to 4 x BB size which is a bit smaller than I would like, but I find they fish really well. I sometimes change the stem for a slightly longer one for deeper swims.

Modified Drennan alloy-stemmers

I have replaced the alloy stem on some of the Drennan's with a slightly longer one for deeper, steadier swims. My fishing pal, Mick Hughes must have had the same thought and, being a brilliant float maker, he discovered that with a firm steady pull using a pair of pliers, the stem is easy to remove with nil damage to the float; then just glue a longer one in, allowing scope to trim.

I am only talking about a ¼" up to 1½" maximum for the extension. It is more of a personal thing, really, that develops over many years of stick float fishing; you learn to recognise what looks right about a float. As they are, they are fine for most situations, it is just that on the odd occasion you feel that to slightly modify the float you are using would improve it. After the session I'd go home and make the change, in case I was in the same situation again. Over time you learn to be able to look at a float then hold it and visualise exactly where you would use it and in what circumstances. Ultimately, we can only really tell how well a float fishes by using it.

To find a commercially manufactured range as good as the Drennans, which lends itself to this type of adaptation is great as it extends your range of options. That said, I remember many years ago winning an Angling Times Yorkshire Winter League match on the Ouse at Widdington with 12lb of roach on a 4 x BB Drennan Alloy Stem (unmodified) in a swim about 12-foot deep. On the face of it the float looked a bit short for the depth of water, but it certainly worked superbly on the day, whereas a longer stem, I thought, would not have worked so well due to the pace of the river. It is about how well the float 'sits' in the water when you hold back or slow it down even slightly: you don't want any riding up for instance.

I like to fish a stick on the Aire and Calder Canal, and Drennan alloys are ideal for this (the canal flows at various speeds) with depths from 4 or 5-foot to about 12-foot. The 4 x no. 4 for instance, takes 8 x no. 6's on average, so I have given some a slightly longer stem to create a 7 x no. 6 stick which is dead right in, say, 7 or 8 feet of depth. Likewise, with the bigger sizes, I have a range taking from 11 up to 17 x no. 6's (seven sizes in three floats: 6 x no. 4, 3 x BB and 4 x BB).

Some are helped by a variation in the density of the balsa, of course.

Winning the World Championship on the Stick

Dave en route to his World win

The build up to this World Champs was like nothing I have seen before or since. It was on home ground: the Warwickshire Avon. We had a great team and expectation of England's first gold was high. Two days before the team match (day one) the river came up and was still carrying for the event. Although the French were now fancying their chances, I was confident of winning but also determined to enjoy it. There can be no higher honour in our sport than to be chosen to fish for your country in a World Champs in front of a home crowd. I had a great match, catching on a stick and waggler to win with 10lb of small chub. The crowd were fantastic, loudly acclaiming every fish I hooked and again cheering and applauding enthusiastically every fished landed. It was a unique and brilliant experience I will never forget. The question then was could I do as well on day two? The individual event consisted of the top five anglers from each section on day one, plus one angler from each team selected by their manager, forty anglers in all. I was confident.

The river came up again overnight and we knew this would keep weights down and make the venue peggier. Most of the finalists would be hoping to draw a slack peg, myself included. Teammate, Clive Smith, had walked the length that morning and seen the pegs. I showed him my peg number; he looked at it and said: "Your peg is in the last four." He didn't think I had any chance off it. It had always been my policy to accept whatever I drew and just go and fish it one hundred per cent and let the result take care of itself. Today was, of course, no exception. Disappointing as it was to hear Clive's words, I knew I had scored off plenty of so-called no-hopers in the past by refusing to give in.

Walking to my peg I saw some lovely slacks before I arrived at my swim and could see why Clive said what he did. It was going through a bit, even on the inside, and my options were limited to one, as far as I could see. That was to fish off the rod end with the stick where I could get behind the float at full reach and ease it as slow as I could through the swim. By choice I would have laid on, but that's not permitted in the World Championship rules. You are not allowed to fish a still bait where the water is moving.

I had the perfect tool for the job, my centrepin reel, unbeatable in this situation. I fed steadily with bronze maggots, getting through hardly a pint over the three hours, and inched the float through at snail's pace. The river was highly coloured and I needed to give any fish that might be there, time to find my bait. The swim was five to six feet deep, my float a 6 x no. 4 stick with single maggot on a 20 hook. Clive told me afterwards that people were coming to me after winning the day before and he was saying to them: "Don't watch Dave today, he's got no chance off this peg."

After about 90 minutes of hooking leaves every cast and trying double maggot on the hook, then returning to single halfway through the three-hour match, the float went under and instead of a leaf my strike met with solid resistance... the rod bent, the crowd shouted loudly. Clive said afterwards that he could hear my heart thumping from where he was. In that moment I had the biggest decision of my match angling career to make. I knew that if I took it steady and played the fish in the normal way there was a fair chance that it might find a snag (chub are good at that) and, with the river in the state it was in, there was probably plenty of unseen vegetation for it to find. The alternative was to go for it and just lift and try to take the fish by surprise and net it before it decided what to do. It felt a decent fish and I knew this option was not without risk. Either way, I knew if I got it wrong I'd never forgive myself. It was a win or lose decision. All this went through my mind in a second. I sensed the fish had hesitated and I said to myself "you're coming out."

I think what really swung it was my Craddock rod. I knew from experience on the Trent that with a chub under the rod end, the stage where they dig into the stones to try and snag or shed the hook, I could just lift steadily and they would come, even fish up to 3lb on a light bottom. It was all down to the rod, incredible in that situation. I eased it up in an unhurried but firm way and it came. In a flash my net was under it and it was mine. It went crazy then but it was too late. The crowd cheered, the atmosphere was charged. I sensed from their reaction there was not much being caught. That fish was a good one, above average for the Avon at that time, maybe 1¾lb. About fifteen minutes later – a repeat performance, this time a smaller fish. I gave it the same treatment and it was in the net before it knew what had happened. The crowd had grown after that first fish and the response was loud and enthusiastic.

The BBC Grandstand cameras were behind me. Pete Thompson caught my eye and asked if Tony Gubba, who was more used to commentating on football, could come down and have a word with me. It might sound strange but I somehow knew that my name was on that trophy now. I admit, with time left to go, anything could have happened. There were 39 other anglers in that match, including Kevin Ashurst, John Dean and Max Winters who was on the peg below me, but I never doubted the outcome. Tony Gubba came down very quietly and asked me if I thought I would win, I replied: "I think it might be enough today." He had no sooner gone back up the bank, when I caught a roach. And that was it, no more bites but I felt confident.

Ian Heaps appeared at the edge of my area and gave me the thumbs up as the all-out signal was sounded. He didn't speak, but his lips said: 'You've got it.' I had never been so sure of anything in my life.

I was pleased to have won it for Stan Smith and for England, to give us something to come away with after the disappointment of being pipped by the French for the Team Gold. It meant a lot. The smiles on Stan's face and other NFA Officials such as Joe Betteridge, Harry Lodge and journalists Colin Graham and Rod Coldron, as well as my wife Avis, in fact everyone who was there, said it all. On a personal note, I suddenly realised I had become the first Yorkshireman to win the title and that made me doubly proud, as any Yorkshireman will understand.

It also went through my mind that nine short years ago, I was still a club angler. I just thought: 'Wow, who'd have believed it!'

Dave Thomas floats with green plastic stems (thinner and slightly heavier than the Dean black plastic), at the lighter end – 4 x 4, two 3 x 4 and a 2 x 4, and two stocky Middy Warrens. Note how they take up to 7 x 4s for a similar length

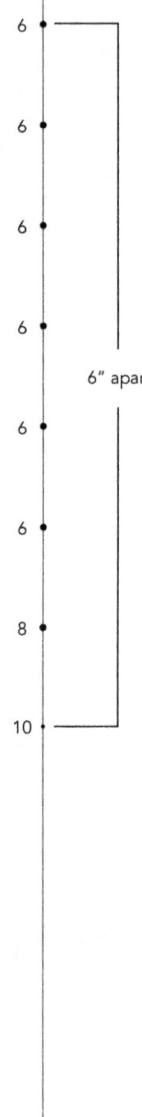

Note the 18" gap from the tell-tale shot to hook, starkly contrasting John Dean's rig (ch. 16) with a 3" gap for a more sensitive presentation. This shot is always adjustable, on many days it will finish up somewhere between the two.

6

6

6

6

6" apart

6

6

8

10

Chapter 22
Denis White – a lignum stick to Bolo' journey

Former England international (17 appearances at all levels) and evergreen Barnsley Black, Denis White, has enjoyed a long and glittering match career. This famously feisty competitor burst onto the big match scene on his open match debut in 1964 when, aged 18, he spectacularly topped a 300-man Trent field at Burton Joyce with 11lb 12oz using a home-made stick and a simple shotting pattern.

With the sixties decade only just getting into full swing, the stick float was still in its infancy despite a group of Mancunians profiting from it along with caster bait. What some of the surprised regulars on this match didn't know, however, was that Denis had already won a few club matches. He was a competent Trent angler, *and* he had an ace up his sleeve: he'd made some special stick floats that he'd every confidence in and was in no way overawed on the bigger stage.

Taught by his dad, Herbert, and two Barnsley anglers from his mid-teens, Billy Howarth and Micky Wood, he'd shown great promise and, in one memorable season, he won 21 club events! Even at the tender age of 10 or 11, fishing the Derwent at Hutton's Ambo, he won a club match junior section with a 7lb-plus catch consisting of five big roach on bread, laying on with a crowquill. Herbert followed suit to win the senior event but fell short of his son's weight by 2lbs.

Showing both his lack of experience and an early craving to win, Denis had no landing net with him on the day so had to ask the lad pegged above him to borrow his net, and five times he obliged. But when the same lad asked how he was catching the roach, he cheekily put him wrong, saying they were coming to 'three pinkies.' Denis, now 74, admits it was perhaps not the most honourable way of returning a favour!

Billy Howarth was keen enough to pick up Denis and take him fishing to Newmiller Dam, even on occasion after working a double shift at the pit, while Micky Wood introduced him to the stick floats he'd made with a lignum base and a flat top to the balsa. Fishing the Swale above Topcliffe Weir, on a deep and steady stretch where ten roach over a pound in a day was not exceptional, he taught his apprentice how to hold the float back then let it go and a bite would follow. "Just a half-day lesson with these experienced anglers put me on the right track and it went from there," said Denis.

Denis started making lignums himself but with a domed top, and, come the day of his first big open match, this was naturally his float of choice. Drawn three pegs above Gunthorpe Bridge, he was faced with an inviting gentle upstream wind and was able to cast his lignum out to five rod-lengths and conjure up 11lb 12oz of silvers – comprising mainly roach, some gudgeon and the odd dace. This pushed Trent star of the period, Ken Parr[14], into second with a lower 11lb. His reward: a cool £220, a small fortune at the time considering he was earning only £4 12s per week as a trainee

14 Ken Parr finished a close second to Dick Ward in one of the Manchester vs Nottingham challenges when all the main Trentmen of the sixties lined up to do battle; he was also the seven-hour weight record holder with 50lb of roach from Shelford in this decade.

miner! It was the thrill of his young life and with partner Tony Wilson they left for home, starry-eyed and full of what they were going to win next.

Denis remembers using a Sundridge Benny Ashurst 13-foot glass rod that day, coupled with the massively popular casting reel of the time – the Mitchell 300, and everyone's favourite line, the reliable Bayer Perlon 1.1lb strain tied to a Mustad 39855 round bend hook.

The lignum stick divides opinion among river angling's elite because this heavy wood tends to cock a float a bit too sharply to stay in line with small shots descending. Undeniably though, it has one major advantage over other sticks: it offers superb casting power wherever fish are shoaled well out. To recognise this so early in his career and craft his own lig' sticks before they were available commercially showed great foresight.

He's believed to be the first Yorkshireman to build lignum into his home-made floats, and among the first in the UK. Ultra would later put a lignum float on the market, which is ironic because Billy Lane, the float maestro and tackle dealer behind the company, was no great fan of any stick float other than the wire-stem version.

Unable to get a ticket for the following weekend's match, he ensured they booked quickly for the Saturday after that. From a 10-foot deep swim near Cocker Dyke mouth, Denis used the same float to fish just past his rod end, and plundered even more roach for 14lb and fourth place. Days later *Angling Times* headlined the match report: *'Young star proves it was no fluke.'* What the angling world would soon realise was that this angler was on a mission.

"The bonus of making a great start in these two matches was how the established stars reacted. Ken Parr could not have been more generous after being beaten, and I got a friendly reception from the likes of John Toulson, Roy Toulson, and Ted Stokes – and what a gentleman he was, respected by everyone. To be quickly accepted by some of the cream of the Trent circuit was marvellous.

"I'd got some lignum sections from a railway fishplate, which is bolted onto rail tracks to maintain their position. After cutting some quarter-inch sticks from it they then had to be shaped. I would fasten these sticks in a drill held between my knees and taper them with two files. It's not the easiest wood to whittle down but the result was a boss float that could be cast as far as you'd ever need it to – a third way across the Trent was easy in an overhead wind.

"The one problem with long casting a stick, of course, is the potential for the dreaded back-tangle. I decided that three shotting points was the least risky way of going about it. A bulk of 3 x BB shot would sit just below half depth, with a no. 4 below and a no. 8 tell-tale, adjustable but usually starting off some 12 inches from the hook. But, and this may sound a little contradictory, the reel choice also mattered: much as I like the Mitchell Match, a closed face reel like an ABU, or in my case a French Contact (Crack) 400, is best for chucking a stick well out. These closed face models release line less freely than an open face one by the thinner spool creating a slight tension and braking effect, but this assists a smooth feathering of the float on landing. If the float overtakes the shot, as it can with a lignum without slowing the cast down before impact, tangles will occur. But make that landing of the float smooth with a subtle feather, helped by the right reel, and all the shots will extend nicely beyond the float."

All the talk about distance begged my next question: what float type did Denis prefer for close-in work when the swim and conditions demanded it?

"I'd still use a lignum as I like the way it never rides up when held back, but I also liked John Dean's plastic stemmers and at times a wire stem too at venues like Collingham, for example: in swims where it might be 10-foot deep and boily. Another float I've used is a pheasant quill, tipped with balsa. I remember that float helping me win a South Kirby Colliery AC match in 1967, taking 14lb of gonks [gudgeon], putting a small nugget of groundbait in every cast. A young tall and thin kid came up and watched me briefly that day. He quickly learned what it was about; returned to his peg and came third with 9lb: his name was Tommy Pickering. He soon joined me in the first Barnsley Blacks team of four and became my travelling companion."

A great all-rounder, Denis would learn the Bolognese method from the Italians (incorporating their long telescopic rods and bigger floats) while they exchanged notes with the English on waggler and slider methods on international duties all over Europe. The best I saw on Bolo' was Roberto Trabucco in the World Championship at Belleek, Northern Ireland, in 1992. Fishing a 7-metre telescopic in an 18-foot swim with an upstream wind, he held the rod high with the butt in his groin and the line acting like a yacht sail; he inched the float through in midstream to catch enough bream to win his section. Denis meanwhile, in a different section saved a blank by catching one micro fish on half a squatt. Denis admired Trabucco's skill.

"He was the best of some very good Italians on Bolo'. They had grown up with it on venues like the River Mincio. Swims on this river run to 20-foot deep but it has a stringy weed growth up from the bottom and this can reach up to half-depth. Using a 7-metre rod and Contact 400 reel, I've seen him boldly lashing a 5 or 6-gram float out a long way – some 30 metres, fishing three maggots on a 14 hook for scardola and carassio – a crucian-like fish, both shy biters that require a finesse approach. They did get the occasional tangle, of course, they are only human, but their answer to that was carrying many identical spare rigs on winders and only had to tie a knot to be back in business.

"The Italian aces are never scared of putting lots of shots either side of the bulk with their heavy Bolo' floats. They'll taper a chain of shots away from a central BB or AAA shot both down towards the hook and back the opposite way towards the float, in say a no. 1, 4, 6, 8 shot sequence, and I have seen rigs employing small 5mm or 10mm gaps, tightening up towards the hook, as well as them opening up slightly, not far removed if you can imagine from a double taper fly line in miniature. They will also feed balls of groundbait containing floating casters which obviously rise up from the weedy bottom as the balls disperse, attracting fish as they go. Films of this tactic can be seen on You Tube, and there are deep UK rivers where this could work.

"When we first pipped the Italians by just one point to win the 1985 World title, on their own muckheap on the River Arno, we did it with the help of slider-caught catfish. But that's another story."

Back home on the Yorkshire circuit Denis has won many matches in recent years on the Bolo' method, notably on the deep Ouse and lower Aire. He's used both an 8m Daiwa Amorphous rod and two customised 7m Maver telescopic models. To improve the rods for windy conditions he's added extra rings on sliding sections of carbon – a total of 19 on one and 17 on his spare.

Fishing Altofts on the Calder he took 26lb of big dace on a 3-gram rig in three hours to break the match record for the stretch. He started in mid-river but only really found the shoal when he moved close in after two hours. He's also won with 20lb nets of roach from the lower Aire on the method. For the Yorkshire rivers Denis shots up simpler than the Italian style, bearing in mind he can be forced to cast underhand wherever trees get in the way of an overhead delivery.

The simple rig for UK waters is configured as follows: an olivette bulk just below mid-depth and three droppers below – a no. 4 shot, no. 6 then a swivel as the tell-tale to replace the standard no. 8. "The swivel is essential with the Bolo' to prevent hook spin and hooklength tangles," adds Denis.

So if the heavier Bolo' method has taken over from the stick in modern times, incorporating approximately half the weight down the line as a medium stick, just what are the criteria that decide its selection? Well, some anglers may have other reasons for using the popular float and its attacking style, but Denis insists it is all down to the *depth* of swim he's faced with on his match circuit.

"In a six-foot swim, say, a 5 x no. 4 stick is perfect. In one of 12 or 13-foot, especially with the advances of technology and today's lightweight long rods, a heavier stick on a 16' rod will cover most situations. But if you consider the deeper Yorkshire Ouse, or the lower Aire at 20-foot or even 25-foot deep, then a 3g or more size Bolo', or top and bottom balsa slider, are the best floats to master them."

The photograph below shows a part of Denis's top and bottom float arsenal. From left to right:

– a balsa-bodied pheasant quill, 60 years old, used for close-in work on the Trent, rated stronger and better than a crowquill

– top and bottom balsa slider (Denis stresses the

importance of its stainless steel eyes as weaker wire ones would too easily bend off-line and ruin the float's sliding facility)

– a non-sliding straight balsa, three lignum sticks also ancient and treasured

– two Allerton-style short lignums – all of which are home-made

– a final group of short wire-stems with fat tops are for fast, three-foot or shallower swims where long-trotting and a surface ripple can test visibility. These were made by floatmaker Mick Hughes (see chapter 54) who camouflaged the floats in green paint to match the colour of the silkweed that is often seen in shallows on the River Calder.

Chapter 23
Keith Hobson: he'd only one stick
but could make it talk

It could be said that Barnsley's Keith Hobson fits the Yorkshire creed in that he's a creature of habit who knows what he likes. He has only fished for the one team as a proud member of his local Barnsley Blacks, and has loved river fishing as long as I've known him. His enthusiasm for matches has never wavered and his attacking style has helped him achieve some prestigious victories in the last half-century. Now 72, he is still

competing on the popular Yorkshire river circuit. Stick float fashions might come and go, but he has never lost his affinity for the John Dean sticks with the black plastic base. They first served him proudly on the Trent, especially at Burton Joyce where he and teammate Dick Clegg collaborated to win more than their share, though really any river holding roach and chub was on their target list. In comparing how Keith fishes in Yorkshire today with his early style, my first question for him was about this particular stick float...

Q: We have fished with and against each other for many years, in matches on many waters. I never really took to a plastic-stemmed stick but you certainly did. So what is so special about this stick float in your go-to 6 x no. 4 size?

– I liked the pointed tipped version which was sensitive, and the way it could be cast a long way out. It was heavy enough in the base but it followed the shots. Casting anywhere the wind allowed, in swims up to eight-foot deep, it never caused me any tangles and never let me down. I never found a lignum float that would cast quite as neatly.

Q: I'm guilty of a bit of artistic licence with the headline to this chapter, but it is not far off the mark that this was the *only* float you used at Burton Joyce; you surely used a handful of alternatives though for special situations?

– Yes, occasionally. In shallow swims I'd use a lighter Dean version – of say 4 x no. 4, and in water over eight feet, I might fish the same float with a dome top in 8 x no. 4 size. And if the swim was fast and/or boily, I'd sometimes change to a Drennan wire-stem Avon which had a rugby ball-shaped body (brown coloured). I liked to fish a bulk of up to 6 x no. 4 with this float and 3 x no. 8 droppers. I once won an Angling Times winter league semi-final at Willington with 36lb of dace and chub with this float and remember it coping well in a facing wind. But the Dean stick suited me best of all.

Q: Your stick shotting back in the day was with 2 x no. 10s closest to the hook and a fair distance to the tell-tale shot. And you liked to present the bait at least a foot overdepth to start with and take it from there. Has this changed in recent times?

– Not really. I measure my hooklength at about an arm's length and only 1 x no. 10 is placed on it. Above that would be

8s and then 6s equally spaced in the lower half of the rig. I have never been one for moving shot about, unless I make a drastic change, but I might change depth several times in a match until I feel it's working right. Get the shotting right first time and you don't need to mess with it, is my motto.

Q: And is back-shotting preferred?

– Only in a very tricky downstreamer.

Q: Moving onto the all-important hook, you were tempted to use a size 24 on the Trent before most risked it, around the late seventies. What particular match led you to drop down so small?

– It came from a Burton Joyce match and a draw above Gunthorpe Bridge, and a frustrating day. I was getting bites on a 22 hook but not connecting with much. Too late in the match to do any good, I switched to a 24 and those misses turned into fish and I put 6lb of roach on the scales. The following week I decided to use a 24 from the off from a draw opposite the Cherry Orchard. The river was out of sorts and I only had four bites for three fish: a perch, a chub and a 4lb bream to win with 7lb. The next day in the Winter League I was drawn below Winthorpe Bridge (Burdett's), and as it was snowing prospects were not brilliant. But fishing a tiny stick in three-foot of water close in, again with a 24, I took five chub to win again with 5lb 12oz. That convinced me I was on the right track.

Q: I think the reel lines we used in those days were perhaps more durable and reliable than some of the pre-stretched, clear ones of today. What say you?

– You make a fair point regarding reel line. I liked the brown 2lb Racine Tortue Nacrita for stick float back then, and 2.5lb for waggler, with 1.1.b or 12oz Bayer Perlon hooklengths, or 1.7lb for the upper Trent where bigger fish were more prevalent. I use a .15mm modern reel line these days, and it might well be stronger but is not necessarily as hard-wearing.

Q: So let's fast forward to your Yorkshire river circuit of today: the 'give 'em a gallon' (of maggots) days are long gone, I imagine?

– Yes, I have had to cut it right back to two pints of caster in summer, often using only a pint to one and a half pints, and in winter two pints of maggots and a pint of caster in reserve as a rule. The Ouse is a harder river than the Trent was at its peak, and so you have to tailor the feed to the catch potential.

Q: Now fishing overdepth is ideal along a smooth river bed, but the Ouse can be snaggy I'm told; what if you can't drag line through on the deck?

– Well if a snag is in the way I'll shop around trying to find a clearer run. I remember a peg I won from on the Calder where I won on the pole with an all-dace bar one chub 22lb. Then I drew the peg again but the water level had come up. Fishing the same distance with pole and a 2.5-gram rig it was a snag pit. I was able to find a clean run through with the stick closer in but it was unproductive. Using the pole on the Ouse does help in the sense that you don't trot as far, but try bringing the fish up to a bed of groundbait instead.

Q: And do you fish the Bolo' method on the deep Ouse?

– I have done, but wherever I'm familiar with the peg and conditions are normal, I now try catching on the pole if possible. I had a 7m Bolo' rod – a Shimano fully ringed job, and won a couple of times on it, but in some pegs overhead trees limited its use, so I sold it after tearing my shoulder muscle. Beyond pole range now I fish a fourteen-foot rod and a top and bottom slider of 4g or even 5g. I find this more comfy. The slider is a Dick Clegg Avon-type with peacock stem and balsa body which takes in 'old money' 10 to 12 x BB.

Q: And I hear you've had an epiphany with regard to your faith in the tiny maggot hook?

– Well yes, I can't deny it. Believe it or not, I now use a strong Kamasan B560 in size 18 or 20 with maggot or caster. I don't know why, but if I'm getting few bites, a smaller hook does not seem to make much difference – it often won't get me more bites. Of course, with the Ouse's depth a finer wire hook might not cope with the water pressure.

Q: And you also like the Calder circuit?

– Yes, it is more like the Trent used to be, at Mirfield for instance where six-foot is a good depth, or at Altofts which is deeper and wider and I also like as it's local at only fifteen miles from home. I like the Ouse because it is a challenge, while the Aire can be tough as it is bottomless (up to thirty feet) in places.

Q: Tell me about any recent memorable matches?

– My best winning weight on the Calder was memorable

for being a different kind of day. I had 38lb on the stick from a peg below Bailey Bridge – all trout bar a 2½ lb grayling! This was in a summer match when trout are allowed. A near miss in the Calder Championship was unforgettable in a different way when drawn in the marina at Brighouse on a rising river. After catching a chub on the waggler, I then ran a little stick down the edge, ladling maggots in heavily like old times, for a 21lb total. I lost one good chub on a big clump of floating weed, which was costly, pushing me into second with 22lb!

But my best fish came from the Ouse. I drew Middle Linton on a cold, clear winter river. I plugged away for three hours for nothing, loose feeding the pole line over a bed of groundbait. This was a deep swim and I had on a rig of six sections to hand. With an hour to go I caught a roach, then a second and a third. With twenty minutes to go I got a better bite and thought I'd hooked a snag: then this 'snag' moved out slowly to mid-river at full elastic stretch! I'd scaled down to a 22 hook to a .10mm bottom. I was thinking 'big bream' but after a tense battle I netted a chub with a mouth I could have got my fist in. It gave me a 6-14 total so it had to have weighed over 6lb.

Q: I'd call that a stylish finish in anyone's book! So what was the secret, groundbait?

– I like a mix of Van den Eynde Super match (black) and VDE Secret in natural brown or black, which adds a binding quality.

Q: And do you use hemp on these Yorkshire matches, and ever as hookbait?

– I'll feed it sometimes in summer, and occasionally put it on the hook too. A last day of the season match at Middle Linton springs to mind – March, but it felt like summer at 20 degrees warm. I'd been fishing caster on an 18 with a 3g rig. It wasn't really happening so I put hemp on and it worked immediately for a roach, and I went on to win with 11lb of quality roach.

Q: So who do you regard as the men to beat on the Ouse and Calder?

– There are so many who are able to win from a decent draw. My old mate Denis [White] can never be written off in any peg, is such a hard worker and so experienced. Ian Bowman stands out as another who can do it all, is very versatile, and match organiser Martin Highe can't be overlooked, is also dangerous and knows every peg well.

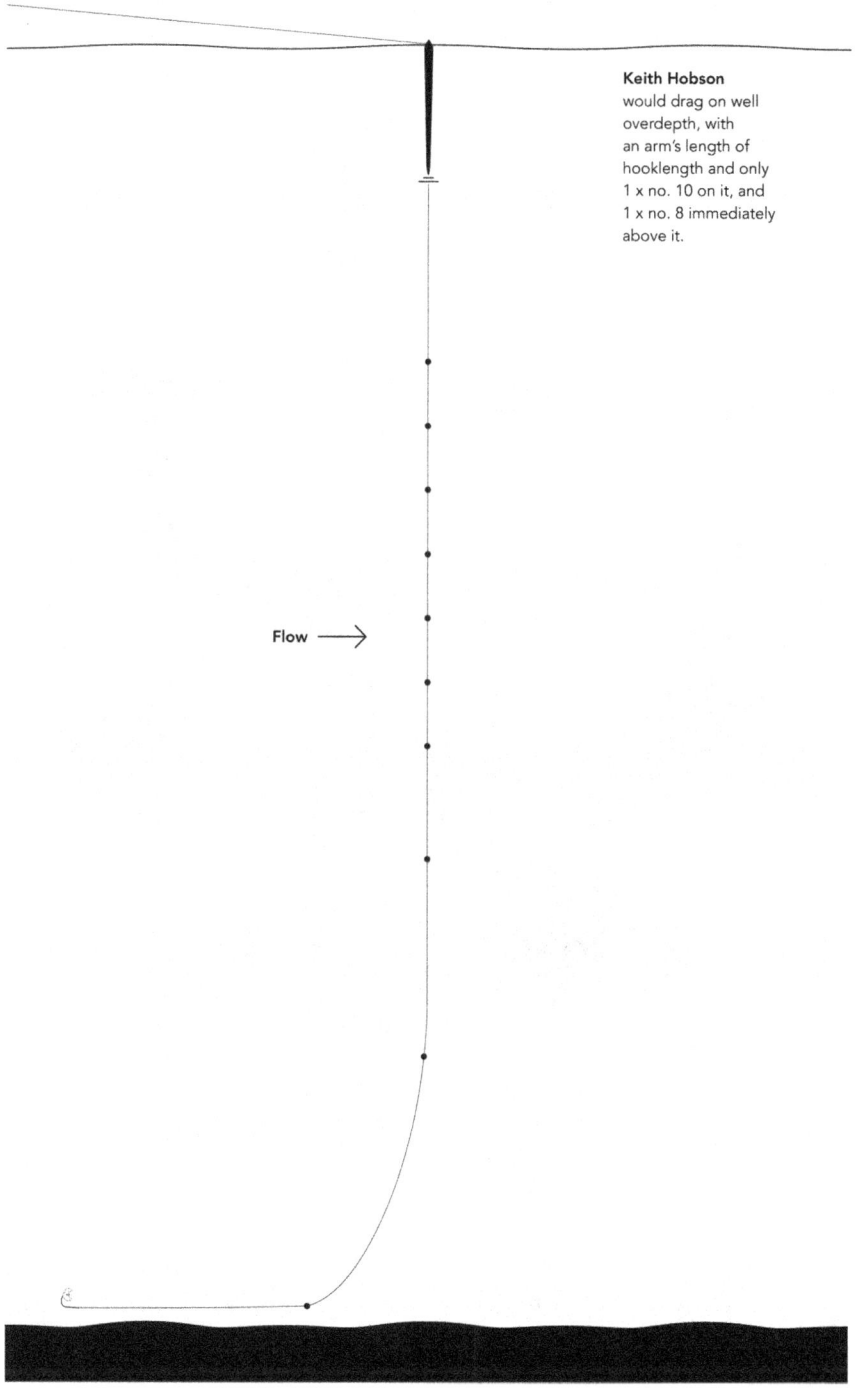

Keith Hobson
would drag on well overdepth, with an arm's length of hooklength and only 1 x no. 10 on it, and 1 x no. 8 immediately above it.

Flow ⟶

Chapter 24
John Allerton 'Mr Cool'
– and a new stick design

With a prestigious Kamasan Matchman of the Year title win, back-to-back Trent Championship wins in '93 and '94, and 50 years of consistent open match success under his belt, Selby's John Allerton is still going strong. A former Barnsley Black team colleague and for many years Tri-cast sponsored, he must rank highly among the finest anglers never to have fished for England. Although John is a proud and slightly reserved man, confident but never boastful, his approach to

angling is totally professional. However, he was never sure he could give the total commitment that winning gold medals for his country demands. John has always regarded his match winnings as a supplement to his day job as a car technician. John made his name catching silver fish in the big river matches of the seventies to nineties, before switching to commercial carp lakes where he carried on winning almost seamlessly. The late Trent ace, Jan Porter, once described him as 'the alien' for his fish catching efficiency combined with the Spock-like detachment shown by Leonard Nimoy in his Star Trek role. John's match record with the waggler on many waters is exemplary enough, but it is his ability with the stick float for which he is best known. His own commercially produced JA stick broke away from the traditional cane base and also incorporated a shoulder and very slender tip. I interviewed John recently to learn more about his float, how it evolved, and more...

Q: When did you first develop the commercial 'John Allerton stick' and why? (John's once unique stick has an aluminium stem and shouldered balsa tip)

— I'd be in my late twenties, 45 years ago, circa 1975. I was not that happy with the presentation of the heavier standard sticks on the market. I experimented a lot, looking for a lighter float that the shots would, in effect, pull through the air, not the other way round. At that time I was also doubling up the number of rings on my rods, to reduce the wind effect and aid trotting by a smoother reel to float line connection.

Q: Who/what influenced your design?

— It was a time when many anglers made their own floats, as good shop-bought floats were uncommon. Bradford team angler, Eric Wright, gave me the idea to try an aluminium stem after I saw him using one, but the shoulder and slim pointed tip was my own innovation. I wanted a more sensitive float than I'd seen around, one allowing a no. 12 micro shot to serve as a tell-tale, and to shot it down to a pimple.

Q: The top of your float looks very similar to the profile of the dumpy carrot float pioneered by Lancastrian Gerry Lees. Did you know of this float; did it influence your own?

— I knew of Gerry from matches at Winthorpe and

elsewhere, and he was a very good angler, but no, I never studied his float.

Q: What convinced you your new float was right?

– Well one immediate benefit was the way I could see the angle of the float when holding back thanks to the fine tip, unlike the view of a dome-topped float for example. This almost told me where the bait was in the swim. The float was also sensitive and seemed to cope well with all types of swim. I never looked back.

Q: What became your most used size on the Trent?

– Five x no. 4.

Q: Prior to this you fished with a certain Stan Brown of Goole; wasn't he your mentor?

– Yes, Stan was a great angler. He worked hard in his job then would take time off and fish a lot. His feeding and presentation was fine-tuned and he took some big Trent weights. But there were three of us: Roy Duckett made up the trio, a character who, like Stan, has now passed away and is sadly missed. We learned from each other. In those early days we'd often change our floats three or four times in the first hour until we found the right one for the swim on the day.

Q: Do you expect all sticks to cock of their own accord when laid on the surface?

– It doesn't bother me that much, though mine do, but to make a float that tilts enough to break the surface film is advisable.

– For slow swims do you ever use a slim traditional stick, e.g. with a cane, lignum or plastic base?

I have used all thicknesses of cane stick at times, but mostly prefer my own design. What I tend to do in slow swims is use lighter shots – say no. 8s six inches apart, scaling up to 6s in a normal flow.

Q: So can you offer the reader a go-to shotting pattern for Burton Joyce road stretch, say for a six-foot deep swim?

– A no. 12 tell-tale six inches from the hook, a no. 8 six inches above that, a no. 6 six inches above that, then enough no. 6s above that 4" apart to dot the float.

Q: I have my own reasons for liking two micro shot closest to the hook, but I'm not sure this is common practice? It is all about finessing the presentation isn't it?

– Exactly. It is about trying to make the hookbait behave in the same way as the loose feed. I work to find the hotspot in the swim then cast the float close to it, then hold the float back and release, lifting and dropping the bait to entice bites. A foot of hooklength with no shot on it can be a bit long, but, with the micro six inches from the hook, the bait will lift higher than with a bigger shot and drop back down slower. I even used this pattern on faster water like the upper Trent.

Q: Did you over-shot the float when holding back?

– No.

Q: But you do like the control of a back-shot?

– Yes, and would use 2 or even 3 x no. 6s behind the float: as far back as four feet on occasion, if the swim's not too deep.

Q: What was your favourite stick float venue back in the day?

– I loved the Calder, and the Witham later on. And even when the wind was awkward the stick could work providing you limited yourself to a shorter trot under full control. This might be the bottom third of the peg, casting downstream to it. I'd always advise casting to the hotspot especially when conditions are difficult.

Q: So your first job is to plumb the depth, then what is your starting depth you set the float to?

– I will start at the exact depth of the water, then will add or remove two to three inches as required. It's about a feel for the way the fish want to feed; every day is different and we can only be guided by experience.

Q: So you are presented with good conditions, warm with a slight breeze, and you think the peg can produce double figures. You're a fan of the Kamasan B510 barbless hook I know, so what is your starting size?

– A 24. It took me a few years to change down from a 22, but the lighter and smaller hook gives better presentation which means better bites.

Q: Would that have a maggot or caster attached as your number one roach bait?

– I don't mind which, but it varies. If in any doubt then I'll feed two or three of each per cast at the start of the session then take it from there. The fish dictate the rules.

Q: Moving onto feed rates: the key to good catches – what would you call an average maggot requirement for a Trent peg, and could you maybe compare heavy to light feed?

– Well, I have never fed that heavily. On a 50lb potential flier I'd only be thinking of three pints at most, and at the opposite extreme, say on the Wharfe, fishing for dace, one pint is ample. You can feed just three maggots per cast and still find the dace reluctant to move up from the bottom of the peg, but still make a 10lb catch.

Q: What is your best stick catch or match win?

– Probably a Daiwa qualifier for a team final in Sweden, held at Dunham Bridge when fishing with Barnsley. I won with just under 30lb of roach on stick with a few very good anglers drawn round me. One asked me "why stick and not waggler?" I told him it was simply a case of better presentation.

Q: I associate your river style mainly with loose-fed maggot or caster, but did you ever feed cereal, hemp or pinkies?

– I have sometimes combined caster with groundbait, but not as a rule. I have fed hemp in the warmer months up to one and a half pints only, but not pinkies: these have been reserved for smaller Fenland rivers like the Glen.

Q: What is your proudest or most memorable day?

– When I won the Kamasan Matchman of the Year on the last match of the season on the Ancholme. The minimum number of anglers fishing had to be 60 at the time, and it looked like I would be disappointed with only 59 there. Then a late arrival boosted the entry to 60 and I managed to win it with 9lb of roach and earn the extra points to nick the title. That's life: without the latecomer I was an also-ran!

Q: One way of fishing the stick we have not covered is laying-on or 'ligging-on' (as some refer to it) in flood conditions. Do you share my passion for this way of presenting a still bait with the stick, and what is your take on it?

– Well yes, lovely method. In a gravel swim it is easy, but if on a stony bottom you can sometimes find one that sticks out and creates a small eddy downstream of it. This might be four feet out from the bank and anywhere from two feet to a rod-length down the peg. Plumb up and fish the eddy which is where the fish should be. In this case I'd overshot the float and fish anything from a foot to three feet overdepth. Adjust the shotting until the float is dotted down when held still with a tight line.

Q: When it comes to maggot colour, everyone used bronze back in the day unlike now where red or white are more popular. Which colour were you most confident with on the rivers?

– Well I believe the right colour made a lot of difference to results. For me the darker the better with bronze (chrysoidine) maggot, occasionally I'd catch on red.

Q: And did you ever go down the additives and flavours route?

– Nothing other than turmeric, which is in line with so many river anglers.

Q: Who was your most respected match rival?

– I can't possibly name one, as I've met some lovely people over the years. Ivan Marks and John Illingworth were both gentleman in their own ways. And Kevin Ashurst, the list goes on.

Q: For deeper and/or pacey swims do you ever fish the modern Bolo' float[15]?

– No, but a long time back we fished the Ouse at Alice Palisades in swims 22' deep. We tackled it with 4AAA sliding balsas. That's the deepest I've fished a top and bottom float.

Q: I understand that you have a John Allerton Mark II float out, slightly different to your original. Please give details.

– Well our old friend and Barnsley Black, Jimmy Leach is making them for me under the label 'DJ.' It is going well and shops are asking for them. The tips are as slim as my originals, and the only other difference really is they come in bigger sizes than before up to the 3-gram.

---

15 John's leaving the river scene in 1997 to concentrate on commercial carp lakes, coincided with the time that the Bolo' was just starting to gain popularity in the UK.

John kindly arranged for Jimmy Leach to send me a set of the John Allerton Mk II sticks (shown in Thomas chapter p.141).

These are my observations:

⌣ The stems are longer stems than the originals and all cock naturally without any shots added, giving more stability

⌣ They are sized to perfection. I put 8 x no. 6s on the '5 no. 4' size float and it was almost dotted with just enough tip showing to add a no. 8 or 10.

⌣ The longer tip above the shoulder must show lift bites better than any dome-topped float. And whenever roach hold up shot and the float rises they are often good fish.

⌣ As the float tip fully settles as the last few shots register, the angle of the line below the float can be appreciated as it corresponds with the angle of the tip. This might only be seen as a minor gain over a standard stick, but it does give a good clue to where the bait is positioned underwater. – *JB*

Chapter 25
Barry Rudge – Goole's motivator (proving that a balsa wood top is not essential)

In terms of the Trent Championship, it could be said that Goole's Barry Rudge, now 75, is about the unluckiest angler who ever fished it. He came second to Benny Ashurst in 1971 with 14lb when Benny finally achieved his ambition to win the great match, and was bridesmaid again to John Toulson when he weighed 17lb 14oz only for John to scale ½oz more! He also scored a third, fifth, seventh and a ninth in the prestigious event without ever getting his hands on the cup. However, Barry trained as a river angler with the same two anglers who

fished with John Allerton when he was a youngster climbing the matchfishing ladder. He enjoyed an inspiring National Championship debut fishing for Hull in the 1967 Relief Channel match (below) and this probably helped him better ride the huge disappointment of just missing out in the team stakes a few years later. In every other sense, former tackle dealer Barry has enjoyed a great match career, both individually and as skipper of Goole Avengers. His favourite venues were Welbeck Lakes and Burton Joyce before the bream and barbel came on strong, or "anywhere with roach feeding." His wins include: Newark Advertiser Trophy with 23lb of roach on caster, 1983 Welland Champion with a modest 5lb 8oz, 1975 Courage Team Champion, Evesham, W. Avon with 16lb of roach and chub on stick float, Cambridge Open win, R. Cam with 26lb, Welbeck Lakes Charity open with 14lb 4oz of roach and the Lincoln Hospital Cup, R. Witham with 8lb.

My dad and uncles took me fishing to local spots on their bikes from being about five years old. I joined Goole and District AA when I was about thirteen. The club ran bus trips to far-off venues. Our town was surrounded by canals at that time but it was difficult to get bites; no comparison to what it's like today with anglers bagging up almost everywhere.

In my late teens I was managing to win a fair number of the club's matches, often on the Ancholme. In 1966 I won a match run from Ferriby Sluice to Hawkstowe with 34lb of skimmers on the float, which stood as a record for a few years. I also won three of the Inter-club matches there, notably one in 1967 with 18lb of silvers on the float. This was before the bream shoals and feeder fishing took over.

Stick floats were rapidly becoming a cult in Yorkshire as news spread from the North West via the Trent circuit, and I made up a couple a bit different with a peacock top and cane base. One was eight inches long and took 8 x no. 4 shots and the other was 6 x no. 4 size and seven inches long. A quarter of an inch down from the tip I made two tiny holes in the peacock and glued in the ends of a folded piece of 8lb nylon thus replacing the top rubber with an eye. I think it was 1965 and the club held a Saturday afternoon/evening open on the deep steady water above Sutton Weir on the Derwent, and I used one of the sticks to win with 7lb of plump dace. It worked a treat. The bigger of the two floats also worked for me on the Yorkshire Ouse at Aldwarke when I caught 20lb, and in a North-East regional match at Dunsforth where it helped me win my section with 8lb of roach.

I helped with the running of the Goole club in the later years along with a few chaps who did more than their share to keep the club afloat. John Palmer, for example, put loads of time in coaching juniors from the area, including my son Kirk, taking them to matches including Junior Nationals etc. I don't think he got the credit he deserved.

My first National was in 1967 on the Relief Channel, Cambs. fishing for Hull DAA. I had a mate from Hull called Geoff Plaxton who worked with me at Brough Aerospace. His wife, Elsie, used to make apple pie to die for with sugar and cheese on top, unbelievable taste. I arrived at my peg in the morning and was met by a crowd of a hundred, gathered behind this chap drawn next to me. He turned out to be none other than the late, great Billy Lane. He fished a big slider about thirty yards out and balled in groundbait by hand to regular applause from his spectators. Unfortunately he failed to catch. I fished a ¾ oz bomb on a spare float rod with a black catapult elastic butt indicator and caught a few dog roach for 3½lb which gave me second in the section! After the match Billy came up to me, introduced himself and said "well done." He seemed a top bloke and I was naturally chuffed.

In future years we managed to enter a team ourselves in the NFA nationals under the Goole and District banner. Local lads such as Paul Cannon, Mike Baverstock, Pete Kitwood, Dennis Bradley, Stan Brown, John Palmer, Roy Duckett, Pete Skinn, Dave Whittaker, Geoff Teanby, Rob Sugden, Trev Harvey and Mike Moore was the nucleus, and we were joined by John Allerton, Derek Sharpe and Dave Povah.

From 1968 I started fishing some Hull and District matches as well as some York matches, and had a few good results on waters like Westfield, Hoehill and Pelican Lakes. I won a Pelican match with 27lb of bream in the last two hours, and one at Houghton Hall Estate Lakes with 90lb of bream on waggler and caster. My best river match of that time was on the River Nidd above York when I managed 42lb of chub on stick float and casters. This stood as the four-hour record there for some years. By 1969 I was fishing the River Trent a fair bit with Roy Duckett and Stan Brown from Rawcliffe, near Goole. Two great guys to fish with and we had some good times on the way to, during and after matches.

All was coming along nicely but in the 1975 Division 2 Trent National Championship our young team suffered a setback. We thought we'd won the title only to be devastated when Dave Povah got disqualified for missing the coach back to match HQ. That cost us seventy-four points and placed us second, two points short of Long Eaton AC. It seemed a harsh decision for something outside the match duration, especially as it was rumoured the winners had one of their lads do the same. On a personal level I won a medal for runner-up spot with 11lb 14oz, but that left mixed feelings with the team's defeat hurting.

Probably my best Trent years were from 1970 through the 1980s, fishing mainly casters on stick float or waggler. I frequented the Nottingham Federation Saturday opens at Burton Joyce, plus some midweek and Sunday matches they ran, and they were great times. One year I won the prestigious Notts Fed Copper Kettle trophy, not bad when you consider I was fishing against the skilful Trentman lads!

But there are days when you think you have won, but haven't. In the two hundred and fifty-peg Shipstone's brewery match at Burton Joyce I scaled 19lb of roach and chub on stick float and caster, only to get beaten by Newark's Colin Walton. At that time Colin was on a good run using a nine-foot feeder rod which had a two-foot white glass quivertip coupled with an ABU 501 reel (not the best feeder reel with no line clip facility!) plus a selection of feeders, a bowl of groundbait and some casters. Over the years he knocked my float weight down into second on several occasions.

My biggest catch of roach on stick float and casters came in a match at Clifton above Nottingham. I think it was 44lb. There were bales of straw and debris coming down the river all day long but the fish were ravenous beneath them. Every time I found a gap in the rubbish I cast in and 'clunk,' caught a big roach. That day I used a small lignum stick with a pointed tip taking 2 x no. 4s, 2 x no. 6s and 1 x no. 8 shot. Arguably my best Trent run was in winning a Brennan and Hickman sponsored league when I won six matches out of the ten fished.

With regard to floats, I tended to use the John Allerton alloy stem sticks, which he gave me, for up to three rods out, and lignum sticks beyond that. My shotting was usually shirt button using nos. 4, 6 and 8 shot with an 8 as the tell-tale.

I also made a couple of mini sticks for shallower swims like those below the Star and Garter pub at Hazelford for example. These were pieces of peacock with an inch or more of 1.5mm brass (brazing) rod in the base. The biggest was only three inches total length including a 3/8" peg of the wire at the base, but they caught me plenty of roach. I won one match with 14lb on one of these floats.

Feeding, of course, is just as important as presentation. Sometimes before the fish were settled we might catch away from the feed, then later tight over it. I fished casters mainly on 18 hooks, but sometimes dropping down to a 20 when it was hard. I would use a .08mm hooklength most of the time and . 10 when I thought there were a few chub about.

Around 1978 a young lad called Steve Canty turned up in my shop. He was emerging on the fishing scene and promising big things. Together we enjoyed some good results in a series of Doncaster evening league matches on the Stainforth Canal at Kirk Bramwith including a few wins.

A few of us were ready to travel up to Scotland to fish the Scottish National Champs in a van with Frank Barlow in our company, and Frank christened us the 'Goole Avengers' to try to put right the Trent National disappointment. Everyone seemed ok with this title and after having a good laugh, off we went. The name stuck. We enjoyed many happy times, managing to gain sponsorship from Conveyor Improvements Ltd, then Tortue, Shimano and Shakespeare, until things changed when the rivers declined and anglers went their separate ways.

Although sadly, during my time with the team, we never won a National team event, we had some success individually with Phil Jennings and Mike Baverstock also taking medals for runner-up spots, as well as Steve Canty winning a national (Leeds-Liverpool Canal) as well as a raft of prestigious titles in an unbelievable run of success! After I'd left the team they managed to win the Division 3 National on the Trent.

We were lucky to have the likes of: Kevin Ashurst, John Allerton, Neil Parkinson, Tony Barker, Rick Tweddle, Adrian Broomhead, Alan Warren, Willy Eyre, Nicky Harrison, Keith Kotchie, Dave Sharp, Kev Holvey and Dave Jubb, who all fished for us at times. Many teams would gladly have recruited them.

Goole Avengers team roll of honour:
- Six times winner of Angling Times Winter League Humberside division
- Two Birmingham Parks team titles, with Mike Baverstock taking a 1st and a 2nd
- Several canal team championships on Stainforth/Keadby Canal, with Willy Eyre leading the way
- 1985 John Smith's (Courage) Team Champions, and 1986 runners-up
- 1986 River Thames Team Champions
- 1991 Drennan Super League KO winners, three-day festival at Lough Muckno, Ireland, with Paul Cannon top individual.

We have now heard from the mentor, the next chapter introduces his talented understudy.

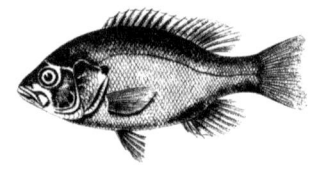

Chapter 26
The man with the Midas touch – Steve Canty

Born in 1960, Steve Canty started fishing at the tender age of six with junior friends at the local Goole Brickponds. He caught very little at first but was "immediately fascinated" – in his words – and "iin awe of some of the adult members who would regularly catch half a dozen roach and perch in a single sitting." It reveals a youngster's perspective, but from there his rise to an advanced skill level when still in his teens was nothing less than phenomenal.

Early coach trips with Goole DAA enabled Steve to fish more venues further afield, and he began match fishing aged sixteen. With the club's encouragement he enjoyed the competitive side with his pals in the junior section. Matches were typically held on the Trent and South Forty Foot drain, and inside twelve months he was beating most adults in the club and keen to go further. Recruited into the Goole team by Barry Rudge, he fished his first National Championship for Goole in that year.

Steve graduated from Hull University with an honours degree in economics and this would lead to him running the family's care home business, but he was soon seeing a dividend from his other studies... on the bankside. In a dramatic ten years, in his twenties and early thirties, he became not only a classy Trent angler, but a prolific winner of prestigious events UK-wide too, and as Barry Rudge recalled: "He was one of those naturals who took only a casual interest in practising midweek, but when the chips were down on big match day he reliably produced the goods." First and foremost a float angler and Trent lover, Steve was in his element wielding a stick float for roach; a man after my own heart who liked catching on the drop. Sadly, the collapse of the Trent as a match Mecca probably broke his heart and he retired from the match scene early, aged 44. Steve explained:

"Prior to 1990 I could hardly put a foot wrong on the Trent and other waters. But the river was changing by the turn of the century, becoming ever clearer and rock hard. I fished a dire Super League at Shelford where only six caught from a 100-plus entry, and a new scene was opening up to tempt anglers onto commercial carp lakes. I also had other things going on my life, so that one match probably caused me to retire, but I respect anyone who made the transition and took to it."

Here's his story:

The club matches were great days out and I learned that you could pick the brains of other anglers on the coach and learn from them. This was something I always did later. I remember in my early twenties travelling to an angling meeting with John Allerton and Pete Wadsworth, both fishing with the Barnsley Blacks and at the top of their powers at the time. To say I grilled them like the Gestapo was an understatement. I think they were glad to get out of the car by the time we arrived. I was so hungry for knowledge.

As a team angler with Goole Avengers in the 1980's and 90's we fished all over the country so had to be adept on canals, lakes and rivers. I prided myself on being able to catch fish on all methods and have won matches on all three types of water, but for pure enjoyment my favourite was float fishing – either waggler or stick on rivers, ideally when the fish were feeding freely.

When the going got hard I was less inclined to stay at my peg! It was during these walkabouts that I learned a great deal by watching others, usually late on in a match. After the match I'd interrogate the anglers who were catching and having a good day. Anglers generally seemed to be a lot more open about methods and baits back then than they are on commercial waters nowadays, and were often happy to tell you about how they had won the match.

Of course, at that time, on the Trent, almost everyone would fish with bronze maggots and a few casters, and were mostly using the same methods. You could be open about methods fished and baits because you knew that the way you caught your fish was often down to the invisible things, like what was going on in your head and the subtleties of feeding and protecting the shoal.

I became captain of Goole Avengers in the mid-eighties and it became a major goal of mine to win a national team competition as captain. Team fishing was very big back then and the matches were generally a hundred pegs or more, so they were great for winning Kamasan points if you did well, which was also a good measure of how you were doing as an individual angler. By attaining certain points levels you could win a cap, and I was very proud to get a thirty-plus points version in the 1989/90 season.

We entered all the major team events such as the summertime Super League and the Angling Times Winter Leagues, National and many others including the knockout team events. We would also travel down to the Thames in September and had a great record in the Thames Championships. We even won the event in 1986 which we felt was a great achievement as we just rolled up and fished without any practice, but the Thames at that time suited us as a team of waggler and stick float anglers, skills that we'd learned on the Trent. We also won the Birmingham Parks Festival in 1988.

It was a great time to be involved in match angling. On a weekend the Trent banks were lined with either open or club matches, and any pegs left would be taken up with pleasure anglers. In winter the Goole anglers would be either booked in to the Burton Joyce Saturday Opens or Long Higgin Opens. Sundays would be winter leagues or 300-peggers at Holme Marsh. My only regret was the pegs were a bit close, many just fifteen yards apart. This meant that on Sundays the feeder often dominated results, as it was hard to put together a frame weight on float due to the close pegging. This was when many

Trent anglers stood up to fish and, if your loose feed was hitting the bottom where the angler below you was standing, he was effectively sky-lining your fish. If I was fishing close, as you often had to in winter, I'd usually try to get my stand in the water and sit down to fish. This definitely helped, but I preferred midweek when we had the luxury of fishing two pegs apart.

A Special Day

To underline the importance of correct feeding, I'll re-visit a midweek event that I won at Long Higgin, where many good Trent anglers of the period fished. I drew in the Parkside field in the 50's and everyone had two pegs. It was notable because the extra room allowed me to fully exploit two swims, which was a bonus. Higgin is a slow-moving section and the water up to a rod-length out was slack, but by casting two to three rod-lengths I found some flow. I decided to loose feed both these lines and to use the still water close in to rest the main line when I wanted to settle the fish on the far line, and vice versa.

The match went like a dream and I managed to catch on both lines for most of the day. The inside line was only marginally shallower than the far one and I could use the same stick float rig for both, only needing to change depth by about a foot.

The wind was very light and upstream (a rarity on the river). My float was a John Allerton-style 6 x no. 4 stick. As the flow was slow I had the shot near the hook very light – 1 x no. 11 nine inches away, 2 x no. 10's spread out ten inches above, a couple of no. 8's above that, and then no. 6 shot spread equally up the line to about two-thirds of the depth, which was from nine to ten feet. As mentioned, I was a big advocate of sitting down to fish to keep off the sky line, especially when aiming to catch close in (Steve is 6' 3" tall). In those days we hadn't started using very long rods and my favourite rod was a fourteen-foot Shimano Triple X with a spliced tip.

The wind allowed me to do what I wanted with the rig and for long periods I had the fish queuing up to be caught. I knew just where to mend the line in readiness for stopping the float, how many seconds to stop the float, and then by letting it go again the bite would come almost instantly. The float continued going under like this with stamp roach.

Periodically, if I went a couple of casts without a bite – after bumping a fish, for example – I would switch to the alternate line. I continually fed both lines and invariably, after resting one, I'd resume catching when returning to it. I even picked up three or four chub on the inside line for good measure. What was most satisfying about the outcome was I had one of my angling heroes in the peg above and he weighed 16lb to my 28lb. An extremely enjoyable day when everything went right.

Steve looking happy despite having only three fish to show: unusual for him.

The Verdict

The only downside on days like this with a perfect wind is that there may be lots of fish willing but they soon wise up to the consistent bait presentation that the negligible wind allows. It is no exact science, but on many occasions a minor change – like a good mend of the line above the float to straighten the rig, or a slight move of a shot, would produce a fish. Was this because the fish were cautious – heavily fished for, and with some having been caught before? Probably.

The key to making such a nice weight, I believe, was the feeding. For this all action session I still only fed three and a quarter pints of bronze maggots total on the two lines. I'd a habit of trying to assess how many fish were in the peg and to step up the feed gradually until bites tailed off. This was not only a positive approach for roach and other small fish, but it would catch more chub than maintaining light feeding. If greedy chub are the predominant species you have to catch them because they will bully the other fish in the swim anyway, not allowing them to settle.

In winter Trent matches of the 80's and 90's when it was really cold, it was often only chub that wanted to feed. On such days you still had to be positive, and I found that some chub would only take the loose feed if there was enough

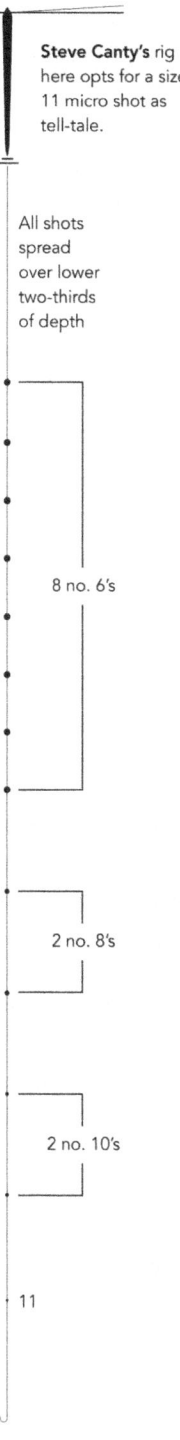

Steve Canty's rig here opts for a size 11 micro shot as tell-tale.

All shots spread over lower two-thirds of depth

8 no. 6's

2 no. 8's

2 no. 10's

11

coming towards them. Feeding lightly you simply wouldn't catch one. In these chub or bust matches I would introduce say fifteen to twenty maggots per cast, and then, once every fifteen minutes, would give them a good handful of maggots. It was remarkable how reliably I'd catch a chub after throwing in sixty to seventy maggots. Often, with chub in the swim, it was almost predictable when I'd catch one this way, and bizarrely the bite often came *before* the handful of bait had got down. It was as if they knew by sight or sound that they were in for a treat in advance of the big mouthful of maggots arriving.

A word about tackle: my reel line for stick float was always 1.5lb Maxima, which seems fine but was actually a thick 1.5lb diameter. It peeled off the reel beautifully and could either be left floating or sunk as required. On bad winds I would often back-shot, all other days I wouldn't. With the back-shot it is more difficult to mend the line and get everything straight, so I'd experiment in bad winds and would often push the back-shot down tight to the float. It all depended on the day. If I could pinpoint where most bites were coming, I'd mainly prefer no back-shot and rely on mending the line before the float entered the hot zone.

Hooklengths were 1lb Nacrita (Racine Tortue) or occasionally 1.5lb Nacrita if I was bagging or expecting a few chub, or there were snags. The 1lb bottom might sound fine (thin) but if careful it would land chub to 3lb-plus in heavy winter flow conditions. Hooks were usually Kamasan B520 size 22, occasionally a 24, but I found that the increased chance of bumping and losing a fish on a 24 outweighed the extra bites I might get. When knowing that the fish would be small I'd happily use a finer wire B511, but there was risk of it opening up on a bonus fish. But with softer-actioned rods fine hooklengths and fine wire hooks came more into play.

Floats

I carried sticks from 4 x no. 6 up to 4 x BB size in both black and red tops, both Allerton-type and lignums for casting well out. Although I probably carried about twenty-five sticks, most of my float fishing was with a half-dozen that seemed to perform better than the others. Is it all about a perfect ratio of heavy base to light balsa top? I'm not sure. Where previously

I'd used the Pete Warren models of conventional cane and balsa, when the John Allerton floats came to the fore I stayed with them for most of my stick fishing.

On days where I had to cast a bit further out I enjoyed using lignum vitae which simply flew due to the heavy base. One other float that I really enjoyed using for a couple of seasons was the balsa slider which was effective on the deep River Don at Sprotborough when it was out and out roach fishing. Fishing mid-river with a two-swan float was not a method I had needed much, but for a while in deep swims it was very effective and enjoyable when it worked.

Regarding Mr. Allerton, when I was walking about and learning I would watch many class anglers, but John was one of the few that looked good as well as being good. His float presentation was second to none. His own designed floats would hold back really well and not ride out of the water as most others' did. It would remain more or less dotted during the stationary period and, when he let the float travel again, the float would often settle a fraction and keep going under with a fish.

I remember thinking 'why don't my floats do that?' So I put my head into gear and tried copying John's shape of float with its shoulder and quite fine tip. This improved things but they would still ride up when checked. It seemed like the line coming out of the top float rubber was catching in the surface film and affecting the settling of the float. I decided that I had to move the line away from the float somehow and ended up  straightening an eyed hook and gluing it side on into the pivot point of the float tip where the rubber had been. This definitely helped, and I caught lots of fish using John's stop-start method of trotting the swim, but I never looked as good as John!

Finally, we consider the dotting of the float, shotting it as low to the surface as possible. On most days this was absolutely vital, in fact even with a speck of float showing some of the best bites would still not take it fully under. I believed the fish were following the bait downstream as some bites would take two or three yards to develop. Only by dotting the float and allowing it to travel unimpeded would it result in a bite. It may have worked for many, but I was never one to drag much line on the deck and rarely fished overdepth on the Trent. I didn't like wasting time getting fast on the bottom and the inconvenience of changing hooks and traces which interrupted the catching/feeding rhythm.

Favourite Memory

I would have to say the day I won the Courage UK Championship. It was a big moment for me. I first had to get in via a qualifying match, which I was lucky enough to do. On the big day I drew the fancied upstream end peg (1A). Setting up three rods – a 5 x no. 4 Warren stick on one and two waggler rigs, I estimated that 10-12lb would be needed to frame. After four hours I thought I was on course for that with five chub for 4lb or so, and maybe 6lb of dace from both my mid-river (waggler) swim and an inside (stick) line. Then a 2½lb chub on waggler set me up for a good last hour and a 17lb 13oz total, which was a weight record for the match at the time. Don Slaymaker came second with a brilliant all-roach 13lb-plus.

My favourite species are roach and skimmers, using a stick or waggler and catching on the drop. As for the perfect venue, I'd select Long Higgin for a midweek match or Holme Pierrepont in the eighties before they put straw bales in to make it clear, and then the cormorants ruined it.

Top Tip

Never stop feeding the swim even when it's difficult to do. I would still feed religiously even when trying to undo a tangle or completely setting up afresh. And keep ringing the changes if you are not catching – lines, depth, hookbaits, also avoiding plundering the fish too heavily, never 'ploughing a furrow' as we used to say in Goole, i.e. do not keep trotting down the swim in exactly the same place incessantly, as before long the fish will avoid the baited hook altogether.

Steve's Best Wins (1984 onwards from age 23):

1984 *Newark Advertiser* Trophy, Winthorpe and Holme Marsh
1985 Central TV Classic, Holme Pierrepoint
1987 Courage UK Championship, Evesham, R. Avon
1988 Wards Gala, Kirkstead, R. Witham
1989 MacPherson's UK Championship (originally the Whitbread UK)
1993 Division 1 National Championship, Leeds-Liverpool Canal
1997 King of Clubs, Ireland
1998 Embassy Pairs Final, Horsens Lake, Denmark (2nd pair, partnered by Pete Kitwood)

Note: In a more high profile sport at least three of these wins would be classed as 'majors' – the MacPherson's UK certainly, as it spanned four rounds on points and was fished by many of the country's top rods; similarly the Courage UK, and the Division 1 National titles, of course, and all three of these achieved by age thirty two. I should add that his National victory was won by a proverbial street with 5.02 kg, with only Jimmy Leach getting close on 4.32kg in second, and without having practised on a tough canal where most of the one thousand and eight competitors struggled to catch a pound! From this match and the MacPherson's alone Steve earned £13.5k, a cool haul for the time in anyone's book. Matchmen reckon to peak in their forties, so what other magic could he have weaved had he kept going? In recent years he has started visiting Ireland to fish in the odd festival with his great friend and former team mate Pete Kitwood, but this is for fun and he has no desire to return to match angling in the UK.

Chapter 27
Tony Scott – the groundbait and caster ace
– by Paul Dennis

A word about Tony Scott. When I watched Tony fishing the Trent in the seventies he was in his pomp and exuded star quality. This England International and Birmingham National angler could throw groundbait so smoothly and accurately to almost hit his float well out on the waggler line, but it was the apparent ease with which he did it that impressed, coupled with his quiet focus on the job at hand. And, of course, Tony

was just as content fishing a stick on his local Burton-on-Trent waters where he won regularly. I think it was Tony's faith in feeding large and small maggots when bleak fishing to keep them going that gave me the idea of feeding pinkies for Witham roach. Only recently he told me a tip that Johnny Moult gave him back in the early days for when a river is flooded: "Put enough stones (if available) in your keepnet to try securing it as a barrier one yard out from the bank, and through the day bleak may well arrive at this artificial feature. Once the bleak start feeding then there's a chance of catching roach later on in the mini slack behind the net... but ensure you remove all the stones before the weigh-in!" Simple but smart, wish I'd have thought of it. - JB

Burton-on-Trent's Tony Scott was one of the first anglers to embrace the waggler as a match-winning tactic on the pacey waters of the River Trent, ultimately winning the Trent Championship on the method. But prior to that, Tony had cut his teeth on stick floats or big balsas on the River Severn, as well as his local River Trent around the Willington area. Both of these venues were very different to the middle Trent in the Nottingham reaches, and the problems that they posed accelerated his development as a brilliant all-round float angler.

I began by asking Tony about his stick float tactics, usually based around the caster and groundbait combination, and how he used the experience gained in his formative years to become a consistent winner on the method.

Tony explained: "Back in the 1960s the River Severn was a very mixed river fishery. Barbel had not yet become the dominant species, so you were looking for chub, dace and roach to compile a decent catch. Matches were run along most of the river, but the length from Bridgnorth down to Holt Fleet was particularly good for float fishing. I used to visit the River Severn a lot, initially on club matches with the Alrewas and Burton Mutual clubs, then branching out into open matches. The River Trent, local to me, was still heavily polluted and no matches were held in the Burton-on-Trent area.

"Downstream of Newton Solney, where the much cleaner River Dove entered the Trent, there were matches held on the

Derby AA and Derby Railway waters from Willington down to Shardlow, but these matches weren't as frequent as the ones on the River Severn.

"The Severn was known amongst anglers for having a 'heavy flow.' It's hard to describe, but compared to the Trent, in a swim of apparently the same depth and pace, you would have to use a much heavier float. Where you could use a five or six number 4 float on the Trent you would need a 5 or 6 x BB float on the Severn to have any sort of control.

"The upper Trent, from Willington down to Shardlow, posed some similar problems. Faster water than the lower river, and, on average, quite a bit shallower.

"The first problem that anglers faced was that the commercially available floats in those days weren't up to the task of tackling fast water, so we had to make our own.

"I used to work at Midland Joinery in Burton-on-Trent, and my charge hand, Joe Ellis, was a very keen and talented angler. We used to spend our lunch hours making floats to tackle the sort of swims we regularly faced. It took a lot of trial and error just to get the materials right, but we were thinking along the right lines.

"One of the first problems was getting the right sort of cane for the stems. The commercial floats almost always had cane that was too light for the waters we were fishing. They didn't cast well, they didn't settle properly, they were too light to 'boss' the swim and they were also, in our opinion, the wrong shape. You have to bear in mind that the stick was first designed for fishing very sluggish waters and was a natural progression from the crow quill. But like the crow quill it wasn't good on really fast water.

"For the stems we searched hard for the heaviest cane we could find to give the floats the stability that we needed, but that reduced the shot carrying capacity, so we used the softest, lightest balsa that we could get for the body. This turned out to be a big advantage. It was easier to work, and we could get away with a slightly smaller body which helped the float settle faster and gave it more stability.

"We even experimented with polystyrene as a body material, but it was very fragile and had to be coated in epoxy resin to make it tougher, plus you had to be careful what glues you used as it was prone to dissolving if you used the wrong type!

"Quite early on we discovered that dome tops performed better than the pointed ones, and that giving the float a bit of a shoulder was another advantage. In time these float designs became commercially available, and nowadays you can buy them over the counter."

Lignum stems

"A couple of our local float makers, Ken Anderson and Les McEwan, used to make very long stick floats with lignum stems. These cast brilliantly and you could fish them effectively a long way out. I remember Burton angler Alan Torr winning a lot of matches fishing a stick down what would normally have been the waggler line using these floats.

"We also experimented with wire-stemmed sticks. These settled a lot faster than cane-stemmed floats, so you did sacrifice catching on the drop, but in the main these were the floats that we used in very turbulent 'washing machine' pegs where catching on the drop wasn't really a factor and the increased stability of the float was what mattered."

One of Tony's notable achievements was bucking the trend when the 'maggot revolution' driven by Dave Thomas was in full swing. Tony still used to fish open matches in the Nottingham area and win on the caster and groundbait combination – something he had perfected on the upper river where caster fishing still held sway. I asked him why he had stuck to the caster in the face of evidence to the contrary.

"Caster is a much cleaner bait and I enjoyed fishing with it more than I did with maggots. Using casters also allowed me to use groundbait, which I felt was quite important to the method I was fishing."

As a World Championship angler, Tony had gained insight into continental groundbait mixes, and was able to apply some of the knowledge gained into his own fishing at home. In particular he was one of the first anglers to use 'soil' in his groundbait to achieve a soft mix which held together well and didn't overfeed the fish. Fine river silt, deposited after floods, was one source of this additive, with the now popular molehill soil another.

Silt, soil & dust

Tony said: "Obviously the continental anglers used what we now know as 'leam' but I needed to find something locally to do the same job. The silt and the molehill soil both worked well. It made a great mix for roach and dace, not so good for chub, but you needed to know what sort of fish you would be targeting and what weight you were after to decide the exact proportion of soil to cereal, which was fine brown crumb.

"In the first few years on the Swadlincote stretch at Newton Solney, chub were a rarity, so that made the decision a lot easier.

"I started off by using the silt as this was obviously a natural material, but finding the right sort could be a bit of a problem as you didn't want it to be too sandy. The right sort was very dark and fine and had an almost silky feel to it. Molehill soil was easier to get hold of, and once it had been dried and riddled it worked almost as well."

The proportions of soil to crumb were quite important, as Tony explained: "The bulk of my groundbait was soil, the crumb was used to add a little feed as an attractor, but mainly to help bind the soil and get a soft but sticky mix that could be thrown as far as you wanted and would get down fast before quickly breaking up on the bottom."

While I knew from years of watching Tony in action that this combination worked very well, I asked Tony about another additive that I had seen him mention in a book by the late John Carding (*Match Angling*) – malt dust, which came in two forms, a very fine, grey powder and coarse, orangey/brown fibres known as malt culms. Tony's contribution to that book had been focused on canal fishing, but I wondered if he had used it on the River Trent.

Tony laughed: "Now you are asking me a question about something that we never used to mention. I used to get malt dust from the old mill at Newton Road, but when that closed down it became very difficult to get hold of. (Note: I used to work at the brewery and it was very hard for me to get it!).

"The grey dust was very fine and very light. It did have a bit of chaff in it, plus a few specks of malt culms (the dried rootlets of the malt produced by the malting process) but you didn't need to riddle it. When wetted it turned dark brown and gave off a distinctive malty smell. It was sticky and a very good groundbait binder and you only needed one or two big handfuls to about 7lb of groundbait for it to do the job. It was also a great additive for attracting roach – and they were usually of a better stamp running 10oz and upwards which obviously was a huge advantage when the scales came round."

Casters and hemp are a favoured fishing and feeding combination, but for many years hemp was banned on the Nottingham waters. I asked Tony if he had been a big user of hemp as feed on venues where it was allowed.

"Yes, and I used plenty of it, as I remember you doing as well. I used to put a lot in at the start, often about six pints, then drip some in with the casters over the top. It was something that the late Clive Smith did on the River Severn opens at Stourport. He was convinced that the roach liked to settle over a carpet of hemp and his results there suggest he was right. I used to talk to Clive a lot on the telephone and he was always a mine of information."

I recalled one of the matches that Tony was thinking about when I had put half a gallon of hemp in right at the start and finished with just under 29lb of roach – not enough to win though as Tony put 34lb onto the scales after a very slow start.

Tony said: "I remember that match very well. I was drawn just below the outfall at Newton Solney and wasn't catching at the start. After about two hours, the river started to come up quite quickly so I pegged my keepnet down and fed hemp behind it. With two hours to go the roach moved on top of it and I was catching right off my rod end – it was like shelling peas.

"The most I used as an initial feed was on the River Trent at Cuttle Brook. I drew a known barbel swim and put a gallon of hemp in at the start. I didn't catch for two hours but then they arrived and I finished with a big weight. It was a good method back then, but it doesn't seem to work so well now."

I asked Tony what he thought his best performance was on the stick float. After a moment's reflection he said: "I won the Derby Railway Institute Tom Draper Memorial match on the River Trent at Shardlow with 48lb of roach and 'soldier' chub. I was drawn above the Crown Meadow, on a peg just running out of a bay and had Loughborough's Ron Stacey at the next peg. Ron was a very good angler but his peg was a bit more difficult than mine and he had 28lb which I thought was a brilliant performance. I was very lucky that day.

"Looking back I think we certainly had the best of the stick float fishing in those days. With the tackle we have today I think the weights would be phenomenal if the quality of the fishing was the same.

"Nowadays to catch well on the stick on the Trent the river *must* be carrying some colour. It runs very clear now and the fish are wary of predation. Add to that a lot more weed, and plenty of natural food in the river, and you can see why results aren't as consistently good as they used to be – but get the conditions spot on and you can still catch a decent net of fish."

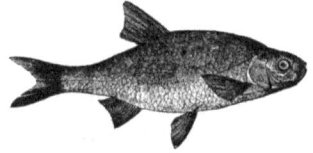

Chapter 28
Taming the upper Trent – John Harper

John and a precious bonus fish – 6lb chub

John Harper recalls the 'bonanza years' on the upper Trent around Burton-on-Trent dating from circa 1978 to the mid-1990s. Drakelow power station had three different stations on the one site - 'A,' 'B' and 'C' which all fed into the same outfall that pumped warm water into the river. This had a major influence on fish stocks – it is believed the fish spawned twice a year, and when all stations were in use the river downstream of the outfall was always warm, and large catches of roach, dace and bream were taken even in winter. Anglers would use lots of bait for these active fish. In the mid-eighties 'A' station was decommissioned and in the mid-nineties 'B' station ceased to operate. That marked the river's decline and anglers increasingly switched to lakes and commercial carp fisheries. In 2003 'C' station was also closed and the river became colder and clearer. Anglers today can still find good sport but the river only fishes well for roach and dace up to November/December; thereafter it becomes a chub river with the small silvers often almost impossible to catch, and two pints of casters or maggots is usually sufficient bait...

During the 1970's and 80's the upper Trent around Burton-on-Trent came to life after years of pollution. At first in the early days the local angling clubs started to run club and open matches. The Bass and Allied brewery clubs both controlled stretches of the river through the town, as did the Drakelow and Swadlincote clubs.

Fishing on the river was new even to local anglers when the town waters started to improve. Many only fished stick float methods in the early years as the pole or waggler hadn't really come into play locally. Upper Trent anglers used tactics and tackle that was seen by many outsiders as crude. Burton anglers often used size 18 and 16 hooks and strong hooklengths, finding they could catch the roach and dace with relative ease. Many of the fish had never seen a hook before so anglers could get away with the cruder tactics, unlike on the middle Trent where more finesse was required. Tom Pickering said he thought I was a butcher when he sat behind me in a match and saw that I was catching on a size 18 hook. He told me the Barnsley lads started on size 22 hooks on the middle reaches of the Trent.

The Bass Burton club and the Swadlincote AA both held regular open matches on the Trent at Burton, often attracting a very good field of anglers. Top names attended the 100-peg Swadlincote opens, such as Keith Hobson, Ivan Marks and Frank Barlow to name but three. We enjoyed a great learning opportunity by mingling with the likes of John Dean, Pete Warren and John Allerton – great stick float exponents displaying their skills week-in and week-out. The best of these matches in this early eighties period was when forty-seven weights of double figures or more were recorded, John Dean coming out tops with 35lb!

I fished some opens run by Keith Evans and Larry Billings on the Broadholme and Andressey islands in Burton. One particular day I drew one peg below the town bridge and I fancied it for a few nice roach. On the next peg downstream was none other than Dick Clegg, Barnsley's England team manager. I set up a Pete Warren 6 x no. 4 stick with a shirt button-style string of no. 8 shot for the six-foot deep steady glide. I fed about a dozen bronze maggots every cast and soon started to catch some good roach to 12oz. Dick was slower off the mark and I was feeling confident, but I noticed how heavy he was feeding with bronze maggots...

After the first hour Cleggy upped his catch rate and really bagged for the rest of the match. I was amazed to hear he had fed a gallon of maggots, and even more gob-smacked when he weighed in 41lb of roach for the win. I doubt he's ever forgotten that day, I certainly haven't as I finished 5th with 29lb which would normally have been enough to win.

Another day on the Broadholme, my mate, Pete Vernon, was treated to a lesson in feeding from Jan Porter on the next peg. Jan had fed heavily from the off with bronze maggots, and although he was using stick float tactics he was feeding all over the river. Pete thought his feeding tactic was strange at first but as the match progressed he realised what Jan was doing. By feeding all over the river the 'man in red' (an all-red outfit was his trademark) had drawn fish up from downstream. Eventually Jan had the dace lined up three rods out and he kept them coming to win with 21lb. That match was to change the way I fed maggots and the amount I would take to a match, and I ordered a gallon of bronze maggots from Tony Scott's shop most weeks thereafter.

Keith Evans, match organiser on the Bass waters, was a fine exponent of caster fishing. His stick floats were something to be admired. They were made from a combination of materials, some of which included porcupine quill which I found unusual. He was a dream to watch with these floats and, as the saying goes, he could make them talk.

Another memory I have of a match on the Broadholme,

was a day when the river was carrying a foot of water. Although I didn't fish this one, I went along to watch Keith Hobson. Keith was pegged at the top end of the island facing the town and he had set up a heavy stick with a centrepin reel. I was mesmerised by his float control and he went on to blitz the opposition with 21lb of roach.

Very often the upper Trent was influenced by the influx of warm water from the power stations. Drakelow power station, just above the town, could make a massive difference on how the river fished. On days when the hot water was not flowing into the river it would often be essential to use a stick float to achieve a slowing of the bait through the swim.

Drakelow AC ran opens on their stretch of river at the sunken gardens, directly below the power station outfall. One particular match I remember was won by Loughborough angler Ron Stacey. There was a strong downstream wind blowing and no hot water was coming in. In almost impossible conditions Ron fished one of his home-made pacemaker-type floats at four rods out to bag a nice net of dace. I was on the next peg and no matter what float I used I could not match his ability. It was one of the best displays of stick float fishing I'd ever seen.

Some may ask why not fish a waggler in those circumstances? Well, yes, the waggler could work when the warm water was coming in and the fish were more active, but there were many times when it just wouldn't work. There were many days, as there still are today, when the fish, especially roach, would only have a bait that was slowed down and only a stick float could achieve that presentation.

Of course, today a long pole and long line will achieve that, but I'm old school and I still prefer the stick. A friend of mine, Pete Fern, made some very long and thin stick floats with a long, heavy cane base. The eight or ten-inch floats could be used to good effect in a downstream wind and often we would back-shot the float to get the line above it to sink. The thing about the Trent is that whilst an upstream wind will make good stick float presentation easier, it's normally a cold easterly. In my experience the river fishes better when the wind is downstream even if float control is harder.

One of my most memorable catches was made in a

brewery club match held on the river one February on the Ferry bridge stretch. I drew a peg between St. Peter's bridge and the Ferry bridge. There had been a sharp frost and there was no hot water coming in, so weights were expected to be low. The peg I drew was about four-foot deep with a steady pace. I set up a light 3 x no. 4 Pete Warren stick with a few no. 8 shot strung throughout the rig. I decided to feed very frugally with bronze maggots, in fact I counted five or six maggots for every cast. After twenty minutes my float buried and I was into a substantial fish. I could barely believe my eyes when a bream of about 3lb graced my landing net. At the halfway mark I was catching bream steadily and anglers began to gather round to watch. The word was that 2lb would be a good weight and I already had about 20lb in my net. Pat Ryan on the peg upstream hadn't had a bite so I invited him to cast his lead into my peg. Paddy cast his bait into my peg but, unbelievably, he still couldn't get a bite.

I finished the match with 46lb of bream and the next weight was around 2lb. I came to the conclusion that the reason Pat couldn't catch was because his bait was nailed to the bottom but it seemed the bream wanted it slowly moving, and the only way to achieve that presentation was with a stick float.

The following Wednesday I couldn't resist going back to the peg to try for some more bream. I took along another mate, Pete Barlow and (being the gentleman I am!) invited him to fish the peg I'd won the match from. I went on Paddy's peg and decided to fish it exactly the same as I had in the match. Although there was snow on the ground we both had an amazing day's fishing. Pete had 80lb of bream and I had 109lb all on stick float and with less than a pint of maggots.

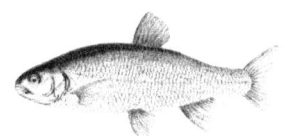

Chapter 29
A bream way to win a National – by Alan Wright

In National Championships on Fenland rivers with a thousand or more anglers competing, the angler who does it right on a shoal of bream with a ledger or swimfeeder usually wins the individual title. But on the Witham in 1973 Alan Wright, fishing for Derby Railway Institute, found a favourable wind at peg M4 on the Langrick upstream section, and struck gold on a stick float, Trent style. What a wonderful way to win!

The team plan was to feed well across with groundbait for fishing the swingtip later in the match, then start just over the marginal weed with cloud groundbait and pinkies, to get some fish in the net. I started well and after about ninety minutes had 4-5lb of small fish. Now was the time to change to the tip.

Casting a small bomb rig three-quarters of the way across to where I'd thrown six groundbait 'jaffas' at the start, I gave it an hour for just a few small fish. There was no sign of bream apart from three screaming 'liners.' While sitting waiting patiently for a proper bite, I noticed that John Illingworth, two pegs to my left, was catching net roach on the stick float about two rod-lengths out, so I started feeding hemp and casters on that line. I had set a stick float up with a home-made balsa/lignum stick taking 1 x BB bulk with 1 x no. 4 dropper and a 1 x no. 4 under the float. I was doing well with this set-up on the Trent at that time. The depth was about seven-foot.

First cast on the stick I had a 2lb bream on double home-bred gozzer on an 18 hook. "That's a bonus," I said to the steward, who was sitting behind me. However, over the next ninety minutes I kept busy and added seven more bream of a similar size and a few roach. In hindsight I was sure the line bites I'd experienced earlier had come from these bream on the inside line. The last hour though was unbelievable; I landed ten more bream, all like peas in a pod at about 2lb. My last fish was just before the whistle following a re-rigging when the line got knotted behind the reel spool. And I got back in action just in time, needing that last fish because my weight of 41lb 10½oz beat Dave Downes of Leicester by just 4½oz!

Note: *We could fairly say Alan absolutely blitzed his 80-peg section of the match. Leicester skipper and Fenland supremo, Ivan Marks drew downstream of Langrick bridge in the same section and attracted a crowd of 200 spectators to watch his every move. He didn't disappoint, beating the anglers around him easily, but his fourth in section was achieved with 11lb 13½oz of small skimmers. Section second was Brian Hull of Loughborough with 26lb 13½oz from a peg near Alan's, while John Illingworth made sixth with 11lb 1oz. For Alan, who modestly claims he has been 'a very lucky angler' over the years, this big win was no flash in the pan. Two years later he won a 1,200-pegger on the Shropshire Union Canal with a 3lb catch on swingtip and gozzer on a day when all the favoured areas failed to produce. And in 2003 he completed the rare feat of winning a second National – the Division 2 on the River Soar with eleven bream on bomb for 18 kilos, a weight ironically similar to his first win.*

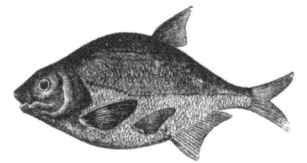

Chapter 30

The Shakespeare Professionals
– Ken Giles & Clive Smith (Part 1)

Clive Smith in familiar pose

Although one retired over ten years ago, and the other sadly passed away far too early (1982 aged 41), the mighty reputation of Birmingham duo, Ken Giles and the late Clive Smith still reverberates in the West Midlands and far beyond. They formed one of match fishing's most successful partnerships in the big match era of the late 20th century. What a force they were together. What a collaboration!

They reached angling's pinnacle individually, both winning England caps – Ken in 1973, '74 and '76 and Clive in '73 and '81. In 1973, in France, they helped England take the bronze medal. On the home front they enjoyed Angling Times Winter League success with the famous Cofton Hackett club, and led the BAA to rule the National Championship medals table including three golds in the seventies. Clive Smith, as skipper, commented in 1978: "In the last seven years, since the National has been decided on section points, the Birmingham squad have chalked up three victories, a seconds, a fifth and a seventh placing."

With Clive ably supported by his deputy Ken, Brum's super consistency at this time set the standard for other great teams of the future. They head-hunted key outsiders with natural ability like Kevin Ashurst and Johnny Toulson, and with sound man-management of local stars, and a dedication to practice, they took team fishing to a professional level not seen before.

If Ken possibly had the edge over Clive on the waggler, then Clive maybe shaded Ken on the stick float, but both were all-rounders who could shine on several winning methods. Ken's best match was arguably his Woodbine Challenge victory in Denmark when he caught half his 110lb catch on stick float and the other half on waggler. After Clive's untimely death, Ken became the driving force behind Shakespeare Professionals, putting new (younger) Birmingham teams on the path to further National Championship glory.

Clive and Ken also jointly wrote two books (entitled *Match Fishing Our Way,* and *Championship Match Fishing: Ten of the Best,* in 1978 and 1982 respectively) and the float fishing lessons within them are as relevant for rivers today as when written thirty years ago.[16]

First, on the stick itself, the illustration shown in their first book reveals the Giles and Smith attention to detail. It presents a classic stick float design with an elliptical balsa top section and a cane base. The balsa shape mirrors Benny Ashurst's original design from the diagram in his own book of ten years earlier. Key details include the fulcrum point where the float

---

16 Pat Newman kindly sent me excerpts from the two books referred to. They evoked memorable days on the Warks, Avon, River Severn and beyond, and I later bought both books. They informed this chapter and the next with further information from Ken. Long retired from the match scene, Ken now fly fishes for trout with that same love of the sport but at a more leisurely pace.

cocks one-third down from the float's pointed tip. The radius of the tip is 1/8" while the cane base tapers down to 1/16" at the lower end. These sticks come in sizes from 3 x no. 4 (or 5 x no. 6) up to a maximum of 4BB (or 16 x no. 6). We'll return to this stick and the shotting pattern shortly, but first let's look at the steps that led to it.

Mark 1: Ken and Clive began to experiment with making stick floats from information spread on the angling grapevine. In the early Sixties the finer details were not travelling South-West that fast from the Trent valley. Initially they would shot up an average five no. 4 size float as follows: one x BB shot at mid-depth. Four x no. 8 would be spread out above this shot, and 4 x no. 8 droppers below the BB down to the hook. This created a double taper with the BB the only shot that mostly stayed in position halfway along the rig. The top no. 8s could be moved close under the float or dropped down to the BB as the depth and flow speed required, and the four dropper shot positions would change according to how the fish were feeding.

Mark 2: Experimenting in a downstream wind – the most awkward direction for stick float control, Ken and Clive then started adding a chain of micro shot close together below the float, five or six shot extending to about six inches below the float, even as far as a foot. This cocked the float quicker and gave better control within seconds of the float entering the water, having the effect of lengthening the float and improving its stability.

We must always be open-minded for clues on how to improve. Ken was taken aback one day in the early years when drawn near to a Yorkshire visitor to the Avon. This stranger was using an overhead cast with a sizeable stick, punching it out to mid-river and catching well. Previously, Ken and Clive had reserved the method for the inside line. That man was John Illingworth, and in a state of shock Ken and Clive put in many hours practice with bigger floats at range for weeks afterwards.

Mark 3: This introduces the shotting pattern shown in the 1978 book. Here the shotting tapers down towards the hook starting with 1 x no. 1 under the float down to 1 x no. 10. In an average six feet of water, the shots would be positioned shirt button-style in the following sequence: 1 x no. 1, 1 x no. 6, 1 x no. 7, 1 x no. 8, and 1 x no. 10 as the tell-tale shot placed ten inches from the hook. When every shot has registered on the float there is just 3/32" of float tip showing on the surface, good light conditions permitting. Needless to say the gaps between each shot would change according to the depth of swim: for example, somewhere between six and twelve inches apart.

"The bottom two shot especially," said Ken, "the 8 and 10 were the most important to get right to suit bites on the day, and we might call them the alternators. But nothing is written in stone with regard to where each shot goes, it is all about adjusting the rig to suit the day and how the fish want the bait presented."

Experimentation led Ken use a lower top rubber placement on the float to dot it down better when fishing close in; conversely when casting the stick well out, he would place the rubber as high as possible on the tip, as this made the job of line-mending easier, i.e. sweeping the rod upstream to lift the line and lay it back behind the float whenever the wind pushes the line off course, or away from the ideal straight line from rod tip to float.

Mark 4: Before the new millennium, anglers were carrying stick floats on winders similar to the way they stored pole rigs, and this led to Kenny's final development with the float: he dispensed with the top rubber and replaced it with a tiny eye. This was achieved by drilling a hole through the balsa ¼" down from the tip and gluing in a wire eye. "By running the reel line through the eye instead of a top rubber it meant the quick-change facility of the double rubber set-up was lost, but we'd begun putting stick rigs on winders by then so it didn't matter; we'd just reach for another winder to change floats," added Ken.

To further illustrate their dedication to angling's finer points that can make or break success, consider the popular Swedish closed face reels: the ABU models 506 and larger 507. These became the cult reels for stick float in the golden era of the big matches, *despite* its one fault: the line spilling over the rim of the spool and two turns of the handle later the resultant time-wasting tangle. In fairness to ABU the reels were made for spinning with thicker lines than a stick float angler would generally use.

Clive Smith researched this spillage problem by putting some powder on the spool and seeing what happened to it when winding in, and found that it was as simple as the draught of air drawn into the reel by the winding in process. His remedy was to drill two 3mm holes in the back of the spool housing either side of the central shaft, and hey presto, no more line spillage and a perfect reel. Now that's what I call a smarter answer than binning the reel as certain anglers were known to have done in bad temper. These ABU reels had the 'marmite factor': they were almost as hated as loved.

Ken had a golden rule he observed when tackling his local Avon at Evesham and elsewhere: "Never skin the peg." He was always conscious of taking too many fish from a shoal to the point where they shut up shop, and to overcome this he was a big fan of alternating swims between a stick line and a waggler line. "My maxim, whenever the size of fish dropped smaller, was to switch and rest the line, building it back up while fishing the other," he added.

And for good stick presentation, Ken is a big fan of Mucilin fly-fishing grease. He coats the top of the float and 18 inches of reel line above the float which enables a cleaner strike or pick out of the float from the water surface. Also, if light conditions deteriorate and he finds it hard to see the float tip, he's not averse to coating the tip with more grease to lift the float a shade by increasing its buoyancy.

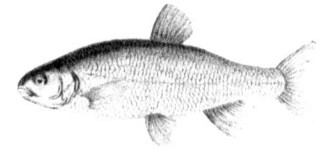

Chapter 31

Giles and Smith – Part 2

Leaving their individual skills aside, the winning record of teams that included Ken Giles and Clive Smith was more than impressive in the 1960's and 70's. As their two books of 1978 and 1982 show, they brought a professional approach to an amateur sport at a time when it was booming. Clive was some strategist, and, if he was not winning or leading the team to glory, Ken was always there ready to fill the void and inspire the squad in his own way.

The 1978 *Angling Times Yearbook* had this to say about Clive, in a short feature entitled 'Top team tactician': "In the world of match team fishing, Clive Smith is simply the best. In the last fifteen years the softly-spoken Birmingham tackle dealer has emerged as the greatest team captain in the country. The teams he has captained, Cofton Hackett and the Birmingham Anglers' Association National squad have piled up trophy after trophy. And most of the credit is entirely due to Clive."

For the benefit of younger readers, Cofton Hackett was Birmingham's Angling Times Winter League side that won the Winter League final twice in Ireland in the mid-sixties, then again in 1971 and 1975.

As for rivals in the National, Coleshill were another great team from the West Midlands who won the inaugural Division Two National in 1972, then upstaged Brum to win Division One in 1978 and 1984. A young Barnsley team were also gaining momentum and won in 1979, and Notts Fed, denied by just two points that year, began their great run in 1980 with a record points win on the Trent. But for the moment Birmingham AA's supremacy in the National was unequalled and their medals collection from 1971 onwards spoke volumes, only twice missing from the podium in seven years, viz: 2nd, 1st, 7th, 5th, 1st, 1st and 2nd!

Was Clive the right man in the right place at the perfect time? Let's consider the makings of this great team. First, the BAA is a huge angling association and, unlike London AA which adopted match size limits at the time, their match rules were consistent with the majority of clubs and every fish counted. Birmingham's canal network also helped develop young anglers' skills with small fish, and in a National Championship, decided on points, such small fry became known as 'points fish.' The senior matchmen added bream-catching skills, learned on lakes, to bleak and barbel methods from the Severn, plus roach and chub finesse honed on the Avon. All this served to make any twelve-man BAA team extremely versatile, so Clive had a rich vein of skill to pick from to add to his winning mentality.

The Showdown

Changes can occur very fast in the angling world, and two years after Stockport's compelling Division Two National win on the Warwickshire Avon, they found themselves drawn beside Birmingham in the twelve sections of the 1976 Division One on the Trent. Freshly-promoted Stockport would dearly have loved to have scalped the bigger association; their team knew the Trent's moods, had grown up with the stick, and had the glory of their '69 Trent National win on their side; Birmingham were playing away. Brum however, were buzzing with confidence as reigning champions from the '75 Nene National.

Alan Mayer won 'A' section for Stockport with 8lb 1oz, but this was countered by Ken Giles winning 'K' section and taking the third individual medal with 16lb 1¼ oz on the stick float. Game on. But of the other team members Birmingham beat their Northern neighbours comfortably to defend their title with 776 points. Stockport had to settle for 10th with 623. This was generally a harder match than the Nene national with the Trent carrying floodwater and, as in all points matches, tiny roach and bleak in the hardest sections would earn big points scores. Clive Smith and his friends were well versed in the art of bleak snatching learned on the River Severn. The waggler also played a part and Brum were quite adept with this float too.

Clive describes his battle with Stockport's Harry Jackson in book two, here is a condensed version:

"When match day arrived we found that rain had affected the river. My peg was at Holme Marsh and with our big rivals, Stockport, drawn next to us the five hours' fishing ahead was going to be interesting indeed. The pace of the river had already started to accelerate when fishing started, and I made my opening gambit with a stick float. On the half-hour mark I hooked and landed a chub of about a pound and hoped that

206

this was the signal for others to follow. But a couple of gudgeon later, and with a good hour of the match gone, I was struggling to attract bites. At the next peg Harry Jackson was in front of me and managing to take roach at odd intervals. Ninety minutes on, after only adding a couple of roach, I reckoned I was a good three pounds behind Harry... I needed a different approach on the rising river to put me back in the race.

"I took a chance on going across the river with a three-swan waggler, dragging the bait two to three feet on the river bed in a nasty downstream wind. I'd previously fed a line some six to seven rod-lengths out in anticipation of this possible desperate move. It took me a good twenty minutes to achieve the correct tackle set-up, and then what a relief when I caught a roach. It came just as I was beginning to doubt the wisdom of making such a bold move on a fast-deteriorating river. As the match progressed my catch rate increased and I finished with just short of seven pounds of fish... I had managed to catch up with my rival and beat him by a pound. This was very satisfying for me because we had arrived at the conclusion that if we could beat the talented Stockport men it would remove the biggest obstacle to us notching up our second successive victory."

Leading by example
But it was on the stick float that Clive really excelled. The story that impressed me most in book two was of his 'Favourite Match' at Stourport-on-Severn. He reveals a small detail about the stick technique which I confess I'd never thought of in all my adventures with top and bottom-style fishing on rivers. This was the theory:

"The current was gentle, so that the light shots at the terminal end were important if I was to obtain anything like an overdepth situation. This is essential when stick float fishing because, with a fish facing its orthodox position, upstream, it is far more desirable for the caster or maggot to arrive in front of it without a column of line standing out, vertically, right in its sight."

The author's point seems obvious now, but subtle: given light shotting in the lower part of the rig, with the float set overdepth and held back in the flow, the rig angles downstream and any fish tempted to take the hookbait will see it arrive before noticing the string of shot above it, unlike if the rig was arriving to them almost vertically. The bonus, of course, is that a shallower angle of presentation allows the bait to ride over stones and snags better, and the bigger fish often respond to the rising bait when the float is stopped in its tracks.

This point was made with regard to a Courage match at Evesham where the flow is steady, but the same principle was applied in the 'Favourite match' that appeared in a later chapter. It is worth noting that the light shotting on the yard of line nearest the hook echoes Dave Thomas' Trent stick approach. Remember those bottom two shots mentioned earlier, the no. 8 and 10, and how their positions in relation to the hook are adjustable. The book diagram shows the no. 8 to be well above the 10, which suggests the authors liked this delicate presentation low down the rig.

The favourite match in question was a four and a half-hour afternoon event held late in 1976 at Stourport-on-Severn, a true float fishing Mecca for West Midlands anglers in the seventies. Over a two-year period at Stourport, Clive was the man to beat, enjoying an amazing winning ratio of over fifty per cent of all the matches he fished – hundred-peggers at that!

Just before this match Clive had won a West Midlands League match with 37½lb of roach, a magnificent haul of redfins beyond the scope of most Severn regulars. A fortnight later in the regular four and a half-hour Saturday match, on a river in perfect condition, he drew a peg which he fancied – "I had not previously fished the swim but when I saw it I was immediately convinced that it should hold a fair head of roach," he wrote. "I tackled up with no little enthusiasm!"

In any sport, any contest, plans do not always work out as expected, and for three and a half hours of this match it was stop-start battle for Clive. He was catching roach of six to eight ounce size, but try as he did to get them to feed at the head of the swim, they would not respond and with an hour to go he estimated he had some 12lb in his net. At this point he sensed that the simplest of changes might help; he made himself less visible, and the effect was magical.

"In no way could I see 16lb being enough to win, and this seemed to be my ultimate catch on my present course. I needed to take some sort of gamble in an effort to speed up my catch rate. As it was such a calm day, giving the fish a good view of me, I surmised that my standing position was deterring the fish from coming closer. So, unusually for me, I decided to fish the rest of the match sitting down," wrote Clive.

"The transformation was quite startling. Almost immediately I was catching roach just beyond the end of my rod! Not only were the intervals between each fish cut down drastically but also larger roach moved in and seemed keen to feed. At this shorter distance, my rhythm was sweet and I well remember developing a knack of casting (perhaps a better description of such close-in action would be 'dropping') the tackle on the water and holding it tight until the float assumed a correct position, and just edging it through the 3-4ft course."

In a glorious final hour Clive added 20lb to his catch for a winning 34lb 13½oz – some comeback! "For four and a half hours I had enjoyed my most pleasurable matchfishing experience. But I don't think it would have impressed me so much had I caught the fish during, say, the second or third hour. As with all sporting events, the ideal finish coming in the 'home straight.' Exciting cup finals are won in the last seconds, great horse races are remembered for 'last ditch' efforts, and to me this Lyttleton Open contest was no exception for the same reason... the swim had been paced out and I believe I had achieved a near 100 per cent return for its potential... it was an event which I cannot see ever being surpassed in terms of providing everything which fishing means to me."

So let's analyse what made Clive's method special enough to give him such wonderful catches and great consistency. He used a 2BB stick float, which is 8 x no. 6 shots (or 5 x no. 4's), the average amount of weight for five feet of water. He baited with casters and a 'liberal lacing' of 'well-cooked hempseed' – an attacking policy, and at the business end of his tackle was single caster on a size 18 crystal bend barbless hook. He shotted shirt button-style with 1 x no. 10 tell-tale, eight inches from the hook and slightly increasing sizes of 8's then 6's up towards the float.

But the key aspects for me was his light shotting in the lower half of the rig, and how he held the float back well overdepth to slow the presentation down, thus: "After some fine adjustments I was fishing at a depth between the float and hook of nearly eight feet, three feet more than the true depth of the water... I continually edged the float down the swim, at times stopping it completely and then running it through at varying speeds in an effort to simulate the hand-fed samples."

Clive reveals he would be lifting his bait well up off the bottom when he stopped the float, despite presenting it overdepth in theory, catching on the 'lift' (as John Allerton calls it) and letting very little line peel off the reel. This can be a deadly way of picking out the bigger roach in the shoal. As for the decision to sit down, well, better late than never. It reminded me of Kevin Ashurst's remark about Harold Booth sensibly sitting down when drawn near him on the day he (Kevin) made his '65 Trent record catch. Keeping a low profile must be right in any shallow swim or fairly clear one.

The heavy artillery
The mammoth 4,000-peg Birmingham AA Annual match, or 'Big 'Un,' was regarded by Clive Smith as his lucky event. Billed as the World's biggest match, it encompassed four hundred miles of pegged-out banks along the Severn and Warwickshire Avon. Few anglers could boast a better record in this match and Clive developed his balsa float skills over several years in his ambition to win it.

His first success came in 1966 from a swim just below Worcester at Diglis, nine swims above Teme mouth, where it joins the Severn. Fishing a large balsa float taking 6AAA and two droppers below, over heavy groundbait and maggot, he won his five hundred-peg 'section' with just under 10lb of dace and chub, also taking 7th spot overall. This was despite a boat churning up his seven-foot deep swim and killing it for an hour. With only 17½lb winning the whole event, this was a killer blow, but it served to spur Clive on.

In 1970 he drew the Danery stretch just above Quatford, in thirteen feet of water running slow which he did not really fancy. By now having progressed to fishing caster in groundbait, again with a balsa float and three casters on the hook, he weighed 10lb 15oz to win his five hundred pegs again and gain 17th overall. The 1971 match placed him at Grimley, near Worcester, which would be part of his practice schedule for September's National Championship, the last ever to be decided on weight. As team skipper of the pre-match favourites, Clive put in many hours on the river trying to work out tactics for both the National and the upcoming 'Big 'Un.'

He drew Boreley in the National, finding water similar in nature to that which he expected at Grimley. Manchester's Brian Lees was drawn a few pegs away and he won the section with 25lb to take fourth in the National, while Clive scaled 11lb 8¾oz. Although this was no mean individual score, Birmingham were pipped to the title by their main rivals Leicester in what was the biggest National match to date. Some consolation for Clive was he'd noticed how well Brian's sliding balsa float worked, and this was his cue for the BAA Annual. Adapting a cigar-shaped slider to his own style, he warmed up with a second in a Kidderminster Open at Boreley with just short of 40lb of chub. With confidence boosted, he banked on the slider again to catch 11lb 0½oz in the BAA match which both topped his five hundred-man section again and earned a winner-take-all prize for his thousand-peg section, also finishing thirteenth overall.

In 1975 he drew at Atcham, taking 17lb 11oz of barbel on feeder to finish second in his five hundred-peg section and joint seventh overall. Then his final chance to win it came a year later when drawn at Mythe Farm on what he called the 'Cinderella' river, the Avon, in a noted bream section. This time the Severn was more than a bit out of sorts and this paved the way for a top overall catch from the Avon. Groundbaiting with four 'tennis-balls' including casters and squatts two-thirds across the river, Clive quivertipped a ¾oz bomb with two white gozzers on a 20 hook and a four and a half-foot tail. He conjured up a dozen bream and three roach for 23lb 11oz, only to be pipped by his teammate, Tony Reece, from six pegs away with 1lb 11oz more! Clive lost one good bream in mid-match and was left to rue this forever, when Tony won the whole event and he had to settle for third. Perhaps we could say luck does not always go to the most deserving, but what a man for the big occasion!

Chapter 32
Paul Newell – turning plastic into gold

Paul with a 6lb 8oz chub, part of a netful from the Avon below Marlcliff, caught with a 6 x no. 4 homemade paintbrush stick and maggot on an 18 hook

We can all relate to those days when fate seems to play a cruel trick on us, when a wonderful day and expected victory is eclipsed by someone else's perfect day. The philosopher might use the phrase: the haunting spectre of the 'might-have-been.' Take John Dean in the 1975 Woodbine Final in Denmark, for example. About to embark on his years of Trent dominance, he had all but won the event by beating the majority of the 80 finalists with 80lb 7¼oz and top score on the River Guden, only to learn that three anglers drawn in one section on the adjacent lake had edged him out, topped by Ken Giles' ton-plus of fish that took the title. Argh, a painful discovery!

On the Warwickshire Avon, form angler, Paul Newell, was in for a similar shock after taking a bulging match net of roach from Evesham. Scaling a magnificent 26lb 15½oz of quality fish on the float he was looking like an easy winner, when up strolled Swindon's Steve Liston, tackle over his shoulder having weighed in, and announced: "I thought you'd beat me – I was doing well with the chub on a block-end feeder [26lb-worth no less] but then the roach moved in."

He'd not only caught on treble maggot on a 16 with a 'plastic pig' [as the feeder was disparagingly called by float anglers at the time], but he twisted the knife by moaning about the roach costing him more than the 42lb he'd won with! Such are the ups and downs of match fishing.

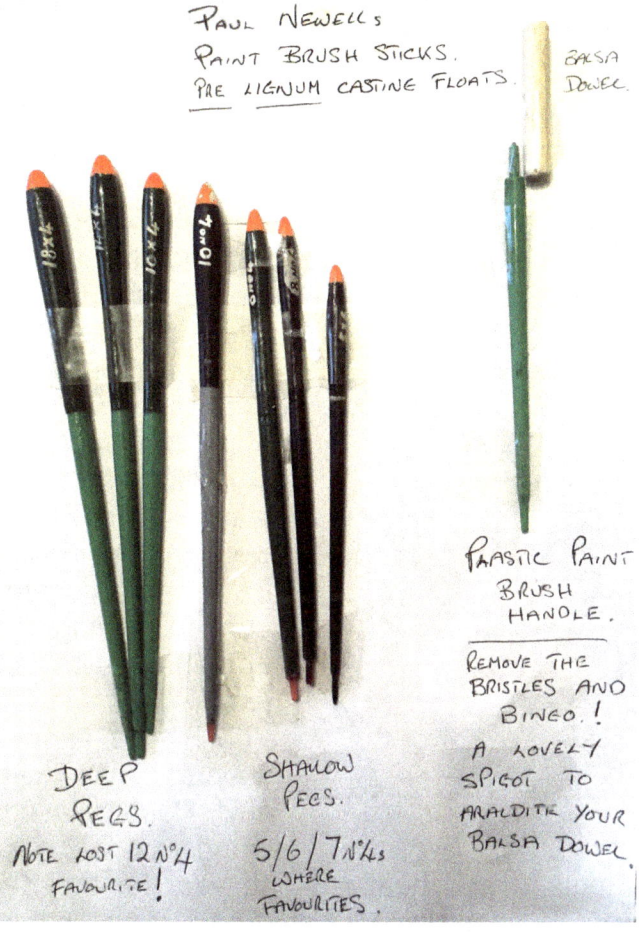

PAUL NEWELLS
PAINT BRUSH STICKS.
PRE LIGNUM CASTING FLOATS.

BALSA DOWEL

PLASTIC PAINT
BRUSH
HANDLE.

REMOVE THE
BRISTLES AND
BINGO.!

A LOVELY
SPIGOT TO
ARALDITE YOUR
BALSA DOWEL

DEEP
PEGS.
NOTE LOST 12 N°4
FAVOURITE!

SHALLOW
PEGS.
5/6/7 N°4s
WHERE
FAVOURITES.

In the early seventies, when good stick floats were hard to come by, Paul Newell designed his own for casting well out, to plunder chub from the middle of the Warwickshire Avon. While cane or wire formed the standard stick base, he made a set of floats with plastic paintbrush handles and they helped him make a major impact on the Avon match circuit. This included a victory in an England trial for the 1981 World Championships at Luddington, where, in spite of taking 14lb of chub in three hours, he did not gain selection.

A very confident angler, Paul was opinionated about good and bad pegs, floats and life generally. But like many anglers I have met, I found him generous with local information on the river. I hardly knew him at the time but during a brief chat he kindly gave me one of his plastic bases which at first glance told me it would deliver a mighty cast. A beefy length of tapered plastic with a diameter of around 7mm at its widest point, it also had a ready-made spigot which the metal sleeve holding the brush bristles fitted onto.

Tony Eaves, another Redditch river angler who came good in the eighties

As one of a quartet of talented youngsters from Redditch, Paul came through the ranks after the trail blazed by Midlands' finest Ken Giles and Clive Smith, and the likes of Lloyd Davies and Max Winters. The other emerging Shakespeare stars alongside Paul, were Pete Rice, Tony Eaves and Richard Kings, all serving their apprenticeships on the Avon.

"I have known many superb Avon anglers," said Paul. "Dave Harrell stands out as brilliant. He fished for England and beat me one year for the Kamasan Matchman of the Year title. He came back from England duty with long Bolo' rods, matching floats, and continental groundbaits, all suitable for fishing the middle Severn at Shrewsbury where he was the man to beat. Gloucester's Kim Milsom was another outstanding England man and someone with an intense focus. A fine line and small hook fan, he'd target all species and any size of fish required to win. But another favourite of mine, less of a household name but still brilliant, was Chris Taylor. Chris was a bit loud and boastful, but he could back it up with winning catches and was a great angler at his peak in the eighties when most pegs on the Avon were worth a few fish.

"But as good as Dave Harrell's floatmaking skills are today, he tried for two years to discover the secret of my paintbrush stick, and I don't mind saying I kept it from him best I could as it worked so well for me.

"Pete Rice and I learned and improved together. Unlike me, who liked to catch chub well out, Pete was at his most dangerous fishing close in for roach. He really was the master of the light stick, up to 3 x no. 6 size maximum. If the big roach came to his method on a good peg, he'd reliably frame or win the match."

When Paul realised the possibility of turning the paintbrush handle into a stick it was a true eureka moment. It dawned on him one day in a shop when he picked up a cheap paintbrush. Weighing it in his hand, and he realised it had a ready-made spigot over which the brush part fitted. He left the shop very happy indeed. Thinking it could well outcast most sticks he knew about, he was soon buying more brushes for stick manufacture.

Max Winters of Gloucester enjoyed some big wins on stick float

"It is a long time ago, but I'd say it was around 1975 when I made my first paintbrush stick. A friend of mine and a top angler, Roy Hall saw the first sticks off the production line and liked them, believing, I'm sure, that we could both gain from their distance potential. Roy fished for leading Brum team Cofton Hackett, and became my mentor in the early days. When he gave the float the thumbs up I knew I was onto something.

"Ricey and I thought Roy was the best chub angler on the

Avon. Roy told me never to be frightened of using lead, and that led me to use floats as big as 10, 12, and even 14 x no. 4's. He also taught me the common sense stuff like when hooking a maggot not to lose any of its juice, and if ever I thought of something to change to do it immediately.

The plastic brush handles had a consistent, heavy density and Paul made them for different depth situations, but mainly in five sizes – 4 x no. 4 up to 8 x no. 4. But if the float material was ground-breaking, the way he shotted it was rare, if not unique. Paul told me how he shotted a 5 x no. 4 size paintbrush float for example, with no dropper shot but those five 4's spread in a reverse taper over 18" of line, meaning the gaps got slightly wider going away from the hook, above a 30-inch hooklength. This helped reduce tangles when casting overhead.

Occasionally though, when he pushed his cast to the limit in an adverse wind, he'd find himself wasting time undoing tangles sooner or later. "If I have one regret about those great days it was before the use of pole floats on winders," admitted Paul. "Had I put a few spare rigs on winders I'd have saved many hours over a season and caught many more fish. Hindsight is fine but always comes too late, of course."

But this float often gave Paul the middle of the river to himself with the stick, to spots where others relied on the waggler. Feeding anything from four to five pints of bronze maggots he'd often catch on the drop with the float set about six to seven feet irrespective of the swim depth. "The float would only travel a yard sometimes and then bury as the chub hit the bait. It would be double maggot on the hook six times of ten, on the harder days they'd prefer a single."

But our subject didn't always use the paintbrush handle. In boily swims he'd revert to a wire stem and liked the Drennan Pin stick. He recalls a special day in the Stan Lewis Businessmen's match which he won at Bewdley, on the Severn with 9lb 14oz. With two feet of water on the river and rising, he inched a 9 x no. 4 pin stick through off his rod end and included three roach in his catch for 6lb 6oz no less! In recent years Paul has also used Woody's (of Hereford) shouldered wire-stems on rivers like the Wye and Severn.

Paul used a Tri-cast Diamond 13-foot rod back in the day

(and still does, owning three of them). His main hook choice for the chub was a Mustad 90340, later changing to a lighter wire Kamasan B510 – "and the originals were the best" he says, in sizes 20 down to 24. Trace line was Shakespeare Omni. Today he's moved on to new hooks like the Matrix Stillwater Feeder size 20 and the Preston black nickel N40 size 18, a pattern with which he caught 18lb 4oz of Burton Festival Trent roach, only recently.

So what are Paul's ideal stick float venues? "I'd have to plump for Stourport on the Severn and Twyford Farm on the Avon, both being such lovely places to catch fish when the rivers are in perfect nick."

With the spread of plastic through every household as time went by it wasn't long before other anglers followed Paul's lead with plastic/nylon in varying ratios and densities, producing floats equal to or of a better quality than Tonkin cane or other woods. The bonus of a suitable cheap paintbrush, of course, was that aside from the ready spigot they were already tapered. These floats were easier to make with only the soft balsa top needing any serious shaping.

Around the same time as Paul produced his float, leading Trentmen like John Dean and Dave Thomas further North were discovering plastic's potential for themselves and, along with Pete Warren who later endorsed Middy sticks, and Peter Drennan, they all designed and put their names on commercial sticks with plastic bases. Peter Drennan called his 'glass' as they were a clear colour offering less of a shadow in crystal clear swims. The fact that plastic or plastic/nylon composite could be reproduced by the thousand in the same density, was its major commercial advantage over wood, for when joined to balsa of a consistent density almost every float off the production line was almost identical in both looks and behaviour. This removed the chance element in trying to make two hand-crafted floats that performed the same.

Chapter 33
Pete Rice – master of the light stick

Pete Rice in action playing a good fish at Evesham

"With the advent of poles up to 14 metres, much of the water formerly covered by the stick can now be more fully exploited, as optimum presentation can be achieved more easily. That said there are still thousands of waters where the stick float dominates – pacier waters, wider and steadier waters, and even some of our favourite pole waters. I sat next to Pete Rice on this year's Courage Team Champs and we'd both drawn poorly and 3-4lb would give good section points. For the first half of the match we had to fish the pole and I went 1½lb up on Pete. In the second half when the rules changed to 'any method' Pete adopted his usual killing stick float method and ended up beating me easily 4lb 4oz to 2lb 10oz. He fished just three metres out halfway down his fifteen-yard peg." – Mark Downes, England Team Manager.

The above quote, courtesy of *Match Fisherman* magazine, shows how challenging five hours of competition river fishing can be, no matter how good our equipment is. Personally, I don't recall the Warwickshire Avon being quite this tough in the years I fished it except in the depths of winter, but, as in our other major rivers, the roach and dace sport declined as the last century came to an end. What the quote also tells us is that Pete Rice famously had a 'killing method,' and so I'd like to explain more about it.

I had not fished the Avon many times before I came across the ever-enthusiastic Pete, from Redditch, and his dry sense of humour. Described by one of his rivals as "a most untidy angler but clever tactically and with a razor-sharp mind," his inner self-confidence came across and I marked him down as a man worth listening to. The Avon today is not the match Mecca it was, and where the target species at Evesham used to be dace, roach and chub, it has changed to big bream and barbel, with fewer roach shoals. Pete has long since drifted away and switched to carp commercials (more's the pity, I say, as I'm sure at heart he's still a river roach angler) but his impact on this glorious river lives on.

Among the key questions any angler needs to ask himself when faced with an unfamiliar swim on a stretch of river is: 'what size of float should we use, considering the depth and flow?' in the knowledge that, with the stick float in particular, two or three shot either way could be the make or break in compiling a decent net of fish.

Accepting that a 6 x no. 4 size stick float is probably the average size on many of our bigger rivers and working on the old guideline of 1 x no. 4 for every foot of depth, then Pete Rice broke all convention with regard to size. For his style was all about 'ultra-light': often one-tenth of the average!

Pete became a star performer on the Avon in the 1980s, and he built up his consistency by mastering this lighter technique, the lightest approach I have come across in fact in my research. Using an Austin Clissett design of mini stick float, he was dominant wherever roach could be caught in numbers, at Twyford Farm and Evesham Town in particular. Now we are not talking sticks taking no. 4 shot or even 6's here, but no. 10's! And although this style evolved over time, it was rare for anyone to shot quite so lightly forty years ago.

Being a close friend of Austin, a Birmingham tackle dealer, Pete had the luxury of searching through and singling out a dozen floats from three hundred of Austin's hand-made sticks before they went on sale. He sought the lightest sizes of 3 x no. 10 shot up to 5 x no. 10 capacity, with pointed tips, and he was only interested in the floats that almost cocked before any shot were added. The varying density of the cane base (i.e. the familiar green garden cane) meant some of the floats did not have this facility. He wanted the heavier bases so they would register an early bite on the drop, as with tiny shots and a slowly falling bait, a bite high in the water column is always likely.

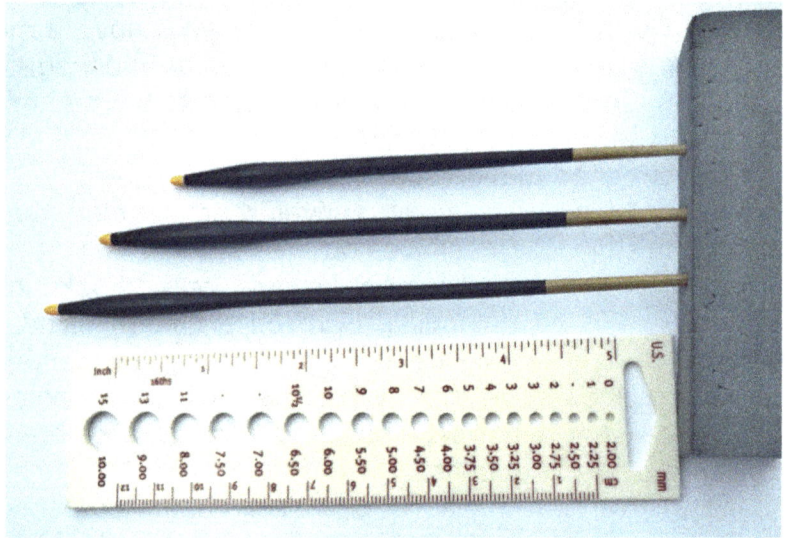

Clissett/Rice sticks

In the shallower pegs, up to five feet deep, Pete would select a 3 x no. 10 size float and check it took exactly three and no more – re-shaping the float if necessary, and then evenly spacing the three shot down the line, then adjust the float if necessary and space the shot out down the line. The tell-tale shot would sit fifteen inches from the hook and the others added at eighteen-inch gaps above that. In a deeper swim Pete would scale up to a 5 x no. 10 model. His standard size 20 hook would be tied to thirty inches of 12oz (or .08mm) Bayer Perlon – "which was the only 12oz line available when we started," says Pete. When finer lines came onto the market, if sport was really hard, he might scale down to a .06mm trace and a 24 hook, but in case he hooked an early chub he'd prefer to start a match on .08mm to a 20.

For Pete to ensure he had precisely shotted the floats down to their limit, he would shot them up at home in a tall jar until they sank, then remove the required number of shots on each until the float re-appeared.

Pete determined to make his light, 3 x no. 10 size stick (or 0.1g capacity) work. Once he found he could almost trickle it downstream just beyond his rod tip and take quality fish, in various swims where a majority of anglers would not think twice about tackling up a far heavier string of upwards of 6 x no. 4's (or 1.0g), his confidence soared. Sometimes he had to find the flow by casting further out, of course, and in fairness I should add that he always carried heavier sticks for days when the river was carrying extra water and pushing through hard.

With regard to the rest of his presentation, he would initially set the float to fish from four to six inches over-depth which ensured his bait was touching bottom when he held the float back. But if the fish were unresponsive, he'd push the float up to fish the bait anything from eighteen to twenty four over-depth which would also put his tell-tale shot on the bottom.

Pete was targeting roach but in the first half of a match he might take more dace. "Roach on the Avon can be slow to respond and it might take half the match, or even three hours to get them feeding properly," he said, "but after searching well down the peg for roach for say two hours or more, in the second half of the match they'd tend to become more active, coming up the peg and often up in the water too to intercept the loose feed, and with the light shotting I could catch them – and these would be quality roach."

"Austin Clissett really designed the small sticks for dace," added Pete, but he found out that quality roach came best to his slow drop approach, usually only two rod-lengths' distance out from the bank at most, though he could occasionally catch roach well out in perfect wind conditions.

Pete used a 12-foot Archie Harrison rod, hand-made by a local rod-builder, combined with a Mitchell Match reel and 2lb Maxima line. To underline the quality of the roach he could catch, Pete described his most enjoyable catch on the method: "It was a qualifier for the first Courage Championship and I won it with 18lb of big roach. It was probably my best match, winning with 8 or 9lb clear. The fish got bigger as the day wore on and I netted eight or nine roach of 1lb-plus in the latter stages. A wonderful day's sport."

Paul Newell, Pete's Redditch colleague and Avon rival, credits Pete as being 'the master of the light stick,' though he never attempted to copy him. Paul based his approach more on a heavy range of sticks for fishing mid-river instead.

Pete reflects on those 'good years' on the Avon and how vastly different the fishing was to today's carp lakes and big weights. He believes a lot of anglers look back with 'rose-tinted glasses' as the saying goes. A catch of 5-6lb was often enough to win money, and definitely offer a good section winning chance, with a double figure net more the exception unless drawn on one of the 'flyer' pegs.

Feeding maggots on the 'little and often' principle, Pete would generally feed two or three pinches of bait per trot to continually maintain some bait going through the swim. A total quantity of maggots used would be 2½ pints maximum. For hookbait he liked to start with double maggot, then change to single if only small fish were showing, but always scaling back up to double maggot for the last hour and chance of a late bonus fish. "You get nowhere by being too cautious," he says.

One special memory of Pete's occurred with a little help from his Aquarians teammate and long-time friend, Richard Kings. It was a hard day, but Pete had drawn the favoured peg just upstream of Evesham Town road bridge. Pete takes up the story: "Richard was walking the bank and when he reached me and asked how I was faring, I admitted to 7lb or so. From others he had seen struggle, Richard thought I was winning the match, but, while I could see small chub in the shadow of the bridge, I was missing lots of bites on a 3BB waggler with 2 x no. 10s down the line. Richard offered to go up on the bridge and point skywards when he thought a 'chublet' (small chub) had taken the bait.

"Richard saw clearly that the chub were seizing the hookbait almost immediately on it hitting the water, but by the time the float moved the bite was missed. So a fraction of a second before the fish struck he'd raise his arm and I then connected almost every time without seeing the float move. I won the match with 18lb, even though we were surely guilty of breaking match rules had we been spotted. We were young and a little crazy then but that's my only excuse, so let me apologise now for what was a foolish bit of cheating!"

But what Pete considers as his best result on the method left him with pangs of heartache – we might call it the haunting spectre of the might-have-been? He finished second to Jan Porter in the 1989 Courage Champs when Jan edged him to the title by an agonising 4oz – 14lb 10oz to 14lb 6oz! Jan caught small chub on the waggler casting well across the river, beyond where he could catapult his maggots. But it was a lost bonus fish that was really Pete's undoing.

"I made a mistake that took me a while to get over. Of the three rods I set up one was intended for big fish with a 1.7lb hooklength attached. I'd been catching steadily when the peg suddenly went quiet. I said to myself 'a big perch has moved in,' and changed to the rod with the stronger line. Three runs down later my next bite produced a 2lb perch – nice. But then I switched back to my light rig. Next trot down I hooked the perch's mate and it broke me. Agony! In hindsight I remembered that big perch usually swam in pairs and I should have stuck with the strong gear for longer. I still won £1,000 on the day so should have been jumping for joy, but was so gutted I could hardly speak at the after-match party in the club."

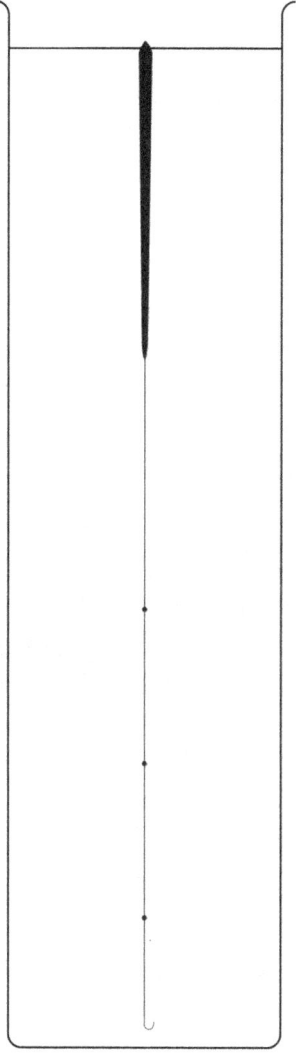

Pete Rice would test his stick float in a jar, shown here dotted down with 3 x no. 10s. If it didn't sit perfectly like this he'd re-model the float.

Chapter 34
Lloyd Davies – the clever feeder

Teammate Ken Giles called him a 'brainbox angler' who never skinned a swim (cleaned it out of fish) and the best stick float angler he ever saw (some accolade from him), while his Birmingham skipper, Clive Smith described him as the 'wonder boy of the early seventies' in his 1982 book referred to in the previous chapter. We are talking about Lloyd Davies of Droitwich.

Lloyd, now 78, told me how he would take four pints of casters to a match and "come back with most of 'em." Noted for being a 'mean' or should we say a defensive feeder, it was good enough to get the better of Ivan Marks in their classic West vs East Midlands peg-to-peg encounter in the 1975 Lawden Masters at Evesham.

With both anglers on peak form, Lloyd chose to loose feed caster, the standard method for the river at that time, while Ivan groundbaited with a caster or worm on the hook, and they matched each other fish for fish. At the final whistle Ivan was a mere 8½oz short of the Brummie's 21lb 10½oz winner! Ken Giles came very close too by finishing third on 20lb 2oz. Lloyd caught mainly small chub, dace and roach on waggler, but coming inside on the stick line in the last hour he clinched it with three fish in the dying minutes!

Many other anecdotes about Lloyd however, reveal that aside from his waggler and stick float prowess, he could turn his hand to big fish when required and he proved versatile whether the fishing was easy or hard. He won the Severn Championship with 36lb of bream from Upton-on-Severn when only 8lb made second with 800 fishing: "which tells you what a flier I was on," he admitted, and scored a second in the same event with 21lb of chub using legered wasp grub. He also won a Birmingham Parks match with a double figure carp. Knowing the high value of the fish with little being caught around him, he smartly took both his keepnet and landing net well away from the water before tipping the bonus fish from one to the other. And as a left-hander, he converted an ABU 507 reel to wind it right-handed, prior to the company's introduction of their 508 model.

Lloyd arguably came to National prominence when he won the 1964 Hampshire Avon Championship with 65 quality roach for 44lb 6oz. Roach catches this big were rarely heard of at that time.[17]

The match attracted some of the UK's finest of that period including Ivan Marks and Billy Lane, and was fished from Ringwood to Sopley. Lloyd's Redditch-based Dalesman AC four-man team, supported by Austin Clissett's 36lb 11oz of chub for fourth place, and backed up by Clive Smith and Jim Ryder, also stormed to the team title with 103lb 8oz, leaving Billy Lane's four well back in second with 54lb.

Lloyd's total included six specimens of 1lb 12oz each, and the match report told how he caught most of his weight in the second hour before a marauding pike killed his swim for the last two hours! In the lead up to the match he'd also won on his local Warwickshire Avon with 8lb of roach and again on the Severn with 15lb 13oz of dace.

The match report added that he fed only a 'few handfuls of maggots.' I dare say this meant the total amount, as to feed a handful at once would be alien to the man. Let's speculate that he fed it lightly, unlike Austin who fed four pints of maggots for his chub catch. As for the actual float used, the West Midlanders had not acquired the stick float at this time, and it is believed Lloyd used either a balsa or Crow Avon. Austin Clissett recalls using a 5 x BB balsa himself.

As for Jim Ryder's team effort, he had a minor confrontation with the angler drawn on his downstream side. Pegged near the lower end of the match course, Jim wasted time playing several sea trout in the first hour of the match before deciding to mix up a bowl of groundbait. As soon as he fed a couple of balls, recalled Austin Clissett, a voice came up from below: "That's not the done thing on here my friend, not on this river." His neighbour was none other than Dick Walker, captor of the 44lb record carp in 1952 and the man still widely revered as the godfather of specimen angling.

Undeterred and unaware he was breaking any rule, Jim

---

17 A stunning catch of roach in anyone's book, but for this remarkable roach river it was not exceptional. Dob Chislett of Christchurch took 64lb of roach on an Avon float and bread in a four-hour local club match to set the river record in 1970. This lasted almost 20 years until a mainly-roach 73lb catch beat it in 1989.

did not respond but proceeded to catch double figures of roach while Dick soldiered on towards a low weight.

Both individually and in team events for Cofton Hackett and the mighty Birmingham A.A, Lloyd would perform to a level equivalent to his famous contemporaries Giles and Smith. In the grim 1969 Trent National when many top anglers returned less than 2lb, Lloyd was tops for Brum with 5lb 6oz, and in the 1972 Bristol Avon National he led for them again with 9lb of roach on stick float to win his 80-peg section. So what made this light feeder a consistent stand-out performer?

Lloyd said: "When I was young and strong, in the pre-carbon days, I'd use a sixteen-foot glass fibre rod, which was a handful, but it gave me better float control. At Evesham we were looking for 12lb to 15lb of roach and dace before the chub explosion, and sometimes 10lb could win. The river was full of dace at that time and only later became full of chub. I'd often start the match on waggler while building up the inside line for later – for the last two hours especially. My feeding rate was normally geared to a 10lb target, starting with four to six casters per trot and using a pint to one and a quarter pints of casters total, but every day was different as swims and conditions vary so much. I had no set pattern with floats or shotting: a 6 x no. 4 size stick on average, shotted with 6s and 8s, and always with a tell-tale no. 10 starting at six inches from the hook, adjustable to how the fish wanted it on the day.

"Clive (Smith) had great belief in a lot of hemp and he'd feed plenty all the way down his swim when targeting roach and chub, but I could never quite get on with his style; probably I didn't quite have the same faith in hemp. In the early days it was banned, of course, at venues like Fladbury, so I did not bother with hemp much generally."

Final word to Ken Giles on his teammate: "Lloyd was a finesse angler with all-round skills who could conjure up a result from anywhere with a stick float on his line. A tall guy, he could handle a fourteen-foot rod with ease when the standard length was shorter, and when working on night shift in the car industry he would regularly practise on midweek days. More than just a good river angler, you could rely on him to deliver for the team almost anywhere, but on a stick float it was a case of watch him go – he was absolutely brilliant."

Chapter 35
Achieving a dream – Joe Brennan

Wolverhampton's Joe Brennan is one of the match world's true gentlemen. A former Gladding Masters champion and Warwickshire Avon champion, his CV also includes a sixth spot in the 1976 Trent National with 12lb 3oz on a flooded river when a lost big carp certainly cost him bronze medal position and possibly the title itself. But the ex-boss of the popular Brennan and Hickman tackle company can reflect on his match career with much pride as he made it count. Here he describes his favourite match and catch on a stick float.

The last Sunday in October was always special to me each year, it being the date of my favourite match, the Wye Championships. The River Wye was very good to me in the 1970s with a number of frame positions from third down to tenth, but never a first or second.

On the way to Hereford in 1979 I was, as usual, mentally listing the pegs or section I hoped to draw. If I remember the river was in good nick and I was hoping for some broken water or a long shallow glide. I was convinced that you would need to catch chub to win, and was always happier drawing chub pegs believing that some anglers would find them difficult as they didn't have the range of floats I carried with me. A lot of my success had come from wild water areas which called for home-made balsa float carrying in excess of six swan shot.

In those days the draw was made in the Hereford Scouts' hut and, with two hundred and fifty or more anglers competing, it was a hive of activity, banter and anticipation. I was very lucky that every year there were three or four local guys who, although not fishing the event, always gave me whatever information they could to help me either find my peg, or advise me of the prospects of the peg I had drawn. Well, it looked like my hopes were dashed as I had avoided all the wonderful wild water swims above and below Hereford. Instead, I had drawn a peg at Belmont in the town centre. It was midway between the boathouse and the disused railway bridge and not at that time an area anyone wanted.

My friendly locals apologetically suggested it was a good roach peg. But in those days very few matches were won with roach; you needed to be on a shoal of chub or dace to get a weight that gave you a chance. On the bright side I could park behind the boathouse and walk the six or seven pegs to my office for the day. There are some horrific walks on the Wye Champs but they take you through amazing scenery and to some wonderful looking pegs. In those days the walks didn't bother me even though we carried all our gear, as trolleys weren't around then. I was young and buzzing with adrenalin and it was up to me to get what I could from the peg drawn.

On arrival at the peg I was dismayed to see a bed of weed the length of the swim that extended out from the bank for about a rod-length. Added to that the bank was very steep indeed and the only space to place my seat box was about six feet off the water. I was in for an uncomfortable day's roach fishing.

Heeding the advice of my learned friends, I proceeded to tackle up with roach in mind. A tip actioned, thirteen-foot rod was matched to my ever faithful Mitchell Match reel loaded with 2.6lb Bayer Perlon line. The chosen float was a 4 x no. 4 stick float with the shot spread over the lower half of the rig. I considered this suitable as I intended to start just past the weedbed where I thought I might find five feet or so of depth. In fact it was just over six feet deep.

A size 18 hook to 1.7lb Bayer completed the rig and after careful plumbing I set the float at six-foot deep to just trip the shelf beyond the weedbed. I have never been one to place all my eggs in one basket so I also set up a thirteen-foot, through actioned rod, Mitchell Match reel loaded with 3.2lb Bayer and a six-swan homemade balsa float completed with a size 6 forged hook to fish mid-river for any stray chub that might grace my net.

A bomb/feeder rod was also set up as a last resort and I was then ready to make myself as comfortable as possible. With barely enough room to wedge my feet in front of the box, I awaited the off. I felt over-armed as I had brought the usual pile of bait for a Wye match: four pints each of casters, hemp and maggots, plus an unsliced loaf and as much groundbait as I thought I could carry.

With the roach in mind I mixed half a bowl of brown crumb and soil laced with hemp and casters, with the intention of an 'easy as you go' approach. At the off I introduced three balls of the groundbait mix, the first two firmer than the third. The idea was for the first two to slowly break up at the head of the swim and the third softer ball to break up and waft down the swim and tempt fish up from below. These were followed by loose maggots. I then baited the size 18 hook with two bronze grubs.

First run down and I thought, although a little light, the 4 x no. 4 rig was coping with what was quite a sedate swim. Retrieving the rig I checked the bait was untouched and laid the rig out for another run through. Two-thirds the way down the swim the float buried and whatever was attached embedded itself in the weed. After pulling at all angles and, bearing in mind I didn't have room to safely stand up, I eventually pulled for a break. 'Didn't expect that,' I thought, and routinely added a fresh hook baited with two bronze maggots.

'Blow me,' I said, when exactly the same thing happened

the next run down. I couldn't swear as my eldest daughter Sarah had come with me for the first and last time. But I was seething and, having always believed in 'if you think it, do it,' I reached for my heavier tackle.

The balsa float was obviously far too big for this situation, but I needed a strong reel line and hooklength plus a rod with some backbone. By now all thoughts of roach had been banished from my mind. It was Joe vs chub, but as the fish were so close to the weedbed I needed to react quicker so felt I must have a tighter line between rod tip and float. To achieve this I pulled out a heavier version of the Drennan glass stick I'd been using – 8 x no. 4, and changed the shotting to spread the shot equally along the length of the rig. This combination, along with my position high off the water, meant I could apply pressure immediately a fish was hooked.

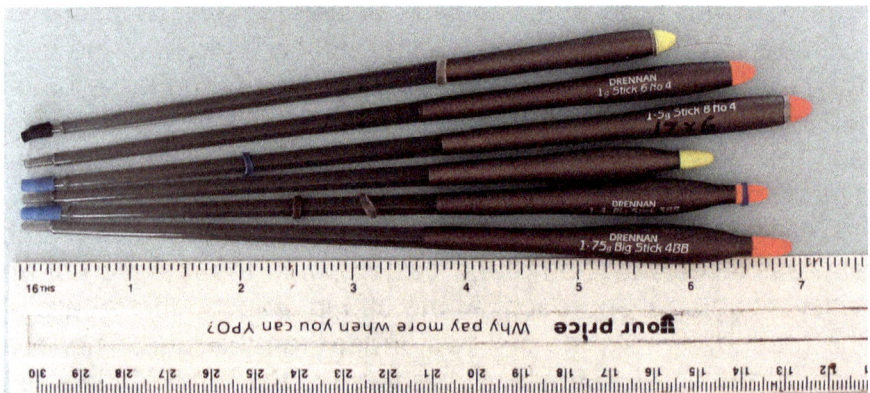

Drennan 'glass' stems, a clear heavy plastic: 'sticks' with domed tops and 'big sticks' with finer top and shoulder up to 1.75g (over 17 x no. 6)

A size 14 hook to 2.6lb Bayer completed the rig and three or four bronze maggots were to be offered to whatever was still interested. I mixed up another bowl of groundbait heavily laced with hemp and casters with the intention of feeding a single ball each run through. I also dug out a little more room for my feet in case I needed to stand up to apply pressure to a fish, trying to give myself a better chance should the fish still want to play.

Not surprisingly, it took half a dozen runs down before the next bite but this time I was ready. As the float neared the bottom of my swim it disappeared and it was 'GAME ON.' The fish desperately tried to bury its head in the sanctuary of the weedbed but I clung on and kept it out, and although it must have been brutal to watch I had no intention of losing this fish. Seconds later a chub of around 4lb graced my net and I felt a whole lot better.

There's not much more to add as the rest of the match was plain sailing. I never lost another fish and ended up with 58lb of quality chub to achieve my dream and win the Wye Championship.

Although I was lucky enough to be able to win an even bigger match – the six hundred-peg Warwickshire Avon Championship – the Wye match will always be my favourite win because I practised what I preached. I didn't think 'Oh, I will try this later.' No, and the same for you if ever in the same dilemma, hesitant to make a change when all your instincts are telling you to switch – don't spend time pondering it, do it NOW!

Chapter 36
A lignum for the Witham – Dave Ashmore

A weed-strewn summer River Witham when eels would show to stick float tactics before the long pole took over

Dave Ashmore, from Grimsby, was one of the big names on the Witham back in the 1980s when the river peaked for roach. A modest man who quietly went about his business, he let his consistent results do the talking. Dave thwarted my plan to complete a hat-trick of Super League titles by posting a perfect section winning score in winter 1984-85 for maximum points from his best eight matches out of 10. Although the waggler method dominated on a winter Witham back then, the stick was often better when the flow speeded up on an outgoing tide, though either float could throw up some surprises by working well on days when conditions didn't seem right for it. Dave had a knack of seizing an advantage at such times to run the stick float over his waggler line and change bait presentation. In one particular Grimsby winter match I scaled 16-11 of stick-caught roach, beating quality anglers like Edgar Purnell and Mal Talbot in the process, only to get licked by Dave with an outstanding 19-15 of roach (story below). Come in Dave…

Whether on the Trent or Witham, I favoured two types of stick float. My first choice was the Ultra lignum stick in sizes 6 to 8 x no. 4 shot which cast beautifully and sat really nicely in the water. I didn't use no. 4 shot, of course, but no. 6's and later no. 8's (after 6's were banned). I reckon the 8 x no. 4 version took around 20 x no. 8 to set it. In a gentle flow the shot would be spaced evenly along the line (shirt button-style) but in heavier flows I would use a bulk maybe placed at half-depth and spread the rest out below that. Position of the bulk and number of shot in it would depend on the pace of the river.

If the flow became too heavy the John Allerton aluminium-stemmed version would come out. It didn't cast anything like as well as the lignum base but sat better in the heavier flow. In perfect conditions (wind slightly upstream, off your back) the lignum base would cast comfortably past the middle. Bites were often hard to spot with the float holding up a little or travelling downstream a bit quicker, and a bit of fiddling around with the bottom few shot would help; in fact, one of my favourite dodges would be to put a little bulk of 2 and very occasionally 3 x no. 8's near the hook. There were definitely occasions when this got some positive bites.

I also doctored some of the floats by putting a fine two-inch insert in the tip of cane or peacock quill. These were usually used if there were heavy upstream rollers on the river but I still wanted to use the stick float instead of the waggler. I suppose, on reflection, these were like a slightly smaller version of the now very popular Bolo' floats. The obvious advantage of the stick float was the fact that you could slow the bait down much more effectively than with the waggler. I caught lots if fish on it when the river was hardly moving. In the right conditions you could stop the float dead, something you couldn't do with the waggler.

Feeding was pretty much as with the waggler. I was always a very light feeder, working on the assumption that the fewer maggots there were in my peg, the quicker a fish would find the one with the hook in it. Obviously you had to feed enough to keep fish in front of you, so it was always a bit of a guessing game, a gut instinct if you like, and the better guessers did the best. I do believe there were (and still are of course) a lot of very good anglers out there with similar abilities with regard to tackle control etc, but generally the ones who got the feeding right for the fishes' appetites on the day did the best.

One good example was a Boxing Day winter match I managed to win with 19lb 15oz of good roach, and I kept them feeding throughout with only around 1½ pints of bronze maggots. My Grimsby mate and travelling partner, Tony Hepburn also came third with 16-4, but the biggest thing I remember about that match was being miffed that I didn't top the 20lb mark!

Another day I remember well was a round of the keenly contested Witham Super League. I don't remember the date or exact weights, but I recall it was an unpleasant day and the river was out of sorts. I was next to Edgar Purnell (a brilliant angler) and well into the match we had caught next to nothing. In desperation I threw the stick out (everything seemed wrong for it) and much to my amazement had a bite or two to win the match with 3lb-odd. If my memory serves me well, Edgar was second with only 1lb-plus.

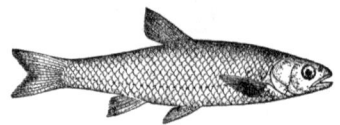

Chapter 37
The London and Southern influence – from crow quills, porkies and the 'Dumpy,' to the stick – Keith Arthur

When I started fishing the mighty River Thames, in my teens, the classic floatfishing style was a crowquill, laid-on, directly under the rod tip. *The* rod back in the day was the famous Apollo Taperflash in 12ft length. They made a 13ft and even a convertible 10ft/14ft model too; the rod was made from tubular steel, by the famous Accles and Pollock company, who are still producing high-quality metal tubes at Oldbury in the West Midlands.

Each quill would take, on average, 1 x BB and 1 x no. 4 shot but anglers used the amount of shot necessary to hold the bait still on the bottom – usually a minimum of 2 x BB but up to as many as eight, even nine shot when the river was high. Bait was introduced via brass droppers, which were made by only a few anglers, so being 'in the know' was essential. The classic 'pan' dropper in use today didn't come into existence until Bob Gleed, a very good London angler, founded Thamesley Tackle, who also produced high-quality moulded lead shot, leger weights, feeders and, ultimately the first mass-produced block-end version.

The reason for the use of these tactics on the Thames was that Thames Conservancy bylaws insisted that only fish over certain sizes could be retained in keepnets, and 'laying on' sorted out the 'goers,' as sizeable fish were known.

By a large margin the most prolific fish were dace, with a size limit of 7ins from tip of snout to tip of tail. A goer roach needed to make 8ins, perch 9ins, chub and bream 12ins, and barbel 16ins. Gudgeon were common but never allowed to be weighed in and neither were bleak which, in those days, were present in plague proportions. The heavy bulk shot and bait dropper tactics allowed the maggot hookbait to be bombed through the bleak to the dace and roach.

The only variation was when fishing with the hemp in summer and autumn, still mostly with the crow quill but either trotted close to the bottom or, quite commonly, fished a foot or so deep as the fish, most often roach, started flashing just under the surface as they competed for the loose-fed hemp.

Many anglers on the Thames used 'roach poles,' hand-crafted from bamboo, often with real silver ferrules. If you were strong and either rich or clever enough, poles could be as long as 21ft but at that length they weighed a ton: 18ft was more the norm but the crowquill, laid-on, was still de rigeur.

These were more North London methods, this being the London Angler's Association (LAA) stronghold. South of the river was where CALPAC (Central Association of London and Provincial Angling Clubs) held more sway. Their members tended to fish more 'open' matches than LAA anglers, sometimes on the Thames but further upstream, towards Oxford. Most of the lower river was free fishing, so impossible to peg as every decent swim would have an angler in it by 8.30 every Sunday morning of the season, but further upstream there were more club-controlled stretches that could be reserved for matches.

Because the 'sarf-London' boys – and very occasional girl – match-fished more diverse waters, including the Kentish rivers such as the Medway and Rother, they used a much wider range of float-fishing styles. This contrasted with the LAA roving events, where the Thames, and occasionally, its main tributary the Lea, suited the laying-on style better (a 'rover' entails anglers choosing their own swims after a walk-off, with number one walking off first).

Us North Londoners fished with our clubs, always travelling on the Sunday morning club coach. Before motorways, the A4 and A40 would be almost a solid line of charabancs each following the other Westwards from 'The Smoke' hoping beyond hope that the section of free Thames they had chosen to fish hadn't already been populated by earlier risers.

The southerners seemed more independent, travelling to venues in groups in their own cars or vans, not tied by the club and coach structure. When I bumped into some of the southern anglers who ventured onto 'our' matches – Ray Mumford would have been the most famous of these – to catch a glimpse inside their float box was a real eye-opener. Not a crowquill in sight but porcupine quills, with or without a balsa enhancement, or combinations of balsa, cane, and reed, all mind-boggling to us crowquill slaves.

This float diversity came about because they fished more pegged-down matches and couldn't guarantee sitting in a swim with 3ft or more of water under the rod-tip, essential for the crowquill, so floats that could be cast and then trotted down the swim had to be created. Because fishing 'bottom only,' a style eventually becoming the waggler, had yet to be adopted on rivers, some of their floats had bodies at the bottom instead of the classic Avon-type floats.

These were used to beat downstream winds and for fishing deeper water. The most famous of these was created by a wonderful angler: Pat Richardson. Pat loved the River Medway, the lower, match-fished sections of which were deep and flowed at a more leisurely pace than the Thames did in those days. Pat wanted a float that he could cast to the middle or just beyond, within range of the new-fangled catapults which were creeping on to the scene, and either trot his bait mid-water or drag it along the bottom. His float became known as the 'Dumpy.'

I'm fairly sure that the original was indeed more a reverse Avon, that is a crowquill with the body at the bottom but when it came on to the scene it boasted a cane stem with a bulbous body at the bottom of the cane, fished top-and-bottom style. The originals took 1 x SSG shot with 1 x no. 4 dropper, the shot set so the smaller weight could be dragged or fished just off. Any bites occurring as the bait fell through the water – often between 10 and 15 feet deep – 'on the drop' as it's known today.

It was also fished with the now more readily available caster, a bait which had been made popular on the River Trent by top-rank match anglers led by Benny Ashurst. What didn't travel simultaneously with the caster was Benny's stick-float tactics.

In the 1970s the block-end feeder, despite calls for it to be banned as 'an infernal machine,' became the method of choice for many LAA anglers, but variations on the Dumpy, fished at maximum catapult range feeding hemp and caster, and in the hands of the South London anglers who started to fish the occasional open match, began exploiting roach shoals that suddenly appeared – or had been there all the time, just not fished for.

Some anglers were so proficient and confident with the style that they formed 'The Team,' a sort of angling version of a supergroup of top anglers from the South-east, which included: John 'The King' McCarthy, Ken Collings, Mick Thill, Billy Hughes, Andy Partridge, and Dick Vetterlein. They entered and won the team event in the 1,000-peg 1971 Trent Championship. This win earned them much respect at a time when the local Nottingham anglers, and Lancashire visitors were winning everything in sight! It was a phenomenal result with catches taken on stick or waggler.

As well as The Team, other South-east match groups began making a mark: Essex County, formed from a base of Roding Valley anglers including Jimmy Randell, Dennis Salmon and Graham Fletcher and ABC (the initials of John Alma, George Butcher and Dickie Carr).

Ken Collings

These anglers travelled far and wide to fish matches all over the country, there being very few opens back then. Around that time I paired up with Peter Burton, in my opinion the best angler ever to come from London. To describe him as a loose cannon would be doing a disservice to cannons. He was a nutcase who didn't care what he did or who he upset, but boy, could he fish. I started travelling and sharing with him in 1970 and we fished together for six or seven years, bouncing ideas about.

I had been a stick float fan for several years even though no decent sticks were available – none worth having anyway – in my local tackle shops. I purchased them via mail order from Tom Watson's in Canal St Nottingham and used them successfully on both LAA matches such as the locally famous knockout 'Shield' competition.

I remember winning the first-ever pegged down match on the famous Crown Fishery on the River Lea in 1977. It was fished to size limits and caster sorted out the bigger roach. Everyone thought it would be a chub match as roving matches were invariably won with bags of chub. I drew badly for chub on the day – peg 4 at the bottom of the stretch, with no far bank cover but, fishing a 6 x no.6 cane and balsa stick down the middle with caster, the chub didn't figure and I came good with seven 'goer' roach for 2lb 14oz.

Often I'd use the stick when other methods would have probably been better, for example in a fierce downstream wind which prevails on the Thames, but it helped me learn the style to a decent level.

Once the restrictive size limits were abolished for matches more anglers came to the river, more opens were organised and the stick float became a very viable tactic. The Thames flow isn't as quick as the Trent and it is a bit deeper on average, so the same floats that worked at, say Burton Joyce, weren't as effective at Kingston, something I learned by increasingly regular sorties to the stick float Mecca, fishing several midweek opens from the famous Nelson pub with some success.

One section of Thames where the stick worked best was the semi-tidal reach between Teddington and Richmond. The full tidal influence is controlled by a lock and weir at Richmond which maintains a navigable depth of water upstream to Teddington. The river rises to maybe 3.5m in two hours or so on a huge tide then falls again at the same speed. That leaves eight hours with the river steady... perfect for a five-hour match. Matches were held fortnightly to prevent the place being hammered and the twice-daily flow kept the fish fit and hungry.

For around fifteen years until the early nineties – before a perfect storm of cormorants, zander, the recovery of perch stocks and sewage discharges saw the dace population plummet, the fishing was remarkable. It was rare not to fill every single swim in the fortnightly 60-pegger on the river – between Petersham Meadow and Eel Pie Island (where the Rolling Stones amongst other honed their craft).

It wasn't everyone's cup of tea as it meant negotiating a

steep, rocky bank to stand knee-deep in waders on the gravel riverbed for the entire match, but the fishing more than compensated, and it was 99 per cent stick float fishing. The amount of boat traffic meant very few summer matches but once the butterflies had gone it was Tidal Time.

My usual target was 120 dace and I knew if I caught that many I'd probably frame, possibly win. Roach sometimes came into play in the early days. I recall drawing next to Andrew Partridge who fished for both Essex County and The Team. Andy liked using plenty of shot and his balsa/porkie quill float took double that of my Watson stick, but we had a battle royal. We both had a single dace but I managed 19 roach, one more than Andy, but his heavier float probably helped him catch bigger fish. He weighed nearly 14lb to my almost 12lb for first and second.

Once the dace took over, though, it was stick all the way. One of my most memorable matches resulted in another second place with 119 dace and a flounder (that Steve Gardener said shouldn't count...) for 27lb 13oz. That was pipped by Steve Sanders with 28-4-0 from a peg above the match length that was put in at the last minute, when it was discovered 61 names were on the entry list! Unbelievably, that was on New Year's Eve 1981.

By now a far greater range of stick floats was available from makers such as Drennan, Ultra Floats and others. Names such as John Allerton, Kevin Ashurst, Pete Warren and Max Winters had their own ranges, all different and all suiting different circumstances. I adapted some of them for the deeper stretches of Thames, my most successful conversion being removing the aluminium stem on an Ashurst model and replacing it with the same material double the length, converting a 6 x no. 4 to a lighter 4 x no. 4 to work the 8-10ft deep swims on the famous Bargewalk section above Kingston Bridge. The float was more stable and definitely went under a lot!

The confidence we gained enabled us Thames anglers to take our stick float skills and beard the lion in its den. Now some of us became regulars at Burton Joyce, Gunthorpe and on the upper Trent around Burton-on-Trent and Swarkestone. I recall travelling through inches of snow with Peter Burton to an invitation match at Bass Island. The river was verging on the nasty with a drop of snow water coming down, and the driving conditions made us late, missing the draw and having to put up with the last two numbers. Luckily for me, I spun for it with Pete and finished up in a decent peg opposite the baths.

Leicester's Stan Piecha, recruited by Ken Giles for the Professionals squad

Fish were coming fairly regularly to my favourite tactic: feeding caster, bronze maggot on the hook, under a stick float of course. They were mostly 'tonkers' (a Thames nickname for big dace), plus a few decent roach and an odd chublet up to 12oz. My 21-6-4 was enough to win but the most exciting part for me was my 'gallery' who drank my tea and offered 'advice.' When I tell you that the crowd, as well as some workers from the brewery, included Stan Piecha, Ivan Marks and David Hall, mickey-takers to a man, you can guess how helpful they were.

The mid-1990s seemed to bring about a decline in float fishing sport on most major match rivers. With the shutting down of power station outflows and the clean-up of sewage outlets, rivers became ultra-clear. Flows seemed to decline at the same time, especially on the Thames, coinciding with the Environment Agency taking over from the old National Rivers Authority.

Amazingly, at virtually the same time, we had the revolution in Sunday Trading, taking thousands of mostly men away from sport as some families were forced to work on what had previously been their fishing day, whilst others decided Sundays were better spent shopping than engaging in sport – *all* sport, not just match fishing by any means.

To top it all off the close season was abolished on most still waters, encouraging the growth of commercial fisheries stuffed with carp that required a completely new set of tackle and stick floats became redundant for Southern match anglers.

However, those of us that love the stick float can find succour in pleasure fishing some of the old haunts, but most of lower Thames sections have sadly lost 80 per cent of their swims to encroaching undergrowth. Sunday riverside parking has also been lost – it costs on average £14 to park in Kingston; there's no free parking any more. Those few matches that survive – at Molesey and below Kingston – are evening affairs dominated by pole and feeder... and big bream. Where 5lb was a decent weight there in the 80s evening matches, it can now take 100lb to win a two and a half-hour match at Kingston!

My Big Three

I've been asked to nominate my top three stick float anglers from London and the South-east and, believe me, it's not an easy task. I've racked my already overworked brain and think I have a trio that would be difficult to argue with. In fact I have two trios: one for the stick, the other for those who fished other floats, usually heavier, 'double-rubber.'

For the stick list, in no particular order, I have two names you will probably know (over a certain age), and one less famous but nonetheless brilliant. I had the privilege of being invited by Ken Collings to fish for his otherwise youthful Banstead team in the late 1980s, along with top rods such as Simon Wheeler, Darren Davies, Paul 'Tommy' Hiller and 'Ginger' Nick Howell. We worked our way up the Nationals and even beat Dorking one famous year in the Surrey Winter League. Ken was a master of small stick floats on rivers such as the Mole and Wey – both Thames tributaries, as well as the Warks. Avon where he made a huge mark. Ken quit fishing several years ago.

The late Mick Thill, aka Capt. America, is in too. Mick fished the stick at long range as well as anyone I've seen, certainly in the South and, despite flitting back and forth between London and the USA where he set up a float making company that exists to this day, was a brilliant angler. He was part of the Trent Champs. Winning team 'The Team' too.

Finally, a lovely man called Keith Speer. Keith hailed from St Albans and passed away on the banks of his favourite upper River Lea. He could virtually make the stick talk and it told a few tales! He fished club matches in the past but adapted his skills to catching big fish and had dace to over 1lb, roach to over 3lb, chub over 7lb and barbel to 17lb, remarkably all on the stick.

As far as the bigger floats were concerned, I'm going for 'King' John McCarthy, who could never be accused of hiding his light under a bushel, but a great mate and wonderful angler. Pat Richardson has to be right up there because it was he, probably more than any other, who changed the way a generation of top anglers fished. He was all-but unbeatable on the Medway. Finally, Chris Love who was simply a master craftsman fishing a float, big or small in a river. Inevitably using caster on the hook, Chris could catch roach from a flowing muddy puddle.

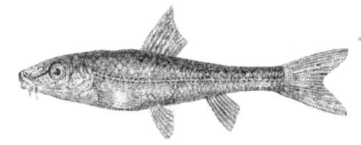

Chapter 38
Stick vs pole interface – why I love the float, any float – Tony Marshall

A friend of a friend describes our subject thus: "He never promotes himself, just quietly goes about his business, but is a good guy and a phenomenal angler." I have yet to meet Tony Marshall in person but, from our few short phone conversations so far, I have no doubt that the compliment fits. Tony, 50, from Mountsorrel, Leics, dedicates himself to fish 100 matches a year. Catching roach on pole and hempseed is his speciality, but he's a bit handy on running line too, and happy to hook a big barbel or carp if one comes along.

Tony has fished with Quorn AC for 30 years, and for 23 of them has been their match team captain, as well as representing Shakespeare Superteam (now Cadence Superteam) for the past 10 years. He has well over 100 open match wins to his credit including several big festival wins on the Trent and Warwickshire Avon, and has shown remarkable consistency this century.

A major change to river fishing in recent years has been the advance of carbon pole technology. Longer and lighter poles can be more easily manipulated with one hand while feeding the swim with the other. Tony has put long hours into perfecting his pole technique on the upper Trent around Burton. The river here is full of character with glides and eddies, and is mostly shallower and streamier than the lower reaches. But his schedule also takes in the wider river all the way downstream to Newark and the tidal stretches beyond, as well as his local Soar and the W. Avon.

While he often fishes his Daiwa Airity pole with a longer line than he would on a lake – up to six sections (7m+) to hand for anywhere deep, with extra sections ready at the rear to thread out as he eases the float downstream, he's just as happy fishing a shorter line on a long pole and shipping down to three or four sections to hand in slow/shallower swims.

Comparing his pole and fixed line method to stick float, Tony, says without a flicker of a boast: "Catching on pole is so easy at times it is almost like cheating." So eat your hearts out, stick float lovers? Well not really, because Tony will also fish a stick beyond his pole line when the swim and conditions demand.

The story below confirms how much Tony puts the accent on finesse with his rigs and his tactics. Though he sometimes feeds groundbait, he's more inclined to loose feed than balling in cereal. In good conditions he might occasionally fish maggot or pinkies with the hemp for roach, but he's also been known to start a match on bread punch as a kind of litmus test for how hungry the fish might be on other baits. Having developed hemp fishing to a fine art, it's been said that he treats its preparation with the care of a Michelin Star chef!

My match apprenticeship began in my teens with club matches on the River Soar with the only tackle I really knew: rod and reel. This posed problems early on, like fishing in a bad downstream wind, for example: potential weights were halved due to bad presentation, and stick float fishing was at times nigh-on impossible. I can recall once having to fish a match with a three-swan waggler but only two rods out on the stick line. Let's just say it didn't work well, but we all have to start somewhere as the saying goes.

Then, with every passing season, the long pole grew more popular as competition within the tackle trade led to gradual improvements in quality. Whilst competing in club matches, I found that anglers with poles greatly enhanced their chances of winning a prize on days with strong wind conditions as their float presentation improved dramatically; it felt almost like they were cheating. Although for a time I had to accept that a good pole was beyond my means, by the nineties I'd saved up enough to buy one and began using it for pleasure fishing and club matches.

I was used to loose feeding and float fishing with rod and line, so continued to feed and fish similarly even though I was using the pole; even to this day I still fish the majority of my matches this way. Over the years I've found a light pole float coupled with styls[18] positioned shirt button-style works best in complementing my loose feed approach.

Regarding pole floats for this style of fishing, for me they are mainly slim-bodied, carbon-stemmed, and have a cane

---

18 The cylindrical leads already described back in Roy Henson chapter

bristle. On slower moving rivers such as the River Soar, Nene and Warwickshire Avon, I found using floats ranging from '4 X 10' up to '4 X 16' best[19], and the lighter the float I could control in the conditions resulted in a superior fish to bite ratio.

In the noughties I began fishing more open matches on the River Trent and, faced with a wider, faster river, I first approached this on the stick float because of the extra flow – the pole limiting the distance which the float can travel downstream.

I wanted my stick floats to be heavy enough to cast well and tried lignum sticks for this reason. They are still my number one choice today. To achieve the required distance, I recommend casting in a loop over your shoulder and from behind (lasso style) and, with practice and perseverance, your hook should land downstream of your float. This needs sufficient room behind you, of course, with no overhanging branches etc; without that you are limited to casting sideways. Another way to gain distance is to fish a fine diameter reel line. I mainly use a good floating 2lb line, sprayed with floating line spray (wind permitting), and would advise spraying the line on the reel spool before threading it through the eyes of the rod.

Tony's sticks

19 i.e. number of styls and size respectively, the latter size equivalent to .5 gram

I like to keep my fishing simple where possible, and what worked years ago for my granddad, dad, and uncles, still works today. They used the shirt button-style of shotting as I do. As for shot size, I only use number 8s, ranging from 6 x no. 8, up to 40 x no. 8 (yes, 40 shots on a heavy stick!) which serves to streamline the cast. Losing or tangling such a well-prepared rig however, almost reduces me to tears, so beware if tempted to try it!

As for the actual stick floats, they range in size from 2 x no. 4 up to 12 x no. 4. But rather than using small shots for my lighter floats (up to 7 x no. 4). I use styls in sizes 9, 10 and 11. When using styls I avoid mixing sizes, but use one size per rig. All my stick rigs are pre-made and kept on winders like the pole rigs.

The chain of styls (or shot) starts with the tell-tale 8" from the hook, with the rest equally spaced towards the float measured by finger widths. A 'two finger' gap is the narrowest at 4 centimetres approx, or three fingers (6cm), up to four finger widths at 8cm. I tend not to move the weights around much throughout a match, only occasionally shuffling them closer together, or spreading them wider apart for a faster or slower drop.

Thinking back to my early Trent stick float matches on the middle Trent, I often fished 7 to 11 feet deep, at a range of three to six rods out, and would start fishing a 5 x no. 4 lignum stick, shotted with 29 x no. 11 styls. This rig led to many enjoyable matches with double figures of fish.

Due to the fact that the Trent flows from west to north-east, with the prevailing westerly wind, it is a river that can suffer from some brutal downstreamers in many sections, and for this reason I started fishing the pole for better presentation. But with my preference for loose feeding and wanting to cover a long distance off my peg, this posed problems. A short, fixed length of line on the pole for instance, means the float has a natural tendency to arc towards the bank once you cannot feed extra line to it, and the fish wise up to a hookbait behaving unnaturally cross-current. To counteract this I have surplus sections of pole attached and gradually ship out more pole to keep the float on track parallel to the bank.

40lb of redfins

Practice taught me that fishing long lines with rigs made up to the top six joints of my pole, and shipping out the extra sections of pole as described, greatly improved the float presentation. This boosted confidence and helped me achieve many 20lb nets of fish topped by a 40lb of roach net that helped me win the three-day Burton Festival at Shardlow in 2014. To attain these big weights I relied on a hemp method, typically using hemp both on the hook and for feeding, and on average I would feed from one and a quarter pints minimum up to two pints.

A common question I get asked is: "How do you hook your hemp?" I use a 16 fine wire hook with a long shank. I pick a grain of hemp that is slightly open with a tiny bit of white kernel showing, put the point of the hook into the kernel, squeeze the grain to open it, then bring the point of the hook through the now open side of the grain. So in effect I am just hooking the kernel. With a gentle strike it will stay on the hook, although it is important not to overcook the hemp or it will become soft and watery resulting in it not gripping on the hook.

But as much as I love fishing hemp with the pole, it is not always the best way to get the most out of the swim. Here are three examples from my Trent matches in 2020 – not once making top spot, but all very enjoyable, combining the pole and stick float.

Three choice matches

1) My first was a busy a match on the upper Trent at Burton: the river here is mainly shallow and weedy with a brisk flow. I started the match on the pole at 11 metres; the pole held two joints-worth of solid number 5 elastic. I potted in one fist-size ball of groundbait with pinkies. I use a short line when potting or using a bait dropper as this is an accurate way of baiting, effectively setting a trap. On this day I used three and a half joints of line to hand.

For this sort of fishing, I use a diamond-shape bodied float with a carbon stem and cane bristle, sizes ranging from 1 – 3 grams. Today's choice was a 1.5g float to 0.12mm main line, with a 0.10mm hook length to a 16 fine wire hook attached. The shotting pattern for this rig was simply a 1 gram olivette plus 8 x no. 8 shot spread two inches apart below the olivette. When bites slowed up on the pole, I potted in another ball of groundbait which improved bites, but after thirty minutes things didn't improve so I changed to the stick float.

I had fed a pinch of maggots regularly from the start of the match slightly downstream and further out than the pole. I then moved onto this line, with a 4 x no. 4 lignum stick shotted shirt button-style with 19 x no. 11 styls, coupled with 2lb reel line (sprayed to keep it floating), a 1lb hook length and a size 16 fine wire hook. The stick was cast between 13 and 18 metres out: so far because the river was shallow and clear.

Knowing how easily the fish can spook in such conditions, my strategy was all about catching a fish in one area then changing to a different area of the peg. When I get a bite, I lift the float out as little as possible; if I feel tension from a fish I continue with the strike, but if there is no tension the float does not move far so I can continue running the float down the peg. This results in a better fish per cast ratio.

When the number of bites declined on the stick, I switched to the pole and potted in a ball of groundbait and pinkies and fished this for a further five minutes. Then when I returned to the stick things had improved. I repeated this process five or six times during the match. With the last hour approaching, bites were diminishing, and I knew I had a good weight in my net. So now I loose-fed pinkies on the stick float line to top up the total and continued catching until the end of the match. Overall, I had a lovely day's fishing and finished with over 180 fish in the net for 18lb, consisting of roach, chub, dace, and perch, to gain runner-up spot in the a 60+ peg match.

Summary: I have no doubt the stick was faster in both casting and catching, also the stick could be fished further out and further down the peg than the long pole. But both methods complemented each other contributing to the end result.

2) The second match was the Newark Trent Championship fished by 90 competitors, upstream and downstream of Newark where the river is deeper and wider than Burton. I drew at Rolleston where I started on the pole at nine metres over the weedy margin, using chopped worm fed via a bait dropper into eight feet of water. For this sort of fishing, I use a round-bodied float with a wire stem and a plastic bristle ranging from 3g to 5g, shotted with an olivette and then number 8 shot below arranged shirt button-style. I sometimes double up number 8 shot on fast pegs. These rigs have a half-inch piece of pole float silicone below the olivette, which enables me to pinch big shot onto the silicone to over-shot my rigs but does not damage the line.

On this day the flow over the weed wasn't too fast so I used a 3g float to four joints length of line, and because this style of fishing can attract big fish – i.e. barbel, carp and occasionally eels, strong line is required, so I used 0.19mm main line to a 0.17mm hook length. Hooks need to be equally strong and size 14's, 12s, 10s are commonly used. To give sufficient cushion, the pole's top set has three joints of solid number 12 elastic inside. The need for the heavy elastic was justified when I was lucky enough to land an 11lb 11oz barbel on the pole, proving what a handy tool the pole is for catching big river fish. This specimen contributed hugely to me winning the Drennan Coors 2020 Final.

But back to Rolleston, over the first thirty minutes I fished the pole for ten perch, but then decided a better option was to fish further out. I changed to a 10 x no. 4 lignum stick cast 20 metres out and at times a rod-length beyond. I fished this way for the remainder of the match, again with the shirt button-style shotting of 40 x no. 8 shots and using the reliable 2lb reel line, 1lb hook length and a 16 fine wire hook.

I was fortunate to have a very kind wind blowing from behind which enabled me to loose feed to the float. Straining to fire bait out in an unfavourable wind can leave the feed falling short, a pile of broken catapults and, at worst, blood pouring from knuckles resembling more of a boxing match than a fishing match! But today it was possible to reach the target zone throughout the match with half a pouchful of bait, alternating between maggot, caster and hemp.

The peg was about eleven feet deep. I adjusted the float depth up and down with the hook going no higher than two feet off the bottom. I cannot stress enough the importance of constantly adjusting the depth, also experimenting with different baits and quantities. No two days are the same, and in this match I found that feeding only maggot later on proved the most successful.

All told, I had a good day's fishing and put over 170 fish in the net for 14lb, consisting of mainly roach, dace, and perch, which earned me third prize, only being beaten by two all-barbel 'plastic pig' feeder weights (dare I say, not *proper* fishing?).

Summary: I only really used the pole in the beginning to get some early fish whilst loose feeding the peg, before moving on to the stick float.

3) The third match was my last Trent open of the season in late October. This was again on the Trent below Newark, and the river was carrying four inches of extra water, but was not that badly coloured. I was faced with ten feet of water with a brisk flow and drawn in a good area for chub. So I tackled up with 3½lb reel line and a 2½lb hooklength to a strong 14s hook. Float was a 7 x no. 4 lignum stick, shotted shirt button-style with 24 x no. 8 shot. I fished between 13 and 18 metres out and worked my way through three pints of loose-fed maggots and a pint of casters.

Overall, I had a great day, even ending with an aching arm, taking six chub, the biggest at 5lb 11oz, three barbel weighing between 6lb and 8lb, and a handful of roach and dace. The finishing weight was 41lb to take second in the match. I remember the weight of the biggest chub because the club put a special cash prize for the biggest chub caught on the day, which I won. How lucky was that?

Summary: when fishing in rocky, snaggy, pegs, it's often easier to land big fish on the float because you are not tethered to a big bomb or swimfeeder that assists the fish to stay deep and close to danger, so using the stick on these quality fish I had no serious trouble.

I'll close by saying that fishing rivers with either a pole and a fixed line *or* a stick float with rod and running line, and keeping busy with regular loose feed, is at times hard work but is enjoyable and so often rewarding at the same time. So whether you fish for pleasure or in matches, give the float a go. Tight Lines.

Chapter 39
My approach to stick float – Alan Barnes

Alan with a specimen 2-8 Ribble roach caught on hemp

Angling journalist Alan Barnes managed to catch a number of specimen roach in a 19-month purple patch on his local, and beloved, River Ribble around Preston. He caught eight 2lb-plus roach up to January 2017, five of them on the stick, two on waggler and one on a link-leger. His personal best Ribble roach scaled 2lb 8oz, a rare creature for waters in the North of England. These results came with a number of fish just shy of the magical 2lb mark. Knowing Alan to be such a stick float fan we needed to ask him to elucidate on his method.

Stick float fishing is one of the most rewarding and magical styles of float fishing you can ever experience – and one I have been working on for almost 45 years. Most people associate the Preston area with canal fishing and, in particular, people like Dave Roper and the Lancaster Canal. The Izaak Walton (Preston) side was an emerging team in the mid to late 1970s when the canal match circuit was thriving in the North West, just as it is, I am delighted to say, once again today.

But being aged 14 and with no prospect of a lift to the canal – a good five or six miles from my house – it was a case of getting on the old pushbike and fishing wherever was nearest to home. And the Ribble, I joyfully discovered, was rammed with quality fish – big roach, chub and dace – all of which liked maggots and my local Elston Lane stretch was only three miles away, a ten-minute bike ride at most. It was there in August 1977 where I first cast out a stick float in anger. I caught three tiny chub, all about an ounce apiece. Utterly clueless – no gear, no idea! On my second trip, on a flooded river in the October of that year, I caught a roach that must have been at least a pound and a half using a Peter Drennan 7 x no. 4 cane-stemmed stick I had bought a day earlier. The love affair had begun.

Fortunately for me, my local length of river attracted high-calibre river anglers from the Manchester area. People like Tony Simcock and Steve Roach, plus another fantastic float angler called Keith Tomlinson, who now lives in Australia. They were all friendly, good-humoured guys who fast-tracked my understanding of stick float fishing as they had all fished on the Trent Open circuit. They showed me the right rods, floats, shotting patterns, hooks and the need for top quality bait. The trade-off was that they could ring me to find out the river level and, if it was looking promising, they'd travel over to fish and I would watch, listen and learn.

In this way I soon saw that catching roach on the stick requires a bit more finesse than when targeting dace or chub and understanding the behaviour of roach is all important.

Location

Success with roach depends on a variety of factors: water temperature, water clarity, pace of the river, light levels, even water quality. But what is an absolute certainty is that you will not catch big roach if you are not fishing where they live. On the Ribble in the Preston area I can safely name three hotspots in a mile and a half length where you may catch a 2lb roach if it is your lucky day. But fish fifty yards from any of these hotspots and your chances are drastically reduced. The fact is that big roach are creatures of habit and tend to show in the same swims time after time and often in the company of other species.

The fact that so many big Ribble roach get caught in darkness on 14mm boilies used by barbel anglers backs up that theory. Big roach can also be aggressive. They will bully smaller roach out of the way when they decide they want to feed, and will come high in the water to intercept those free offerings, climbing the trail of feed almost to the point where it is hitting the water. I have had days on the Ribble when big roach have fed like this and the rod has been virtually wrenched from my hand when they have hit the hookbait on the drop. Conversely, roach can be incredibly hard to catch when the water is clear and the sun shining and super fine tackle becomes essential.

Another 'redfin' trait that I have picked up on over the years is how, when the shoal numbers start to dwindle, they will become wary, often hanging just off the main feed area, maybe 10 yards further out to mid-river. The bigger roach will often sit at the bottom end of your peg, happy to intercept the odd maggot or caster that washes down to them past the main shoal of smaller fish competing higher up the swim.

Good Presentation Is Everything
I firmly believe that the best stick float anglers always worked out how the roach wanted to feed and then imitated the rate at which their loose-fed maggots dropped through the water.

The late, great Clive Smith once wrote of a contest on the Severn at Stourport in which he caught 37lb 8oz of roach on caster over hemp. Describing that particular match, Clive observed that it took half an hour to catch a fish and a further half-hour to work out the contours of the swim, allowing him to adjust the rig so that he was putting the float through almost three feet overdepth (eight feet deep in five feet of water). This was achieved primarily through correct choice of float, the shotting pattern and how the line was controlled so as to inch the float through the peg. Clive placed 1 x no. 10 shot ten inches from the hook, with 1 x no. 8 just above that, and the largest shot used was a no. 6 (this was prior to the lead ban on sizes bigger than an 8).

Presentation is everything. Some pegs require a 4-gramme capacity (20 x no. 4 stick), others you can fish with an 8 x no. 8 stick shotted with a fine string of no. 11s, 10s and 9s. The evidence for the above is perhaps best provided by describing some of my more memorable days.

Making Light of it at Burton Joyce

It was June 1993 and I put a call in to Terry Dorman's tackle shop and he told me to head for the famous Roadside stretch at Burton Joyce, where anglers had been catching some roach despite it being so early in the season.

I found a peg I liked the look of and set up two identical 13ft rods with matching closed face reels and with identical main line (Bayer 1.7lb) and hook lengths of .010mm Force, finished off on each with a size 24 B510 barbless hook. Any barb, however small, tends to cause a blob of liquid to ooze from the bait which may be enough to shy away from it.

John Dean 'Stabilizers' for turbulent water, and two slimmer wires

The swim I had chosen was approximately 5½ feet deep a rod-length and a half out from the bank. On one rod I tackled up an original Pete Warren 5 x no. 4 stick, shotted shirt button-style, starting with a single no. 10 nearest the hook, then 2 x no. 10s together, then 8s up to the float. The second rod was tackled up with an original 8 x no. 8 pointed top, John Dean wire stem model. This had 1 x no. 11 nearest the hook and the rest of the shot comprised more 11s, and 10s, shirt-buttoned up to the float.

After fifteen minutes using the Peter Warren model I netted a roach. But then nothing for the next twenty minutes, not a dink, not a chewed maggot. Yet the peg was screaming fish. It was a real puzzle.

I reached for the other rod with the much lighter John Dean wire stem stick on it and flicked it out to run down the exact same line. It only went four yards, buried, and there was that satisfying clunk as a quality roach turned flank-on in the current. For the next half hour it was a roach a cast, then I decided to try the rod carrying the Warren float again. Nothing. Eight trots later, still nothing.

A change back to the John Dean stick float resulted in ten roach in ten trots. Switching back to the rod carrying the heavier-shotted dome-topped Warren pattern. Nothing again. So the lesson learned was that the fish wanted the hookbait to match the speed at which the loose feed dropped through the water. The lighter rig with no.11s and 10s worked a treat. The slightly heavier rig with no. 8s did not.

Fine Margins count

In his heyday at Burton Joyce, legendary Barnsley Black, John Allerton, used tiny hooks whilst fishing caster hookbait. When asked why he used such small hooks, John said that while he lost the odd fish by fishing with a size 24, it did not matter because he was getting three times more bites than rivals using sizes 18 or 20. More bites, more fish in the net, bigger weights than your rivals. When you look at it this way it seems perfectly logical, and no one could argue with his match record. If I needed a reminder of the importance of fine line and small hooks, it was brought home to me a few weeks after my red letter day at Burton Joyce, when I returned to the Roadside length again. I was fishing with a friend who was a bagging specialist but who refused to drop below .10mm hooklengths and a size 18 medium wire hook. He also used a 5 x no. 4 stick, shotted with 8s bar 1 x no. 10 nearest the hook.

My approach was finer: a 1.5lb main line an 8 x no. 8 John Dean wire stem model with a fine pointed tip and no.10s and 11s shot only. The hooklength was a piece of .06mm Ignesti

Special to a Tubertini size 24 2T hook. This is a tiny and very light hook but also quite strong.

On that second trip to the Roadside at Burton Joyce I caught 14lb of big roach. It wasn't easy and required hard work and real perseverance, but I'd get a bite every fifteen minutes or so. Those roach were averaging 12oz to 14oz. Meanwhile, in the next peg my pal who refused to fine down, blanked.

The Heavy Approach
Fishing light, however, is not always the answer. I once fished a match on the Nene where I drew a deep peg on the length near Thorpe Wood Golf Course. It was 11ft off the rod end and 14ft deep two rods out. The roach, however, wanted to sit down the middle of the river. That day I was horribly ill-equipped: my 13ft rod was not long enough and the biggest float I had in my kit at the time – a 9 x no. 4 lignum – was too light to make the hookbait 'work' for the majority of the length of the swim. I weighed in 5lb-odd for nowhere and knew I had not done the peg justice.

Back at HQ after the match I sat down with Trent legend Wayne Swinscoe for a pint to talk through our matches and quiz him about what he had done. He had drawn above Orton Staunch and his peg was seven feet deep. He explained that after starting on a 5 x no. 4 stick with a light shotting pattern, he made a decision in mid-match to swap it for a 7 x no. 4 model, basically giving the fish 1 x no. 4 shot per foot of water. It proved a clever move and he ended up framing with 10lb-plus.

Armed with this information I bought some 14 x no. 4 and 12 x no. 4, cane-stemmed MAP sticks that Dave Harrell had designed, coupled with a 14ft spliced tip rod. I decided this would be my approach if confronted with a similar deep water situation again.

Ironically enough the following week we had an inter-departmental match between the various angling publications produced by EMAP, on the very same length of the Nene. Our trio of Richard Lee, Andrew James and myself won the team trophy that day and I was second in the match with around 150 small roach for 8lb-odd. I drew within 30 yards of the peg I had fished on the PDAA Open where I caught 5lb, so I knew what I was facing, depth-wise.

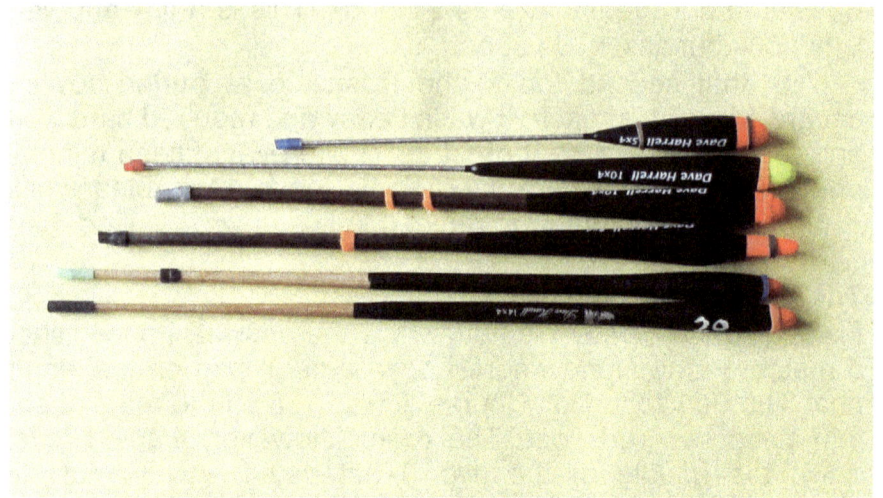

The Dave Harrell brand of big sticks. Boosted by his own successes and reputation as a class river angler, Dave cornered the market for heavy sticks with fatter tips to suit powerful rivers like the Severn and Wye. Wire, lignum and light cane stems shown here

Remembering Swinno's advice, this time I placed the bulk of shot at just below half-depth, then several groups of 2 x no. 8s tapering down to no. 10s, a .06mm Ignesti Special hooklength and a size 24 Tubertini Series 2T. The float went in like a bag of washing with that bulk arrangement just below half-depth. But importantly, with so much weight down the line, it sat down immediately, allowing the business end of the rig to cover a much greater part of the peg more efficiently and bringing bites pretty much every run down. Nowadays we might use an olivette instead of a big bulk of shot, but at that time the really big sticks were only just arriving on the scene.

One week later we had an Angling Times East Midlands Winter League round, in that same area of the Nene. At the time I was fishing with Sensas Mark One, and when our skipper, John Bates, passed me my peg ticket I was happy to find I was pretty much on the peg I'd drawn in the EMAP group match. Suffice to say I used the same approach, catching for the whole five hours and putting 10lb on the scales to win the section and do my job for the team. All of which is why I think it important to cover your options with a minimum of two stick float rods on a match: one with a lighter set-up, the other with a heavier one. Only by trial and error will you discover which one works best.

Sticks of choice

Pointed Top, Light Cane stem

For light shotting and summer 'on the drop' fishing, I like cane-stemmed models, preferably with a fine pointed top. With this type of stick I am not usually tripping the bottom so there is no need for a buoyant domed top. MAP used to make a model years ago and I have included one in the picture to illustrate the point. I tend to use these floats in slow flowing water where the fish are watching everything as the hookbait drops through the water. I like using this float particularly with caster or hemp hookbait. Why light, slim cane? Because it cocks gradually and this is perfect for laying the rig out and not having the float sit straight down, as it would if you used a wire or alloy stem model. These delicate floats allow wonderful, on-the-drop presentation.

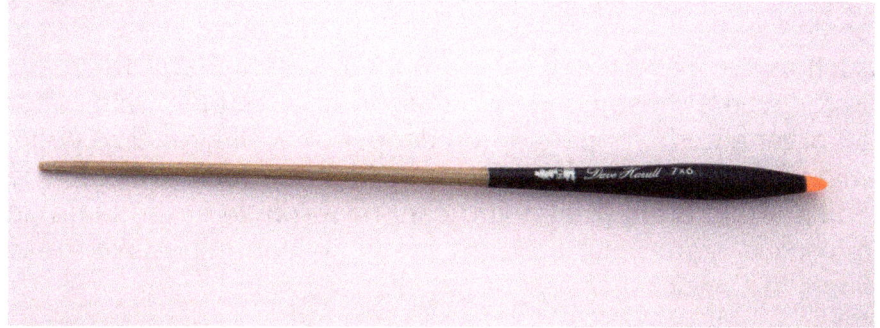

Standard Dome-topped Cane stem

For general work tripping bottom, I prefer a dome-topped cane-stemmed, balsa bodied float, or a balsa bodied wire stem stick. If the water is even, without boils, I tend to opt for something like an original Pete Warren. These floats are the best ever made in my opinion. The dimensions, the balance and fulcrum or pivot point, between the cane and balsa, is spot-on, and they behave so well. I carry these in sizes from 2 x no. 4 up to 14 x no. 4.

Lignum stem

There is still very much a place in my box for 'ligs,' especially when the wind is awkward and you need to fish some distance out. The beauty of lignums, apart from the fact they enable you to cast effortlessly up to four or five rods out, is the density in the lignum wood means the float does not get pushed off line by the wind if it is gusting and picking your reel line from the water surface. Presentation is everything. I carry these from 4 x no. 4 up to 16 x no. 4.

<u>Wire stem</u>
More and more I am inclined to think that if I could only have one pattern of stick in my box, this would be it. I like the fact the slim wire cuts through the water effortlessly, providing stability and sensitivity. Again, because the stem is wire, it does not get buffeted about by the wind or the current like a float with a less dense material such as cane. I carry wire stem models in sizes from 8 x no. 8 up to 12 x no. 4.

<u>Alloy stem</u>
I love these sticks, in particular simple dome-topped, balsa bodied pattern with a reasonable gauge alloy stem. Rivers such as the Severn and Wye are the types of river with 'heavy water' where these come into their own. I use them with either an olivette and droppers or, on deep, powerful even flow pegs, with a lot of strung bunches of no.8s from hook to float. The dome top is great in that you can 'hang on' to it, the large tip making a great pivot point on the float. You can make these floats talk back to you.

<u>Wire Stem Avons and Alloy Stem Avons:</u>
Wire Avons are truly excellent and in boily pegs they behave superbly. I tend to use them with an olivette and droppers and I have had many big catches of roach using them. They are especially suited to powerful rivers such as the Trent, Severn, Wye and Ribble.

Presentation
Let's look at how I make the float go through the peg. There are no hard or fast rules. On some days you can let the float go through at the pace of the current, but on others you need to slow it down. Nine times out of ten I will use back-shot on my rigs, whether they are no 10s, no 8s or 2 x no. 8s together.

There are different techniques that can be used to ensure the smooth passage of the float down the swim. You can let line off the reel then trap it against the spool and 'follow' the float down the peg with a fixed amount of line from rod tip to float, before releasing more line and repeating the process. You can also use a very heavy float and slow it down by virtue of the shotting down the line, or you can back-wind a float down the peg. John Allerton famously did this with his old Mitchell Match reels many years ago – and there is no doubt that back-winding does work. Many Severn and Wye anglers employ the back-winding technique to put heavy Bolo' floats through the peg to devastating effect.

With closed-face reels you can gently peel line from the reel and ease it through the rod's butt ring, controlling the float and slowing it down slightly in this way. This again is a very effective technique which, on its day, can tempt bites when other styles of trotting presentation do not.

Finally, you can employ a centrepin reel. On its day it can still be unbeatable. Not perhaps in a fish-catching race like dace matches on the Severn and Wye when it is far too slow a method in terms of the speed of retrieve, but certainly on days when bites are at a premium and presentation is going to make a vital difference. There is absolutely no question that the centrepin can put a float though a peg in a way that cannot be mimicked by a fixed spool reel. Ask Dave Thomas. That's how he won his World championship title on a difficult, flooded Warwickshire Avon in 1981.

Feeding
This is the final piece of the jigsaw and as important as getting the presentation right. In my opinion the two go together. Golden rule No.1 – Do your utmost to find out how the fish are feeding: are they coming up in the water, are they staying well down the peg and on the bottom, can you catch them by holding back hard, can you only catch them by running the float through at the pace of the current? And then feed accordingly.

Golden Rule No 2 – Be flexible in your thinking. Sometimes, in fast shallow water, you need to feed upstream to get loose feed down in front of you, or you may have to use a bait dropper to get the bait down on deeper, boily pegs. But if you think it, just do it. Your angling sixth sense is often right.

What makes the stick special?

Why do I love the stick float? It comes down to the art of fishing it. The sideways cast, laying the rig out in a straight line, watching the float as the shot drop through the layers, and the anticipation as the float progresses to the hot spot in the peg. The 'dink' of an enquiry... and the float vanishing. The satisfying 'kerlunk' as the rod tip contacts the fish. Seeing the float as it comes off the water, the jig-jag of a big roach, the powerful runs of a barbel. You see it all on the stick. It's such a skill, such a delight to use and so deadly on the right day.

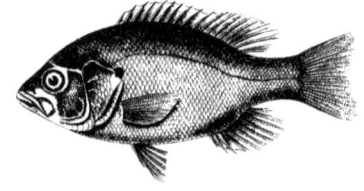

Chapter 40
Stick in Yorkshire – Chris Burton

If you are the type of angler who thinks a centrepin reel is old-fashioned then you might not want to talk fishing with Chris Burton for long. The Tadcaster angler is one of the pin's greatest advocates and has used it to win matches on both his local River Ouse and Trent including winning the Ouse Championship with 16lb of roach. For fun pleasure days, Chris recalls the tidal Wharfe when it was full of roach. He remembers how he could fish peg 24 East Side and for three seasons would catch between 20lb and 30lb every time.

Chris's best roach is a 2lb 1½oz specimen from the tidal Wharfe. His biggest ever fish is a 19lb pike, while his best catches have come from Holland – bream nets to 200lb. Another highlight was winning his local club's centenary match in 1987 with 11lb of dace on stick and pin. He also rates winning a centrepin in a float-only match on the Trent embankment with a hard-earned 8lb-plus as special. A memorable near miss came at Burton Joyce when he weighed 28lb of roach from the roadside. Just as his weight was announced by the scalesman, Frank Barlow arrived and said he wouldn't win, and "it was all wrong because someone near the outfall had thrown out a plastic thing, which was not f...... fishing, and should be banned." Sure enough he was beaten by Robin Grouse with 35lb! Chris, now a veteran of 71, looks back at that match with a smile as it heralded the start of the Trent's feeder revolution, and though not to Chris's taste, the method remains unbeatable at times.

I have fished top and bottom floats for most of my life, on all the main Yorkshire rivers, big matches on the Trent and beyond. From early sorties with plastic chubbers, I moved on to crow quills with small cork bodies, then porkies (porcupine quills) and finally stick floats in various forms.

Initially on the Trent I used the original Benny Ashurst sticks – one of 6 x no. 4 size and another of 2½ x BB. I then progressed to the John Dean sticks with the black plastic stem and domed top in 5 x no. 4's size, but modified the top by creating a small shoulder. Also, I used the John Allerton alloy stems in 7 and 8 x no. 4's, and for very light work a Dick Clegg cane stem of 4 x no. 4's with a modified top. If conditions were bad or I needed to fish further out I'd switch to a 7 x no. 4 Ultra lignum. These floats were my weapons of choice back in the Trent's heyday, but in recent years I've moved on.

My biggest change now is that nearly all the sticks I use have alloy stems and large tops with a shoulder. I like these when the Wharfe is pushing through in winter and I fish overdepth. The larger top allows shot to be dragged along the bottom smoothly without going under all the time like floats with thinner tops.

Despite the thicker tops I seem to be able to read the bites better which led to fewer bumped fish. I used to make my own but no longer need to as there are some very good – almost identical brands – available in the tackle shops.

John Dean's iconic plastic stems with domed and pointed tips, the grey one marked up to take 10 x no. 6

Influences

My early lessons on fishing stick float style were given to me by Brian Mallory, a local angler who showed me how to use porkies and how to tie spade end hooks to nylon. A few years

264

older than myself, Brian had already left school and, working as an apprentice, could afford to buy plenty of maggots. In those days over a pint was a lot, and he would give me some of what he had left after his weekend match. This allowed me to fish for dace and roach, rather than catching mainly chub, perch, eels and flounders on natural baits.

The next stage of my development came when I started working in Leeds and met Stuart Thompson in Kendall and Watson's fishing tackle shop. Later Stu took me for my first visit to the Trent and invited me to fish with Dene AC, a team which included Dave Thomas, Stan Haigh, Tim Harrison, and other top Leeds youngsters who all did a lot of stick float fishing. I had no direct mentor but was lucky enough to meet and chat to the talented John Allerton, Dave Thomas and Yorkshire legend, John Illingworth, all of whom gave me good advice.

My favourite venues have always involved roach fishing, with some dace at times, starting with the Burton Joyce/Gunthorpe Saturday opens, then opens at North Muskham, on the Wharfe at Smaws Ings, and now parts of the Calder at Altofts, the lower Aire and Ouse at Linton/Hunters Lodge. All these local venues respond well to my stick float and centrepin approach.

In spite of taking on board all the advice offered by greats like Jan Porter, John Dean, Wayne Swinscoe and Kenny Kendall, I like to think I have developed my own style. I do obviously listen and talk to other anglers after matches, however: analysing how they have caught, and trying to gauge if they are doing things differently, and how I might use it in the way I fish.

I'll now describe some of my favourite haunts:

River Wharfe

Although I very much prefer roach fishing, I have no local venues where they can be caught in summer, so I go to Ulleskelf where dace are the predominant silver fish, but a lot of matches are now won with big fish – mainly barbel with some bream and chub.

My 2016 season was very good and I averaged 7lb of silver fish over the matches fished, winning one with 13lb of silvers. I could not match this in 2017, however, only catching silvers in two matches with every match dominated by barbel. I usually feed about 1 pint of maggots for 7lb of dace plus a few roach, using a 4 or 5 x no. 6 stick float, shotted in the classic shirt button style with my first shot usually set fifteen inches from the hook. I mostly start with a 20 hook to 0.14mm line which gives me a chance if I hook a barbel, but if the dace become difficult will soon drop down to a .10mm. I always start at full depth, but with my light shotting I often catch at the start on the drop at the top of the peg and, taking a leaf out of the old master Kenny Kendall's book, I will lay the rig out upstream and hold it into the feed, before the dace drop down the peg, at which point I fish conventionally by casting the float downstream.[20]

The Aire & Calder

Because the Lower River Aire is mostly a very deep water, I usually carry two twenty-foot rods, two of seventeen feet, and one of fifteen feet for waggler fishing. One of my rods will always have my trusty centrepin on and the lightest float I feel I can use on the day, which is usually a 10 or 12 x no. 4. Until recently I always loose fed with hemp and maggots slightly downstream. This approach, even with the depths involved, is helped by the fact that most pegs are thirty yards long, offering a far longer trot that the standard eighteen yards at Burton Joyce for example. However, as a lot of matches are now being won on the long whip – eight metres to hand, or pole, over large amounts of groundbait, I have now started introducing four balls on my float line at the start. This seems to get me bites quicker than building the swim up and has resulted in me catching some fish initially above the feed. I do not know why this is, but gratefully accept that it happens.

Just like on the Aire, the whip/pole to hand method has also been used by many anglers on the Calder, and is a fast method. I do not use the whip to any extent, always trying with my sticks to catch a better stamp of fish. It does allow me to cover more of my peg which I think at times is an advantage.

---

20 See Mick Hughes' chapter for more

Favourite Sticks

As mentioned earlier, I like alloy-stemmed floats in sizes 4 x no. 4 right up to 16 x no. 4, though occasionally use cane stems of 4 or 5 x no. 4 in water up to seven feet deep if I want a slower fall of the bait. This enables the float to cock in line with the shots as they descend, rather than forming an angle between the bottom of the float and the rig below which I believe, in shallow water, allows the fish to feel the stem and reject the bait prior to registering a bite on the drop.

Sometimes on the Wharfe I use a small wire stem taking 5 x no. 8 when the dace are difficult to catch, but more often a shouldered alloy of 5 to 7 x no. 4. On the Calder the float size varies between 6 x no. 4 and 12 x no. 4 depending on the depth. On the Aire it is usually 10 x no. 4 to 16 x no. 4. If I had to use one type of stick float it would be a shouldered alloy stem carrying between 8 and 12 x no. 4 which seems the correct size range on the venues where I currently catch roach. If the bites are shy, I will, as Dave Thomas says, put on extra shot until I can see the bites. However, with the thicker tops I use, I seem to be able to read the bites better, and at times this results in me catching fish without the float going under.

The Pin

Using the centrepin is the thing I am best known for. In my opinion the reel gives far better control as you never have any excess line and it is always direct to the float. It is easy to stop and start the trot as required in order to find how fast the fish require the bait presented on the day.

Other than in very shallow water I always like to back-shot my sticks irrespective of conditions. If conditions are very bad I'll sometimes use two shot. I do not spray my line with any floatant or other treatment, having always found a good floating line which I change when it gets old and starts to sink. As for keeping rigs tidy, I always mount my stick rigs on winders now, and do not know how I set everything up and started on time before I did so. These days even with the benefit of winders I am not always ready when time's called!

Ninety per cent of my summer fishing is done with red and white maggots and hemp then, as temperatures fall, I switch to bronze and red with a few fluoro' maggots for a change of colour. If dace are the main target I'll try and obtain some yellow maggots but this is not always possible. When roach usually start feeding well in late summer, bronze maggot becomes my main bait. And if ever chub are likely to show up anywhere, I'll feed hemp and caster and fish caster or red maggot on the hook.

Changing times

I feel that very little has changed in shotting and feeding over the last thirty years as these were always adapted to the

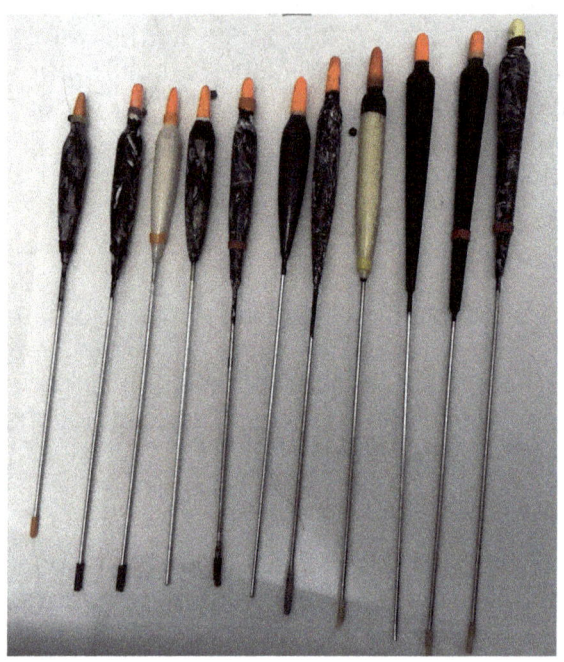

conditions and number of fish/weight required. The main changes to my style have been in the float size I now use due to the depth of my local rivers – Ouse and Aire for roach venues in particular. On the Trent it was very rare for me to use a float over 7 x no. 4, but now they are from 10 to 16 x no. 4 (see photo) Also, there seems to be no need to use the 24s any more, with a 22 being the smallest I use and usually my starter hook is a 20.

The most significant change for me has been the availability of long rods, especially the lightness and quality of 17-foot and 20-footers, which aid control, and I wonder how much more we may have caught at Burton Joyce with seventeen-foot rods. The other development which helps is low diameter line which floats very well and allows hooks to be tied to very thin line with no loss of strength.

Main rivals

Who do I rate as the best stick anglers? I think few would disagree that when the Trent was at its peak it produced some exceptional anglers. I'd have to name John Allerton, John Dean and Dave Thomas as stand-outs, but sadly, not one of them still fishes river matches. So I'll select three others from the Trent's big match era: Pete Warren who was about the only caster man able to compete with Dave Thomas's maggots. Pete Palmer, who gave me the best tip at Burton Joyce when I came back after one of the earliest matches I fished, complaining about the number of gudgeon I had caught: "Keep shallowing up six inches at a time until you catch no more." It was alien to me at that time to fish off the bottom as nearly all my fishing was done overdepth. Finally, Keith Hobson, the waggler man, who at Burton Joyce also won a lot of matches, fishing his favourite John Dean 6 x no. 4 pointed top, plastic stem stick. But there are many other good anglers around today. If I had to name a local angler to catch a fish to save my life on current form, I'd go for Dave Armitage. He has been consistent on the Yorkshire circuit for many years now.

Other Methods

Considering the depth of some of my local rivers I mostly avoid slider fishing and cannot say I have ever mastered it. I think I have an aversion to too much lead. Years ago I did use 5 x BB size sliders above our local weir in one or two deep pegs for dace, but found they did not hold onto the lead in a bulk, so I spread the shot out and found that sliding from about twelve feet proved lots better. I have neither really used the Bolo' float much, or hardly until last autumn on my long rod. I did try a 4g Bolo' with an olivette and 2 x no. 8 droppers, with maggot over groundbait. The river was up and I caught 10lb of roach. Sadly, I could not manage to repeat the performance despite two more tries.

Pointers for the beginner to river fishing and matches:

1) Learn the pin reel. I use my pin a lot which I believe helps me vary my float control more than other reels and therefore hopefully helps me catch a better stamp of fish.

2) Shot lightly near the hook. I always shot my floats very

lightly in the bottom quarter of the set depth, using in most cases 3 x no. 11's starting with the tell-tale no. 11 placed fifteen inches from the hook, 3 x no. 10's above those, then enough no. 8s to fully cock the float working upwards to the float. I believe this gives a more natural presentation.

3) Never give up on a swim as rivers are always changing and experience shows that you can win/frame in the last two hours with quality roach.

4) Ensure your stick bosses the conditions. Make sure the float you use is heavy enough to reach where you wish to fish, that you can control the float at that distance, and that it takes enough shot for the river's depth.

5) Never be afraid to put a back shot on above the float to help control.

6) Always use a floating line as it also makes float control so much easier.

7) Locate the fish by trial and error, noting that the stick can explore more of the peg than anglers using a whip or pole on rivers.

The Interrogator
Chris and match colleague Mick Hughes travelled together to Burton Joyce many times in the eighties and nineties to fish the popular Saturday winter opens. One day Mick caught 23lb of chub to win the match and Chris had also done well so naturally, as the happy duo set off on the drive home the match inquest naturally began. Chris wanted to know all about Mick's approach, which his pal revealed down to the smallest detail. The following week Chris won the match with 23lb, but when homeward bound he was again picking Mick's brains. Suddenly Mick stopped him: "Hang on a sec Chris, *you* have won with roach today, so how did *you* do it?"

"Maggot," was Chris's reply.

"On what rig?"

"Well I had three set up…"

Mick pressed hard but Chris (well known for keeping his cards close to his chest) kept his answers vague. Mick was laughing about it for weeks after, and tagged his mate with the above title. They remain close friends and still fish regularly together.

Chapter 41
Chub Bonanza and an Aire record
– Nick Chaffer

Nick Chaffer, from Bingley, is a marketing consultant for Selby-based bait and tackle company Willy Worms, but he grew up in a world where maggots for river fishing were in far greater demand than worms, and before any modern commercial carp waters had been created. Nick, now 66, was taught how to fish a stick float by team colleague, Roger Patrick whose claim to fame was winning the Woodbine Final in Denmark in the early years of the competition that evolved into the Embassy Challenge. He was also influenced by Bradford team man, Alan Tremethick who won the final two years later. These days Nick fishes venues like Linton on the Yorkshire Ouse with the Drake range of alum-based stick floats in all sizes up to 4.5 gram, targeting roach and dace in swims sixteen to twenty feet deep. But back in 1989, using a small stick in a shallower swim on the upper River Aire, Nick made an outstanding catch to set a match record that still stands to this day...

The details of the day, method, match and catch are still as clear in my head as the day it happened in 1989. The river was fining off nicely after carrying water most of the week, it had a tinge of colour and just the right pace. There was little or no breeze and it was cloudy and overcast – perfect in fact for the Keighley Open. I knew the peg drawn was good for a decent net and had won a match three weeks prior from three or four swims upstream with a near 30lb catch.

The River Aire here, just below Kildwick, is no more than fifteen yards wide and around 8ft deep, shallowing slightly towards the end of a thirty-yard run when it turns sharply right over some shallows. It was just a simple case of running a stick right down the middle in the deepest water.

My favourite rod at that time was a Bruce and Walker 13ft XLT which had a spliced tip allowing the use of lighter hook length, but plenty of power too to subdue the hard fighting chub. My choice of reel was the same as I still use today, a trusty Mitchell Match loaded with 2.6 lb Waterqueen 'Special Anglaise' line.

On the day I started with a 4 x no. 4 lignum stick and a Mustad 90340 barbless 21 (20) hook on 1½lb hooklength of the same line. The float was made for me by an old friend, Charlie Makaitis, who had settled in Yorkshire as a Polish refugee. He put a lovely wedge-shaped taper on all his lignums and made a seamless joint where the balsa met the base. They cocked nicely, shotting tangles were rare, and he made them as small as 3 and 4 x no. 10 sizes for very shallow water.

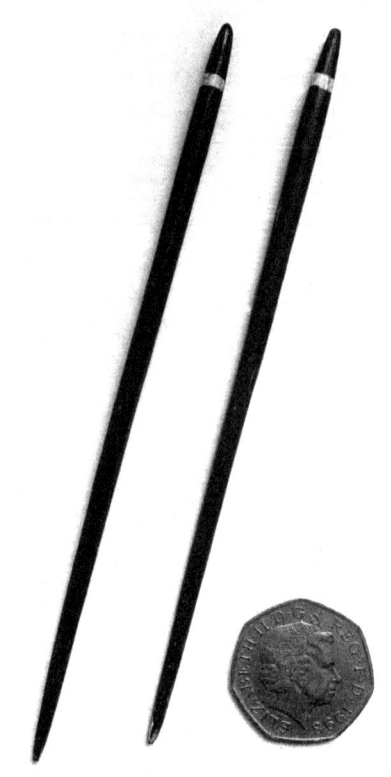

Makaitis lignum sticks

Due to the narrowness of the river I always made a point of sitting down on this stretch and using a catapult to feed. I felt this was important in avoiding spooking the fish instead of standing and waving my arms about throwing maggots into the swim. The first fish came along after about half an hour but, with the swim seemingly full of minnows, I began to feed more heavily with hempseed and maggots. My usual bait supply for an Aire match back then was four pints of maggot and a couple of pints of hemp.

Shirt button shotting was the order of the day with 2 x no. 6's and 6 x no. 8's evenly spaced, then 2 x no. 9's nearest the hook. After starting at full depth it was not long before I was able to shallow up and catch six to eight inches off the bottom.

A good hour into the match my swim was solid and I was

catching a chub almost every run down, ranging in size from 12oz to 3lb-plus. By now I'd stepped up to double maggot on the hook. I remember thinking 'this will not last much longer,' but it did, and by the end of the second hour I had about a dozen chub and they were moving up the swim and taking my hookbait within eight yards or so of the float settling.

This swim shallows up near its downstream limit twenty yards below me, at which point I'd normally hold back hard to trot a few more yards, but today this was not necessary: it was more a case of holding back then releasing the float towards the closer hotspot.

I then lost two in two chucks which I thought were foul-hooked and, after netting two of around 1lb apiece, I was then broken for the first time in the match. With an estimated thirty pounds already in my net, I scaled up to a 90340 19 (18) straight through and continued to catch chub after chub sometimes with three maggots on the hook. Knowing that I was on for a big weight I was conscious of and quite vocal about keeping bank walkers off the skyline. When the match ended the thrill of it all kicked in. I had caught forty-three fish to total 115lb 13oz, using all my four pints of maggots and all the hemp in the process.

I'd lost six fish all day, three of which I was sure were foul-hooked, along with two bigger ones that ran me into a snag on the shallows below. The fish averaged a little over 2lb 8oz with the biggest on the day an estimated 3lb 12oz. The previous record had been just over 50lb. The river was solid with chub back then all the way from just below Skipton to Keighley, and the Keighley AC opens were almost always eighty or ninety-peg sell-outs with anglers travelling long distances to get a piece of the action.

My record still stands today, in fact I do not think that a catch over 50lb was recorded after that year. The River Aire five-hour match record will be broken sooner or later I'm sure, but probably not on the Upper Aire. I'd expect it to come from the lower Aire with bream as there are some big bream down there and plenty of them. The Aire is my lucky river as I also hold the record for the biggest single bream weighed in a match at 9lb 3oz caught in last year's Aire Championships.

Chapter 42
Darrell Taylor rotates three swims to set an Aire roach record

Some say he's lucky, has a golden arm at the drawbag, but, as Darrell Taylor usually catches lots of fish, it invites such comments, often laced with a touch of envy. Truth is, none of us can catch much from barren pegs, but when an angler seems to get more than his share of good ones, might it not also be true that they are thinking confidently, making sound decisions and performing to a high standard?

His record seems to confirm it: twice River Ure Champion, runner-up in both the Ouse and Calder Championships, a recent 17lb of 'chublets' and dace win from the Aire on a waggler, a 67lb net of bream from the Ouse on waggler in a Bradford City match, and twice champion on his local River Nidd.

In the same way as a canal angler rotates several swims to keep them alive and ticking over, Darrell fished three swims in a triangular formation to set a new record roach catch for the river River Aire at Beal in the Yorkshire Winter League Round 1 in October 2020 with an impressive 37lb 10oz of quality redfins. He caught fish off a groundbait line immediately in front of his box at nine metres range, then two swims at 19 metres out – one a yard or so upstream and one several yards downstream. He fed these two lines with casters and hemp separately because the hemp sinks faster, and past experience told him that the fish would settle close to where each bait hit the surface.

On this occasion he did draw a corker of a swim, two below the bridge at Beal where a huge eddy forms in the river, locally referred to as a 'dub.' Some swims here plunge to over 20-feet deep, but this peg offered a far more manageable 11 feet. A good peg is only the first step towards a big catch; however, Darrell could see the odd roach rising and swirling before the start and he seized the moment.

Darrell resides in a most convenient location for an angler – half a mile from Yorkshire's River Nidd at Knaresborough. He started fishing aged 15 after reading a 'Mr Crabtree' book and has learned his trade mainly by trial and error. He thinks we learn best from our mistakes and, after any fishing session where he senses a weakness or that something may have tripped him up, he has never shied away from consulting his peers.

Now 52, Darrell has almost 30 years match experience, many of which were spent fishing commercials. Back in 2003 he was plundering new lake venues like Woodlands (Thirsk), Sessay and Cudmore, and finished runner-up in the Kamasan Matchmen of the Year with 58 points. He also took runner-up spot in the Kamasan final the following year.

But after what he calls his 'mis-spent years' on the carp lakes, the shine wore off and he decided he'd grown complacent, fishing the same venues in the same way week after week. Feeling he'd more to learn, he went back to his river roots on the Nidd and Ure in club matches, before venturing to the Calder open circuit three years ago.

"I felt a lot sharper after going back on a few river matches and was then inspired to try deeper waters. I spent two years on the Ouse Winter League then joined Leeds Anglers World on the Yorkshire Winter League, which led to this brilliant day on the Aire."

Confirming how the Bolognese method is now a vital weapon for any aspiring river matchman, Darrell describes how sixty per cent of his catch fell to a 2.5g Bolo' float and the rest on a six number 4 stick, alternating the two and switching between his nine-metre line and two far lines, one for caster and a third for hemp in mid-river (19m estimated). Darrell caught mostly on a boss float with red maggot on a 16 hook, and topped up with some bonus fish on caster and others on giant hemp. Other than losing the odd big roach to marauding pike, he caught fish from 4oz to 1lb throughout the match.

His teammate, Tom Gausden said of his performance: "John Allerton, no less, had told a friend that the peg was a flier at certain times, and Darrell did have a spare peg upstream. I think a few of our team might have won the match from it. But to conjure up 37lb was a bit special. Darrell has a very positive mind-set, he attacks a swim and makes good decisions, and he has an impressive winning record on many waters, notably the Calder in recent years."

Darrell now takes up the story of his catch of a lifetime:

"I fancied the draw having been next peg downstream once before. Conditions were inviting – overcast and mild and no wind blowing. The river had a touch of extra water on but thankfully not enough to spur the bream to feed. I plumbed up to find 11 feet of water and set my stall out to fish just touching the bottom in three areas. The first cast was nine metres out where I'd feed groundbait – carefully as I had already seen fish in the swim – two golf ball-size balls only at the start, and the two others in mid-river at 19 metres range where I fed upstream with casters and four yards downstream with hemp.

"The peg is usually slack up to the crease at 9m beyond which it flows steadily, but today is was backing up on the inside and I wanted to utilise this on the whip or stick.

"My groundbait mix was a third of a kilo each of Sensas River, Gros Gardons and brown crumb, with a pint of ground hemp (boiled) added. Most of it would stay on the bank. I believe the Aire roach are quite migratory and I noticed that fish were topping as they moved upstream before the start. I thought it would be unwise to ball it in when fish were already shoaled up. Teammate Tom Gausden said he thought the peg had 20lb potential and such a comment always helps.

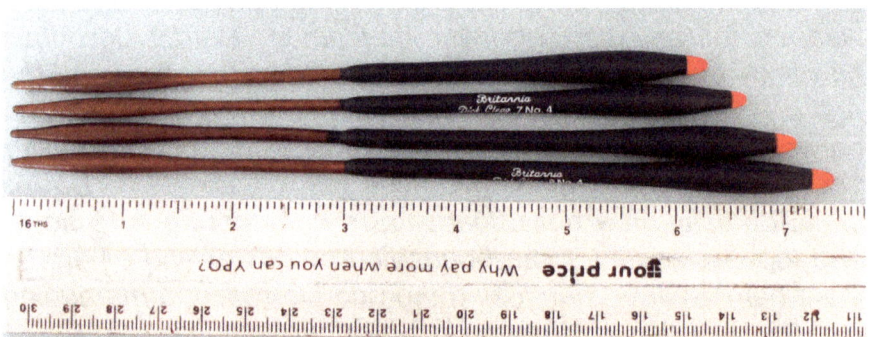

Dick Clegg's 'weight forward' lignums from his Britannia label. Here in sizes 6 x no. 4 up to 9 x no. 4, some rate these as his best range of sticks

"The tactic for the far lines was a 17-foot Daiwa Tournament rod and Dave Harrell 2.5g Bolo' float with an olivette and two sets of droppers below it – three x no. 10s bunched ten inches from a size 16 Colmic B957 hook and three x no. 8s bunched eleven inches above that. Reel line was DH 3lb float line to a .12mm Silstar trace. The bunched droppers would give a positive bite, but they could also be separated according to how the fish wanted to feed.

"For the near (groundbait) line I opted for the stick float on a 15-foot Tri-cast Finesse rod and 3lb DH reel line to a six x no. 4 Dick Clegg lignum stick with shoulder, and .10mm Preston Powerline hooklength to a Colmic B957 size 18 hook. I also set up a 6-metre whip and long line and tried this briefly, but had some issues trying to lift fish quickly enough before a pike struck.

"Over the first hour the basic plan was to start steadily with a bulk-down Bolo' rig, and to alternate with the stick and its slower drop. Shotting for the stick was shirt button-style with a one x no. 10 tell-tale ten inches from the hook, four x no. 9s spaced out, three groups of two x no. 8s above that, and a bulk of three x no. 6s just below half depth.

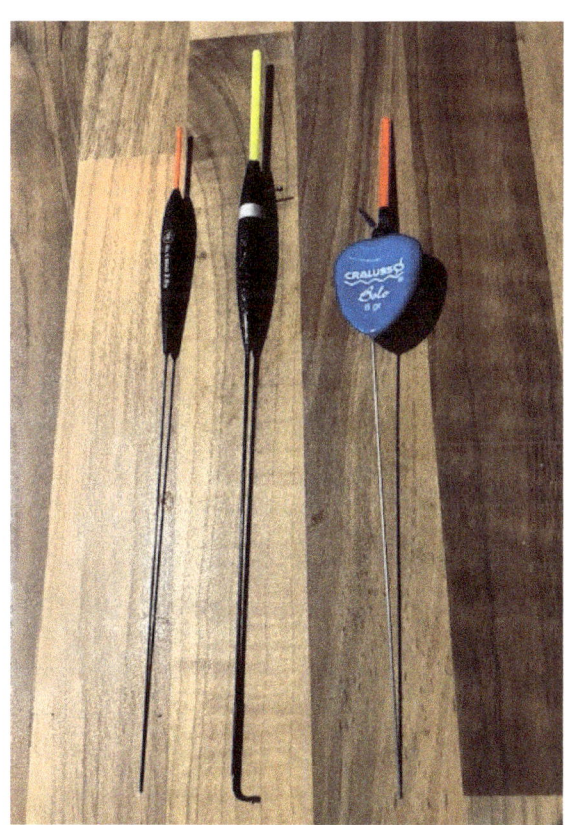

Bolo and sliding Bolo floats

"My baits included a pint of casters, same of red maggots and a one and half pints of hemp. Single red maggot over caster tempted most of the roach, but sometimes a double would get one. The match went like a dream! I caught roach steadily on the Bolo' rig running the float through over the caster line, most taking red maggot, but occasionally I'd get one on a caster or a piece of giant hemp further downstream, hence the choice of the big 16 hook.

"The better bites came to the maggot from good roach, while on the hemp and caster they were more ponderous. So, as the match wore on, I'd stay with the maggot if the bites kept coming. If ever the bites went off on the Bolo' I'd switch to stick and keep the rhythm going. When I missed a bite on the far line, I could sometimes wind back and run through on the 9m line. Holding back harder over the groundbaited area I'd often get a fish of similar quality. All told it was a great thrill to win with such a weight and days like that help us keep going when the rain is lashing down and bites are hard to come by."

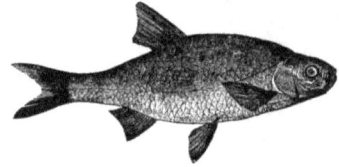

Chapter 43
Stick float with a bit of Bolo' and slider on the Tees, Tyne and Wear – Mick Broadley

For both his float skills and longevity as a champion angler from the North-East, Yarm's Mick Broadley has few peers. He might be a veteran of 78 now, but is still fit enough to wade into the upper Tees and win matches with dace like he's done for over half a century! Mick came to the fore as a member of the Yarm team that reigned supreme in the AT North-East Winter League division from 1971 to 1982 then added a thirteenth win in 1984. A float lover through and through, Mick excels on stick float and he learned the Bolognese method back in the eighties on visits to France where he's also won his share in the best of company.

Before the barrage was constructed in 1994, the Tees was tidal and the method at Yarm was to groundbait heavily while the tide was running off using a 4 x BB stick float with shots well down the line to catch at full depth, then later switching to loose-fed maggots to catch roach and dace 'on the drop' (the 'killing' method for winning matches) using a 6 x No. 4 stick during the three hours of steady flow before the tide backed up again.

For this method it is important to have a light but stiff, fine wire stem so that the float follows the bait down in an arc and any interception of the bait by a fish up in the water is easily noticed by a temporary halt in descent of the float. As I prefer the line to fall evenly down to the fish, I'm not a lover of shotting with a heavy bulk. Also, I never hold back the float hard because it does not give a natural presentation to the fish. The latter principles have provided the basis for many of my two hundred and forty victories.

Since the construction of the barrage at Middlesbrough, the depths at Yarm now range from three metres up to six metres.. In winter, the dace migrate from the upper reaches and are mainly caught on the three metre deep stretches from Yarm down to the barrage, where an 8 x no. 4 is perfect for fishing with a fourteen or fifteen-foot rod with the shot well down the line.

I use a lot of no. 8 lead shot spread out evenly with two separate no. 10 shot on the hooklength. These soft lead shot can easily be moved up or down the line without damaging it, so I steer clear of Stotz leads on whose square corners the line can catch and cause tangles. A key point to remember when you fall on a shoal of dace in a match is that, for speed (and to minimise fatigue due to the leverage), you should generally use the shortest rod you can suitably get away with for the depth of the swim, and for me this would be a thirteen-footer.

For depths greater than two and a half metres I like to use a stick float modified with an inserted antenna as the small top of a standard stick can become ineffective. In fact, I also use such modified stick floats on all reservoirs and lakes that have drift. I never use stick floats with large bulbous tops because they make such a noise upon striking due to their resistance in the water.

The big advantages of the stick float over the waggler on the wild Northern rivers is that you can use one in all sorts of currents, while waggler fishing in my opinion is more suitable when the flow is constant all the way across the river. With a stick float, control and instant connection to the fish is possible with the line being on the surface, whereas fishing across a dead bay into a current with a waggler means that the friction of the dead water on the line can pull the waggler off course. Also, another key advantage of the stick float is that you can check the float for a second or two to lift the bait in front of the fish's mouth for an irresistible take.

As a general maxim: light, stiff rods are essential for connecting the bites when stick float fishing, and a closed face reel is a must for fast close-in work.

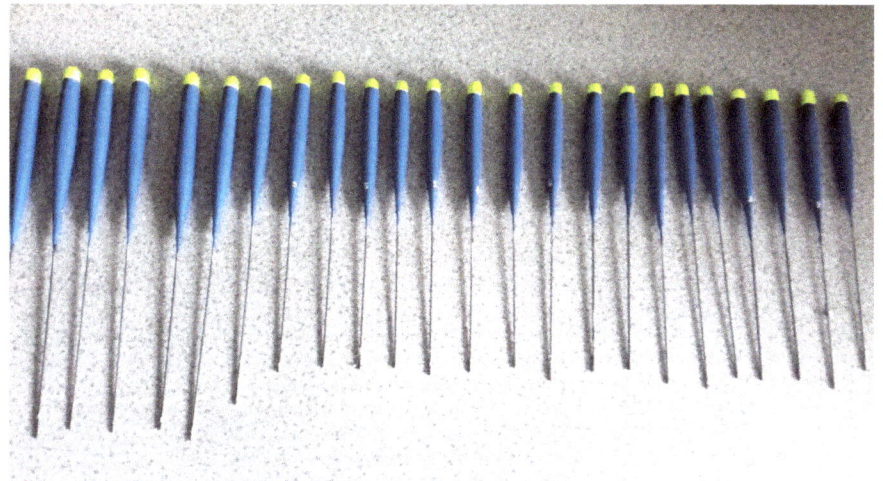

Mike's new stick floats

I find that a 4 x no. 4 stick suffices for most cases, but I'll often change to a 3 x no. 4 float, especially in clear water, giving a lighter fall on the water upon casting. For light stick float work for dace and roach I always take a range of spare sticks set up on winders complete with hooklength, shot and hook, but if chub are present I may well set up afresh and change the float if necessary.

Stick float fishing for roach requires a more cautious approach than for dace [see 'Food for Thought'].

For most of my dace fishing, in the streamy swims, I prefer single maggot (saves time over double maggot and avoids spinning) on a size 18 hook, though for steadier water, for dace and roach, I may use a size 20. When fishing for dace or roach with maggot, contrary to what many anglers do, I do not add casters in the feed. I want to get the fish feeding on the same bait as I'm putting on the hook. The hooklength is normally 0.10 mm diameter but I may reduce to 0.08 mm diameter in slower, harder swims. I will also scale up to 0.12 mm when I am 'bagging' in moving water.

Food for thought

‌ I was once fishing a big open match and had drawn a peg containing only roach, but lots of them. A strong downstream wind was blowing, causing many waves. The swim was two metres deep so I fished my trusty 4 x no. 4 stick float fitted with a short antenna. Anglers each side of me were casting long wagglers to counteract the wind. I caught only small roach and in the waves it was a case of 'now you see me, now you don't,' so I had to strike when the float didn't re-appear. Halfway through the match, a chap walking the bank, asked me how I was faring, to which I replied that I'd only about four and a half pounds of roach to six ounces. He said that I could win the match if I carried on the same. I then decided to change the float to an 8 x no. 4 stick to provide more buoyancy. After twenty minutes without a fish, I changed back to the small stick and caught steadily again till the end of the match, weighing in 7lb 8oz for third place. A costly mistake because 8lb 1oz won the match! The moral of the story is don't change tactics when catching steadily, fishing light for roach is often right anyway.

‌ The old saying that you must cast the stick float so that the hook lands downstream of the float does not always apply now. I've noticed that on venues where the pole is popular, I can do better by casting slightly upstream with the hook landing upstream, waiting for the hook to sink while the float stays in the same position in front of me, until a bite comes when the maggot has settled beneath the float. The fish have got used to sitting directly beneath the pole and feeding cup!

When it comes to the River Tyne, however, the dace are large and, when bagging, it is not uncommon to use a size 16 or even 14 hook, baited with two or three maggots, to 0.14 mm line. To win on the Tyne when big weights are expected, it is essential to also use a stronger rod to haul out the dace from the strong current.

When the dace are in the deeper water, the Bolognese method is very effective using a Bolo' float with an insert; a seven-metre Bolo' rod is ideal for all the deep swims on the Tees.

The lightest float that should be used with a Bolo' rod is three-gram. A two-gram float takes too much effort to cast. Some anglers prefer to use heavier floats, but I have found that any float heavier than three-gram results in more missed bites. In all cases, the Bolo' float should be appreciably long, as short floats tend to double back on themselves.

When Bolo' fishing for dace I prefer to use a bunch of medium-sized shot over an olivette – usually positioned about three-foot above the hook, which enables me to split the bulk to move some of the shot up the line should the dace start to feed off the bottom.

I like to use the Bolo' method early in a match as it can tell me plenty about the nature of the river bed, but if I start catching regularly I often switch to a sliding float attack as I find it much quicker and easier on the arm! I have used top-and-bottom slider floats for many years, but more recently have turned to simpler waggler sliders. These are more practical in windy conditions as the shotting can be adjusted to vary the length of antenna above the water to ride the waves and give me a good reading of the river bed and better indication of lift bites. All slider floats must be pre-loaded slightly at the base so that they stay with the terminal rig upon casting.

Much of my fishing in shallow waters requires wading. I find that, rather than being rigidly seated on a 'station,' it is more practical to stand and place bait, groundbait and accessories on an adjacent platform to which the keepnet and landing net are attached, so that, when the fish move out, the platform assembly may be quickly moved out to a new position.

When fishing the stick float for chub, I use a 0.17 mm reel line, and, although the float size can generally be as for dace, I use a size 12 fine forged hook holding four casters. A hook any lighter will simply result in lost fish. Chub are usually located very near the far bank close to many tree roots, so a powerful rod is essential. Chub have a particular liking for casters so in such swims I'll feed heavily with casters and hemp, and indeed sometimes also with all the red maggots in my possession, trying to get the chub into a feeding frenzy.

Groundbaiting

As the upper Tyne is a salmon river only four matches a year are allowed with each match a sell-out of around ninety anglers. I always pile the groundbait in to attract the dace shoals as these dace have rarely seen a hook before!

I use ninety per cent breadcrumb with just enough black 'River' to darken it, and with maggots mixed in. The river is wide but generally not much more than one metre deep. However, each of the three times time that I've caught over 38lb, all on the stick float close in, I eased off the groundbait to catch most of the fish on the drop.

In contrast to the Tees dace, the Tyne fish do not like the fast current and prefer the slacks. But it is chub that can really boost your weight, having vastly increased in number over recent years. I've found that when the dace tail off in the last hour, I pile in casters which can result in a few big chub.

The average depth in the upper and middle stretches of the Tees is 1m and dace is the most predominant species. When the water is clear I tend not to use groundbait, especially when the sun is shining. However, on cool, overcast days, I've had regular success by flicking in small balls of well-wetted groundbait as an attractor. I also do the same when there is a small amount of coloured fresh water running. Once again, I use 90 per cent bread crumb with some black 'River' to darken it and maggots mixed in. Dace do not seem to like commercial groundbaits.

I never groundbait where there are chub. They just don't like it. However, I will catapult a few soft balls of moistened white bread across into two far-side swims, accompanied by casters and hemp. When the chub are in feeding mood I have no hesitation in using a size 12 with four casters, tied to .017 mm line. On certain days though, simply using three pints of red maggots can result in big weights, and at such times I use two red maggots on a size 16 super spade hook. I do not like wide gape hooks, preferring instead to use a hook with a longer shank for stability.

Only when fishing the deeper lower Tees in winter, where the dace have migrated downstream, do I break my rule and use groundbait. Again, it is the same mix as above including maggots, but with leam added. Because the undertow is strong here, I never loose feed. The deeper the water or heavier the flow, the more leam I add.

More food for thought

⌣ I remember a good angler once saying to me: "Nine times out of ten, fish the stick float – and if in doubt the tenth time, still fish a stick float!" He was my kind of angler.

⌣ Before casters became the 'in' bait circa 1960, most rods had a soft through-action. But when we needed to strike fast to connect with caster bites, the spliced-tip, stick rods came to the rescue. Soft action rods are more suitable for waggler fishing, but even then I prefer a stiff action rod.

⌣ Even as far back as the seventies, we always added a second butt ring three inches from the original butt ring. This enabled a smoother line feed off the reel and helped a light stick to be cast a few yards further. This still hasn't ever been incorporated in rod design!

⌣ How often do we hear anglers complain that the hooklength has snapped at the hook when losing a good fish like a chub or barbel? Against all rules (as shown on hook packets), the line should come from the back of a spade hook in my opinion. This is because when you hit a fish and put tension on the line, the line tries to get to the back of the hook and cuts on the sharp edge of the spade.

⌣ Sadly, there are very few good reel lines on the market today, due I believe to the concentration of manufacturers on carp fishing. I use Preston Reflo Power in .13mm and .15mm, but choice is limited in my opinion.

Chapter 44
A Lakeland nirvana – Nick Butterfield

Born and bred in Teesside, Nick Butterfield crossed the Pennines to live in Cumbria when deciding to 'semi-retire' as he describes it, aged 51. After travelling widely with his work in manufacturing engineering with companies like Toyota, BAE Systems, and the Sellafield nuclear plant, he left it all behind to become club manager for Windermere and Ambleside DAA (or WADAA), Cumbria's largest angling club. He now looks after a dozen waters holding both coarse and game fish.

I was introduced to angling as a boy in Middlesbrough when joining a very junior-orientated club called Preston Park AC which led me into match fishing. With a core of young mates, we were taken under the capable wing of Jeff Herbert and the Middlesbrough AC team. We formed a young team nicknamed 'the Pound Puppies' and, aged 15, I managed to win a series at Albert Park Lake, beating some top seniors en route including John Smiles (Barnsley Blacks), and Dave 'Tweedy' Harris (1978 Div. 1 National Champion). My £50 tackle voucher prize was like winning the Pools! Still on a high, I won a club match on the Swale the next day with 30lb of chub and barbel! Other early influences were Ian Worton and Mick Ward and Yarm AC team members I saw 'battering' the dace on the tidal Tees in winter. They inspired me to then get up at 4am in December to catch a bus early enough to get on a decent peg there!

While studying at Leeds University I fished alongside Leeds team anglers and tackle dealers, Stan Jeffries and Paul Clark, and they too helped me along. I enjoyed a spell in the nineties living in Nottingham which fostered a love for the Trent, and once got the better of John Allerton at the next peg at Burton Joyce Rack, fishing stick and caster and taking big roach right at the end of my swim. I later dabbled with a few commercial lake matches and won a big charity open at the Glebe, Leics. with 252lb. But odd as it may sound, that result scratched the itch for me with that type of fishing.

Moving to Windermere to work at the shipyard in Barrow-in-Furness in 2006, gave me more time for fishing and I joined the local (small) match scene. For the past two years I've been dedicated to improving the WADAA venues, as well as spending many hours working on float designs and other tackle ideas. My own stick and Bolo' floats have helped me take some nice catches from several rivers in my adopted county.

We have some fantastic roach fishing up here in Cumbria, and my very favourite stillwater venue (pre-cormorants at least!) was Killington Lake, just off the M6. My best catch here was 286 quality roach for 115lb on the waggler. The River Ribble in Preston is another absolute favourite, my best catch being 80lb of dace on the stick float a few winters ago – real 'clonkers'.

Having been brought up fishing on some of the big North-East rivers like the Swale and Tees, fishing the stick float was always a really important part of the armoury. In the days pre-barrage, the Tees was heavily tidal, with vast shoals of big dace migrating to the downstream reaches in winter. Big, deep and powerful, it presents interesting challenges to get the correct presentation for the big, but shy, dace.

The upper reaches of the river offer a somewhat different challenge with shallower, faster water, very similar to that of the Swale. Here the fish (again dace, but also chub, perch and grayling) hug shallow runs and pools which were often well out in the river.

The challenge: how to fish at distance without using a big float, which would be overkill, catching these species in shallow water? This is where my interest in distance stick float fishing really started. Whereas light sticks are generally associated with trotting close in to the rod tip, I was wanting to fish at a range of 30 metres or more. This requires a fairly significant overhead cast and at these sorts of distances, initial efforts invariably ended in tangles and frustration – the dreaded 'flick-over'. It became obvious that the key was balancing the weight distribution and this is where the distance Bolo' (or what I termed my distance-sticks) came to the fore.

Using the principles of a dart, the casting weight needs to be at the front of the rig, with a length of lightweight material acting as the spine of the float and a shaped body stabilising the flight. I learned to see the whole rig as a casting method, not just the lead shot and the design evolved.

What also became obvious was the importance of the weight and shot placement and here, simple is best. I settled on an olivette for the 'bulk' with a simple one or two-shot dropper – no smaller than a no. 6. Though really wanting to use more sophisticated and delicate shotting patterns this proved unnecessary and was actually a hindrance – more of this later.

These floats were made up in a variety of sizes and I started to catch a lot of fish. This led on to the next problems to solve: 1) How to see a tiny dome top on a stick float at distance – especially in the wind? 2) What was the best body shape when the rig needed to be slowed down, particularly relevant in winter when teasing those big dace onto the hook?

The body shape evolved through trial and error and looking at shapes that were being used elsewhere. The 'hard wedge' shape proved really good at being held almost still in the water – even at distance.

The solution of visibility was easily solved with the addition of a pole float bristle – obvious really. The bristle serves no purpose other than to aid visibility and as such was made of solid material as buoyancy is irrelevant; the weight loading is still made to the balsa tip, as would be the case on a traditional stick float. I was now getting close to the perfect solution and although the floats and set-up look very unusual, the method was catching a lot of fish.

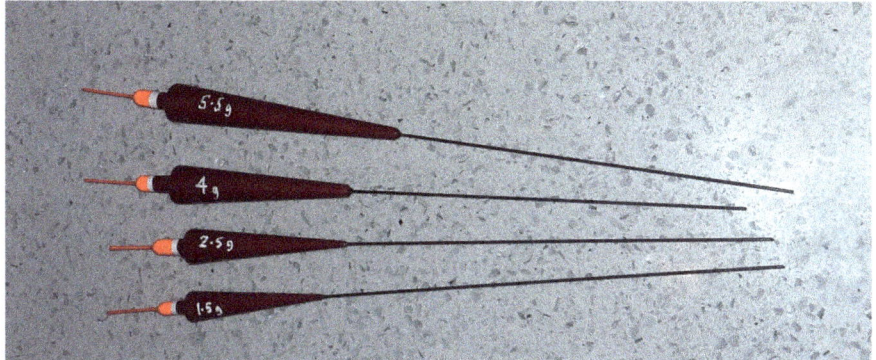

Nick's long cast Bolo's

At about this time I had moved down to Nottingham and was fishing the middle reaches of the Trent a lot (which, unfortunately for me, coincided perfectly with the demise of this great river in the late nineties). As the river became cleaner and the water colder and clearer, the fish became much more difficult to catch – often sitting well away from the bank.

Once again, this proved to be perfect for distance stick fishing, but the Trent added a further complication. Often, especially in winter, the fish (much more roach dominated here and generally of a smaller size) wanted the bait slowing down almost to a standstill. This called for a degree of over-shotting, the amount of which was determined by the flow on the day.

Wanting to keep the shotting on the rig as simple as possible for casting purposes, I now needed to design a method to be able to quickly change the weight of the olivette. The solution, which is now obvious but was not available at the time, involved gluing a short length of yard brush bristle (the same as I used for the sight-tips) into the olivette and fastening it to the line using pole float silicone. This allows the olivette to be quickly changed without altering the rig at all. This same idea is now commercially available, of course, from various tackle companies. So now we had the perfect, flexible set-up for long-distance stick float (later termed 'Bolo') fishing on a variety of rivers.

I later built some of these adaptations into my standard stick set-up. As a big river, the Trent is sometimes subject to 'rollers' on the water created by the wind. With a 'dotted-down' stick, the float would disappear into troughs. By gluing a short length of bristle into the tips of my standard stick floats the problem is eliminated and without any detriment to the rig at all. If you think about it, it is little different to fishing a pole float.

So that is how the design of my river floats has evolved and, having seen many of our major rivers from living and working all around the country, I'm confident that they will work successfully far and wide.

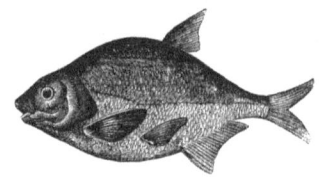

Chapter 45
'Sticking at it' – the birth of a river angler
– Dave Pilgrim

Dave and a nice catch of Irish tench

My friend and former regular contributor to Angling Star magazine, Dave Pilgrim, describes a tough learning curve as a youngster when only inferior pond fishing was available. It all changed when the junior coaches at Ryburn AS introduced him to a new world of trotting rivers with a stick float. It became Dave's favourite method, and he eloquently describes here the sheer joy of trotting a stick and hooking a quality fish like a chub, a feeling so well appreciated by thousands of river anglers nationwide. Dave also relates how badly polluted rivers can recover and make first class fisheries given sufficient respect and time for nature to rejuvenate life…

The river was in full midsummer splendour. Emerald fronds of water-crowfoot swayed calypso-like in the current against the fragile, daisy-like flowers reaching sunward through the early morning mist. The domed red-topped float, dotted against the slate surface, glided downstream carrying the baited hook gently fishward?

And suddenly it wasn't there! A firm sweep of the rod was not this time met by a splashy dace but by firm resistance. I gingerly gained a few turns on the reel and was suddenly aware of the weedbed between me and my prize. The line sang in the breeze, a sound I'd never heard before, eerie in the stillness. The fish found the sanctuary of the weeds and went still. I pulled steadily, line taught and howling. Something gave, the fish freed itself, and I slid the net under it before it got chance to recover. It was mine. Parting the folds of the net, I revealed the bronze head and rubber lips of my first proper chub, the hook neatly nicked in the corner of its cavernous mouth. It was the biggest fish I'd ever seen.

Non-anglers will never know the sometimes almost spiritual joy of our sport. Moments, fish captures, special days, places, all forever accessible by just closing your eyes. And so, this day when I finally cracked the stick float, is burned in memory: unforgettable. But I'm getting ahead of myself, because the journey to that fateful day was faltering, and on the way I suffered agonies that only my fellow anglers will understand.

I lived in Sowerby Bridge, West Yorkshire, land of cotton mills, brass bands and Webster's Ale. The place was not known for its fishing. As a young and enthusiastic beginner I'd got precious few angling opportunities to choose from. Our river, the Calder, was an open sewer. As the saying went, you might catch something from it, but it wouldn't be fish.

We had a derelict canal festooned with shopping trollies and choked with Canadian pondweed and chickweed, though it did hold some small roach, perch and jack pike. And because the land tilts so much the still water options were also few – dams; small reservoirs built to serve our dark, satanic mills, most being deep, cold and featureless. Even the shallow ones were only shallow because they'd been drained. That said, with considerable effort I, and a few die-hard mates, caught a few fish from them.

Willow Hall Dam, on my doorstep was very deep but threw

up a few micro perch, odd roach and the occasional exotic such as a skimmer, brown trout and (take a deep breath) tench. Swamp Dam (a brilliant name for a fishery if ever there was one) also held some enormous gudgeon. But these waters were hardly prolific and our catching window was generally limited to late spring until late autumn. Winter fishing involved chucking a tiny Mepps spinner into the Hebden 'ditch' once the weed had died for the odd micro 'jack.'

There was another largely untapped alternative. The Calder had a number of unpolluted tributaries, and these were explored to the nth degree. The River Hebden, Crag Brook, River Elphin, River Lud, River Ryburn, Mill Bank stream, all held trout and because we were clueless on how else to fish we caught the odd one by accident using a crude 'bomb and worm' tactic. And therein lay the problem: there was some half decent fishing to be had on the streams but we didn't have a clue how to catch them because the water didn't stay in one place long enough for our basic waggler tactics.

So we just about got by, but with so few opportunities it was no wonder the number of young anglers in the area was dwindling. It was easier to sack it off and spend time on a skateboard or bike or playing football at the 'rec.' By age 14 I was starting to get fed-up of catching 'not very much' on our local dams.

Enter the Ryburn Angling Society, in particular three individuals within it: Brian Gibson, Dave Collins and John Graham. Bri and Dave 'ran' (very loosely) the Match and Junior sections of the club. They did a great job training some Ryburn youths to later became very good anglers – Darren Taylor, Phil Stansfield, Paul McCabe and others; all had (and still have) an impact on the Northern match scene. They helped me too, and Bri in particular is a lifelong friend, but my major influence was John Graham. John lived near me and took a few of us under his wing. He was always available to help with home-made floats, bits and pieces of gear and, more importantly, encouragement. This ultimately led to the awakening of a stick float angler.

The Ryburn Club ran matches and John encouraged 'his' juniors to take part: "It's a great way to learn," he'd say. So when the club match list for summer 1976 came out it included an event on the River Calder on the Gravel Pits stretch near Brighouse. I'd heard rumours of this length – warmed by a power station and oxygenated by a series of weirs and fast water. It was allegedly solid with roach and gudgeon. But it was off the beaten track, two bus-rides away, and even if we got there we'd not know how to tackle it, as the water didn't stay in the same place all the time.

In stepped John. "If you fancy entering the match we can go for a practice. You'll need to fish the stick float..." And so the 'top and bottom' float was unveiled, explained, and off we went to the venue for a pleasure chuck. It was a grey, early June day, just before the scorching summer of '76 exploded upon us. The river was actually carrying some water, said John, and armed with a couple of stick floats, I peered anxiously at the oily and boily surface with some confusion. With only a year's real angling experience and little watercraft gained, I plumped for the dub[21] below the Bailey Bridge at the top of the length.

My rod was a 13-foot (glass) Sealey Black Arrow to a Mitchell 300 reel loaded with 2.6 Bayer. The 'stick float' was what was then also known as a 'caster float' – slim and with an eye in the base. It would have been part of a Christmas gift set bought by my parents which had previously rested in my wicker basket untroubled as I'd no use for it. The hook was an eyed Mustad of some description, almost certainly with an evil barb.

Still naïve about plumbing the depth, I set the float three-foot deep, deciding to shallow off, if it dragged the bottom and deepen if it didn't. Hookbait was an ASI (our local tackle shop) special maggot. I dropped the float off the rod end whereby it wobbled hypnotically around the eddy, line going all over the place, the float being left to fish itself. Handfuls of maggot peppered the float at various points in its traverse around the swim, and to my surprise I was getting several rapid 'dips' on the float. An extra shot (probably a no. 6) dotted the float down far enough for the dips to become 'go unders.' The sinker bites were tiny gudgeon and at the end of the session I'd accrued 79

---

21 A 'dub' has various meanings including the now obsolete way of tying a hook to line with silk thread and varnish, but in this context it is a Yorkshire term for a back eddy

of them for less than 1lb. This introduction to river fishing had been satisfactory, and I figured that if I was getting bites that would do for starters.

And so came the day of the big match – a forty-peg sell-out, I'd never seen as many anglers all in one place at one time. We paid our pools and then awaited the draw in the bankside car park. The peg I drew was different in that it flowed only gently but I felt I'd be able to use the 'successful' set-up of my previous attempt. So I sat there on my wicker basket, dropped the float in off the rod and let it wobble gently down the river, peppered occasionally by a fistful of maggots. As before, I plucked these ubiquitous gudgeon from the grey depths completely thoughtless of any roach that might be only yards from my float! I did actually manage to 'fool' a four-ouncer, the crowning glory on top of my 100-plus gudgeon, to end up with 2lb 4oz. I'm smiling as I write because when I knew the river better a year later, I realised I'd wasted an absolute flier that day.

It would be great to report that I won the match, but that honour went to Andy Parker (one of my mates) with 3lb of roach from a streamy peg above the bridges and earned the spoils, but I was still happy with my result. The Senior event was won by the club's 'crack' matchman, Ernest Shardlow, with 8lb of roach, from the peg below me, but he might as well have been fishing in a different world as far as I was concerned.

So I was now quite keen to get this 'stick float' thing sorted out. I'd seen its fish-catching potential and, as importantly, saw its potential to take me to fresh fields away from the deep dark dams of my embryonic angling career. A trip to the local tackle shop saw the addition of some new, proper 'stick floats' to my meagre collection: nothing scientific in their purchase other than none of them had eyes in the base – I'd managed to figure out that double rubber made that feature redundant.

I guess we'd been badgering John Graham too, as the next weekend we were introduced to the river that has entranced and beguiled me ever since – the Nidd. The venue was Bradford No 1's water at Nun Monkton. The river here is narrow and pacey with features dotted throughout – streams, pools, willows, stakes in the water, weed beds, undercut banks, the place was mind blowing to a kid who spent most of his time sitting on dam walls. Add to this the venue was in the middle of nowhere, none of the industry or machinery that I was used to; background noise was birdsong, gurgling currents, lowing cattle, willows and reeds – secluded but never silent. Hypnotic and entrancing. It would also mean a step up in 'degree of difficulty' as there were no slacks or gentle glides for me to rely on here. I would finally have to do some serious trotting.

It was another glorious summer's day as I stood in the edge of the tiny stream watching the torrent rush past. What surprises lay beneath the tumult? Said new stick float was lowered into the current and off it went, wobbling and bobbing crazily down the chute. It took me a bit of time to understand checking the line against the reel spool, and this required co-ordination in loose feeding, but, little by little a modicum of control was achieved and I started to get signs on the float that it was not alone in the water – dips, jabs, barely perceptible movements in its trajectory.

Additions of shot and amendments to depth further improved control and presentation and bites began to develop, followed by a veritable aquarium of·fishlets. My old friends the gudgeon first up, soon followed by my first ever dace and chublets, plus the odd roach and perch, all tiny but each one building confidence and anticipation of what may come next. The day flew by and, chuffed to bits, I returned maybe 3lb of allsorts back into their home. I'd learned a lot but also realised I'd loads more to learn. Probably the biggest lesson of all was to fish the streamier water, as it 'forced' me to learn to control the stick by keeping the line behind it.

And so to the day I will never forget, the day that would make angling a part of my life forever. My fourth river expedition, to the Nidd again, this time at Cowthorpe. It was the height of summer and we'd to be off early to make sure we'd be fishing by first light. We walked from the van to the river through dewy fields and rising mist, the sounds of the babbling stream in the distance, owls and the overture of the dawn chorus. John directed me to a glide above a sharp bend and set off to a peg not far below. I proceeded to set up in the slowly lifting gloom. Threading the line through the rod rings was a nightmare, a combination of anticipation, shaking hands and semi- darkness hampering the task.

And then the stick float itself, a little 4 x no. 6 job held on the line by three float rubbers. The shot were tooth-squeezed onto the 2.6lb Bayer line, which, in turn, was tied direct to a size 18 Mustad. Bait was caster with the hook buried to try to fool the clever dace.

But before all that I'd need to be able to see the river to fish. Time slowed down, the light imperceptibly increasing but rising mist still made it impossible to cast. Finally, day began to clear and I could see well enough to begin fishing.

I cast my stick float slightly downstream keeping line behind float, float behind hook and bait, a big pinch of casters behind the float, line checked and tight against the reel spool, peeled off by hand allowing the float to travel downstream as naturally as possible. Minutes passed and finally the float simply vanished. My resultant strike connected with thin air, but the empty shell of the caster was testimony to a bite.

And so it continued, the fabled million mile-an-hour dace bites, all missed... but this was fun, I'd get one in a minute. And eventually I did: a satisfying 'clunk' of the strike connecting with something alive, not the micro dace of Nun Monkton, but a plump 6oz 'herring,' pristine in its silver-bronze chain mail and full of the casters I'd been feeding. This was proper fishing! More bites were missed, hair was pulled out as I tried to learn and adapt – depth on, depth off, more feed, less feed, cast behind the loose feed, past it, short of it. The odd decent dace was swung to hand.

So this is where we came in. With 'old rubber lips' safely deposited in the keepnet I got back to trying to capture a few more, but that was the end of my day. That chub weighed 1lb 10oz but, for a young lad living in a fishless desert, whose previous biggest fish was a pound tench, it looked enormous and had an equally enormous impact on me, igniting a love affair with stick floats and rivers that has never diminished and is stronger today than it ever has been.

The stick float liberated me, and allowed me to escape the shackles of those deep dark dams. Suddenly all those Calder tributaries were accessible and the trout we knew lived there were catchable. Back in the seventies we were still able to fish maggot on our rivers and streams from March 25th. A gang of us would be out most weekends, travelling light with waders, bait apron, rod, reel and landing net, covering many swims from the top of a beck down to its confluence with the Calder. Catches of forty-plus trout were regular. Those faltering first steps taught me a lot and I carried on learning every time I picked a stick float up. At John Graham's suggestion I invested in an ABU 506, *the* reel for stick floating. We started making the two-bus trip to Brighouse and other reaches of the 'proper Calder.' Soon we were catching double figure weights of roach ourselves. Still a junior, I was ready for the next Ryburn club match on the Gravel Pits and came third overall with 9lb 10oz of roach.

The stick float has taken me to rivers all over England, Scotland, Ireland and Holland. I've caught fish of all species, shapes and sizes, I've had big weights, blanks, won matches, been battered, sung, whistled and laughed my way through thousands of hours on the river bank. The stick float has made me some very good friends and still does, and I've met and fished with some of the very best anglers in the country.

Looking through my stick floats at the start of a new day, picking one out to thread on the line and the anticipation of that first cast and what might be to come: well it's just as exciting now as it was back then, forty-five years ago looking at the inky, oily, smelly Calder.

Best of all, the once open sewer that ran through Sowerby Bridge had surprises in store. They say hope springs eternal, and once I'd got confidence in the stick float it was almost natural that as we explored the tributaries we would stray on to the main river as well. So after several disappointments, fast forward a year, another day burned into memory, when the dotted red-domed stick disappeared as it travelled down my peg at Copley... but that's another story!

Finally, I cannot find the words to express my appreciation of all the encouragement and help John Graham and Brian Gibson gave me back then, so I dedicate this piece to them, and to my dad who started me off in the first place on the Hebden 'ditch' with a tiny perch in 1967. Thank you.

Chapter 46
Finding the winning touch – Jim Baxter

The author with a frame-placed catch at Long Higgin

Looking back over fifty years to my early floatfishing days the details can get sketchy. Luckily, I started keeping records during the 1972-73 season and wrote fishing diaries from 1978, so know how tentative my early steps were in what we old guys refer to as the golden era of the big matches. I read and soaked up every page of Benny Ashurst's 1968 book like a sponge, so knew a bit about the principles of a stick float and casters (maggot chrysalis) as bait. I avidly followed Ivan Marks' weekly *Angling Times* columns too, but putting into practice all that these legends made sound easy was not always straightforward.

I had self-belief but found success hard to come by up to age 20. A next peg mauling on the Witham proved my inexperience when Leeds skipper Howard Robson stuffed me one November day with a 6lb 6oz frame score to my one lonely roach! In fairness, the 'stick' I used had dubious provenance and was made from hardwood with a hair grip glued in the base!

I was no Trent regular by then, but in my late teens (late sixties) I remember finishing second in a Crookes WMC autumn match at North Muskham with 14lb of mainly roach on caster. This was a breakthrough: fishing against some experienced men. I recall using a medium weight stick float, possibly made by my friend Ian Wiggins, an excellent float-maker. The green glass rod, too, I can still visualise – a fourteen-footer with a chunk of lead pipe sealed inside the butt which aided the overall balance nicely.

In spite of the occasional success, I knew years later I could have learned quicker by having a good coach or mentor. On the stick I was still raw but aching to improve. It was years later when I discovered how to back-shot the float in a strong wind, for example. I missed a chance to get to know Denis White well after meeting him at a Barnsley maggot farm in 1973. He could have taught me more in a day than I'd take a season to learn. There are endless examples of how coaching, assisted by videos, has flattened the learning curve for modern sports participants.

Early stick fun

Teaming up with another mate called Ian (Bray), we fished Rolleston upstream of Newark and also enjoyed the tidal Trent around Dunham Bridge. The stocky roach here, not unlike the upper river, always seemed that bit fitter than the non-tidal and fought harder in the strong current. We used fibreglass rods built from Lerc or Hardy Fibatube blanks, finished with matt black paint and with spiralled strip cork to form the butt, cycle innertube for the reel fittings, and home-made sticks, baiting with caster and hemp. Later I'd upgrade to the glass Shakespeare International rod, which had a lovely soft tip action. When carbon fibre rods came on the scene they took some adjusting to. For half a season I was losing fish that I felt the Shakespeare would have landed.

Those early carbon models were either too whippy or too

stiff in the middle section. I bought an okay Normark, improved on it with a Kevin Ashurst then John Dean model, before Terry Smith (of tackle dealers, Terry & John's, Sheffield) built me a new 13-foot rod from a Sportex blank. This had a long solid spliced tip and became my main weapon – nice and forgiving on the strike. Today's anglers are lucky to have a wide choice of superb rods available at the right price. As for reels, a closed-face model like the ABU always had a serious Marmite factor, but I was, and still am, a fan of the 507. Reel line choice was always Racine Tortue green while hooklengths were usually Bayer Perlon 1.1lb in Sorrel colour.

One way of fishing a stick that I much miss, is laying-on, or ligging-on as the Trentmen would term it. More than once on the narrow section of the lower Witham at Bardney I made a fair catch of roach on this method, fishing a yard from the bank with the river well flooded and chocolate coloured.

Years later this style could also produce well at Long Higgin when trotting was a waste of time and the only chance of bites from lethargic fish would be with a still bait. One day on the River Soar, around the start of the new millennium I fished a three-way friendly with Terry Gough and Brian Elliott on a rising river at Normanton. Laying-on with a 13 x no. 6 stick, inched through at intervals, got me 9lb of quality roach up to near 1lb size, fishing less than four feet from the bank. As the river deteriorated, my swim actually improved, while my two mates fishing further out in the flow with poles struggled. Almost every roach that day was a netter and fell to double maggot.

Our routine was to fish the Trent on a Saturday then drive past it en route to a big Witham or Welland match on the Sunday. And in winter on the Darnall Horti' WMC club trips we learned from the old hands, including at least a dozen members of Sheffield's two National Championship teams, the 'Amalgamated' and 'District.'

Then in the 1973-74 season the planets aligned and I actually won my first open – a Newark Piscatorial match at Winthorpe – beating a field of three hundred and fifty with 8lb 10oz of roach and chub. Newark's Col Walton came a close second with 8lb 5oz. I used a 4BB balsa float, possibly inspired by once meeting Johnny Toulson who showed me a 3 x AAA balsa he used in boily swims, and caught three chub topped up with roach and gudgeon.

The win was a huge confidence boost, as Sheffield anglers were more successful on the Witham at that time. The Trent was changing in nature too: the river was gradually getting cleaner and clearer and the roach, at Winthorpe for example, were increasingly responding to waggler tactics further out than the stick float zone. It made me even more eager to have a proper go at the open match circuit. Trying to generate some momentum, I'd even boasted in the 1974 write-up how a 7lb 1oz catch in the Trent Championship had made the 'top thirty' (from 1,000), though this was probably an educated guess: an unchecked stat.

This same year, we were introduced to the upper Trent at Bass Island, Burton-on-Trent, where the river divides and narrows considerably. Here in this streamy water, full of character with glides, riffles and back eddies, I caught my first 20lb match catch with 21lb-plus for third in the 1975 Wincil Charity Open fished by sixty. On this day I tried something different: holding an overshotted float back really hard to catch big roach in the last two hours. Ian did even better with a match win from the downstream point of the island with 21lb.

It was all caster for me at the time, but more change was in the air after Dave Thomas and other Leeds anglers began taking the Witham and Trent apart with bronze maggot. The caster men suddenly did not want a maggot angler drawn above them putting twice their amount of bait in and more. In 1976 at Burton Joyce I managed 12lb-odd for runner-up spot to Roy Toulson, but still only had the one good open win to my credit in five seasons.

Then, in 1977, I had a good season and, in sixty-four matches fished, I won a frame or section prize in half. I won only two matches: one on a whip on the Witham, the other a Walkley club match on stick float at Long Higgin on Trent, but achieved some consistency at last with ten section wins and twenty-five results as section top threes. The following year I only fished forty-eight matches but won eleven sections, and so it went on. Sections were usually 50 in size though at that time. It had taken ten years or more, but now I could hardly go wrong with a confidence that carried me right through the eighties as those early struggles finally bore fruit.

The discovery

Consistency in any sport boosts confidence and by gaining a momentum of success we can surprise ourselves at the ease with which a victory takes shape. I never concerned myself with what the anglers either side of me might do. By the late seventies I felt my methods and tactics were good enough to win matches on several venues, but tried never to get too cocky about it: a bad run of draws soon brings an angler down to earth with a bump.

One result from two weekend matches was a good average for me. A money win would usually lead to another decent performance next time out, while a stinking result could put me on a downer for a couple more as diary comments show: 'fished like a pillock' or 'a day of cardinal errors,' for example, and these reversals juxtapose the positive stuff.

When the River Witham roach were lethargic and the water very cold in winter, the stick float could be better than the waggler, holding the float back and inching it through. So the stick became my back-up method to waggler. I particularly liked a 7 x no. 4 cane and balsa float which got me some good results when the river was out of sorts. As noted elsewhere, the stick was also a good eel catcher in summer. I tended to experiment more with the size of stick on the Trent; a small Warren stick, and later various Dave Pearson models, brought me success at Long Higgin in particular.

Pinning my faith in the waggler all too often probably made every stick success all the sweeter. In the 1984-85 season I enjoyed a three match burst, finishing the season on good note at 'the Higgin,' a popular match course not too far downstream of Nottingham's Trent Bridge on the river's right bank. It was almost Christmas and I was having a good season. I'd won only one big match – the Scunthorpe Open on the Witham at Kirkstead – but had a few near misses and won sixteen sections over the six months since June 16. I was on my third visit to Higgin having blanked in the first on a flooded river, then come nowhere a fortnight later with 6-6-8. Could it be third time lucky at this venue?

It was. The match led to a brief but telling diary comment: 'At last a stick success – went like a dream.' I weighed 15-5-8 for third from peg 49 on Parkside and pocketed an early Xmas present of £75. My notes record that 19lb won the match including a 12lb carp, but not who caught it, plus a key detail from the day: '18" tail' (ie. hook to tell-tale shot gap). That shot, most probably a no. 8, was standard, and the hook a size 22. This distance was longer than normal for me, not dissimilar to how I'd shot a Witham waggler for a slow drop. This was also my best weight from Long Higgin to date, and this likely influenced what was to follow.

After this confidence boost I enjoyed two decent Trent match weights of 11-15 at Higgin and 13-2 at Shelford respectively in February; neither won me anything, though I placed eighth from a hundred and thirty in the latter. A few weeks later I fished a pleasure session on the Burton Joyce Road stretch on a trip with another mate, Steve Koc. The date was Thursday 7th March and seven is my lucky number.

I decided to add a couple of 'pilot shot' to the stick rig – no. 13 micros below the tell-tale no. 9, with the latter a full twenty seven inches away from the hook. Possibly the previous Higgin match led me to instinctively give the fish an even longer drop and slower fall to the maggot, but over two feet was pushing my luck? The drawing in the diary shows the no. 13 nearest the hook was placed approximately sixteen inches away, with a second five and a half inches above that, and then the no. 9 the same distance above this. The other shots placed shirt button-style were 2 x no. 8s and 4 x no. 4s beneath a six x no. 4 lignum stick.

Catch details remembered from the day are sketchy: it was quite cold after a frost, but I recall beating Steve with a net of roach that fell just short of double figures. But the important memory (and it was entered in capital letters above the diagram in the diary) was the success of my experimental shotting pattern. I don't think I missed many bites on the day, prompting me to get excited in the analysis: 'THE DISCOVERY made at Burton Joyce 7th March involving no. 13 shots.'

Two days later and I was back at Long Higgin for the Toone Open, and it was almost déjà vu when I drew peg no. 50 on the long outside bend below the fast straight, one above where I'd made third place. This was always a handy draw. The only issue for me was upstream on 52 where my former Barnsley teammate, John Allerton was standing. Always a class act, and hard to get the better of, John also had the luxury of a spare peg that separated us.

But, riding high with confidence both from the earlier

success and the recent practice, and in the knowledge that I'd done well before with John in my section, I could hardly have imagined a more successful outcome and end to the season. I would have been the clear underdog on paper, but I was simple buzzing and in no way overawed. I won the match with 21-2-8: mostly roach and a few skimmers but including three bonus chub for around 8lb, while John had to settle for 10-11. He took the defeat very well I have to say, but if there is a 'zone' state in angling I was in it that day. Feeling buoyed up by this result, twenty-four hours later I managed second on the Witham with 11-2, and was second again at Higgin with 11-5 to round off the season in style on the final day March 14th.

Shotting patterns are always subjective and vary greatly as this book demonstrates, but these pilot shot, or 'canary shot' as I called them in my first book, have definitely worked for me far more times than in this one match, and I have never really seen the need to change the pattern much at the lower end of the rig. I see it as speeding up the chain reaction of the shots working on the float and our reaction time with the strike, and just a few hundredths of a second must help, but, at the same time, not placing the first substantial shot too close to the hook in case the bigger, craftier fish, ignore the bait.

I'd never say that a no. 10 shot at ten to twelve inches from the hook at the business end is wrong, nor would I crib others' shot configurations, but the micros and longer gap to the main tell-tale, usually a no. 8, worked for me. The strategy was that at some stage in the day it might bring one or two bigger than average fish, and it worked well enough for bonus fish on different rivers to confirm it. Only by purposeful practice and experiment can you decide if it is right for you or not.

To end on an ironic note, I remember Ivan Marks writing about adding a micro shot to his trace below the tell-tale, saying that is could make a difference to the catch rate but little more. Curiously, no angler in my research other than John Allerton has mentioned the use of micro shot with their stick float presentation. John however, says he shots down to a no. 12. So might a few others do similar and keep quiet about it?

Chapter 47
Bespoke lignum sticks – Dave Pearson

Sheffield's Dave Pearson began making his own stick floats over 40 years ago after discovering that the best models he could buy from tackle shops were inferior and inclined to leak at the balsa/cane joint after a few sessions. Dave thought he could make better himself. It should be added that many anglers made their own floats at the time, a force of habit before good commercial floats were widely available.

A keen river angler, Dave had already made a few peacock wagglers for himself but, a toolmaker by trade, he started making sticks to order. His floats were well received locally and by the time the Trent was booming in the 80s, his lignums had a fan base across Yorkshire and beyond. I have several in my collection that still look as good as when I first laid eyes on them. At the smaller end of the scale is a five and a quarter-inch long, matt black finished, pointed top, 5 x no. 6 model that has caught me plenty of roach at shallow venues like Newark Dyke or on Burton Joyce Road stretch. He's also made me big sticks to order – 4 x BB and 5 x BB all of eleven inches long for the fifteen-foot deep R. Don at Sprotborough – arrow-straight, sturdy and great for easy casting. I've always admired the top to bottom symmetry and seamless balsa to lignum joint, have never had one break on me, and the shotting capacity always matches what's claimed on the label!

Years ago when I fished with Dave for Sheffield, his name was always high on the team sheet. Known first as a classy float angler, he later became a feeder angler of repute in the nineties. He won thirty-one matches with bream catches in one season alone, at venues like Elsecar, Butterley Reservoir and Attenborough Gravels, and set a record bream weight at Staunton Harold, Derbyshire with 104lb. His biggest bream is 12lb 4oz from Clumber Park lake.

Fast forward to the switch to pole fishing and commercial carp waters in particular, Dave now makes mostly pole floats to suit the different demand, but the quality of his stick floats is fondly remembered by all who have ever used one. Precision is his hallmark. Dave's angling hero is the legendary John Dean but his favourite Yorkshire angler is Barnsley's Keith Hobson, "and a lovely bloke too," he adds.

I wanted to learn more from my former teammate about the best stick floats I have ever used. Dave, now 71 and retired from the match scene, tells the story here...

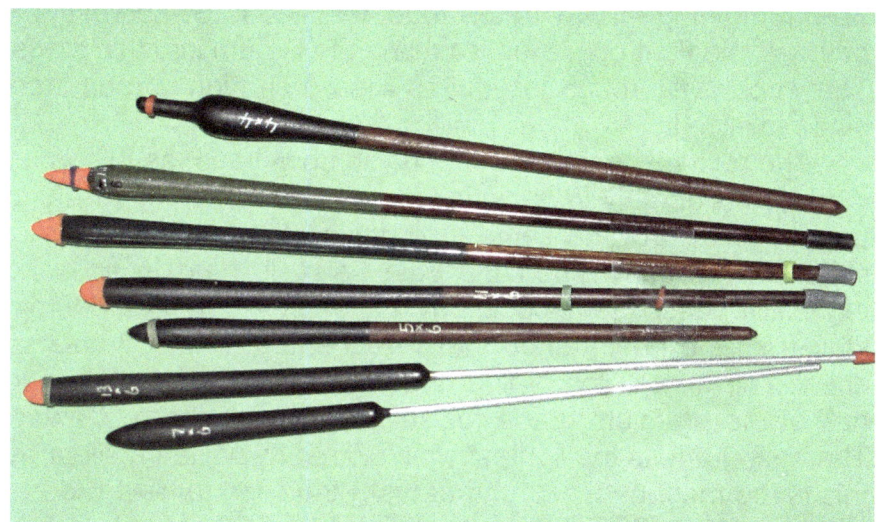

Assortment of the author's Pearsons including a pointed 6 x 4 lignum – all with seamless joints and arrow straight

I'd often make my own waggler floats when I started match fishing, and so it was a natural next step for me to produce home-made sticks. I started using commercial 'Benny Ashurst' sticks in the seventies but found they had a short life span. I think at that time the North West anglers had long been making their own sticks of better quality, but instead of shopping around I started experimenting with my own and it went from there.

My fishing improved because I was suddenly using floats I had more confidence in, especially knowing they would not leak at the joint, for example. I made a few to order for friends and the word got round. I watched Dave Harrell in a Swarkestone match one day and saw he had on one of my floats. "Where did you get the float?," I gently enquired. "Tom Pickering gave me a couple," he said. "A Sheffield bloke made 'em for him." If they were good enough for him it convinced me

I was doing something right.

To make a lignum stick the first job is to acquire some top quality lignum vitae. It is an oil-based wood that improves as it gets older. Fresh lignum is no good as it will warp/bend over time. I started my process with the help of wood from a hundred-year-old fishplate. An apt name for a wood to turn into floats! A fishplate is a large block of laminated lignum that is used for joining railway tracks together. About the hardest part of the whole float operation is cutting the lignum into thin strips. The wood is so tough it requires a six-inch high carbon steel blade to slice it.

The next job is to buy some balsa dowel and, as this wood varies considerably in density, we need a consistent quality to arrive at sticks of the same size, taking the same amount of shot. Unlike today when the best balsa is hard to find and expensive, back then I could buy it cheaply – 10p for a 600mm strip from the hobby shop that I frequented. In fact it was so cheap I'd buy a batch of five hundred pieces and select up to half of the premium grade for sticks and give the rest away. The best grade is the lightest which is nearly white in colour as this is the most buoyant, and at first I travelled far and wide to get hold of it. Sadly, it is hard to even find a hobby shop anywhere today.

The most popular sizes I made were probably smaller than many river anglers use now – a set would include five sizes – 4, 5, 6, 7, and 8 x no. 6s. From the lignums I branched out into longer wire-stemmers, or alum stems to be precise, with or without a shoulder at the top of the balsa, not unlike the John Allerton-style float.

John's name and fame led customers to start asking me for wire stems, though I have never been a wire lover myself. I have watched John fish a few times and he was fantastic with a wire stem. He could cast it out a good distance *and* control it there better than anyone else I'd seen. He, like a few others in his class but not many, made it look so easy. I'd have used a lignum every time at such range.

I'd get orders for pointed tops and domed tops according to taste. I personally liked a shouldered stick for casting three to four rods range, but a dome shape for close-in pin reel-work, running through and sometimes dragging a shot on the deck, and over-shotted and held back so the tip is just visible. Possibly my favourite sticks of all are my upper Trent specials for two to three-foot swims on gravel. At four-inch long or just over, they only take 2, 3 and 4 x no. 6 shots, but will cast from four to six rod-lengths. I used to enjoy running them through fast when the upper river was fishing at its peak. One experiment led me to a reverse tapered stem on some of these floats, and the result was a very stable float for rod end work and laying on in flood conditions. Now I'll take you through how I make my floats:

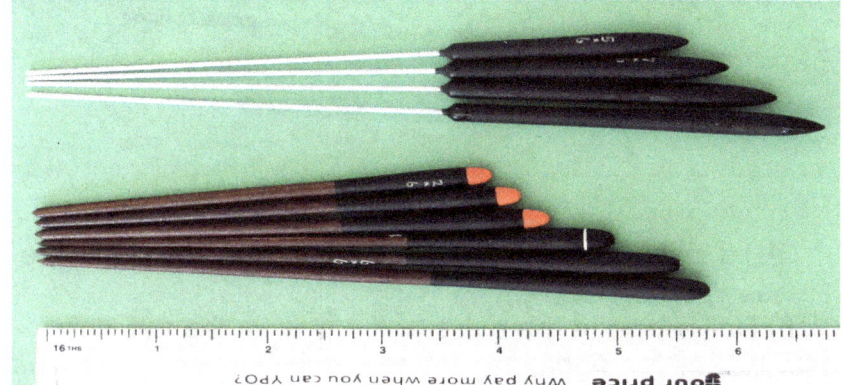

A range of Pearson pointed wire stems and some small domed lignums

MAKING A LIGNUM STICK Step-by-step

1) It is stating the obvious, but start with quality materials as already described – soft whitish balsa and lignum.

2) Using a table saw, I cut the lignum into rough sticks – 20cm long approx. by 5mm square cross section.

3) I file the sticks down to a round tapered shape then put each in the drill to sand down smooth. This involves using a micrometer to give a 160 thou (or approx. 4mm) diameter at the thick end, tapering down to 2mm at the pointed end. On most sizes these stems were just over four inches in length.

4) In the early days I would then carve a 5/8" spigot with a Stanley knife to insert into the balsa, but this was time-consuming. From there I turned the spigots down in a chuck of a small lathe, which was easier.

5) I used a measuring stick to cut the 5/16" diameter balsa to different lengths depending on the size of float required, but in each case would cut it a centimetre oversize, for example 70mm for a 60mm finished balsa top. This allowed 1cm to be

held in the lathe for shaping the top third or more of the float.

6) I'd put the balsa in the drill and gently spin between finger and thumb to align and centre the piece, then shape as required with emery paper.

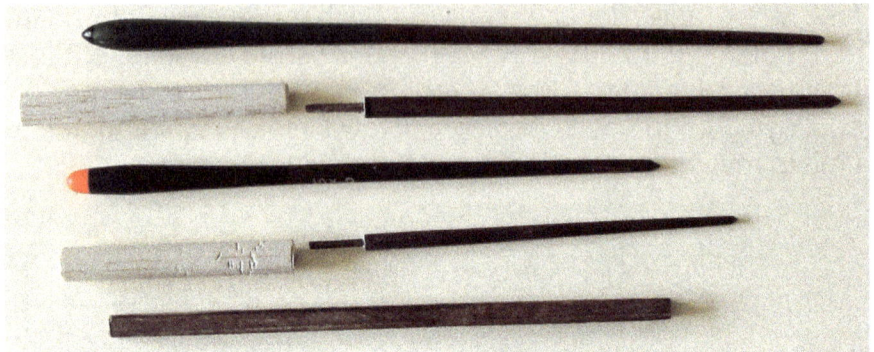

Two stages of the Pearson lignum float process, with rough lignum piece (bottom)

7) I'd mice up both ends of the balsa and re-shape if necessary.

8) Drill a hole in the balsa and marry up the two halves of float. It can be fiddly to get the hole straight, and takes practice. Patience required.

9) Marry up the two halves and glue them together. I used Evo-stick wood glue at the time. I'd advise to avoid epoxy resin unless you are careful with it, as any excess on the joint sets rock hard which makes a smooth finish more difficult.

10) Seal the balsa with sanding sealer then smooth off when dry with fine emery, blending it into the lignum.

11) Paint the balsa tip to your desired colour (in my case it was orange, red or black), add a transfer or write on the shotting capacity as a single figure to represent the number of size 6 shot, then finally add a coat of varnish to the balsa or the whole float. Job done.

One other point, use three silicon sleeves to attach all your stick floats as this gives you a spare in case the top one breaks, and make the top two rubbers slim – 2mm wide, say, is ample. A longer base rubber which fits a shade tighter can be made to overhang the float by a centimetre, and it is this which traps the float firmly in place.

Pearson's Top Tips

⌐ I have mentioned watching Dave Harrell and John Allerton fish a stick float, and walking the banks and watching others can teach us so much. Another angler I learned plenty from by taking a short hike was Castleford's Keith Kotchie, both a noted feeder angler and good float man. Keith, just like so many of the Trent locals, was forthcoming with information and told me all I needed to know. So the message is if ever in doubt: watch others, ask questions and learn.

⌐ Try a quality centrepin. For days when the river is slightly out of sorts I use an Adcock Stanton pin reel with only thirty yards of line on it. This stops the line bedding into the spool. Whenever there is extra flow and colour on the river, I have always found it the best choice, certainly for roach or chub. I wouldn't use the pin in a barbel peg, however – even though some do. Pumping in a big barbel would be hard work.

Chapter 48
The Puller stick for still water
– Jim Baxter & Ant Smith

On any reasonably mild day, if you continually feed a small pinch of casters or maggots into a lake holding a decent head of roach and/or other species, sooner or later (and it can take only a few seconds or minutes), you may see tell-tale swirls as fish take the bait close the surface. You may also see the fish flashing as they feed, subject to water clarity, or you might not see any kind of surface disturbance at all, but the fish can still be there feeding midwater.

Fish have to be competitive to survive and so are naturally inclined to reach a falling bait before it's snapped up by another. The message is clear: if the fish will rise up into the upper layers of water, they are catchable there. The next float to introduce to you is designed to do just that; it also explodes the myth that good fish can only be caught on or near the bottom.

I like to catch fish on the drop, or in midwater, it just appeals to my personality. I have a vivid memory of catching quality chub on a stick float on a winter's day on the Warwickshire Avon at Evesham, fishing half-depth in well over ten feet of water. The fish betrayed their presence early doors by crashing on the surface, and every one hooked put up a great fight and a serious bend in the rod, partly explaining why I still love using a rod and reel a bit more than pole fishing.

The puller stick float functions in an entirely different way to every other stick in four key respects: 1) it is fished on still waters, 2) unlike sticks for rivers that run away from the angler, this one is cast out then drawn backwards towards the rod, 3) for almost all that journey it is fished at a shallow angle, a tilt of around five degrees to the water surface being ideal, and 4) it is a sliding float, but one where a stop knot is not required – the fish self-hook by pulling against the angler's hand so the visual bite detection is secondary to feel.

For anyone who likes to catch fish on the drop, especially with stick float, this sliding float had immediate appeal. But for lake fishing – why? Well, once we begin to understand its function, we realise the puller can target many species –

roach, rudd, skimmers, crucians, ide and chub in particular, but any fish really that will feed in midwater or nearer the surface.

If you have never heard of the puller, you may think it strange that any worthy fish would look twice at a bait travelling almost horizontally through the water but, believe me, they do. Furthermore, it's a way of fishing different levels in the water column in a single cast which quickly tells us at what level the fish are most concentrated.

I first heard about this trolled sliding stick method for roach over twenty years ago. Sheffield's Bernard Bryan was the man behind it, and he was slowly revealing his secrets to any friends prepared to listen. I had limited knowledge of the float Bernard used, and what I didn't know was that the balsa top of his stick float had a piece of metal loaded inside before it was joined to the cane base, hence it took very little shot to cock it. Once I'd realised that the balsa was made to cock before the float was put together, I effected something similar, and began catching more fish. In the early years of the puller revolution, some anglers turned wooden

Ant Smith sliding pullers

paintbrush handles into one-piece puller floats. I have since copied this idea, making pullers from various floating materials because, as long as the float tilts rather than cocks, balsa is not essential.

The method hinges on the float sitting at a very shallow angle to the surface, with a number of no. 7 styl leads – usually from six to twelve leads, or similar weight in micro shot, spread out down the line shirt button-style. In effect it is a 1 x no. 6 size stick that you need.

Why does the float have to lay almost flat, one might ask?

Well the method relies on casting straight out and keeping as straight a line as possible from rod tip to hook. A fully cocked float would simply ruin the direct line with an unwanted angle. Line is slowly drawn from the rod with the free hand by hooking the forefinger over it at a point just beyond the butt ring then easing the float back towards the rod tip. The fish takes the bait, turns its head and the line immediately tightens against the finger and he's hooked. But if a fish is not taken on the drop, as the float is drawn closer to the rod tip and the bait descends close to the bottom, bonus fish can be caught there if a bed of bait is laid down in readiness. Regard this as a second bite of the cherry.

My best weight on the method at Barlow Farm is 56lb-0oz in a three-hour evening match, consisting of roach, rudd, skimmers and the odd bonus crucian. I had a nice run back in 2012-13 winning nine matches from 12 fished on summer evenings and averaging 43lb-14oz in the second series of six, beaten just once with my worst weight of 33-10.

Sheffield's Ant Smith investigated Bernard's method, which was making other good anglers wonder how this strange method could beat their pole approach, and worked things out his own way.

Ant took the basic roach catcher to a new level, applying it to commercial fisheries. He and protégé Chris Smith, no relation but a former Sheffield Junior National team angler, pitted their wits against the pole and carp specialists on Yorkshire and North Midland venues, and held their own with big weights of bream, roach and ide, plus the odd carp. Ant, 58 and a self-employed conservatory builder, moved the dial by breaking several venue records on his version of the method, with suitably scaled up tackle.

After making the right floats for the job, and combining them with stronger lines, a bigger hook in the shape of a 16 and heavy caster feed, his catches improved no end. The penny dropped when realising how the wary bigger roach and other species would habitually lie lower in the water and take a caster presented on a bigger hook among the few samples that had got past the smaller fish. Prior to Lodge Farm's Top pond being stocked with carp, he set the match record with 57lb comprising four tench and lots of small skimmers.

In a feeding bonanza on Lodge Farm's Lily pond he came out tops with 160lb of F1s and bream, ahead of rival Roger Pryor on 138lb, with Chris Smith's 100lb-plus puller net taking third. He added a venue record of 109lb of skimmers, bream and roach at Shireoaks in 2010, and in the same year his 40lb of roach net broke the silver fish record at Elm Tree Farm. He made the best ide catch at the time with 90lb from Lodge's Signal pond, and only last year topped forty-three anglers at the popular Springvale fishery with 158lb of ide and carp. His top carp weight on the method is 170lb-plus from Candy Corner. All told a very impressive record. Below is Ant's breakdown of the method and how it can beat more traditional styles.

My way with the Puller – Ant Smith

Teaming up and travelling with Chris Smith has brought us fair success on the puller method for over ten years. For a season or two it worked so well for ide in matches at KJS Aston's big pond that some of the competitors convinced the organiser to ban the method. They were not prepared to learn the method and so, like in other areas of life, they rejected it and claimed we had an unfair advantage, which was nonsense. It is just another method albeit a very good one on waters where fish will feed off the bottom. I'll now give my reasons why I enjoy the method along with a few do's and don'ts.

1) The puller method peaks in the warmer months of spring through to autumn when many species of fish will chase a bait in mid-water or shallower. I find that caster is by far the best bait for the method and will carry at least four pints with me for an average lake match.

2) A tight line is created from rod tip to float which creates a bolt rig when the float is cast straight out and trolled back by winding the reel slowly or pulling line away from the rod by hooking it with the middle finger and extending your arm sideways and backwards. The fish takes the bait and if the line is straight enough it only has to turn its head slightly to hook itself.

3) No pole is ever wavering over the fishes' heads, which can scare them in clear water.

4) Takes are attracted due to the bait's horizontal

movement. From spinning for pike, to carp 'jiggin,' a moving bait is famous for inducing bites in all forms of fishing.

5) By using a larger than normal hook – the hookbait sinks through the smaller fish to the bigger ones waiting for the odd caster getting through the small fry. These fish are not as fussy due to less bait reaching them.

6) Occasionally carp will take it, mainly I find around mid-May before spawning time, and early to mid-September when carp feed well on natural baits. On quite a few occasions at a venue called Candy Corner it worked really well for carp, and Chris and I were catching fish to 17lb on the puller, obviously with beefed up tackle.

7) As for the long rod approach as pioneered by Bernard Bryan, I have found this totally unnecessary and opt instead for a 14-footer, especially because a 20ft rod cannot exploit the potential catching area nearer to marginal features.

8) The puller is an excellent method for bream in summer when the rig has been allowed to sink deeper and the float drawn back into the rod tip vicinity.

9) The sliding float is shotted lightly with styl weights spaced out shirt button-style, and is carefully balanced so it just tilts to around five degrees from horizontal when the rig hits the water. Fish like ide, rudd and roach can often be caught quickly inches from the surface, but lots more of the water column can be covered if bites are coming deeper. As said, when the bait has dropped to mid-depth or lower, bigger fish, particularly bream and crucians, will often get in on the act.

10) I make my puller sticks by converting a traditional cane base and a balsa top stick. I take the float apart at the joint before drilling an 1/8" hole deeper into the balsa and packing this with number 9 shot before gluing the float back together. This gives casting weight to the float. Then drill the bottom of the float and add weight (lead or brass wire) until the float tilts. Finally whip on an eye at the top, a second on the side and two hard plastic sleeves on the cane (obviously keeping all in line).

11) My average rig is nine to ten x no. 7 styls spaced eight inches apart for an overall rig length of six feet-plus.

12) This method is also rather special for still water chub

as they find casters irresistible. When the caster hookbait hits the water I have known takes to be almost instantaneous, but be ready to release the line from your finger as we all know how fast they can charge off on their first powerful run.

13) Don't expect to catch fish consistently if you are not prepared to keep busy and continually feed them. We mostly take upwards of six pints of casters to a match on a commercial and, while we may only feed half that amount, on a good day will not bring many back.

Pipette power

Pictured are Pullers made for Sheffield's Paul Briggs by Middlesborough float-maker Andy Hartley, built from plastic pipettes with water added for the casting weight. Paul, 53, is a former neighbour of Bernard Bryan and, though aware of his puller method having watched Bernard fish as a young man, he mostly relies on pole for his sport. Prior to the Bernard Bryan Memorial match in summer 2021, he bought a selection of Andy Hartley's floats. He intended to fish pole and pellet in the match, but tried the new puller, liked the result and changed his mind. And bingo! He placed second to Roger Pryor, one of Sheffield's finest on the method, but it was very close – 45lb of bream to 44lb. Paul's verdict on his result: 'ecstatic.' Now well inspired, in a sequel at Milton a few weeks later, Paul hit the jackpot, catching mostly 2lb to 3lb bream from the off, to set a new Milton Ponds match record with 68lb and turn the tables on Roger in the bargain, second with 53lb. Credit also to Andy for making a near transparent float that must help reduce the caution of shallow-feeding fish by its camo' effect.

Analysis

On its day on the right water, the puller with caster on the hook can be deadly. Maggot can also produce well at times but caster seems to bring better fish, possibly helped by the rattle factor when they hit the surface. The method only came to me in the latter days of my match career; I wish I'd known of it much earlier. At a silvers venue like Holme Pierrepoint, for example, when on form, before it was ravaged by cormorants, I believe it could have beaten the pole or waggler hands down. My experience of the optimum depth that fish can be caught with it does not quite tally with Ant's, because at Barlow Farm I find the better fish will often take within five seconds of the bait hitting the surface. Here I have caught well, with as little as 3 x no. 7 styls down the line. But I totally agree that the rod need not be a long one, and the length can vary according the venue – for a large windswept lake with a shallow ledge to get over I'd say a 17-foot rod would be ideal, but on a sheltered pond where the fish will feed close, I have caught on an 11-footer, ergo a rod of 14 feet is about standard.

If you believe that the pole or feeder can deliver the goods everywhere you fish, cover every match eventuality, I'd say think again. The puller is a confidence method and one that rewards a high work rate. On some thinly stocked waters it is not that effective, nor on waters holding too many tiny fish of 1oz to 2oz size that the bigger ones cannot push away from the bait, but anywhere that you can get fish of 4oz and bigger competing for the bait it will catch well.

I had always wanted to catch some bigger fish this way. In the summer of 2021, on a short holiday in Cambridgeshire, I got the chance. The lake was full of carp, but by casting beyond the feed area I caught many chub in the 4lb class and ide closer to 5lb, scaling up the trace line to .13mm. The chub were hitting the bait within a foot of the surface and putting a serious bend in the rod. There must be scores of waters around the UK where the fish will respond similarly to this style of fishing. Finally, I'll stick my neck out and predict that, one day soon enough, good anglers will have got the message for a major match to be won with it.

Top Tip

If you like dark ruby red casters then try turning your own from red maggots. The first time I did this I took a quality roach catch and I have not seen any drawback to reds over white maggots. This follows the likes of Benny Ashurst who preferred the deep red caster, and a crisp dark caster seems particularly suited to the puller method.

Chapter 49
Getting a taste for Bolo': Trent style
– John Small

John's 34-12 top Bolo' catch

Lincoln's John Small, 52 and a roofer, developed his match skills on the Rivers Witham and Trent. He was first shown the basics by his father, Mick, then tutored in the 1980s by the late Paul Andrews, one of Lincoln's top float anglers. John has always enjoyed using a waggler or stick float for roach but, with the Trent becoming increasingly pure this century, he moved towards the Bolognese or Bolo' method and has never looked back. He has notched up open wins on the tidal and middle Trent, Newark Dyke, the upper and lower reaches of his local Witham and River Don. He rates his two best Bolo' results as: 1) the 2016 Trent National when he caught 12.750kg in a 50mph downstream wind, winning his section at

Collingham, and finishing eighth overall, helping his 'beloved' Lincoln side to a 'long overdue' National medal for which he'd been striving since 1985; and 2) a stunning 34b 12oz personal best weight from Burton Joyce. But another match that meant a lot to John for obvious reasons was winning the 2015 Paul Andrews Memorial match at Dunham with 18lb 14oz, a trophy that in his words he's been 'lucky enough' to get his name on twice more.[22]

It might make sense to start by describing why I think the Bolo' serves me well and and how it might help you, the reader. Some may think of it only for very deep water, but I'm quite happy fishing a 3g Bolo' float in depths from 7-foot to 14-foot that ideally has a nice steady flow and is not too turbulent. Any shallower and I will likely turn to a waggler or stick but, if deeper, I will up the size of Bolo' float. It doesn't appear to be too detrimental to hitting bites in deeper water. Similarly, if the water is fairly turbulent I will fish a heavier float to try and improve presentation.

I regard any swim over 10-foot deep as Bolo' territory even if it is close in. The fish seem to like the deeper water nowadays, and we very rarely catch much on the shallower pegs like we used to, likely due to the water clarity and bird predation. At Collingham in the National I was fortunate to find the eight feet of water close in and the fish were there. By casting well downstream and pointing my rod at the float (a Bob Pearson 2.7g) I could present the float well enough to beat the vicious gusting wind. I often find that fish will feed more confidently anyway in a strong wind, so presentation can be less than perfect. Another reason I like the Bolo' is the speed you can catch when there are lots of fish in the swim. The weight down the line helps in casting to the hotspot and getting the float set for another bite very quickly.

It is tempting to think that the extra weight under a Bolo' float might not suit clear water and difficult fish, but I feel the big advantage is that I can fish much further out whenever clear water makes the fish reluctant to come to close to the

---

22 John added a fourth Paul Andrews Memorial trophy win in 2021 with 14lb of roach on the Bolo'...

bank. I can still get away with fishing a light hooklength and the shotting is very light in the three feet below my bulk where I try and concentrate the fish. Another advantage of the extra weight is that a lot of my fishing is done on the tidal Trent where the wind is usually in your face and downstream. With the heavier float I can still manage to get decent presentation when I would struggle to present the stick float at all.

Tackle
I like to fish the Bolo' with a long rod rather than one of the telescopic Bolognese rods. The tidal Trent with its open nature and downstream winds is no place for a six or seven-metre rod with only half a dozen eyes on, although I have heard good reports about the new Bolo' rods coming out recently. I started out on the tidal using a long rod and I see no reason to change. There are lots of very good reasonably priced 16-20-foot rods on the market at the moment. My personal choice of rod length is 17 feet.

Reels are very much an individual choice. I just try to find one that does not create line twist and does not allow the line to go behind the spool in a headwind. I also like a reel with a slower retrieve to help prevent the hook length spinning up. My main line is very old school in the form of Bayer Perlon 2.6lb – a line I have always used and also see no reason to change. It is a very robust line and close to neutral buoyancy allowing the line to float on top of the water or be sunk if needed. I have never used back-shots with the Bolo', but will normally push my rod tip underwater and allow the waves sink the line in a downstreamer.

Rig profile
The setting up of the Bolo' rig I use is not at all complicated. First, I attach the float using four rubbers. Float choice I feel is very important, second only to feeding, which I will come back to later. An olivette .5-gram less than the float loading is then threaded on the line and a quick-change swivel tied to the end of the line. Six x no. 8 shots are then put in a bulk just above the swivel to produce a boom, which helps prevent tangles. The olivette is then pushed down to the boom and a single number 8 placed two inches above to trap it.

322

I then take a 30-inch length of line (or leader) with a small loop at each end and attach this to the quick-change swivel. Three x no. 10 shots are placed on this and my six-inch hook length is added to the bottom loop. The line I use for this leader is 3.2lb Bayer Perlon. Along with the swivel the thicker line helps prevent hooklength twist and tangles. I also believe that the thicker line catches the water flow more, so having just 3 x no. 10s on the line this allows me to tease the bait down the peg by gently slowing the float. The neutral buoyancy of the line also helps the bait lift slowly in the water when the float is held back. Hook choice is usually a size 18 or 20, hooklengths are more often than not 0.10mm. I also have several reserve 30-inch leaders tied up, with 3 x no. 10 shots in place, stored in the old white hook packets that we once used. Should the worst happen and I tangle up, it is just a matter of attaching a new leader to the quick-change swivel. I also carry some 18-inch lengths of line carrying 2 x no. 8 shots, should a more positive approach be needed.

The Float
As for the float, there is only one pattern I use which is home-made. I first saw the float being used when I sat behind Roly Moses at South Clifton one Thursday. The way he put it through the peg, it looked like it would go under at any moment. I believe the pattern was developed by Roly and Paul Goulding for use on the River Don. I knew I wanted some, so went to see the best float maker in Lincoln, Bob Pearson, or 'Bobby Blue Shoes' as he was affectionately known to us.

Bob was a very talented float maker, a gift rating second only to his ability to talk and tell a story. I lost many an evening collecting floats and listening to Bob's stories of playing for Sheffield Wednesday, and of his racing his pigeons that were descendants of the ones Adolf Hitler used during WW2. Bob was not just one of angling's characters, he was one of life's characters and is sadly missed by many. After Bob's sad death, and running low on floats, I decided to have a go at making some myself. I wasn't talented enough to turn the bodies myself like Bob would, so found someone who could make the bodies for me.

The floats I make now have a tear-shaped body, a six-inch long two-millimetre-thick carbon stem and a two-inch tip made

John Small Bolo's

of 3mm cane. The bodies are made of Rohacell foam so will not take water on, even with line-cut. It is a great source of pride that my floats are now used by many anglers on the Trent circuit, including World and Riverfest champions. Float size I find is a real trade-off: the bigger the float the easier it is to fish but the more bites you can expect to miss. I carry floats from 2.5g to 6.5g but for 90 per cent of fishing I will use one of 3g.

I choose now to fish a Bolo' rather than a stick float in most situations because, as suggested the water clarity tends to make the fish nervous and stop them settling too close. A Bolo' allows me to fish further out where the fish feel safer. There is no doubting that a stick float gives a nicer presentation than a Bolo' but there is no point in fishing where the fish are not. However, there are still a few old boys around that make the stick float work, notably Jim Evans, Colin Perry, and river legend and one of my heroes, Wayne Swinscoe. The only time I choose a stick over a Bolo' is if there is a little extra water on, with a bit of colour, and I need to fish close.

Baits

I carry just three different baits on my bait tray – maggots, hemp and tares. Why no groundbait you may ask? Well, I have not persevered with cereal much in truth, but I am planning to try it more next season. It works on many other rivers around the country so I see no reason why it wouldn't score on the Trent, and it should also help to keep the fish low in the water.

For a five-hour match I will take five pints of maggots, 4.5 pints of bronze with fluoro's (fluorescent pink) mixed in, four pints of hemp and one pint of tares cooked with an iron tablet to turn them jet-black. I will very rarely use all the bait but it all keeps for the next match. I have no problem with feeding old maggots, in fact I prefer to. The tares are slightly undercooked to cope with the rigours of long casting. I also have a few grains of hemp which I have prepared at home by pushing a needle through and tying a line around, so it is just a matter of hooking the line. I have real problems with hooking hemp naturally.

My main hookbait is maggot and I have a lot of confidence in a fluoro' maggot. It has caught me loads of bonus fish, and on hard days I will have one on the hook most of the match. However, on some days there are so many small fish in the peg that a maggot will not find its way to the better stamp fish. These are times when a grain of hemp or a tare on the hook can make all the difference.

An example of this was when I drew the famous outfall peg on Burton Joyce roadside stretch. Upon arrival at the peg, it was clear there were millions of small dace waiting to frustrate me. Tiny fish were showing themselves all over the peg. My plan of attack for the day was to feed nothing but hemp with the odd pouch of tares on the Bolo' line, but to start on the whip, loose feeding plenty of maggots by hand. The aim was to attract the smaller dace close in and allow the better roach time to settle over the hemp on the Bolo' line, to at least start off putting some fish in the net.

After an hour and ten minutes of catching dace on the whip, it was time to have a look and see if there were any better roach on the Bolo'. The snag was I spent the next twenty minutes getting a bite every chuck from tiny fish and only catching two small dace. It was time to try a tare on the hook. First cast and the float slid under and a lovely six-ounce roach came to the net. Three and a half hours and 110 roach later I put 34lb 12oz on the scales for my best weight on the method, and a real red letter day!

Feeding

I believe that feeding is the most important element and there is no set pattern to follow. I want to keep the fish in the bottom couple of feet of water and this can involve feeding more hemp than maggots. I will also feed maggots less often if I feel the fish are coming up in the water. Sometimes it can be feeding maggots only every half-hour, but putting two or three big catapult pouchfuls in at a time. It is always down to conditions on the day, but I like to feed them as often as I can, and generally I feed fairly aggressively. I am not fishing for team points, only for a weight good enough to get me in the frame or win the match. Usually 14-25lb is needed for this.

At the start of the match, I will feed a pint of hemp, spread from halfway down my peg to three-quarters and not all on one line. I will also feed four or five pouchfuls of maggots and the same of tares. This gives the peg a good carpet of bait. The first hour of the match is then spent either looking for a bonus fish on the feeder or putting a few fish in the net on a whip, whilst I carry on feeding the Bolo' line with hemp and maggot, allowing the peg to settle. The hemp and maggots I feed in the first hour are fed halfway down the peg on one line, trying to produce a killing zone in which to catch.

Once I start to fish the Bolo' it is a matter of trying to work out the best feeding regime. Some days you get the impression the fish do not like the hemp being fed over the top of them, so I will cut out the hemp in the knowledge that I have a good carpet of it in the peg from the initial feed and will just feed maggots. Other days feeding maggots will bring too many small fish into the peg so I will just feed hemp. But more often than not, it is a matter of feeding a bit of both and trying to work out the best ratio of feed. This could be something like three casts feeding hemp and then one with maggots. It really is a matter of trial and error.

Presentation

To present the bait at a good angle to the rod I like to cast about halfway down my peg. This allows me to get my main line behind the float even with an awkward downstream wind. Most matches these days are double pegged, so you have plenty of room to fish. Even on a single peg I would rather present the bait nicely for half a peg rather than poorly for a full peg. Depth-wise I try to start just tripping bottom and take it from there, making little adjustments as the bites slow or start to be missed. Certainly on the tidal Trent such depth changes are a must as the water level is constantly changing.

I like the float to go through the peg at the same pace as the flow, just checking and slowing it a little from time to time. This very often results in the tip of the float lifting out the water a couple of inches then as you release it and the float starts to settle again it just carries on and disappears. A crisp, upwards strike and hopefully I am playing a nice fish. If the bite is missed the float is left to carry on its way a little closer in. The better stamp fish very often hang off the main shoal and this can result in the odd bonus fish.

My style is largely based on catching small fish – predominantly roach and dace, but I have hooked and caught plenty of big fish too, including barbel, chub and perch. The Bolo' is a lovely way of fishing and less complicated than many people believe. I would recommend giving it a go. The River Trent is just as good as it has even been, if not better! But your local river may well suit the Bolo' method too.

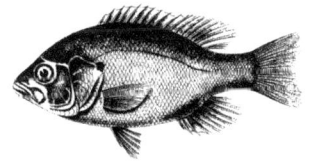

Chapter 50
The Don: three ways – Topper, Bolo' & Stick

John Bromilow

South Yorkshire's River Don changes dramatically from its shallow headwaters to the north-west of Sheffield, then onwards through the city to Rotherham where it doubles in depth. But downstream of Denaby, near Sprotborough, it enters a deep gully offering 14 feet and more of water. Thanks to the decline of the steel and mining industries, the river is now one of Yorkshire's premier river venues, it holds good coarse fish stocks and it is even anticipated that salmon will return. In recent years the feeder for bream and long pole for roach have become dominant match methods, but float and running line tactics will often beat both in the right hands. In this chapter we'll study three such anglers and the different floats that have brought them success: the 'Topper' of John Bromilow and Mick Peverley, the stick of Joe Murray, and the Bolognese of Paul Goulding.

1A) Topper with John Bromilow & Mick Peverley

Maltby's John Bromilow, 59 and an electrician, has been a consistent performer on the Don over the last 20 years. His style is based on the Topper, the polystyrene-bodied crowquill float developed by Bristol's Mervyn Haskins. As stated elsewhere, this float is intended more for an upstream wind than anything, but is a boss float with a very sensitive tip. I interviewed John in 2020 about his choice for the Denaby and Sprotborough match circuit:

Q: John, would I be right in saying that although you have become a winner as a float angler, in your early years on the Trent you were better known for your feeder skills? And while you probably missed the Trent's heyday of float matches, your skills improved with help of the Don's transformation into a good match venue nearer to home?

– Well yes, that's correct. I watched and learned from local anglers on the Don from the days it started to fish well. Before that I had a few years on the Trent when I enjoyed stick float but had most success catching chub and bream on the feeder.

My conversion to the Topper on the Don was influenced by fishing with Maltby's best float anglers, particularly Joe Murray, Brian 'Buck' Butler, and Dennis Pinkos, all a few years my senior. Joe was always steady, but Dennis attacked his swim with caster and hemp and was what we might call a 'muck or nettles' feeder. I learned from them all, but if Dennis didn't kill his swim he'd be favourite to catch most of the three. He adapted his methods to the Don and won his share of matches. Sadly, he's been forced to retire early with back problems.

Q: What is your 'go-to' size of Topper float for the deep Don?

– My regular size is 10BB or four-gram which is shotted with a 3.5g olivette approximately three feet from the hook and strung out droppers below. A typical rig will carry 8 x no. 8s in a close chain immediately below the olivette, then 4 x no. 8s and 1 x no. 10 equally spaced towards the hook, and lastly a size 20 micro swivel as the tell-tale which attaches to the hooklength. My heavier approach would be with a 12 x BB (4.8g) float, using a 4.0g olivette and a similar arrangement of droppers.

Q: So, if you plumb up to find 14-foot of depth at say 10m range, how deep would you set the float to start the session?

– I set the float to dead depth and will start at that after checking I have a clear snag-free run through first. I never fish over-depth but may well shallow up on days when the fish grow in confidence and rise up the feed column.

Q: How do you combat a downstream wind: back-shotting perhaps?

– When faced with a strong downstreamer I naturally try to fish a closer line as there is no sense in presenting the float further out where trotting in a straight line parallel to the bank is virtually impossible. Sometimes I will sink the line to the float with the help of back-shots, but in a bad wind I might also consider changing to a pole or whip to offer better presentation. I might well go up to the 12BB first and try moving the bulk down to two foot to use the slower bottom layers of water in the river to slow the float down.

Q: I hear that the Don runs a bit quicker now than when I fished it a few years ago, but the Topper is not generally regarded as stable enough to avoid riding up when held back – is this ever a problem?

– Yes, the float does ride up when held tight but my float is normally shotted really well down, and the float top is the thinnest I can get away with, so even if it rides up a little when holding back this is not usually an issue.

Q: Do you put down a bed of groundbait to kick-start the peg, and do you lay the float in upstream similar to a long pole style?

– I've experimented with balling in groundbait in the past, but found this always had a negative effect on the catch rate. So now I tend to put a bed of hemp down and loose feed over the top.

Q: So what is the loose feed that's always on your bait waiter; I always remember you preferring caster to maggot?

– I normally take two pints each of casters, maggots and hemp to a match, but the amount fed always depends on how the fish respond. This also varies summer to winter, so less bait is required when the water's very cold and the fish lethargic. These days I mainly start fishing the Don matches in autumn, as we travel to the country at weekends in summer.

On an average autumn/winter peg I expect to feed a pint to a pint and a half each of caster and hemp. We have found more bleak appearing in recent years though, and to avoid them I will feed maggot on a separate line (usually closer in, occasionally further out) to keep the bleak away from my main (caster) line. No two days are ever quite the same of course; I won a match recently with 14lb of roach using hemp on the hook, and I have ended up fishing maggot a few times lately as it has worked better on the pegs I've drawn.

Q: So how far out in the river do you make your play as a rule?

– It varies according to the peg, of course, but generally it's from one third across to mid-river.

Q: What species would an average double figure net of yours consist of?

– I would estimate 80 per cent roach, 15% bream and 5% perch. This can vary quite a lot however, depending on the swim and weather conditions. Bream always come more into the picture, and roach less so, whenever the river is up a bit and coloured.

Q: Would you start on a 20 hook with a 12BB rig, or do you go for an 18?

– I'm always looking for the better quality roach and will fish a 20 hook on a 12BB but if the fish are having it I will not think twice of upping to an 18, and I always hook the caster like I would a maggot.

Q: Do you ever fish a stick and/or Bolo', and if so how heavy?

– I've tried to fish the stick in the past and failed miserably. I do set up the Bolo' occasionally if the bream are feeding and I want to use a heavy bait and hold back really hard. This is in conjunction with a six-metre Bolo' rod.

Q: Which peg or area at Sprotborough do you fancy offers the best win chance if you could draw it?

– I like the late thirties, or early forties pegs. It is always a consistent area and has a good depth close in which obviously makes float control easier if conditions are a bit awkward.

Q: Do you have a best match memory, or, say, a proudest moment on the Don circuit?

– Not really of one match in particular, but I did win the Rotherham Winter League points race twice when it was a 60-pegger and fished over six rounds. That was not all on Bolo' of course but at least half of it was.

Q: Finally John, from all your rivals who gains your utmost respect, in that you'd ideally not want them in your section if both drawn on good float pegs?

– Joe Murray and Paul Goulding are always there or thereabouts if it is a float session. But really we can only concentrate on our own performance; what others catch is out of our hands. We might lose to the guy at the next peg and still come second in the match, for instance.

1B) The Sliding Topper – Mick Peverley

Rotherham's Mick Peverley was one of the best Fenland swingtippers in the sixties. Fishing under the Conisbrough Ivanhoe team banner, he won six prestigious titles, including the Sheffield DAA Haig & Haig Trophy, Middle Level drain, the Stones Gala (twice) on the River Witham, the CIU National Champs (twice) on the R. Welland (one with the tip, the other waggler), and almost all the big Witham association matches of that era. Those six wins were huge matches of 700 or more pegs!

The former Rotherham team skipper, and Rotherham Raider, has also been a consistent all-rounder, respected for consistency with stick float and waggler on the Rotherham stretch of the tidal Trent at Dunham Bridge. Mick's stand-out stick memories include a 100lb-plus of roach to frame on the River Erne, Northern Ireland match when Ian Heaps set the world record catch (166lb 11½oz), and a 17lb of roach winner at Dunham, pushing John Allerton, who "was virtually unbeatable on the Trent at the time", into second from the next peg.

Other float successes include: 2nd in the Angling Times Winter League final, R. Blackwater, Ireland – 23lb 9oz of dace on stick; 1st Charles Haig match at Burton Joyce – 16lb 5oz; 1st Eastern Region Winter League, Sibsey Trader drain – 9lb 10oz; 1st Eastern Region W/L, Nene North Bank – 16lb 7oz; Angling Star Super League final, Rother Valley – 20lb 0oz and the River Don Championship with 9lb 14oz of gudgeon.

Knowing that Mick (now a veteran of 80) was involved with the stick in its early years, I first wanted to ask him about his floats and presentation in the days when Dunham housed many big matches...

"My range of Trent stick floats vary in size from 4 x no. 4 up to 10 x no. 4 originally made for me by the late Garry Oates, from Doncaster. Instead of lignum stems (this hardwood was difficult to get at the time) Garry found a dense plastic used as insulation in the electrical industry that proved to be an excellent alternative. I shotted the floats with no. 6s spread over the bottom half of the rig spaced 150mm apart, and 1 x no. 8 just above the 45cm hook length. The no. 6 shot would be replaced by no. 4s in deeper Dunham swims.

"Regarding float presentation, in the early years with very coloured water you had to slow the bait down to give the fish time to see the bait. We did this by slowly following the float with the rod downstream under a tight line to its limit before it pulls the float off course, then releasing more line and sweeping the rod back upstream to repeat the process. Most anglers feed line direct from the reel by hand to slow the float down; it is personal choice.

"As the river water quality began to steadily improve in the 1970s due to new regulations on discharges from sewage works, coal mines, steel plants etc, the water became clearer. This meant we now had to change the way we presented the bait. Clearer water meant that the fish moved further out in the river, which created problems with presentation in the prevailing downstream winds at Dunham. To overcome this it was necessary to cast the float further out and downstream to keep the float moving on a straight line to the flow.

"Loose feeding casters now became the method but you still had to hold the hook bait back slightly to keep the bites coming. The other thing we had to be aware of, like on any tidal river, was changing depth, as the water dropped or lifted with the tide, requiring constant float adjustments to keep the bait just off the bottom.

"Things never remain the same though, as Dave Thomas proved by using maggots with great success on the opens at Dunham. I watched Dave fishing a centrepin reel with maggot at Dunham one day and was really impressed. I was very reluctant to accept that maggot was now the dominant roach bait on the tidal. Winning a big 290-peg Eastern region winter league match in 1980 from a peg at North Clifton with 10lb 8oz of roach on the stick float and caster made me continue using casters longer than I should have.

"It was always two to three pints of casters with groundbait in my early days with the stick float but the winds of change saw me switch to two to three pints of loose-fed bronze maggots.

"Coming up to present with my local River Don, I have been experimenting with a 'Sliding Topper' float to use with a 16-foot rod at Sprotborough in swims of 15-feet and more. Trials are still ongoing, but early results have been promising with my 16-foot Tri-cast Allerton Premier rod, using a 10 x BB float (4-gram) at Sprotborough and an 8 x BB (3.2g) version for the shallower Denaby section. There are three stand-off wire eyes whipped to the float – an inch from the tip just above the body and two at the lower end and, with the poly body 5/8" diameter at its widest point, the eyes are offset at least a quarter-inch.

"A tiny bead is threaded on above the float that runs up to the stop knot, and under slack line the weight pulls the line through to reach the required depth, but the line will trap against the float body when holding back. I use a bulk of shot a yard from the hook with a string of no. 8 droppers below, and I have also made some short (hollow) peacock ends to slide onto the tip for improved visibility that also allow a change tip colour in awkward light conditions."

2) BOLOGNESE with Paul Goulding

Paul, 55, an arboriculturalist from Harworth, near Worksop, has blazed a trail with the Bolo' method on the River Don throughout the river's improvement in the last twenty years. His best Don weight on the float from Sprotborough is 24lb from a peg in the fifties, and during the very wet weeks of winter 2020 his best winning catch that year was 215 fish for 19lb. That's busy! He has also honed his method well on the Trent and won some good matches there too. But before Paul explains his deadly Bolo' approach here's what two friends had to say about him:
Terry Moroz: "I have fished alongside Paul at Sprotborough on South Yorkshire's River Don for many years. In that time he

has built up an enviable record, with some big wins in most of the key matches held on the river. This began just as the Bolognese method had arrived from Italy and was growing popular here as a way of tackling our deeper rivers. The Don here runs through a steep-sided gully that creates depths up to 20ft in places at normal level. Upstream at Denaby the depth is a little easier to manage, at 12 or 13 feet, but none of it makes a difference to Paul because he's perfected the Bolo' method to cope with these swims. From pioneering the method on the Don he has won with it on the Trent and become an outstanding Bolo' angler generally. His Trent victories include a record three wins at Long Higgin in the Frank Barlow Memorial.

Paul Goulding

"My best testimony to Paul's skill was when we fished in the same winter league team and he gave me one of his floats which I took to Denaby for a practice. I was catching very little until Paul sat behind me, watched for a while then said I was doing it all wrong. Eager to learn from the master, I passed him the rod. Within twenty minutes he was catching a roach every run down! I'm glad he did, as it led me to securing a few brown envelopes of my own which I'm certain I wouldn't have won without that lesson. My main mistake was feeding too far *upstream which he corrected: a real eureka moment."*

Roly Moses: "Paul was already making waves on the Don when he came to me with a request to make him a Bolo' float. He'd been doing all right with a rust-coloured, cigar-shaped one if I remember correctly, but insisted it was not quite what he wanted. I made one that I thought was right, he tried it brought it back. "Not right," he said. So I made another body-down shape in contrast to the popular body-up type. He tried it, brought it back again. To cut the story short, through his trial and error on the bank, and my own in the 'mancave,' we arrived at a float (1.5mm diameter cane bristle, 1.5mm diameter carbon stem) with which Paul won a Don match then told me it was 'perfect.' But then Paul could make a poor float fish well, he had it in spades, so to speak. He is one of the best river anglers I have ever met."

The Don has been very kind to me on various methods but especially the Bolo'. All of us have those breakthroughs in fishing when we try something new, magic happens and we think: 'I've got this – cracked it,' then almost at that exact moment something changes for the worse and we realise we have to re-think our strategy in some way.

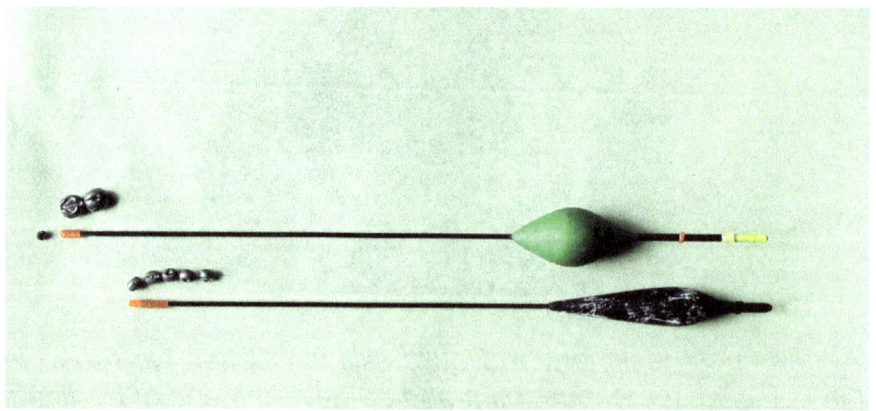

Two Bolo floats from the Roly Moses bench – a 3.3g with rugby ball-shaped body and carbon stem, and a float he calls the 'stick bolo' of 5 x BB with slim balsa tip

For example, it took me some time to find a shotting pattern for the Bolo', which minimised tangling. On a Bank Holiday Monday session at Shelford the wind was blowing awkwardly downstream and in. I couldn't get a bite on waggler.

So I tried using a Bolo' with a shirt button shotting pattern, but had many tangles on the cast. I'd only get a bite when the rig landed in a straight line. I won the section with 4-5lb but went home with mixed thoughts.

When shotting up a Bolo' rig later, it was different in the sense that: a) I used a big bulk, and b) the dropper shot placings were closer together than on the stick, not dissimilar to a double bulk effect. I finished work early one day and decided on the spur of the moment to travel to the Burton Joyce Roadside with the latest float. I caught a roach first drop in, another next drop, and went home happy with the result of three hours fishing.

My next match was an Angling Times Winter League and I drew the Roadside, going on to win the section with 13lb. That same year in the (Burton Joyce) Ferry Field I had 42 fish on the Bolo' when no one else caught a fish on the float.

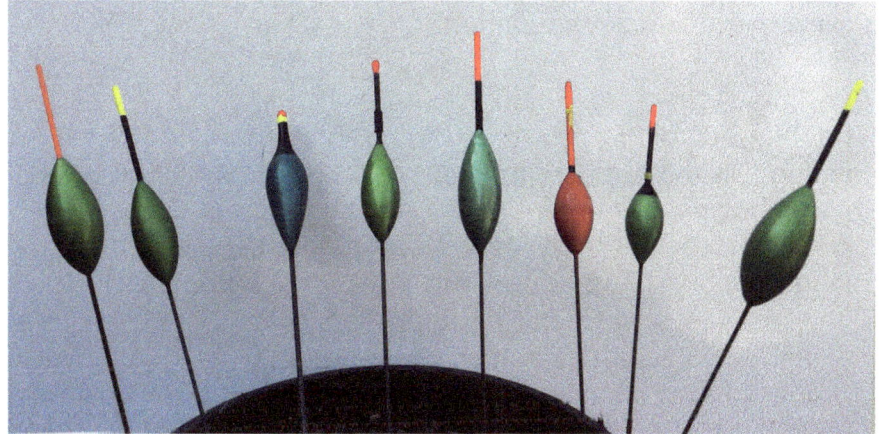

Goulding Bolo's

I have also applied the method when fishing the deep length of the Trent at Long Higgin, notably in the Frank Barlow Memorial. I managed to win this at my first attempt with 18lb of roach on Bolo' and, after framing twice more, eventually won it again when I rode my luck on a flooded river to catch a 9lb 15oz bream on the bomb and a 1lb hooklength.

The Tackle
Moving on to tackle, the longer and lighter rods available today obviously give all river anglers an advantage with float

presentation compared to what they could do with a 13-foot rod in days gone by. Until recently I have used a modified 20-foot Milo Power Era rod with Bolo' on the Don and I have three of them. They give me the necessary control whenever the wind was awkward. But I never liked the hollow tip and changed all of them to a spliced tip. This softer tip greatly improved the rods in my opinion. I also added three extra eyes to the spliced tips, which made them even softer. I still like the 20-footer on the River Aire, but since the Don has seemed to speed up to more like the Trent pace, I now fish a 17-foot Tri-cast Trilogy John Allerton model, again customised on the tip section, teaming this up with a Daiwa Tournament Pro of the same length which is also brilliant. For a reel I look no further than a Daiwa Autocast. When it comes to hooks there are many good brands to choose from. I have long favoured Drennan 'Super Carbon Maggot' in size 20 or 22, but my supply is just about used up, so I have started trying out Colmic and Gamakatsu patterns.

Feeding

The biggest difference with my Don method today is the feeding. The river has changed nature in recent times. I used to feed downstream of the float despite the great depth of 14ft-plus, and would simply cast a yard upstream of where the maggots hit the surface and run the float towards them. So I'd often catch just upstream of where I fed.

In my opinion the situation changed in 2015 when a hydro-electric scheme including two turbines were installed upstream at Aldwarke and Thrybergh. Since then the river flow has been more erratic and generally a little faster which requires a heavier rig.[23] Previously I fished a 3-gram float; now I have to fish 4g.

---

23 With regard to the Don's hydro-electric scheme, Mark Simon, the engineer who built the plant, disputes the belief that they can make the flow erratic or speed up the mean flow, which poses the question what other factors could cause flow fluctuations? A large tanker, for example, which carries oil from Hull upstream to Rotherham via the Don, displaces a huge volume of water on leaving the river through the lock into the adjacent Mexborough Canal. And there are many Don tributaries, the rivers Rother and Dearne included, that feed into the river and could change the speed at any time.

In fact my Sprotborough approach has become more akin to how I fish the Trent in that I feed upstream of the float. With the river's faster pace I run it at 'em too, no holding back; the heavier float sets up quicker and the bites tend to come quicker. I used to feed three times per trot but now I can't as the float settles fast and a bite can follow rapidly. One might imagine catching fish shallow this way but on the Don I can never seem to get them in midwater. Also, if I have a hiccup with something, like the need to change a hook, any break in the feeding pattern can risk losing the feeding shoal and going from a bite every cast to nothing.

One area that some anglers have missed out on, I think, is the bulk, for it regularly has to be adjusted up and down to suit where the fish are in the water column. I also place 6 x no. 10s below the bulk for which I found shots worked better than an olivette. The three shot bulk I favour is an AAA, BB and a no. 4, though this is less important now, bearing in mind the extra pace of river and quality of bites – positive is hardly the word!

The no. 10 droppers also evolved and increased in quantity over time. I have done well with 20 x no. 10s, placed close together below the bulk with gradually widening gaps towards the hook – starting 5mm apart and opening up to 10mm, terminating in the tell-tale six inches from the hook. I've also configured it the opposite way round with the gaps diminishing towards the hook to make a more sensitive rig. A third rig that has served me well is a form of 'double bulk' where a tight bunch of 5 x no. 8s would be placed in the middle of these droppers. This rig has won me a fair few matches (see diagram). In my last win before the Covid lockdown with the river carrying a bit of extra and flowing hard, I used 20 no. 9 shot below the bulk on a 4-gram float. Another development has been to add a Drennan snap (quick-change) swivel to the rig that sits below the bulk. This means the bulk stays permanent but spare shotted rigs on winders can be kept close to hand to quickly resolve a tangle problem.

Top Tips:

⌐ High top rubber: One trick that I've used particularly on River Aire matches where deep swims can be a bit turbulent, possibly where big rocks on the river bed create a vortex, is to add a second rubber on the float bristle (i.e. aside from three on the carbon stem). Using a tight sleeve at the very tip of the bristle, or ¼-inch down, it gives a quieter and cleaner pick out of the float on the strike. If you rely on one top rubber at the base of the bristle it is a fractionally slower contact which I find can make a difference.

⌐ Paper clip trick (*addition by author*): There are several loop-tiers on the market, but for tying small loops take a leaf out of Paul's book and employ a paper clip re-shaped as pictured. Paul has done this for most of his match career. I have always liked small loops myself for attaching the hooklength but not as short as Paul's. Trouble with a nylon loop 1cm long of, say, 10mm diameter is that it can straighten in use. It then gets fiddly to push a replacement hook through it. A shorter loop, however, will tend to stay in shape. Try the system illustrated, inserting the paper clip ends in both the circle and the round end of the line together and pulling gently to tighten the loop as small as you like. Paul also goes one step further by tying his hooklength to the loop with a tucked half-blood knot. It may not always give him an edge but it's less obtrusive to shy fish.

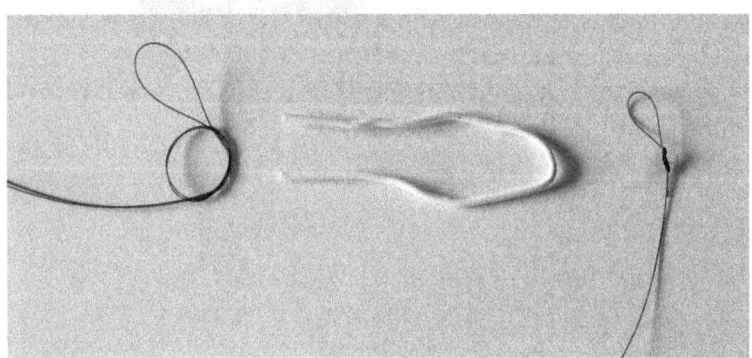

The Float

Experiment led me to try numerous float patterns that changed my thought process totally. Getting a float that's ideal in ALL Bolo' situations, is nearly impossible, but we try. Steve Pinnock's originals, the red ones, were made for pole fishing so I asked him for bigger floats and he obliged, but the bristles and stems would come in various sizes and diameters. That's when the fun started – cutting down one bit, lengthening another, and pulling my hair out in frustration!

My mate, Steve Fretwell got onto Tony Fisher, a fine rod-builder and floatmaker from Harworth, to put some longer bristles in Steve P's floats, who had by this time ceased production. 'Fret' had gone practising at Denaby, and when I arrived to see him he was struggling. Watching him, I noticed the float wobbling in the flow and suggested the bristle was too long. With his agreement I cut off a ¼" and he instantly started getting bites, but it still didn't seem right so I removed two more tiny bits of bristle after which it brought a bite every throw. We both learned a big lesson that day.

Best Win

A nice memory was winning the Weathercall league two years running, a strong league covering six matches, and my team also won the team event. But probably my favourite win was a Rotherham (teams of four) Open, at Burcroft, Denaby, including the Dearne mouth and all of Sprotborough right up to and above the viaduct – the biggest I've known on the Don. It was a full house with loads of good anglers from the North there.

The river was carrying three to four inches of extra water and I drew peg 8 at Sprotborough, and fancied it for a few fish. I was on form so was probably more confident than I let on, but considering the extra water I thought peg 2 was a better one. I'd won the Rotherham fur and feather match off it a few weeks earlier. Now the peg had been drawn by Denis White, who was fishing the Don a lot at this time and was dangerous but I was happy with my draw on his upstream side.

I got to my peg and set up a 3.5gram Bolo' rig plus a token bomb rod and was soon catching steadily.

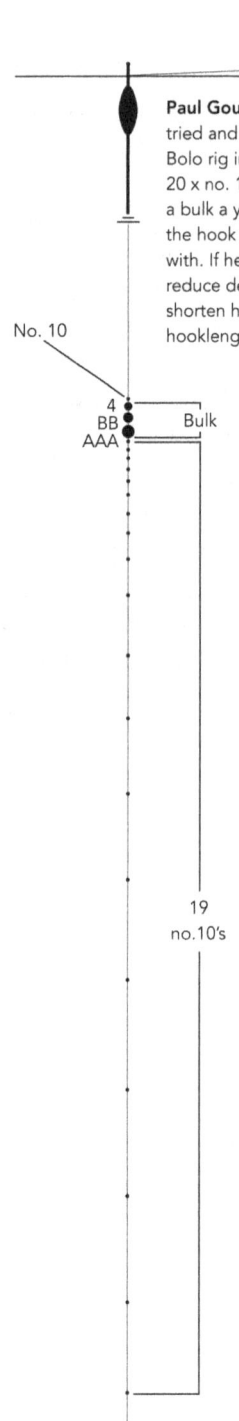

Paul Goulding's tried and tested Bolo rig includes 20 x no. 10s below a bulk a yard from the hook to start with. If he needs to reduce depth he will shorten his (18-inch) hooklength.

No. 10

4
BB
AAA

Bulk

19
no.10's

Halfway through the match fellow competitor Gary Whalley appeared behind me and reported that Denis was catching but many anglers were struggling. Eventually 'time' was shouted and Gary, on weighing-in duty, re-appeared with the scales and I recorded 13lb-plus. Denis's catch was then weighed and Gary returned with the words: "Denis beat you with an ounce, lad – hard luck."

"Well, I've had a nice day," I replied, biting back my disappointment. Then, just as he was walking away, he confessed: "No lad – you beat Denis by an ounce." I might have guessed, as Gary, from Wigan, is known as a character always up for a laugh. So it was a very good day.

3) Stick with Joe Murray

One of many Yorkies who left the Witham scene in the nineties, Joe Murray would soon find his local River Don suited him perfectly. He has won matches on other rivers - the Trent, Aire, Calder and Witham included, but since the late nineties on the Don the former miner, now 72, estimates he's won an impressive fifty times, and is still one of the men to beat. I talked to Joe recently…

Q: Hello Joe, if we can analyse your float first: the Drennan 8 x no. 4 with dome top and 'glass' (clear plastic) base. What makes this stick so integral to your Don approach?

– Well first, the size, i.e. shot capacity, has proved itself suited to almost everywhere I fish on the Don from Denaby to Sprotborough, and has brought me consistent success. The shotting gets the hookbait down fast to where the fish are feeding, and the weighty float base assists in casting to mid-river and beyond.

Q: Do you ever find a heavier or lighter float is more suitable in some swims?

– I very rarely fish the Don lighter, but in an upgate wind I will sometimes turn to a shouldered 'big stick' version of the Drennan in 2g size. The extra weight down helps pull the float through when the wind is trying hard to stop it in its tracks.

Q: Do you add a third silicon sleeve to the float as a spare in case of a breakage?

– Yes, at least three, sometimes four sleeves. The main spare is the same diameter as the wider one that secures the float tip, as this is the most likely to break.

Q: After plumbing up, do you start at the exact depth, or a little overdepth?

– I will start at the swim depth, and as the match progresses I'll generally shallow up a float's length at a time. This can often extend up to five float lengths, meaning I end up catching over two feet off the bottom.

Q: But not overdepth, even when it looks rock hard?

– Well rarely on a normal river and only slightly over at that, dragging around six inches or a float length only on the bottom (note that discounts laying-on in a flood).

Q: If the river is fishing well and bites come on the drop, what is your next move?

– I will shallow up. Two to three feet off the bottom can be productive, and if bites come quickly I'll also gradually feed more maggots to suit.

Q: On a normal river do you do best running the float through at the river's natural speed, or do you hold back to some degree?

– Very rarely do I hold back. The Don roach mainly like the bait running at the speed of flow, or as near to it as possible.

Q: I recall you used a Normark rod when we fished in the same Don team; do you still, and what other tackle do you use at the business end?

– Yes, I have four Normark Titan 2000 rods and they have never let me down. Nine times out of ten, I need to fish at a depth close to the length of the rod. This can be awkward, but I have developed a loop cast that works. My reel is a Daiwa Whisker with trusty 2.1lb Bayer on the spool. Trace lines are .08mm or .10mm Middy Lo-viz. As for hooks, my favourites are now obsolete. I used the Mustad (wide-gape) Match, then Mustad Canal Seed sizes 22 and 24, also a wide gape. On hearing the company was discontinuing the second pattern I bought 100 packets.

Q: What gives you confidence with the stick when others are winning on Bolo' or pole; don't you ever rate those methods as good if not better than yours on some days?

– Well, I have my own opinions about the Bolo' being better. Yes, I am one of a very small minority who fishes the stick religiously (sometimes the only one!), but do think the reason for many preferring Bolo' is they can't cast the required distance comfortably with a stick, with the great depth admittedly making casting awkward. I have faith in my overhead (loop) casting style and can get the stick three-quarters across the river on a good day and halfway on an average day. I only really come unstuck when hampered by trees in what we call a 'parrot cage' swim, and then I'm forced to cast from one side and have to fish closer in.

I don't believe in too much extra weight down the line, which will make the fish let go if they feel it. I once had Alan Scotthorne above me on Bolo', and they don't come better do they? But that day he had a bulk shot down the size of a marble and his float must have been 5-gram. I wouldn't expect to beat him every week, but that day I weighed 19lb and had 6lb to spare over him. I'm sure that roach feel the weight if you go too heavy, but maybe there's a fairer case for using Bolo' on bream.

Q: I think that kind of result would have given anyone confidence in their method. Do you back-shot in a downstream wind; or even grease the end of your reel line in calm conditions?

– No. I find (wash-up treated) Bayer Perlon in 2.1lb can be

sunk by flicking the rod tip underwater. And nor do I ever grease the line.

Q: Describe your favourite shotting pattern for an average 14-foot swim, fishing just over the shelf at say 10 metres distance, and your starter tell-tale shot position?

– Three feet from the hook I put a bulk of 10 x no. 6 shot, and then five tapered droppers: a no. 8 four inches below the bulk and a second no. 8 four inches below that, a no. 10 five inches below that and a second no. 10 five more inches below that, and finally a no. 11 or 12 shot as the tell-tale, a foot or so from the hook. This rig rarely tangles on the cast.

Q: What's your most used hook size and do you always hook the maggot the standard way, lightly at the rear end?

– If the fish are feeding well a 22, but if bites are coming slowly then a 24, wide gape in each case.

Q: Is bronze still your favourite maggot colour, and/or red or other colour?

– Bronze has stood the test of time, and I will take three pints to a match with a handful of reds as a change bait. I also feed hemp and will take a half-pint, usually feeding three or four pouches to start the match, then at intervals. But I rarely use caster as I see it as wasting time; I like to catch a lot of fish and build up a rhythm even if they are small.

Q: Assuming you usually fish maggot, how many times in ten would you catch on double maggot over single; and do you ever fish floating maggot?

– Nine times out of ten it is single maggot for me, and I never use floaters.

Q: How low down do you 'dot' the float?

– On a calm day I shot it so the tip is almost underwater; in other words as low as possible so I can still see it. On a windy day a fraction more of tip may be left showing. Obviously the lower the better for less resistance.

Q: What is your favourite Don peg?

– I like 29 which has an easy depth of 13-foot and you can get a nice slack close in too. I have had some good nets from it over the years. But the best ten pegs are the forties which are always dependable for a few fish, a section where the river bed is nice and even.

Q: Is the roach fishing at Sprotborough still on an upward trend as I hear that the feeder and bream have become more dominant lately?

– The flow does seem to have been affected by the hydro-electric turbines installed upstream at Thrybergh and Aldwarke in 2015. You can be catching roach well one minute, then it is like no fish are there. The flow seems to fluctuate more now from a nice steady pace, to almost stood, to racing through, and this can happen three times in a day. The effect has been fewer roach showing but more bream, meaning more anglers sitting it out on a feeder. My problem with this is that waiting for five or six bites over five hours bores me silly.

Q: Bit of the Ivan Marks temperament there, Joe? So who are your main Don rivals?

– Paul Goulding and John Bromilow are the obvious ones: both consistent. Dennis Pinkos before them was good with caster and hemp, but sadly a back injury forced him to retire. Fishing the maggot could see me take a good lead for three hours over someone like Dennis with his casters, but he was capable of hitting back with bigger fish in the last two hours and blitzing the match. And I have been on the receiving end. We've not seen much of Mick Peverley lately, but he's always been dangerous on feeding fish. And Alan Yates is a new lad who has been doing well on stick over the last few seasons; one I've got my eye on! They are the running line float anglers, but we can't ignore all the young and talented long pole men who also win on the river. Going back a few years I also have to mention the late John Illingworth who used a slider on the Don, and when it worked he was unbeatable on the float, either the balsa top and bottom version or waggler-type.

Q: So finally, Joe, you seem more than content with your stick floats, so guess you won't be changing to the Bolo' or pole any time soon?

– Well, yes to the first bit and no to the second. Does that make me a throwback, not sure? I enjoy the way I fish and it works for me.

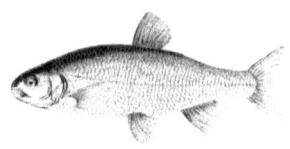

Chapter 51
Other Key Floats: the Avon – by Mark Wintle

Robin Harris winning the 1971 Severn National with 40lb 5oz from a rapid swim

The origins of the Avon float are lost in antiquity. They're a simple development from using a bird quill as a float as it was an easy enhancement to add a body made of a buoyant material such as cork to the quill enabling the float to carry a much greater shotting load than the 2BB of a crow quill.

Whether the float originated on the Warwickshire Avon, the Bristol Avon or the Hampshire Avon is unclear. It was only in the 1960s that anglers such as Billy Lane started calling it an 'Avon' float and the name has stuck.

Billy was a great fan of the Avon float. His three float fishing books extol its virtues over the more specialised stick floats which were incredibly popular at the time. Billy's commercially available Avon floats were a departure from the traditional construction of a cork-bodied crow quill in that Ultra Floats, Billy's float company, made his version using a cane stem and balsa body.

Ultra floats sold by the hundred thousand, thanks both to Billy's popularity and their practical designs. Billy admitted that it was simply impractical to manufacture Avon floats using cork bodies and crow quills as it was too labour-intensive and impossible to source sufficient quills. His design therefore owes more to commercial considerations than a desire to create the perfect float. But the dedicated match angler who craves perfection has the luxury of being able to take the extra time and care needed to try making one.

Notwithstanding the above, Peterborough's top angler and 1969 World Champion, Robin Harris consulted with Billy ahead of the 1971 Severn National, then invested in a selection of his balsa on cane Avons. The Nene specialist showed his adaptability after drawing a plum swim at Quatford, and fishing a 4 x AAA Avon for the first time, with most under the float and just 2 x BB down, promptly won the match with 40lb 5oz to add another major trophy to his cabinet.

I started using Billy Lane's Avon floats when I first fished the Dorset Stour. I also made my own Avons with cane and balsa to obtain a float that took around 9 x BB. Then in the mid-1980s a Birmingham angler took over a local tackle shop and I realised the superiority of the genuine crow quill Avon. Proprietor Ivor Brittain obtained supplies of hand-made floats from Birmingham, and I soon found the ones that had a shoulder with a shot-load of 9 x BB were superb for roach fishing. In time I got some crow quills and made my own versions. The body of the float is fairly slim – 3/8" balsa dowel is ideal for making the bodies and the tip is not too long. The design of the float allows it to be over-shotted and held back whilst fishing over-depth. The increase in diameter at the shoulder makes the float less likely to rise out of the water when held back. This is an important point for bait presentation. It is essential to be able to mend the line and hold back without jerking the float.

The drawback to a pronounced shoulder on the float is that it makes the strike more splashy, something that may scare shy roach and a reason for my reluctance to using many Bolognese-type floats. The Topper-style Avons is more streamlined so this is less of a problem but they're not really designed for holding back[24].

Over the years I have made many of these floats and experimented with materials. For the bodies I like balsa,

---

24 More in chapter 52

although if you want to make your own 'Topper' Avon the blue polystyrene blocks used in wall insulation are better as the float is then ultra-light and follows the weight better when casting underhand, also enabling the flick mend that Topper used to get the float to maintain a straight line down the swim. Use acrylic, water-based paints if you use styrene as spirit-based paints will melt it.

In the last couple of years I have increasingly found the hollow ready-painted pole float tips useful for float making. Initially I used them for insert wagglers, but in 2019 I started putting 3mm tips (seemingly the thickest available) in my crow quill Avons, with a balsa body and a section of quill for the lower stem.

For me the Avon is an excellent roach float for presenting bread, especially punch on a 16 or 14, on a river in swims of even flow and good depth (up to twelve feet). It's best to attach the float with three rubbers: one at the top, one just below the body and a tight one, an inch long, at the end of the stem, letting a tiny bit of this rubber protrude past the end. Increasingly I'm using olivettes taking from 3 to 5 grams for the bulk. I'll place the main bulk between two and three feet from the hook, depending on the depth and flow. I like a second mini-bulk of either 3 x no. 6 or 3 x no. 4 shot about a foot below this, just above the twenty two-inch hook link. As a drop shot, I use 2 x no. 8s bulked about a foot from the hook as a starting point. For fishing at long range, show more of the float-tip for visibility. But, closer in, it may be advantageous to shot the float right down. The Avon float is ideal for water over ten feet deep, this type of water being found throughout the Dorset Stour.

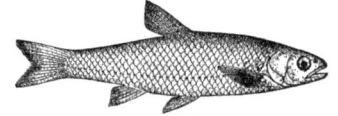

Chapter 52
The Pheasant quill – Edgar Purnell

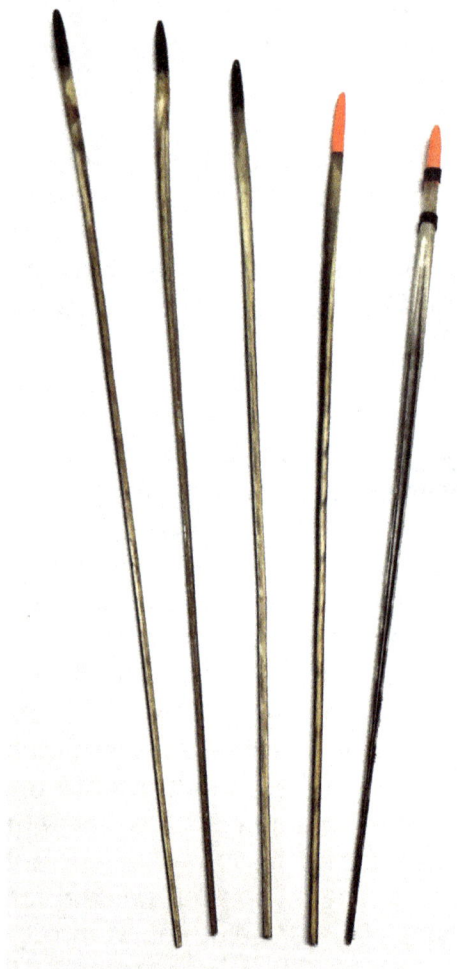

Edgar Purnell, from Ruskington, Lincs., was for many years one of the most popular faces at the big Witham open matches and perhaps, more than anyone, spanned the swingtip era of the sixties when bream won most matches and the roach years that followed with equal success. A member of the Oundle team for many seasons, he's gained wide respect throughout Fenland for match wins with either species. His versatility has also brought him success in recent years on local carp commercials, which he's frequented since the Witham's decline as a match venue.

Edgar's early days on the Witham were in partnership with big Jim Todd, who he describes as a great bream angler and the very best at throwing groundbait accurately. Size is not everything in throwing, but Jim was not only built like a brick outhouse, he was once an AAA javelin champion, who also fished for Leicester Likely Lads! Edgar modestly says he learned a lot from Jim, but he no doubt taught Jim plenty too. They both certainly tamed many a bream shoal in that era. When not catching fish himself Edgar would always go and watch other anglers, who were, saying: "There's so much to learn by watching other anglers. We had some cracking anglers on the Witham – Pete Bagshaw, Roger Wakenshaw, Tony Woods, and the late Jack Pugh to name a few, but one who stands out for me as great on a stick float was Andy Finch, of Lincoln. If you beat Andy at the next peg you knew you'd fished well. Another angler that helped me was Bill Watchorn, great friend and fishing companion. We've been pals now for 55 years and still fish together once a week. One of the nicest men you could wish to meet."

Edgar's home-made lignum sticks are what I'd call 'tasty' and come in two versions: a dome-topped or flat-topped stick for stability in a downstream wind, and a pointed top for use in perfect conditions. With the former stick he'd shot the float right down almost flat to the surface, then aim a sideways cast downstream before re-winding to the point where he wanted to start the trot. This downstream cast shortens the trot but assists the float to maintain a straight line going through. He'd always shot the float shirt button-style and always back-shot with 2 x no. 8s, at ten inches and twenty inches behind the float respectively. The second stick, with the pointed top, would come into play in good conditions with a gentle breeze blowing. In an upstream wind that had 'rollers' to contend with, (peaks and troughs on a flowing Witham), however, he reverted to an old float that had slimness on its side to cut through the waves like a knife – the pheasant quill.

Barry Camm of Newark was a quality Trent angler who sometimes ventured down to fish the big Witham matches. The first time I saw him in action was on Newark Dyke in an open match. I stopped to watch him for about ten minutes and liked the way his float was trotting through the swim. He told me it was a pheasant quill. So the following day, off I went and got myself some quills and made half a dozen floats. These quills were from the long tail feathers of the cock bird.

Historically the crow quill was a favourite float which was used even by the great champion Billy Lane who employed them in favourable weather conditions, but a pheasant quill is stronger, a fair bit longer, and can be fished at depths ranging from four to at least nine feet. It is particularly good at cutting through waves in adverse conditions, better than any other float in my opinion, and it is also handy for trotting down the margins when the river is carrying extra water. I have tried a crow quill many a time but much prefer the pheasant for these jobs.

Making the float is a simple operation: first cut it to length then remove the plume, first with sharp scissors then lightly sand down, being careful not to damage the quill. Paint the tip of the float in black or fluorescent red depending on the venue, and job done. I could never see the need to add more paint or to seal the body as any feather is naturally waterproofed anyway.

Shotting up the quill is quite simple. I use a bulk of 8 to 10 x no. 8 shots roughly two feet from the hook, plus 2 x no. 8 shots spread evenly between bulk and the hook. The chosen quill length is from eight to ten and a half inches, and from early tests I found that its slim profile cut through the waves a treat. The theory is that if the float is going through on a nice level path then so is the hookbait, meaning good bait presentation.

So, as suggested, I saw the advantages for cutting through any upstream rollers on the river, and equally it was good for inching a bait through with extra water on the river. It came up trumps in both situations. I mostly used the quill when the river was pulling, combined with a fairly strong upstream wind causing high waves or rollers as we call them, but sometimes on a rising river which was running a bit harder than normal.

The one downside of the float, which I can't dispute, is its casting limitations. On the River Witham, for example, I'd say the limit is a rod-length out, to just over two rod-lengths, which is roughly eight or nine metres or perhaps one fifth of the way across the river. The best way of casting it is into the wind and downstream which enables laying the rig out in a straight line, and I always use a side-cast or underarm cast.

The difficulty with an overhead cast is the float does not fly that straight. Having only a rough diameter of 1.5mm at its base and 3.75mm approx. at the tip, it is slightly top heavy and unsuitable for a longer cast being attached both top and bottom. This is the opposite, of course, to a lignum stick which has base weight to literally fly through the air. All that said, though, once the float is set up it's a delight to use!

This is a flexible float that you can take hold of and bend the base round back on itself to touch halfway up the stem. However, there is one little dodge I have to mention when mounting it on the line. To use a half-inch long rubber at the base and two more at the tip (one as a spare in case of a breakage), the force of the strike is prone to pulling the line through the top two rubbers consequently twisting the bottom of the float back on itself. It is obviously no good if the float doubles back this way and ends up in the shape of a hook (see photo).

My remedy to this is to leave the top two rubbers off the quill and attach the bottom rubber first. I then grip the line above the base rubber and, holding the float in the other hand, spiral the line round the quill about eight times from base to tip before sliding the top two rubbers into position. This both prevents any distortion on the strike, and stops it sliding out of position.

In summary, my ten minutes studying Barry Camm proved a valuable lesson. The pheasant quill might be the simplest float imaginable, but it's one that can pleasantly surprise in adverse conditions. Then it acts more like a precision tool. Give it a try and you might be surprised.

A word on sticks

If conditions were right for the stick float I would always start on it. I only ever fished the quill when conditions were as described above. Shotting for the Witham was usually about 8 to 12 x no. 8 shots with both the quill and the stick float. Shotting for the stick was slightly more spread out than the quill which worked better with a bulk and droppers. The big advantage with the stick is you can always follow the fish out if needs be due to its superior casting power.

I have a rule of thumb with shotting, involving the position of the tell-tale shot and the one above it, that I will adhere to with every session. I place them further apart than all the shots higher up. This allows the hooklength to rise up better in the water when the float is held back and it is more tantalising to the fish. Specifically, the tell-tale no. 10 goes seven inches from the hook, the next shot, a no. 8, is also seven inches above that, then 1 x no. 6 is placed six inches above that, and so on with no. 6s at six-inch intervals up the line (see diagram). This puts only two tiny shot in the twenty inches of line above the hook.

I could name many anglers who were brilliant on the stick float, but the one who always springs to mind first is the great John Dean. I do think John was in a different class to the rest. But anglers like Dave Thomas, Pete Warren, Wayne Swinscoe and John Allerton were all at the very top at this type of fishing. Dave, of course, won his World Champs title using a stick float, possibly the only angler ever to do so, on a flooded Warwickshire Avon.

I treasure my stick floats, some that are forty-five or more years old, and wouldn't part with them for all the tea in China. Most of my floats, I'd say 95 per cent, are home-made too, including lignum sticks and peacock wagglers.

Asked to describe his most memorable matches on stick float, Edgar recalled two on the Witham and one on the Trent:

In the big matches like the Eastern Region Winter Leagues, with 300-plus fishing, there was such a good atmosphere and buzz around the match HQ when it came to draw time. I remember one I won, not so much for the quality of sport but for the man I just pushed into second place. I drew a peg in the seventies on the outside bend below Schoolhouse bend, and went for roach on a lignum stick three rods out. I was getting the odd fish and word came down the line that nobody was really catching well. To hear that always makes you concentrate! I ended up with 5lb 6oz to win and my mate Jim Todd was second with two fish less for 5lb 0½oz.

Matches could be decided in the last few minutes in those days. Another close one was a winter league round at Gunthorpe and Shelford. I started on a maggot feeder, casting a quarter way across the river, but after 45 minutes had only one roach. I changed to the stick and found a few small roach and small chub willing to feed, and finished up with 3lb 13oz. To win with so little was a surprise, and with only 2oz to spare on the runner-up, had I changed a few minutes later than I did he'd have beat me.

An easier catch to make was my best roach weight from the Witham on a Super League round with sixty fishing – ten upstream of Kirkstead Bridge and fifty on the Pound length. I drew on the Pound and conditions looked promising even with a strong upstream wind, but fishing the stick two rods out I'd nothing much to show after an hour. Then the swim just exploded into life and I started catching roach every cast with some up to 12oz. I won with 26lb 12oz, including many net roach, and it was a good day for others too with fifteen double figure weights of roach and bream.

Top Tip
These days I'd always advise attaching four silicon bands to any top and bottom float. Place one spare band a third of the way down from the tip where it's out of the way. Then add a second spare a third of the way up from the float's base. Then you are well covered in case of any breakages, with no risk of a delay in having to break down the tackle to add more. Important in a match situation.

Chapter 53
The Topper – Mervyn 'Topper' Haskins

Bristol matchman, Mervyn Haskins began experimenting in the 1950s with the crow quill Avon float, and the one he perfected, he christened the 'Topper.' It has since won him matches all over his local River Avon, the Warwickshire Avon, and far beyond on the Great Ouse, Cambs.

Mervyn's early prototypes included wooden bodies from pencils. He'd dismantle them by placing in boiling water to melt the glue before putting the wooden halves back together around a crow quill with the wood's top edge an inch from the tip of the quill. Mervyn admits they were less than successful, so he next tried blotting paper cut into a wedge shape and rolled onto the top third of the quill. This made a more lightweight and bit better body, but it obviously had to be fully sealed. From there he moved on to elder pith bodies – 'brilliant but very delicate to work with' – then to balsa, and finally to (blue) polystyrene. The Bristol Avon is a deep and slow river which flows in a Westerly direction so anglers generally have to contend with an upstream wind that will stop a light float trotting through smoothly... or totally. Mervyn's Topper employs a big bulk of lead that the current will grab hold of and pull the float through at the river's natural speed. Come in Mervyn...

If ever a quill was heaven sent for anglers it has to be that of the crow. Even today I cannot think of a more sensitive float with a hollow tip of the perfect thickness that the crow quill gives us. At the thin end too, a reversed crow quill tip makes a waggler insert as sensitive as any pole bristle. Finding a source of quills is the first task, and I suggest searching in a field adjacent to a rookery in spring.

Some modern anglers may think that 'Crow Avon' fishing is old-fashioned, but when you get it right it is brilliant. Two other good quills that are strong and can be used to make the float deserve a mention – pheasant quills and cormorant quills. I have made some big Avons with cormorant quills.

When I first made the floats many years ago, the Bristol Avon was tree-lined with many awkward swims that we call 'parrot cages' where making an overhead cast was very difficult. A slider would have worked but they are mainly used for deep water, like the trees at Saltford where you don't have room behind to cast overhead. To cast to mid-river underhand I needed considerable casting weight down the line, but the float could be a lightweight material.

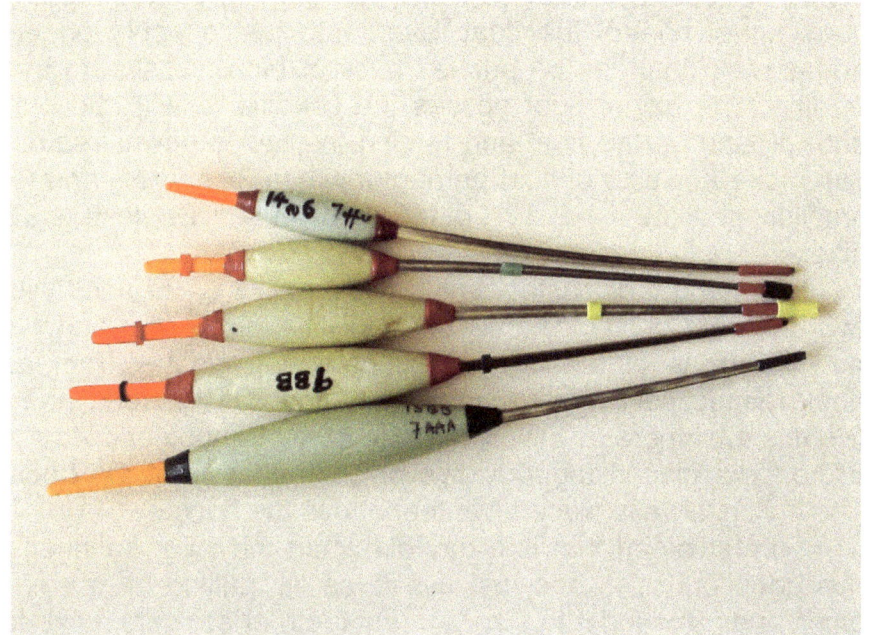

Original Topper Haskins floats designed for the Bristol Avon upstreamers, biggest here is 13BB also marked up as 7AAA which is in fact slightly heavier

So I made some balsa wood bodies and put them on crow quills to make 10 x BB size floats, and they cast out of this world. This was in the early days on the centrepin, when the fixed spool reel was in its infancy. Almost overnight, I found I could get a lot further out in the river with improved bait presentation compared to any other float I knew.

Now I had to perfect the art of fishing it, and a lot of time was spent doing that. And when you put the hours in you learn to do so many things – how to cast properly so as not to get tangles, and different ways of holding back etc. I now started to catch a lot more fish and this led me to make more floats of different sizes.

With the quill being very delicate and easily bent, I like to keep them on the short side. I do have quills of ten inches long but I don't think this length makes them better. So I'll use a stiffer six-inch quill to make the lightest float in the range, then increase the length slightly as they get heavier – from six up to nearly seven inches total length for the heaviest float. My five standard sizes for the Bristol Avon are: 8 x BB, 9 x BB, 10 x BB, 12 x BB and 13 x BB. On the Avon, or any similar river, I would not use less than 10 x BB, as with any lighter shotting you cannot control the float: even with just a ripple on the surface the float can be pushed back or blown upstream and off line. The bigger float bosses the conditions, with the bulk shot picking up the float and forcing the tackle downstream. I can make any size of float an angler wants, of course, and for smaller, shallow rivers I've made them in 4 x BB to 6 x BB sizes.

For maggot or caster fishing I use an 18 or 20 hook with two droppers below the bulk of BBs – 1 x no. 8 shot and 1 x no. 10 shot as tell-tale at eight inches and five inches from the hook respectively. But my favourite Avon bait is bread and I fish this a bit more positively – a size 16 or 14 hook and 2 x no. 8 droppers placed together five or six inches from the hook. The bulk is always placed two feet above the hook.

I prefer bread that is a day old when the 'over freshness' has gone out of it, and just use it 'as is,' pulling off a small pinch and trimming it to size with my teeth or scissors. I like to start on bread and groundbait and gauge how the fish are responding, but if no bites come in the first twenty minutes I'll change to maggot. In a match I will start with two or three egg-size balls of groundbait followed by a small golf ball-size nugget every cast, but the feed rate is something you have to work out on the day. There are never any hard and fast rules: the fish will dictate what you do.

I fish the float with a 20-foot rod using two hands (pushing the left hand forward to hold the rod more like a pole, laying the rod on the left-hand fingers) and that allows me to make a gentle upward movement on the strike. Beware when using one hand only on a 20-foot rod, if the strike is made too sharply the rod tip will go down before it goes up.

I hold the float back to slow it down in three ways: 1) In

calm conditions by holding the rod high so the line goes from the rod tip straight to the float with none on the water; the strike then is just a short upward movement, 2) holding back in a light upstream wind with the rod not necessarily held high, 3) by lowering the rod tip to just above the water surface. I do this when faced with the kind of tricky wind that puts an upstream bow in the line behind the float. This bow will hold the float back too much and, though it can produce bites, it's better with the low rod position to 'mend' the line by pushing the rod tip in a downstream direction. When the bow is removed, flick the line back upstream and start trotting again.[25]

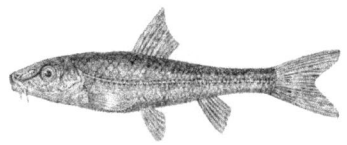

25 The above story is reproduced and adapted slightly from an article published in the former Sheffield monthly magazine, *Angling Star*.

Chapter 54
The porcupine Kendall-style – Mick Hughes

For the record, readers, there was life before stick floats. Mick analyses the methods of former Yorkshire champion Kenny Kendall when a porcupine quill was the popular choice on rivers or lakes in the bygone era before the stick float.

In 1957, writer and leading York angler, Frank Oates stated clearly in Lesson 13 of his book ('Match Fishing – How to join the ranks of the experts') that: 'Porcupine quill floats are the best for match-fishing – sufficiently heavy for accurate casting, yet buoyant enough to carry an adequate amount of lead.' A bold claim indeed, but at that time these quills in different sizes made as good a float as any.

Kenny Kendall, of Leeds, bronze medallist and top scorer for England when beating France and Italy to win the inaugural European Championship in 1953 on Lake Garda (Italy), the forerunner to the World Championship, was another big fan of the porkie. Once the master at catching dace on his local River Wharfe, he won two lucrative post-war Witham opens from over a thousand entrants, which enabled him to open a tackle shop in Leeds. He once told me how he enjoyed a regular 'income' from scores of match wins on the Wharfe in the forties and fifties.

As reported in Midland Angler magazine, Jan. '53 issue, Kenny also skippered his Leeds Amalgamated team to victory in the 1952 National Championship on the River Severn and finished fourth overall with 21lb 9¾oz of small fish. The twelve-man Leeds team also produced a record-breaking winning weight of 135lb 5oz. Drawn in a rather fast, thirty-inch deep swim at Quatford D36, three spectators timed Kenny for an hour and twenty minutes during which he caught no fewer than one hundred and eight fish! His overall total was thought to be in excess of three hundred. He used a twelve-foot Aspindale's all split cane rod, a porkie with a small cork body, shotted with a tapered string of shots – 2 x no. 3 shots nearest the float, 2 x no. 5's below that, and 2 x no. 8's nearest the hook. He baited with white maggot as he never bothered to colour any. In an article about that performance he said in

360

Midland Angler: 'One should not hold too tight a line; just enough to let the bait go first, but still with enough leeway to let them get hold without suspicion. Then, at the very first touch on the float, strike the hook home.' This information is telling. Mick Hughes now speculates about this as being one reason why the former Leeds supremo was so successful on Yorkshire rivers in the days of yore.

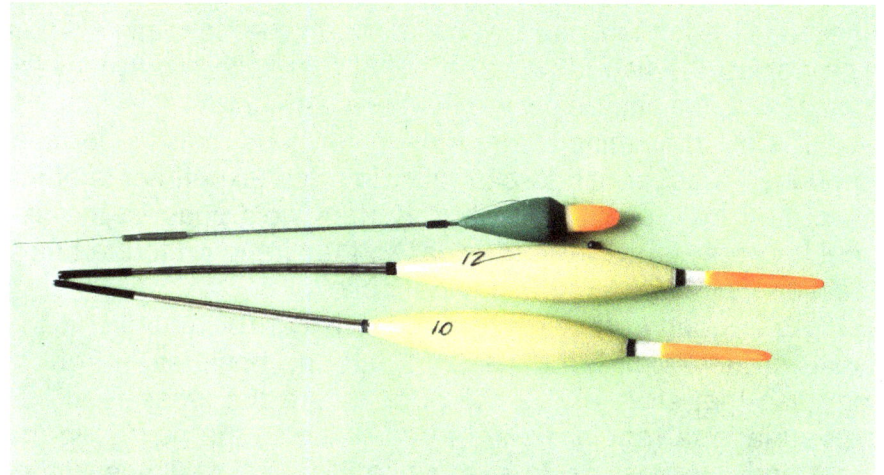

Mick Hughes' floats: (top) a short fat stick for the River Calder with hi-viz tip, foam body, steel wire stem and a tiny hole for the line to pass through the float near the tip replacing the top rubber, (bottom) upgraded Toppers in 10 and 12 x BB size, with a harder resin material than the blue polystyrene for the body, designed for the deep Yorkshire Ouse

The key to catching Wharfe dace consistently is to feed steadily to keep them competing and not to let them disperse, or to overfeed so they drop too far down the swim. Ulleskelf has some short pegs of only 12 yards which can require groundbait to concentrate the fish, but, with cereal or loose feed only, Kenny discovered a way of hitting more bites than others – by casting his float above his feed, and encouraging the hookbait to land slightly upstream.

Kenny's system was to feed downstream at around one o'clock (with river flowing left to right), cast the float straight out (to twelve o'clock), but to try laying the rig upstream. Ideally, in an upstream wind, he could feather the line as the float was about to land on the surface and the rig would land in the correct arc. In this way the bait would fall on a slacker line than with a downstream cast.

At that time Kenny fished a porcupine quill, occasionally with a slim (detachable) cork body added. Down the line he'd spread out six shots or would sometimes use a heavier float shotted simply with a pea bullet (round drilled lead bullet up to 1/8oz) some eighteen inches from the hook.

By casting over his left shoulder from the river's right bank (left to right flow), or vice versa from the left bank, he would effect this upstream curve in the line from float to bait, and as the bait descended and swung round in the flow this slacker line helped the fish to hang on better than with a downstream cast where the line below the float was straighter.

Kenny maintained that this slight upstream loop cast produced a better fish-to-bite ratio. In a few experiments of my own, and from chats with Chris Burton, we'd suggest the fish feel less resistance from the float so they hang on to the bait a fraction longer for a more confident bite.

As a bonus, of course, if the fish can be caught at the head of the swim, it means: 1) it puts the hookbait in front of any fish that stray above the point where the loose feed hits the surface, a regular habit of dace; and 2) the float is in the best possible position to see a bite clearly, i.e. almost under the angler's eyes at twelve-o'clock.

I am not sure Kenny used the pea bullet that often, which is equivalent to a basic bulk shot we'd use today, but suspect the bullet might have given him the idea but he'd have improved it with spread out shots.

I have caught in a similar way on the deep River Aire with a peacock waggler and no. 8 shot down the line, as much as four feet off the bottom. When I thought the hookbait had travelled to the hotspot where the feed was being taken, I'd hold back to sink the float and it would not reappear if a bite came at that moment.

Kenny's consistency with double figures of Wharfe dace was legendary, and similarly nets of roach on the Ouse when others couldn't get near it. Chris and I remember winning dace catches of 17lb and 15lb while we were still apprentices on the river circuit.

Thinking about it, Kenny's method was an early version of what the modern pole angler is able to do easier with a shorter line on today's rivers. They will ball in groundbait slightly downstream, load the rig in upstream, then expect a bite when the hookbait reaches the carpet of feed.

If you fancy trying a porcupine quill float then the all-white dumpier quills take most shot size for size compared to the slimmer mottled quills. I dare say these would be the ones preferred by Kenny Kendall. But all porkies make sensitive floats having such a thin point at either end.

Chapter 55
Other key floats – the all-balsa
with Ivan Marks & co.

If, like me, you have a tendency to err more on the light side than heavy with your shotting, then it might be useful for you to skip the first two floats in this chapter but stretch your imagination by focusing on the heavier ones starting with the 'Pacemaker.' As a philosopher once said 'boldness has genius, power and magic in it.' Fishing is never an exact science and if the fish will accept a heavy float carrying a BB tell-tale shot it would be wise to try it, as this chapter reveals, not play safe with the standard no. 8 which could lead to failure…

1) Small – Jim Sharp-style

In the pre-stick float days of the 1950s Jim Sharp was widely acknowledged at Nottingham's No. 1 Trentman. His biggest achievement was beating 2,000 competitors to win the 1951 Trent Championship with 16lb 2oz. This rewarded his perseverance after a second and a third in the event previously. His Nottingham match colleague, John Toulson, described him as: 'the best angler in the world with a centrepin reel.'

The story of his all-balsa float used to win the match was told in the Sep. '53 issue of the original *Midland Angler* magazine. Jim caught roach, fishing mostly at one rod-length distance, and a few further out when the wind allowed. "Drawn at Hazleford and feeding his swim with groundbait and pinkies (described as 'feeders' in the report), plus a 'sprinkling' of larger maggots fed loose, he fished a yellow maggot on a gilt size 20 hook. The swim was four and a half feet deep and his float was shotted with a BB at mid-depth and 3 x no. 8 shot spread out evenly below that, with the tell-tale placed six inches from the hook."

On the Trent at that time the fish were generally caught close-in with a centrepin reel, signified by the three floats referred to in the article. Float no. 1 was a standard straight balsa tapered at both ends, four and a half inches long and taking 6 x no. 8 shots, for the River Trent. Float 2 was slightly smaller at four inches including an inch of fine gull quill inserted in the tip and taking 4 x no. 8 shots. Float 3 was a three-inch balsa version for 'fast water,' with a slim elderberry pith body mounted on the stem, again taking 4 x no. 8 shots. Surprisingly, no loading is shown on this shortest float considering the added body and that the tip is more bulbous to cope with water turbulence, which begs the question: was the diagram wrong in scale or was the balsa very fine and the elder pith no more than a sliver?

Jim used a braided reel line of 'terylene polyester' of only 1lb breaking strain, and below the float he had a yard length of .006" nylon, then a twelve-inch hooklength of .005" nylon tied to the 20 hook. So 'light was right' for this early Trent champion. Apart from his outstanding Trent record, Jim also won matches far from his home county. Up on the River Wharfe near York in June '53 he took an all dace net of 17lb 14oz for top score. Then back home in the Trent's opening fixture at East Stoke he topped his own four-hour Trent record catch with a winning 17lb 8oz.

When the stick and caster hit the Trent scene in the sixties Jim found it harder to maintain his consistency, yet in the second Nottingham vs Manchester challenge in 1963 he turned on the old style to win narrowly from teammate, John Toulson, and together they set up the local team for victory.[26]

Tom Watson's shop
No, our subject here is not the golfing legend but his namesake, Nottingham tackle dealer Tom Watson. Tom owned the shop where Jim Sharp worked behind the counter. Watson's sold the balsa floats of Jim's design, along with a wide range of other river floats, including the 'Trentcaster,' one of the earliest commercially produced stick floats, and a fluted version of a stick.

2) Tiny – used by Mac Willis with seed baits

Newark's Mac Willis was noted for his Trent success with roach on hemp and tares. With seeds being noted for taking a

---

26 Detailed in Notts vs Manc Challenges

while to get the fish going, Mac would single-mindedly persevere when others around him were already catching on caster or maggot. But Mac had a habit of making a late counter-attack. He has also enjoyed considerable success with weights of Severn chub using tares on the hook. He insisted on fishing close in with the tare, first because he believed it was a bait for light tackle capable of being held back, which he achieved with a small balsa float fished double rubber; second because he was looking for smooth and steady water. In a fast stream or turbulent swim Mac did not rate the tare's chances, claiming they would roll when fed rather than stay in place on the bottom.

"The rolling quality of the bait is part of its attraction but you don't want it to roll too far from where it is introduced," said Mac. "The perfect tare swim is marginal, about four feet deep and steady or slack." Mac's tare floats were always slim, tapered at both ends and their average size were slightly over three inches long, taking up to 6 x no. 8 shots.

3) Medium – the Ivan Marks Pacemaker

After the 1970 Woodbine Final on Ireland's River Blackwater, Ivan Marks came home thinking he had used the wrong floats. Back at the drawing board he shaped a new float from balsa dowel, gave it to a friend who visited the Blackwater the following year, and he returned having caught loads of fish calling the float 'brilliant!' Ivan then collaborated with Ron Pinder, from Newark, and they started making the float commercially, naming it the 'Pacemaker.' It had the appearance of a scaled up Gerry Lees' carrot float.

Ivan was soon scoring well with the float on the Trent in a typical 3 x BB size, but with bigger sizes to suit the occasion. It also won favour in steady glides on the Severn and even the Nene, when it was running. The main feature of the float was the shoulder an inch below the tip creating a slender top inch of float. The shoulder stopped the float riding up in the flow when holding back and the thin tip section improved sensitivity. Ivan recorded wins on different sections of the Trent, at Stourport and Bewdley on the Severn, and on the upper Nene around Oundle.

"I'd got confidence in the float and could make it work. If you think about it the shoulder and slim tip was like a forerunner to the John Allerton stick. John's float was better for casting with the aluminium stem but we would always put a BB under the float and this improved its casting power and stability," said Ivan.

"We shotted shirt button, like the stick, with a tell-tale no. 10 approximately a foot from the hook to start with, to drag on the bottom if necessary, 4 x no. 8's would be placed seven inches apart above that, and say 4 x no. 6 shot similarly spaced above that."

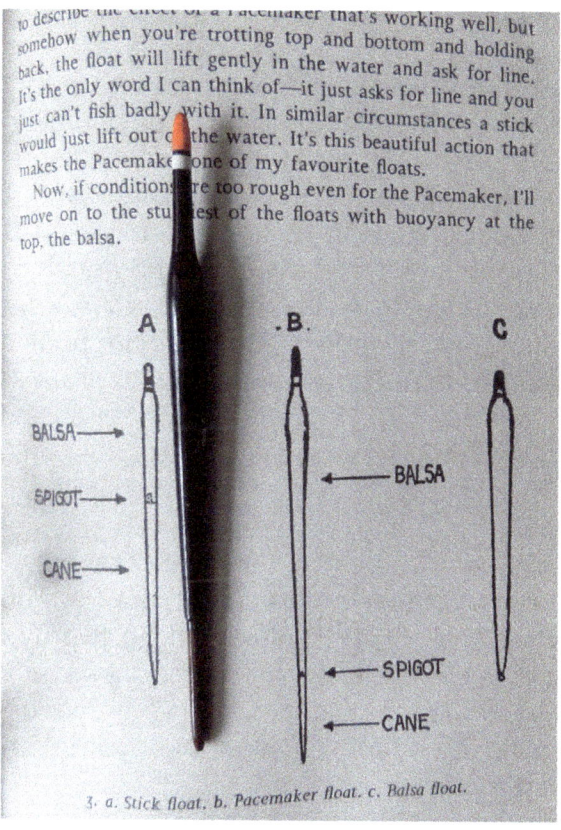

to describe the effect of a Pacemaker that's working well, but somehow when you're trotting top and bottom and holding back, the float will lift gently in the water and ask for line. It's the only word I can think of—it just asks for line and you just can't fish badly with it. In similar circumstances a stick would just lift out of the water. It's this beautiful action that makes the Pacemaker one of my favourite floats.

Now, if conditions are too rough even for the Pacemaker, I'll move on to the stumpiest of the floats with buoyancy at the top, the balsa.

A

BALSA→

SPIGOT→

CANE→

.B.

←BALSA

←SPIGOT

←CANE

C

3. a. Stick float. b. Pacemaker float. c. Balsa float.

Ivan's bait choice in the seventies was mainly caster with loose-fed caster and hemp feed, but he would occasionally spring a surprise, for example when he fed groundbait on the Warwickshire Avon at Evesham and just lost out in famous battle against Lloyd Davies, who beat him by 10oz to win the Lawden Masters. Ivan confounded the pundits with his tactics, and commented later: "Some maybe thought I was mad to gamble with groundbait, but the fish couldn't get enough of the stuff that day, and after another couple of successes with cereal some of the local stars changed their thinking."

Talking about balsa floats generally in *Angling Times*, 1974, Ivan said: "Most people fish far too light. Even many expert Trentmen fall into this trap. John Toulson is an exception. He knows how to make that extra weight work for him. Balsas look much clumsier than a nice slim stick, but shot them correctly and they are just as sensitive. For some reason they are the only floats to use in certain circumstances."

4) Medium to heavy – as used by Ian Heaps

Ian Heaps was never an angler to shy away from putting extra lead on his line when required. In heavy flowing, deep or turbulent water, like Billy Lane and John Toulson before him, he had total faith in getting hittable bites and the fish not minding the weight. He was quite content fishing 9 x AAA in a twelve-foot Trent swim, for example, comprising: 3 x Swan shots set fifty inches from the hook, 2 x AAA twenty inches below that, and a BB dropper a foot from the hook.

In shallower water Ian would try a small balsa with a BB just below mid-depth and 1 x no. 4 tell-tale shot about a foot from the hook. This was usually fished in conjunction with groundbait in line with the other heavier floats in the balsa family.

In a fast, shallow swim he'd also select a balsa of 3½ AAA size, saying how positive the presentation was *if* bites could be hit. In this case a 3 x AAA bulk would go twenty inches from the hook and a BB tell-tale nine inches away. "If there is a shade too much lead for the float, you can do something terribly scientific to correct it," joked Ian. "Cut a lump off one of the AAAs with a pair of scissors."

If missing bites, however, he advises moving all the shots further away from the hook, by first splitting 1 x AAA into 2 x BBs, for example, so reducing the bulk to 2 x AAA and 1 x BB, then placing 2 x BBs below that, and using a no. 1 as the tell-tale. By holding back with this rig the bait will lift a shade better and sometimes this makes a difference. But, Ian warns: "Beware with this rig as it can cause missed bites as they have to register through three lots of shot instead of two."

Normally with these balsas the ideal bait presentation is at the speed of the current, with the lead giving the control and the tell-tale shot dictating the way the bait is presented. Obviously a no. 1 shot will lift the bait more than a BB where the bait might just stop in its tracks, but the latter can be a "deadly bite producer," Ian adds. Lines recommended for these floats are 3lb reel line and a 1½ to 2½lb hooklength depending on the size of fish expected. The top rubber also fits no lower than ¼-inch from the tip of the float.

Ian's heaviest balsa caught him 173lb of ide in a five-hour session in Sweden. This float took a 3 x Swan bulk, a yard from the hook, and an AAA dropper fourteen inches from the hook, combined with bread flake flattened overnight between two boards and a damp cloth then cut into irregular half-inch shapes. His feed was three loaves turned into mashed bread then dried off with a little groundbait to make it easier to leave the fingers when thrown.

5) Sliding balsa – Clive Smith & Ken Giles

In their instructional book of 1978 Clive Smith and Ken Giles pooled their floatfishing ideas to create a very advanced book for the time it was written. Their cigar-shaped balsa floats were made to fish 'more awkward waters' than their home Warks. Avon – e.g. the Wye, Hampshire Avon and faster-flowing Yorkshire rivers. The Balsa, they said, lends itself to a pattern of bulk shotting and it has somewhat cruder uses than the more sophisticated stick float, but is ideal for baits like bread or wasp grub where the bulk of shots is excellent for depositing a buoyant bait on the bed of a fast-flowing river.

The shotting capacity takes over around the point where the stick float leaves off, at 4 x BB, and it is well capable of achieving heavyweight proportions: "Severn anglers go as heavy as seven and eight swan, with excellent results." A diagram of an average pattern was shown as 6 x BB for a seven-foot swim – a bulk of 3 x AAA forty inches from the hook and two droppers terminating in 1 x no. 7 shot. But the next float, the adapted 'sliding balsa' for deep water was the one that caught my eye. This float's size range starts at 2½-Swan.

Here the duo used a piece of hollow fibreglass to fashion a stronger eye at the base of the sliding balsa compared to a wire ring when the large shots bumped against it, along with a .015-inch diameter top ring that runs up to the stop knot tied from the 3lb reel line. Again the simplest of shotting patterns will swiftly deliver a sizeable bait to the fish in any depth. The 3 x Swan bulk goes four feet from the hook, with 1 x BB and 1 x no. 1 below as droppers.

"It is no coincidence that the emergence of this float has come with the chub explosion," said the authors. "It offers the finest possible bait presentation to the chub and can be cast long distances with great accuracy." In their second book of 1982 Clive described a Severn match at Boreley where he bossed the swim with a bulk of four large shots (AAA or SSG not defined) and a AAA dropper, taking nearly 40lb of chub baiting with three casters on a 16 hook.

Kevin Ashurst once described his 'calamity' when he was caught without the right float, quoting a Winter League final on the River Blackwater, Ireland. He had to fish five rod-lengths out in fourteen feet of water, but he was drawn under trees making casting difficult in the kind of peg that's referred to as a 'parrot cage.' He admitted to struggling to fish double rubber and caught 13lb from a swim that was worth twice as much. The match was won with 19lb, "and I blew it because I did not have a balsa slider," rued Kevin.

Finally, a word on the long forgotten Porcupine quill. Billy Lane devoted a chapter in his (1971) *Encyclopaedia of Float Fishing* to the sliding porcupine quill. He added a wire .015 inch diameter top ring near to the tip of a large porcupine and a base ring offset slightly for easier sliding up the line. He liked the tough nature of the quill compared to other quills for fishing heavy. The shotting example on this float shown in the book could not be simpler: 3 x AAA bulked a yard from the hook and 1 x BB dropper in a variable position between six and twenty-four inches from the hook depending how the fish were taking. Last word to Kevin Ashurst with a thumbs up for a sizeable porkie: "They ride well in turbulent water and one of 5 x BB is useful on the odd occasion when the biggest stick is not quite right and the conditions don't really call for a balsa."

Chapter 56
The Dumpy (two versions)
– by Keith Arthur & Tony Gibbons

The late Pat Richardson, of Grebes AC, designed the 'Dumpy' for the deep water stretches of the Medway. He pioneered the float and was very successful with it. It had a cane stem and a balsa body set well down the stem. The standard shotting was simple but effective: one 1 x Swan shot (or SSG) and 1 x no. 4 which was adequate for anywhere on the Medway.

The idea was to fish the SSG three feet or so off the bottom, with the no. 4 set a foot or so from the hook and the hook just tripping bottom. How it was told to me was that the Medway had big rocks on the bottom and when the no. 4 shot hit them, Pat would sort of guide the float around the obstruction.

Pat Richardson and his catch.

The body was down to allow the float to grab as much flow as possible rather than hold back, like with a stick float. Remember this was the early 70s, or before, and wagglers weren't in use: everything was fished top and bottom and a body-up float held back too much. Peter Burton gave me the story and it makes a lot of sense. Remember that Pete fished with Pat in the Grebes back in the day, along with Harry Ball and others.

From there, the Dumpy travelled to the Thames but, being wider, it needed a bigger float. Freddie Gladwin made some from balsa and peacock but peacock and crow quill proved no good as they'd collapse on the strike – the reason why Pat used cane. Freddie overcame that by threading nylon rod, exactly like today's pole float stems, through the centre of his peacock so the floats stayed straight.

The Dumpy and block-end feeder effectively ended the years of domination of laying-on with a crowquill and with it a generation of LAA match anglers!

Dumpy floats and roach

Norfolk's alternative 'Dumpy' and Jimmy Randell – by Tony Gibbons[27]

In the period 1960-80 the River Wensum in the centre of Norwich was a Mecca for winter roach fishing. Matches were allowed on the 120-peg stretch from Cow Tower to Carron Swing Bridge, October onwards, and regularly attracted some of the best stick and waggler anglers, all of whom expected weights in excess of 20lb. This fantastic roach fishing encouraged anglers to travel from far and wide to compete.

At the time, one and a half pints of caster and a pint of hemp was the order of the day on this tidal river. Swims offered six and a half/seven feet of water on a low tide but over

27 Tony Gibbons is a veteran matchman and hard-working stalwart of the Norwich and Norfolk Broads match circuit. He still competes successfully on the Rivers Yare, Bure and beyond, and he himself took a personal best 43lb from the Wensum in those big redfin years. The long-standing Wensum roach match record is 56lb taken on a remarkable day when it took over 20lb of fish to make the top 20 places!

The contrast with Pat Richardson's Dumpy for Kent's River Medway is stark – the float body has been shifted to the top and forms a bulbous tip for the faster flowing Wensum.

ten feet at high water when the fish could be caught close in.

One Saturday that comes to mind was a 100-pegger run by Norwich DAA when the likes of Jimmy Randell and Gordon Blanks from Essex arrived to try their skills. Both fished for Roding Valley and had an awesome reputation when it came to roach fishing. After the draw I was asked if I had any advice to offer regarding their pegs. Gordon drew 68 on the 'Coalyard' stretch – a deep peg but one that could hold some big roach, i.e. 12oz to 1lb 4oz, while Jimmy drew 33 on the Green opposite Jewson's wood yard – a possible winning peg. As it was his Wensum debut, Jimmy asked how he should fish it. I just said: "It's roach fishing," and left him to it.

Five hours and 43lb of roach later, 'JR' had won. He had fished the 'Dumpy' float, or at least that's what we called it – a stocky balsa and cane float only 4" long taking from 4 x BB shot up to 10 x BB-plus, with caster and hemp. When dotted down this float rode the water well and would stay on track when mending the line to it. At the business end it was single caster on an 18 or 16 hook to 1.1lb Bayer line fished just off the bottom. Jimmy went on to dominate the river for the next five years, using this float and method similar to the one we use today with the Bolognese or pole: a bulk and two droppers.

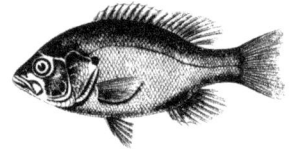

Chapter 57
A float for fast water
– the Pattison Flattie or Lollipop

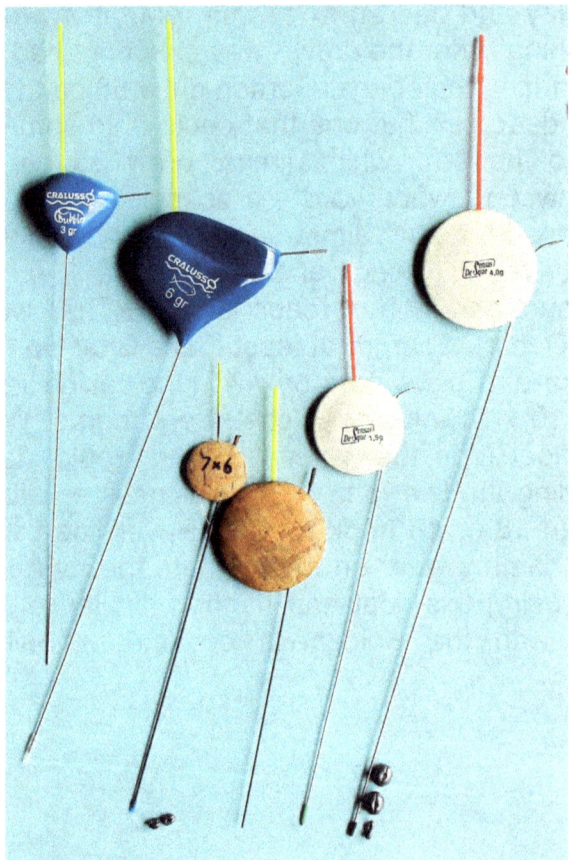

Flatties (L to R): 3-gram Cralusso Bubble, 6g Cralusso Torpedo, Dave Edwards cork & carbon stem patterns in 0.7g and 4g size, and two slim Sensas models

For the origins of this float as far as could be researched, we need to picture the River Bann at Portadown, Northern Ireland in the early 1970s when it was one of the most prolific roach waters in Europe. When Harold Pattison was learning how best to fish it, weights of strong migratory fish up to and over 1lb regularly topped 100lb from this section of the river.

Born and schooled in Manchester, Harold Pattison left his job in England for South Carolina when the textile trade

374

slumped in the early sixties. There he worked as a textile designer before re-locating again and re-settling in Dublin in 1968. His return neatly coincided with a boom in the Irish match-fishing scene. The whole River Erne system, too, had become a fish-filled haven for holidaying anglers from the UK.

Harold won the first Newry Canal Championship with 126lb 12oz of bream in 1973, then the inaugural Benson & Hedges Festival in 1976 on the Erne with a 137lb aggregate over three matches, proving he was a more than capable matchman. But it was his scientific approach to tackle that made his biggest impact on the sport.

Harold had already pioneered the springtip as an alternative to the quivertip in 1972-3, and was now searching for a float to fish the Bann at Portadown when the flow was strong.

"We would use huge floats at the time in the heaviest flows. Instead of thinking of a round body one day, I suddenly got the idea for a flat one," said Harold. "From the first trials it was obvious that a 12-gram flattie would do the job of a 20-gram round bodied one, or a 5-gram would substitute an 8-gram."

From 1/8" flat form balsa Harold cut out a half-moon shape, the straight edge of which he sharpened to a point to face upstream and meet the flow, while leaving the curved side pointing downstream intact. In an improved version he increased the body size to three-quarters of a full circle before adding a two-inch plastic bristle and a seven-inch wire stem, completing the float with a tiny side eye made from the shank of a size 6 eyed hook.

The result was this streamlined float, around forty per cent more efficient that a round body, that sliced into and diverted a powerful current around it. Harold and colleagues later used them on the River Liffey when presented with twelve to thirteen feet of water that was often bombing through.

Today the Flattie is a universally popular pole float design for fast water, and several companies including Sensas and Trabucco make models in slightly different shapes. These are usually fished with a pole, though there is no earthly reason why rod and reel can't be used. Indeed Harold fished his original float on the Bann with a 13-foot Bruce and Walker rod, laying on six feet downstream of his rod tip. He later coupled the float with a pole and fished eight metres to hand to catch big nets of roach in the 12-14oz bracket.

As a variant for shallower rivers like the Colebrook he'd add a second eye at the base of the wire stem and turn it into a slider: "This smaller slider worked brilliant for smaller fish, and sliding the float about a foot up to a stop knot made for a cleaner strike," added Harold.

On the deep River Don at Sprotborough, near Doncaster, flatties with a square profile, not unlike an After Eight mint's shape and size, have proved successful, while Sheffield's Dave Edwards makes mini versions for the shallow Boston drains when they are pulling hard. Dave constructs his from slim cork bodies and a carbon stem and they are hardly bigger than a 5p coin.

One of the most popular commercial flatties on the market today is the Hungarian Cralusso 'Torpedo' which has a mini 'shelf' halfway up the body said to hold the float down and stable in the flow when held back hard.

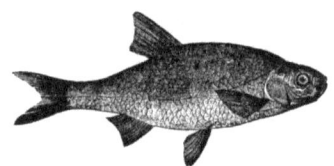

Chapter 58
South Yorkshire Talent

Considering this book has covered anglers from several counties there has been little mention of my home city of Sheffield. It is true that we have had better results on the slower rivers of Fenland than with roach from swifter rivers like the Trent, and the last premier National Sheffield won, in fact, was with bream from the Huntspill in a former era (1955). It would be remiss of me however, not to mention a few of my city's peers – consistent performers with stick floats.

Some local anglers I've fished with and against have shown true class. Sheffield's David Bates was arguably the first angler to win an open on the Witham with a stick float and hemp combination back in the seventies. He presented his bait just beyond the marginal weed with a small Albert Dronfield stick of 5 no. 6 size, taking a BB under the float and a small piece of fine flat lead, doubled over down the line to mimic a slim styl weight. This lead was to avoid "shot bites" in the belief that the fish mistook small round shot for the seed. Dave won a big Grimsby open with 10lb 10oz of roach, and framed a few times backing himself against the bream anglers. He had this summer method to himself for a while, but when asked how he did it by Ken and Steve Bennett, a father and son team from Goldthorpe, he told them and they listened well. The irony of this generosity was felt when Dave weighed 12lb-plus in a later match only for Ken to demote him to second thanks to a bonus bream. In this same period Sheffield National team anglers Keith Boswell and Ken Littlewood scored well with tares on the hook, Ken winning one big open with 17lb of roach when the bream refused to feed.

Former Blades footballer, the late Gerry Dodds, was a handy Trent regular and loved using stick float, and my former team mates Dave Pearson, Kevin Rice and Dennis Bateman have all shown stick skills on rivers. Andy Sellars and Tim Hannon were a bit handy too, before they were recruited by Barnsley Blacks. Brian Shaw won several matches on the Witham including a Super League round with what he called his "super stick" – of 6 x BB size, which the fish liked enough for a 19lb 1 1/2oz total. This was one of the Witham's better roach days when the top 30 in the match averaged over 10lb per man. Brian has since used Bolo' floats up to 6g size to catch roach on the river. 'Perhaps we often fished too light back in the day?' he suggested. All these anglers have known some stick supremacy.

Rotherham's Trent talent includes the likes of Ernie Wilde, Dave Parkes, Jack Pugh, John Powell, Frank Austin and Geoff Newby (before emigrating to Australia); the latter four I fished with as members of the match group Rotherham Raiders. Aside from taking an individual bronze medal in the 1980 National, Frank Austin was very unlucky when winning a Sheffield AA Pairs match on the Witham easily with 14lb of roach on stick float. He discovered he'd not won a bean because all the pools money was paid out to the winning pairs. To leave him empty-handed was most unfair in my opinion. Maltby's Dennis Pinkos was a top performer on the Don circuit before he was forced to retire through a back injury. A noted heavy feeder, he would not shy away from feeding three or more pints of casters and similar of hemp. In a head-to-head challenge against the great John Allerton for *Angling Star* magazine on the River Aire at Beal, Dennis emerged the victor. John took defeat sportingly but Dennis on his day could beat anyone.

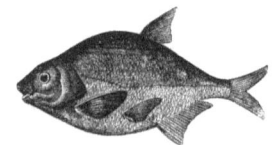

Chapter 59
Some more top tips

A typically bulging netful for Steve Gardener,
England regular and top Thames angler

Divide to conquer

In his 27-year career as an England International up to 2013, Dorking's Steve Gardener won an outstanding 18 team medals including 11 golds. Consistency was his trademark even though his best individual medal was silver. His reliability was undoubtedly helped by his great understanding of the feeding habits of silver fish. Your stick float might be the best in the world, but if your feeding is wrong on the day you won't get the best out of the swim. The clever way that Steve fed two areas of a river swim was first explained in *Angling Times* as long ago as 1981 and featured in Pat Newman's book on Steve, *A Life in Match Fishing*, published by Mpress Media, as follows:

"Look carefully at the swim and select: 1) the (feeding area) downstream where you are going to concentrate your fish; 2) your main 'catching area' closer in, about a rod-length inside this. When the starting whistle goes begin feeding at 1) to build up a main swim, but also feed lighter on inside swim 2) – your main catching area. The objective is to build up a main shoal and a second shoal closer in which may only be a dozen fish. Hopefully, I can keep sneaking fish out of the near line throughout the match, but at times there may be a need to plunder the main shoal. The objective is to time it or pace yourself so that your swim (2) stays alive to as near the end of the match as possible, and if that happens you can justifiably say that you've fished a good match.'"

Try a colour change

Ever the thinking angler, Leicester and England International, Ivan Marks assessed maggot colours in the days of his *Angling Times* articles, so, do we think about maggot colour enough? Here's what Ivan said: "There's little doubt that fish don't see colours as we see them but they do have colour preferences. And that preference is ever-changing – so the angler who is first on to the coloured bait the fish accept most readily is the chap most likely to succeed. I am sure that on any one day, with its varied ingredients – water colour, sunshine, cloud, gales, flat, calm or something in between – helps prejudice fish towards certain colours. Other factors also come into the reckoning such as the amount of hammer a particular water has had, depth, size and species being caught. Pink, for instance, comes into its own when a river has been flogged to death, and pink hook maggots and pinkies have sometimes done good work on the Nene, for example, or on Fen drains in autumn when the fish have taken a hiding. Yellow often does best when the water is coloured or when insects are dropping in from overhanging bushes. Some say dark casters are a flop in coloured water. Is it more about the fish having some difficulty finding (darker) casters when the water's muddy?

"In any 20 matches I fish, I estimate that white maggot is the best colour 11 times, yellow ranks top six times and pink or red scores three times. This means that if you always fish with whites you will be right more than half the time, at least on the waters I fish! But that, of course isn't enough. You've got to get it right all the time. There are days when freshly turned casters are superior, others when a really dark caster is tops. You've got to find out what's right on the day."

Note: It's fair to say that bronze maggot replaced yellow in popularity and red maggot took over for bream as time moved on. Coincidence or not, the very first time I tried a fluoro' pink maggot on the hook on a flooded River Witham, I caught a PB roach of 2-1-8 and won the match easily with over 5lb. The great man called it. – *JB*

Rig Streamlining

The Bolognese float is customarily shotted with a bulk of lead and a few small droppers. But float maestro and five times World Champion Alan Scotthorne does not always stick with tradition. In a feature at Burton Joyce for Match Fishing magazine he used what he described as a 'softer' shotting pattern, discarding the bulk in favour of a close chain of no. 8 shot on a 70cm leader above a 12-inch trace for the session. The float was 2.0 gram and the leader a quite heavy line of . 20mm, which he said reduces the chance of tangles. On this leader he spaced out 28 X no. 8 shots and a no. 10 tell-tale, and this produced a good double figures of dace and small roach for the camera.

Second Cast Leviathan

To win a match with one fish in a three-foot flood might fairly be called very lucky, but few would lay that charge on Sheffield's Chris Garlick who turned up at the Trent ready for almost any eventuality. His reward was the biggest Trent carp we know about to win a match – 26lb 10oz! It was a 2001 Walkley Winter League event at Burton Joyce, and Chris admittedly had the fishing 'gods' on his side. Firstly, he drew a good swim on the roadside outfall peg, and then he met a local on the bank who gave him a handy tip, ie: 'try a worm as carp can show up here in the slack margin'. This was music to Chris's ears. He had some lobworms in his bag and, more importantly, some size 10 hooks and 10lb line which he then decided to use. After one failed attempt with a dendrabaena Chris changed to lobbie and hooked the carp second cast. His float: a 9 x no. 6 Dave Pearson lignum, shotted by the big worm only.

To sink the reel line or not

Whether you should float or sink the reel line above the stick float depends largely on the wind and to some extent the route of the river. Earlier chapters have referred to greasing the line behind the float to keep it on the surface and reduce striking friction, or back-shotting to sink the line in a downstream wind (allied to dipping the rod tip underwater). If the wind is light from any direction then it should be easy to keep the line straight behind the float, trotting parallel to the bankside with an occasional flick 'mend' of the rod. But in a strong facing or downstream wind, life gets harder and a sunken line will pay dividends. The right bank of the northward flowing Trent at Dunham Bridge, for example, is typically such back-shot-country when windy, but this bears no comparison to the right bank of say the Warwickshire Avon at Evesham. As this river flows southwest, the prevailing wind here is kinder on float control, hence a floating line (greased or silicone sprayed or not) makes good sense. So by studying the wind factor on your local river you'll know the best policy.

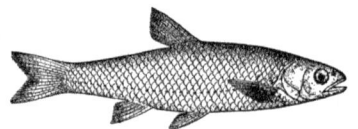

Postscript – a fresh look at the float tip

Why should the tip of a pole float or Bolo' float be so different to a stick float tip when all three floats are used successfully on rivers – the first two being slim, the latter a short point or more rounded? Well, I'd venture to say they need not be. Without wanting to re-invent the thing, or disrespect all the pioneers who have blazed the trail with balsa-topped sticks, be they domed or pointed tips, couldn't we possibly finesse our stick floats at the critical point of bite indication – the piece of tip that we study on the surface, and, *if* the bait is not fished overdepth and dragging on the river bed, need this top third of the float be in balsa wood at all?

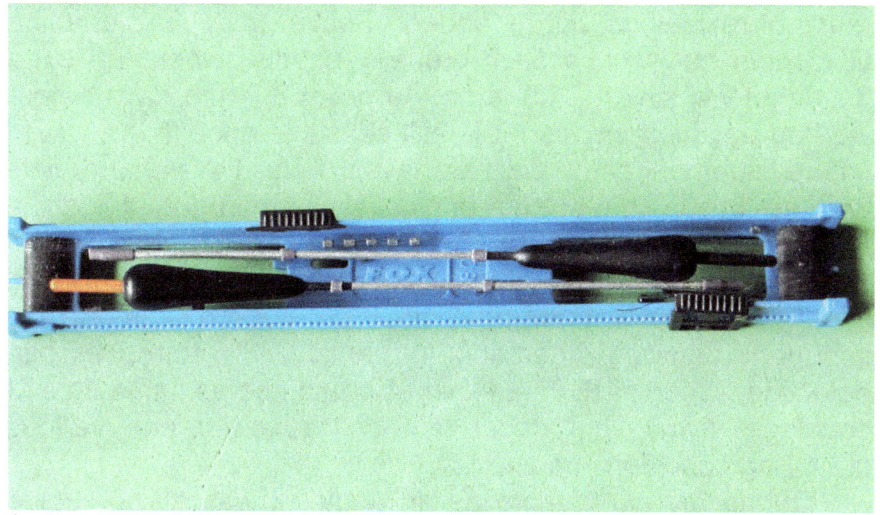

Keeping sticks on float winders is the modern way. These two are converted John Allerton's with a finer tip and a top wire eye to replace the rubber, done by Steve Parramore to beat a deadening upstream wind

There are a few examples of inserts added to the top of sticks working successfully through the book as well as slim stick tips. I suppose the fine (balsa) John Allerton stick top is not far removed from a pole float bristle, and another example is the cane top of the old Carrot float of Gerry Lees.[28] To me that float was like a boat without a keel, perhaps best suited to shallower swims, but Gerry certainly made it work with its

---

28 *Unlike the Carrots made by Drake Floats (p.61), Gerry favoured an 1/8" or 3mm diameter cane tip with a blunter end than shown.*

sensitive tip. The Ivan Marks' balsa Pacemaker with its shoulder and fine tip, too, is another case of one angler going against the grain.

Resistance of the float to the taking fish will cause missed bites and that kills our rhythm and efficiency, so most good anglers will dot their floats down to the limit of visibility. For argument's sake a 3mm showing of a 3mm cane or plastic insert for example, gives a volume of 9mm square, which is half as sensitive as a 3mm show of a bulbous equivalent of say a 6mm balsa semi-circle.

I put this to Kevin Ashurst, the Leigh legend and master of both stick and pole styles on rivers, and someone who learned the stick/caster style almost from the cradle. Kevin agrees with me that the fish feel the float on the bite. Obviously the bit sticking out on the water surface is the offending portion in terms of resistance, but he added: "I have no doubt that a fine tip counts but, with a stick properly shotted where an extra dust shot will sink it – i.e. a no. 10 or an 8 in the days before we had anything smaller, it is still sensitive enough. Yes, with the development of the pole we have got used to slender floats with fine bristle tips, but the original stick when dotted is still a very sensitive float."

Here's how Dave Thomas rationalises the difference:

"There is no doubt that float tip thickness is a very important detail/consideration in particular in terms of bite detection. When stick float fishing I would use as thin a tip as I could get away with dependent on the swim and various prevailing conditions on the day.

During my early years as an angler it was all porcupine quills, then straight balsa floats and eventually stick floats, no mention of poles/pole floats. The first thing that hit me when I started to use a pole (they were only seven or eight metres then) was that the bites I was seeing on that thin bristle float might never have registered on a stick float, it was a huge eye opener at the time. A lot of the porkies I used were naturally thin in the tip and needed to be for the predominantly dace fishing on Yorkshire rivers at the time, a real challenge, but marvellous grounding for improving my float fishing skills.

Naturally nearly all my sticks are more pointed than rounded or dome shaped in the tip. A lot of the time when fishing for roach and dace, the fish will ride with the bait showing barely any indication at all on the float, even with a thinnish tip fished as low in the water as possible you still get the smallest of indications which, as low as the float is, don't pull it under. These are good bites if you can detect them. Sometimes I find myself striking and hooking a fish then on reflection I can't put my finger on why I struck, but something must have told me that there was a fish there, the float must have done something. Sounds crazy, but it has happened to me and other anglers I talk to. The other thing of course is that, with a thinner tip, a taking fish feels less resistance, resulting in better bite detection in general and more fish hooked."

Mick Broadley inserted sticks, left half of picture

Rugby's Dave Burr, who broke the National Championship weight record in 1965 with 76lb of bream from the King's Sedgemoor drain, was no one-hit wonder but a tackle dealer and accomplished river angler in the Midlands. He favoured an inch-long 2mm cane insert in his balsa floats in the very early days of the stick float's emergence. I asked him recently if there was any downside. A firm 'No' was his reply, adding: "the cane insert worked well for me unless it was a flat calm day and then I'd revert to a standard stick."

Years ago Witham anglers would add a cane insert of up to two inches long to a standard stick top for when the river had a strong easterly wind blowing upstream that put peaks and troughs on the surface against the current. The tip extension helped cure that 'now you see it, now you don't' problem whenever the float fell into a trough, with no way of seeing a bite. I saw no drawback of this antenna on the stick in that situation. Others have told me how a fine insert has helped when a cold upstream wind restricts the float's travel.

Even a bulbous tip on a float like a balsa Chubber could be refined. In devising a home-made fluted waggler tip, my friend Ian Bray cut the middle out of a plastic syringe (the profile of which from an aerial viewpoint looks like a plus symbol) and rounded the corners to make some sensitive hi-viz pellet wagglers tips. Similar tips could also be built onto the fat balsa top of the chub float for long-trotting. Some anglers will surely already have tried this.

I'll round off by saying that no float has all the answers, but because a thin float tip will move further on a bite than a fat one, it follows that it must show a better signal on the subtlest of bites. So the sensitivity of the tip might be one area where the stick float can be improved still.

Tightest of lines to you all!

About the Author

Jim Baxter was born into a Sheffield fishing family and has enjoyed competitive (match) angling for over 50 years. He won his first senior match aged 17 which inspired him to take angling more seriously. He was a member of the Barnsley Division 1 National Championship team in 1979 and skippered the Sheffied AAS National team in the 80s.

He coached the Sheffield Juniors for eight years from 1982 and coached his wife Lynne for three years from being a beginner through to her winning the 1987 Ladies National.

He has organised matches on rivers and lakes and the Fossdyke canal and ran his own Northern School of Angling for three years. He has made hundreds of fishing floats – for longer than he cares to remember.

His writing career has included editing four angling magazines, the most recent being the *Angling Star* (1995-2012). His first book *The Rising Antenn*a was published in 2016.

Jim lives in South Sheffield with Lynne and has two girls, Frances and Sophie.

Burton Joyce outfall

Acknowledgments

Sincerest thanks to the following people for helping me in different ways to produce this book, in no particular order: Stuart Thompson, Malcolm Caunt, Dave Edwards, Jeff Herbert, Geoff Wyatt, Steve Parramore, Mark Halksworth, Scott Smith, Dave Burr, Dave Bates, Roly Moses, Brian Shaw (of Stocksbridge, not the World's strongest man) Linda Marks, Pat Bielderman, Lyn and Sarah Ward, Ian Bray, Andy Love, *Match Fisherman* magazine, *Angling Times* magazine, the former *Angler's Mail*, the late John Cardingand, of course, all my talented and enthusiastic contributors.

I am also humbly indebted to: John Essex, Dave Roberts and Pat Newman, each who kindly and keenly supplied archive material, pictures and key facts, similarly to my editor Jim Macdonald, Simon Waller for graphics, and Steven Kay of 1889 Books.

– JB

CPSIA information can be obtained
at www.ICGtesting.com
Printed in the USA
LVHW080601030123
736277LV00003B/114